Documents of the
LGBT Movement

Recent Titles in the Eyewitness to History Series

Documents of the Salem Witch Trials
K. David Goss

Documents of the Chicano Movement
Roger Bruns

Documents of the LGBT Movement

CHUCK STEWART

Eyewitness to History

 ABC-CLIO™

An Imprint of ABC-CLIO, LLC
Santa Barbara, California • Denver, Colorado

Library of Congress Cataloging-in-Publication Data

Names: Stewart, Chuck, 1951– author.
Title: Documents of the LGBT movement / Chuck Stewart.
Description: Santa Barbara, California : ABC-CLIO, [2018] | Series: Eyewitness
    to history | Includes bibliographical references and index.
Identifiers: LCCN 2017056212 (print) | LCCN 2018006167 (ebook) |
    ISBN 9781440855023 (ebook) | ISBN 9781440855016 (alk. paper)
Subjects: LCSH: Gays—United States—History. | Gays—United States—
    History—Sources. | Gay rights—United States—History. | Gay rights—United
    States—History—Sources.
Classification: LCC HQ76.3.U5 (ebook) | LCC HQ76.3.U5 S756 2018 (print) |
    DDC 306.76/60973—dc23
LC record available at https://lccn.loc.gov/2017056212

ISBN: 978-1-4408-5501-6 (print)
       978-1-4408-5502-3 (ebook)

22 21 20 19 18   1 2 3 4 5

This book is also available as an eBook.

ABC-CLIO
An Imprint of ABC-CLIO, LLC

ABC-CLIO, LLC
130 Cremona Drive, P.O. Box 1911
Santa Barbara, California 93116-1911
www.abc-clio.com

This book is printed on acid-free paper ∞

Manufactured in the United States of America

Contents

Preface

Until recently, history courses amounted to little more than reading about the activities of wealthy white men who engaged in war against one another. Rarely did the histories and lives of people of color or women appear, and if they did, it was as a sidebar in textbooks and presented in relation to men. Homosexuality was completely ignored unless it pertained to particular "scandals."

The civil rights movement and women's rights movement in the 1960s and 1970s brought significant changes to historical textbooks. The process of consciousness-raising initiated by the women's movement included reclaiming its history—a process adopted by other marginalized groups, including lesbians, gay men, and transgendered.

Even though people like American archivist Jim Kepner privately collected material on the early American gay movement (the world's largest collection with more than one million items contained in the ONE Institute and Archives located on the campus of the University of Southern California), many of the current lesbian and gay historical collections did not begin until the aftermath of the Stonewall Riots. The Lesbian Herstory and Archives founded in 1973 and the San Francisco Lesbian and Gay History Project (1977) are examples of two new collections. Now lesbian and gay archives can be found on most universities, all around the country, and around the world.

Deciding on which events to include in this chronology is problematic. Before the twentieth century, there are virtually no writings of personal letters or books that include explicit sexual descriptions. Very little information exists about the actual lives of people in earlier times. Identifying someone as gay or lesbian is exceedingly difficult. The primary document created by older cultures is for the ownership, transfer, and taxation of property. With property ownership came the issue of inheritance. Only the wealthy were landowners, and they wanted to guarantee that their property would go to their offspring. Religion and culture combined to create and reinforce heterosexual nuclear family norms. Thus, marriages and offspring were recorded to assure the legitimacy of heirs. Not all marriages and not all offspring were recorded; the poor, slaves, and racial/ethnic outcasts were often ignored. So were same-sex relationships. The documents we have are biased toward wealthy landowners who formed heterosexual relationships and their resultant children.

A second source of documents related to human sexuality is legislation and court proceedings. Beginning in the 1600s America, colonies and states enacted laws to control sodomy. Vague terms were used to describe sodomy and generally meant any form of sexuality disapproved by those in power, which were white landowners. By the early twentieth century, states passed laws to sexually steril-ize persons considered "deviant." With the development of psychology, psycho-pathic laws were passed to indefinitely incarcerate those convicted of illegal sexual crimes. These three categories of laws created a cache of documents that dem-onstrate how confused legislators were concerning human sexuality and moral-ity. Court proceedings and decisions also help to shed light on the relationship between religion and sexuality in early America. Unfortunately, legislation and court proceedings only show the tip of the iceberg concerning homosexual behav-iors and nothing about same-sex relationships—and what is shown is extremely negative.

Finally, we have the problem of identity. The "gay identity" is decidedly a mod-ern term that cannot be properly applied to people of earlier cultures. Also, the gay-straight dichotomy is extremely limiting. How people express their gender, sexual orientation, sex roles, and more is extremely fluid. It seems that for most of human history and most places on this earth, conforming to gender roles was important whereas whom you had sex with was not. Considering that there are no documents showing same-sex marriages, or the adoption of children by same-sex couples, or diaries that explicitly state homosexual behaviors or "gay" identities, it is problematic to tell a history that includes LGBTQ people.

Since Stonewall, and in particular the past 30 years, gay rights have come to the forefront of world politics. Every day there is some act of gay protest, opposi-tion to gay rights, laws being passed or rescinded that specifically identify sexual orientation, and other events. Thus, any chronology, including this one, will be incomplete. Readers are encouraged to use this list as a starting point in their own research.

Evaluating and Interpreting Primary Documents

In historiography, which is the study of the writing of history and the employment of historical methods, a primary source is a document, recording, artifact, work of art or literature, or other information resource that was created at or near the time being studied, usually by someone with direct, personal knowledge of the particular past events, persons, or topics being described. Primary sources are original sources of information about the past, unlike secondary sources, which are works later historians create from a study, citation, and evaluation of primary sources. A modern monograph such as *Chicano! The History of the Mexican American Civil Rights Movement* by F. Arturo Rosales; a modern film such as *Zoot Suit,* directed by Luis Valdez; a modern television production such as *Walkout,* directed by Edward James Olmos and Moctezuma Esparza; or *The House on Mango Street* by Sandra Cisneros may be helpful in explaining the Chicano movement, but they are all secondary descriptions and depictions based upon firsthand experiences and recollections recorded and preserved in the primary documents of the period.

Primary documents—as illustrated by the document selections in *Documents of the Chicano Movement: Eyewitness to History*—come in many forms and types, including letters, journals, polemics, speeches, literary works, and public records and documents. All these types of sources were written by a particular person at a particular time in a particular place for a particular reason. Some were written with no expectation that they would ever be read by anyone other than the original recipient; others were written for publication or at least with an eye to wider distribution. Some were meant to inform, some to persuade, some to entertain, and some to obfuscate. Each exhibits the political, religious, class, ethnic, or personal biases of their creators, whether those attitudes were consciously or unconsciously expressed. Some are the product of poor memories, bad information, or outright deception, but all are authentic voices of someone alive at the time and all can add at least a little to the information we have of an otherwise irrecoverable past age or person. Nonetheless, historians must carefully evaluate and test all primary sources to determine how much weight and credibility each should be given.

How to Read Primary Documents

When evaluating a primary source, historians ask the following questions:

1. Who wrote or produced it? What is known about this person's life or career?
2. When was the source written or produced? What date? How close or far was that date from the date of the events described?

3. Where was it produced? What country, what region, what locality?

4. How was the source written or produced? What form did it originally take? Was it based upon any preexisting material? Does the source survive in its original form?

5. Why was the source written or produced? What was its creator trying to do, and for whom?

6. Who was the source written or produced for? Who was its audience, and why? What do we know about the audience?

7. What is the evidential value of its contents? How credible is it?

Readers of the document selections contained in this volume should apply these same questions to the selections they read or study.

When analyzing a primary document, scholars also seek to identify the key words and phrases used by the author and try to understand what the author meant by those terms. They will also try to summarize the main thesis of the source to understand what point the author was trying to make. Once the author's thesis is understood, historians evaluate the evidence the author provided to support that argument and try to identify any assumptions the author made in crafting those arguments. Historians also examine the source within the context of its time period by asking if the document is similar to others from the same period, or how widely was it circulated, or what tone, problems, or ideas it shares with other documents of the period. Scholars will also seek to determine if the author agrees or disagrees with other contemporary authors on the same subject and whether or not the source supports what they already know or have learned about the subject from other sources.

Primary sources offer modern readers and researchers the actual words of people who lived through a particular event. Secondary sources, like textbooks, offer an interpretation of a historical person or event by someone who did not know the person or witness the period. Reading primary sources allows us to evaluate the interpretations of historians for ourselves and to draw our own conclusions about a past personage or events. Asking the questions listed earlier will help users of this volume better understand and interpret the documents provided here. Because of unfamiliar and archaic language or terminology, or very different modes of expression or styles of writing, some primary sources can be difficult to read and hard to understand.

However, an important part of the process of reading and using historical sources is determining what the documents can tell about the past and deciding whether one agrees with the interpretation offered, both by the author of the original source and by later creators of secondary works based on the original document. By using primary sources, modern readers become aware that all history is based on sources that are themselves interpretations of events rooted in the interpreter's own opinions and biases. This awareness allows modern students to recognize the subjective nature of history. Thus, reading primary sources provides modern readers with the tools and evidence needed to make informed statements about the world of the past and of the present.

Introduction

There have always been and always will be people who engage in homosexual activities and relationships and those who do not conform to the gender binary. Being "gay" is a modern political concept. It reflects the efforts made by homosexuals to fight against a heterosexist society that tells them they are deviant and not deserving of full human rights. LGBT rights are the process of claiming the respect due all people.

Historical Overview of LGBT Rights and Issues

Until the Industrial Revolution, the lives of most people were the same and unchanged. The development of steam power, the use of fossil fuels, and the invention of electricity were technical developments that increased the ability of humans to communicate and be productive. These events occurred during the 1800s. Before that, most people worked on farms. A farmer in seventeenth-century England would be virtually indistinguishable from a farmer in 180 C.E. Rome or a farmer in Egypt or China or Africa in 2000 B.C.E. Cultures slowly evolved, and most accepted homosexual behaviors. In general, as long as a person who owned property fulfilled his or her familial obligations of producing children, whom they had sex with was relatively immaterial. And, in general, the society really didn't care what poor and marginalized people did sexually as they had no need for assuring property rights through family lineage.

What is rarely written about are, what anthropologists term, *all-male societies* (or societies made up of one gender). Jamestown, the first settlement in America by Europeans, was made up exclusively of men. Frontiersmen, the military, and the movement west were conducted mostly by men. The early settlement of the Midwest, mountains, desert regions, California, Oregon, and Washington was by men. For example, in 1848, San Francisco had a population of 812 people of whom approximately three-fourths were male. Within three years these numbers would become more male dominated as 25,000 Chinese men came to California through San Francisco to participate in the Gold Rush of 1851 and to build the cross-continental railroad. Whom did these men have relationships with? We can only conclude that same-sex relationships were, in fact, the norm in all-male societies, yet public documents will have no record of these lives.

LGBT Rights in America

The Americas were populated for many thousands of years before the arrival of Europeans. Hundreds, if not thousands, of languages were spoken, and only a few nations in South America used limited written symbols. In North America, no language group had a written language. As such, we have no original documentation about the lives of First People residing in what is now the United States. We have no specific information about family structure, marriage, same- or other-sexual relationships, or more. What do exist are some of the diaries and reports from the first European explorers who were confused and shocked by the amount of gender and sexual nonconformity they witnessed within the indigenous population. Considering the many reports of "sodomitical" behaviors observed within First People, it could be assumed that "sodomy" was common.

But what is sodomy? A review of historical documents, court cases, legislation, and religious treaties shows a wide variance as to what it means. Sometimes it was defined as any sexual behaviors (regardless of same- or other-sex) outside of wedlock. Many laws vaguely referred to sodomy as a crime so heinous that it could not be named, the public was not allowed to observe the trials, and newspapers were forbidden to report on the outcome of the trials. Other times it was concisely defined as to where vaginas, anus, penises, and mouths were used and the location the sexual behavior occurred. Often the gender, age, or status of the person modified the definition. For example, men could be convicted of sodomy but not women. For centuries, lesbianism was not identified since sex between women was thought to be inconceivable. Also, slaves faced greater punishment for the same behavior. The European explorers most likely identified any behavior that did not conform to Catholic gender and sexual norms as "sodomy."

In a sense, most First People nations were not antigay. Most tribes respected the innate spirit which they believed resides in all things. They looked for the benefits each person brought to the tribe. A two-spirited person was truly special as he or she contained the spirit of both women and men and, as such, often held a respected position in the tribe as spiritual leader, teacher, and counselor. Creation myths often told the stories of how god created a two-spirited person to help men and women in the world. Being central to their creation myths helped nurture tolerance between different sexual relationships, gender expressions, and sex roles.

But all that would change with the invasion of Europeans. The English sent initial settlements to Jamestown and the Virginia colonies as business ventures. The sailors, soldiers, and farmers were all men. It was reported that men were stealing food and trading for sexual favors. Sodomy was so widespread that the military implemented rules against its practice under pain of death. As the English established more colonies, English common laws were applied—and this included sodomy provisions meting out the death penalty. In the Spanish- and Portuguese-controlled areas, Catholic rules were applied. The Catholic world had experienced centuries of religious inquisitions and, as such, was ruled by mysticisms and fear. The form of Catholicism that came to the Americas was fundamental, extremely antigay, and paranoid. Colonies set up under Spanish and Portuguese rule applied Catholic rules, and sodomy was punishable by death.

As can be imagined, the spread of Europeans throughout the Americas brought with them antigay beliefs, sentiments, and legal systems. Homosexuality and same-sex relationships not only were illegal but also couldn't be spoken about. The idea of gay rights had not entered the American psyche.

Rise of the Early Gay Rights Movement

The early gay rights movement began in Germany during the mid-1800s. The rise of Nazism crushed the fledgling movement. But the idea of equal rights for homosexuals did not die with World War II. Instead, it rose again in the United States paralleling the civil rights movement that began in the 1950s.

The German Homosexual Emancipation Movement

Karl Heinrich Ulrich published many social and juridical studies in Germany concerning same-sex love between men. His 12 books represented the largest body of work on homosexuality in the 1860s and were collectively known as *Researches on the Riddle of Love between Men.* He used the term "Uranian" in reference to male homosexuality, a term taken from Plato's *Symposium* in which love between two men was referred to as a beautiful love that belonged to the heavenly "Muse Urania." Ulrich is recognized as the "Grandfather of Gay Liberation."

The word *homosexual* was coined in 1869 by Hungarian doctor Karoly Maria Benkert (who went by the pseudonym K. M. Kertbeny). The term *heterosexual* was not used publicly until 10 years later in 1880. Initially heterosexuality meant sexual deviancy and was used in defense of homosexuality. In 1871, the newly united Germany enacted the New Prussian Penal Code. It included Paragraph 175 outlawing "unnatural sexual acts between men, and men and beast" and specified imprisonment for up to four years (Plant 1988, 33).

British doctor Havelock Ellis continued with the medicalization of homosexuality and coined the phrase "sexual inversion" to characterize homosexual behavior. Sigmund Freud was influenced by the work of Ellis and further characterized homosexuality as an "immature" stage of development. It is important to realize that Freud and early psychologists did not base their theories on any scientific evidence but, instead, cast social and cultural norms and prejudices into the new field of psychology. Unfortunately, their theories would influence psychology for the next 100 years.

Heterosexuality was medicalized as the norm and homosexuality as "deviant." However, not everyone accepted this. Magnus Hirschfeld founded the Scientific Humanitarian Committee in Germany in 1897 to overcome antigay prejudice and to change the law. He worked tirelessly for three decades for homosexual emancipation. The committee distributed over 50,000 copies of the pamphlet *What People Should Know about the Third Sex.* Although there were 40 gay bars in Berlin by World War I, he had little success organizing the many homosexual groups in Germany.

Hirschfeld opened the Institute for Sexual Research in 1919. The library contained more than 20,000 volumes of rare anthropological, medical, legal, and social documents. It employed four physicians and several assistants and included over 35,000 photographs.

German Brownshirts and police often physically beat Hirschfeld. One month after Hitler was named chancellor of Germany on January 30, 1933, all homosexual rights organizations and pornography were banned. Four months later on May 6, 1933, approximately 100 students surrounded and entered the Institute for Sexual Research. They smashed and carried everything out. A public ceremony was held four days later where these materials, along with a bust of Hirschfeld, were burned. (History books contain the infamous pictures of the Nazi burning books. They imply that Nazis were "bad" for destroying books. However, what books were being burned? The first fires contained the institute's collection on sexuality and homosexuality. Why do history books fail to mention this? Perhaps our own culture wants to suppress all references to homosexuality.)

For the next two years, the Nazis staged a campaign against homosexuals. Bars were closed, groups and meetings were banned, and homosexuals were arrested in thousands. On July 3, 1934, the leader of the Brownshirts (SA) and a known homosexual, Ernst Roehm, was executed along with hundreds of other members (during what is known as the "Night of the Long Knives"). By 1935, the entire homosexual reform movement was extinguished, and thousands of homosexuals were thrown into concentration camps where at least 50,000 of them died. They were identified with a lavender triangle sewn onto their clothes. Tragically, some legal-minded Allied commanders forced those who survived the camps to return to prison after the war to serve out their sentences as sexual deviants.

The American Homosexual Emancipation Movement

There is very little evidence of efforts toward homosexual emancipation in the United States in the nineteenth century and early twentieth century. The Chicago Society for Human Rights was the first group in the United States to advocate for gay rights. Henry Gerber, a German American immigrant, along with a number of working-class homosexuals, launched the Society in 1929, which was granted nonprofit corporate status from the state of Illinois. Gerber was aware of the works of Hirschfeld and the Institute for Sexual Research. The Society created a newsletter and was able to distribute only two issues before law enforcement arrested (without warrant) all members of the board. The men were jailed, brought to trial, but ultimately set free. Gerber lost his job with the post office and the Society disbanded (Katz 1976).

The early 1920s saw an increase in the number of novels with lesbian and gay themes published in the United States, although not without great controversy. A growing underground developed in Harlem in New York and in other major cities such as San Francisco and New Orleans. Homosexuals were fairly free to associate with each other yet still under the fear of police entrapment and harassment.

World War II and the Migration of Lesbians and Gays to the Cities

Family patterns, social networks, and entire cultural systems were disrupted by World War II. Millions of men and women left their homes to enter the military or to work in factories to help make war supplies. Many of these settings were segregated by race and sex. Soldiers often had to share bunks, and men were often seen sleeping in each other's arms at train depots while waiting to ship out. Men often danced with each other at army canteens. Women lived together in company-provided housing at war factories. Homosexuality was a criminal act in the military in the 1920s and 1930s, but the war provided an excuse for these behaviors. Under these conditions, lesbians and gay men were able to find each other without bringing undue attention (Blumenfeld & Raymond 1993, 291; D'Emilio & Freedman 1988, 25–26).

An effort was made to reduce the number of personnel in the military after the war. One method was to enforce the 1943 regulations banning homosexuals from all branches of the military. Approximately 10,000 men and women were dishonorably discharged from the military for homosexuality during the war and immediately afterward (known as "blue-discharges" because the discharge document was printed on blue paper). Many did not return home but rather flocked to New York, Los Angeles, and San Francisco to form gay enclaves. The gay community found relative safety and, eventually, its identity within these enclaves.

A number of factors led to the development of the modern gay movement after World War II. In 1948 Alfred Kinsey released his study of American male sexual habits—*Sexual Behaviors in the Human Male*—and in 1953 his corresponding study of American female sexual habits—*Sexual Behaviors in the Human Female*. The reports sent shock waves through American culture forever shattering stereotypes and myths concerning American puritanical codes of sexual conduct. The reports showed, besides other things, that many Americans had sex out of wedlock, engaged in sex in their teens, and had participated in a variety of sexual behaviors, including bisexuality and homosexuality.

Another factor was McCarthyism. Joseph McCarthy led a campaign to purge Communists and homosexuals from the federal government. Although many Communists lost their jobs, many more (thousands) homosexuals lost theirs. (Interestingly, our history books constantly refer to "McCarthyism" as the period in which Communists were routed out with the question "Are you now or have you ever been a Communist?" Yet, the plight of homosexuals is barely mentioned. Have history books purposely ignored this inequality in an effort to continue keeping homosexuals hidden?) However, the hearings gave an unprecedented exposure to homosexuals and homosexual oppression. Roy Cohen, McCarthy's assistant, was known as a cunning, ruthless attorney and gay. Cohen would later become a mentor of President Donald Trump.

The media around McCarthyism facilitated discussions about homosexuality. Much of what was written was negative, but it allowed closeted and isolated homosexuals to know that there were many others like them.

The Homophile Movement

The Homophile Movement is a period in which people who engaged in homosexual behavior and relationships began to self-identify and cast-off the deficit label put on them by early sexologists. They began to overcome their own homophobia and find love for themselves and other homosexuals. This is the period of *homo* (same) *phile* (love) identity formation.

Harry Hay (previously known as Henry Hay) was one of the key founders of the modern gay movement. He was a Communist organizer in Los Angeles and a sought-after teacher of Communist theory. In 1950, he assembled friends from the University of Southern California and launched the International Bachelors Fraternal Orders for Peace and Social Dignity (sometimes referred to as Bachelors Anonymous). The group was structured as a secret society with underground guilds separated so that no one would know all other members—a method used by the old left to keep members safe.

In 1951 Bachelors Anonymous incorporated in California as the Mattachine Society. The name Mattachine was inspired by the *Société Mattachine*, a secret fraternal organization in thirteenth- and fourteenth-century France and Spain of unmarried townsmen who performed music, dances, and rituals while wearing masks, sometimes in protest against oppression. The Society wanted to unify homosexuals and educate people about LGBTQ issues. At the same time, the Mattachine Foundation was established to provide a legal front for the Society.

In the same year the Mattachine Society was formed, Donald Webster Cory published *The Homosexual in America*. He argued that the problems experienced by homosexuals stemmed from societal disapproval rather than from homosexuality itself. This was an important perspective, but American society was not ready to accept it. The publisher was ordered to cease publishing books with homosexual themes.

America was a very dangerous place for lesbians and gay men during the 1940s, 1950s, and 1960s. Bars were about the only place gays and lesbians could meet, and often they were unmarked and required patrons to enter through a back door so no one could see them entering from the street. Police regularly entrapped men and women for lewd conduct, raided bars and baths, and suspended business licenses of gay establishments with no provocation or legitimacy. For example, in some cities and states there were laws that required bar patrons to wear clothing conforming to their gender. Police would enter a lesbian bar and seek out the manliest-looking patron. They would take her outside to the sidewalk and make her strip. They were making sure that she wore at least three items of clothing that were "feminine." If she wore boxer shorts, she could be arrested.

In 1952, Dale Jennings, one of the members of the Mattachine Society, was arrested and charged with lewd conduct. He claimed that a man he was not overly interested in came home with him. When Jennings went to make him coffee, the man moved to the window and played with the blinds. Police immediately entered the apartment and arrested Jennings. Jennings felt this was entrapment, a very common practice used by police at that time (and unfortunately, still a problem).

Most people charged with vagrancy and lewd conduct pleaded guilty and paid the fine so as to avoid jail (where they could be raped and beaten) and to keep it quiet so employers and families would not find out. Jennings convinced the Mattachine Society to help with the fight. At the trial, Jennings admitted being a homosexual (probably the first time anyone stood in a court of law and made that pronouncement) and insisted that he was neither lewd nor criminal. He helped educate the jury about the process of entrapment and how homosexuals were targets of police abuse. The defense attorney caught the arresting officer lying on the witness stand. The jury was hung (11 wanted acquittal, 1 wanted conviction), and the judge dismissed the case. Although this was the first successful defense against police entrapment, none of the mainstream media carried the story.

The Mattachine Society set up another organization to publish a newsletter—*ONE Inc.* It began publication in January 1953 and was the voice of the homophile movement. The U.S. postmaster seized copies of *ONE* on grounds that it was "obscene, lewd, lascivious and filthy" and refused to allow the newsletter to be sent by U.S. mail. *ONE* sued, eventually winning an U.S. Supreme Court decision (*One, Inc. v. Olesen*). The Court ruled in 1958 that homosexual materials were not automatically deemed "obscene" and could be sent via the mail. This was a very important decision. Without the right to send materials through the mail the fledging gay rights movement would have been significantly hampered.

In 1953, Joseph McCarthy called Mattachine Foundation legal advisor Fred M. Snyder to testify before the House Un-American Activities Committee. McCarthy considered Snyder an unfriendly witness and attempted to defame and humiliate him. At the same time, the Mattachine Society held a convention in Los Angeles. With over 500 representatives, it was the largest such gathering of homosexuals in U.S. history. A power struggle ensued between the founders, who were leftist, and those who wanted a more moderate, liberal organization. The liberal factions won out, and the old Mattachine Foundation board resigned.

Over the next 40 years, the Mattachine Society/ONE Inc. evolved, changed names a number of times, floundered, regrouped, but survived. Currently, it is mostly a library and archive collection located on the campus of the University of Southern California (USC) and is named ONE National Gay & Archives. It contains the largest collection of homosexual books, magazines, articles, paintings, and memorabilia in the world with more than two million catalogued items.

Soon after the formation of the Mattachine Society in California, homosexuals in New York began meeting informally in a group called the League. Sam Morford and Tony Segura were frustrated by the flimsy nature of the League and decided in December 1955 to launch the *Mattachine Review* and Mattachine Society New York (MSNY). Approximately 30 persons attended the first meeting of MSNY at the Diplomat Hotel. The organizers had to work with extreme caution because homosexuality was a felony in New York State and punishable by up to 20 years in prison.

Women were always involved with the Mattachine Society, although they constituted a very small percentage of the membership. Inspired by its success, Del Martin and Phyllis Lyon in 1956 transformed their lesbian social club into a lesbian activist organization named the Daughters of Bilitis (DOB): the first national lesbian organization in the United States. (Del Martin and Phyllis Lyon would become the first same-sex couple to be legally married in the United States in 2004.) The name came from Pierre Louÿs's narrative "Song of Bilitis," in which Bilitis is a lesbian poet and disciple of Sappho who lived in ancient Greece on the isle of Lesbos. Chapters of DOB were established in major cities around the country and in Australia. They produced a newsletter called *The Ladder*. DOB was well connected with the Mattachine Society and other early gay rights organizations.

The early 1960s was a turning point for the homophile movement. The Mattachine Society and DOB were conservative in their actions and avoided direct politics. For example, when they were involved in official business, they required members to dress conservatively—suits and ties for men, dresses and heels for women. They excluded members who were overly effeminate or ultramasculine. They wrote polite letters, planned scholarly publications, and invited experts to lecture on "sexual variation" before serious audiences in respectable halls. Most members were secretive, and even the leaders often used pseudonyms. Because of the fears and inhibitions of these organizations, few members were attracted. As such, many homosexuals felt left out and resented professionals who told them they were deviants and immoral. They wanted an organization that would take direct political action to reduce police harassment and to change laws.

Frank Kameny, Harvard astronomer, was an activist who took direct political action. He was dismissed from his army post in 1957 for being a homosexual. He contested the dismissal all the way to the U.S. Supreme Court. The Court would not review the case and let stand his dismissal. The betrayal he felt toward a legal system that denied his right to employment led him to form the Mattachine Society of Washington (MSW). He wanted the group to take direct political action. He rejected the deviancy label and coined the phrase "Gay Is Good" to paraphrase African American militants whose motto was "Black Is Beautiful." He argued

> that discrimination was squarely to blame for the homosexual's problems and that boldly challenging discriminatory policies was the most effective way to make progress . . . [and we should take] a militant homophile approach to gay political activity. (Marotta 1981, 25)

The activist approach for MSW threatened Mattachine leadership in New York, San Francisco, and Los Angeles who wrote

> that Mattachine cannot pursue any path but the educational and research. . . . Our charter is placed in jeopardy whenever we try to influence legislation through any other means publicly. . . . We can endorse the action of other agencies working in this field, and "ride on their shirttails," so to speak, with relative safety. But we cannot lobby on our own, and must be careful how we recommend changes of law so that our charter and the right to solicit funds through the mail is not in danger. ("Letter from Hall Call" 1956)

Other groups formed outside of Mattachine were more activist oriented. In 1964, 10 participants from the Homosexual League of New York and the League for Sexual Freedom picketed along the street in front of the Army Induction Center on Whitehall Street. In this "first" gay demonstration, they protested the army's dishonorable discharges of gay soldiers.

The next year, 1965, the Mattachine Society held its first public demonstration in front of the White House to protest government discriminatory employment practices. Before they went, they agreed that the men would wear suits and ties and the women would wear conservative dress. That same day, 20,000 antiwar protestors were at the Washington Monument. The coincidence of media being there for the antiwar protestors got national TV coverage for this gay demonstration.

In spring 1966, the police began "Operation New Broom" in New York City in which they "cleaned up" Times Square and Greenwich Village areas. They raided and closed gay bars, restaurants, bookstores, and taverns. Many men were entrapped and charged with solicitation and lewd conduct. Seven members of the Mattachine Society attended a public meeting at Judson Memorial Church where the chief inspector for the police was holding a community hearing. Randy Wicker and Craig Rodwell from Mattachine spoke and explained how previous efforts by New York police to "crack down" on gay bars left homosexuals with no social outlet and led to underworld elements opening illegal operations for homosexuals. The illegal bars were sources of police corruption and bribery. The chief inspector responded by saying that gay bars were illegal because of "illicit activities." Wicker pointed out these illicit activities were mostly undercover policemen soliciting bar patrons for entrapment. The chief inspector denied the allegations. Wicker was shocked by the naïveté of the chief inspector and said, "It's alarming to think that the Chief Inspector doesn't know that a large number of police spend their duty hours dressed in tight pants, sneakers, and polo sweaters . . . to bring about solicitations" (Marotta 1981, 36). The audience at the meeting shouted out "Bravo!" Soon after, the mayor of New York issued a memorandum ordering the police to cease engaging in entrapment.

It is important to understand the process of overcoming stigmatization and oppression. Initially, those who engaged in homosexual behaviors had no identity concerning their sexual orientation. In much of history and in many cultures today, as long as people meet their familial obligations by marrying and having children, society does not care if they engage in homosexual behaviors. In these cultures, homosexuality is not spoken about. Only if the homosexual relationship interferes with the family or becomes too "obvious," does the culture crack down, often seeking the death of the offender.

As the science of psychology developed, homosexuality was identified as a "sexual inversion" that was deviant. These characteristics were not based on science but rather the codification of social and cultural norms. Still, it influenced psychologists, legislators, judges, police, schools, universities, churches, and others in power and enabled them to justify the persecution of homosexuals. Those who engaged in homosexual behaviors began to see an identity, albeit one that was negative and enforced feelings of worthlessness. This is called internalized homophobia.

But not all homosexuals felt they were mentally ill or deviant. Instead, they recognized that society put this label on them. It was society that expressed homophobia. The Mattachine Society took an educational approach. It believed that if accurate information got out, it could dispel stereotypes and influence society. It issued newsletters and pamphlets, held educational seminars, and challenged the medical establishment. Its demonstrations were meant to bring attention to problems the media and society refused to face or even name.

The Mattachine Society was the right organization for its time. If gay activists had engaged in direct political action in the 1950s, they would have been jailed and their message would have been obliterated. But by the late 1960s the Mattachine Society proved to be too conservative, and few outside the gay community heard their message. Many homosexuals did not accept the negative stereotypes of society and wanted an immediate relief from the oppression of police and laws. They wanted to be able to keep their jobs, homes, and families without having to stay in the closet. Thus, they took more political action, such as the public meeting at Judson Memorial Church. They wanted a public hearing with the chief inspector of police to bring the issue of entrapment to his attention. As described earlier, the chief inspector denied entrapment occurred, yet the gay community knew otherwise and brought it to the attention of the media, the surrounding community, and the mayor.

Bringing the problem to the attention of the community is the first step toward overcoming oppression. Homosexuality was hidden, but no more. Now the arrests, beatings, firings, and more were brought to everyone's attention. Homosexuals were overcoming their internalized homophobia, but so were heterosexuals. The U.S. Constitution and civil religion emphasize fair and equitable treatment. The entrapment of gay men by New York City police was brought to the attention of the mayor and city council who saw the unfairness of these actions and stepped in to stop the abuse. It was heterosexuals who understood the oppression of heterosexism and took action. Heterosexuals were overcoming their homophobia.

The next 30 years of gay activism reflect this process. Heterosexuals controlled the laws and institutions of the United States. Gay activists, especially in the early years, were few in numbers. Yet the truth of their message of equality between homosexuals and heterosexuals was strong enough to convince heterosexuals to intervene and change the power structure. This is a recurring pattern for overcoming injustice.

Another major change occurred during the 1950s and 1960s. Psychologists engaged in academic research into homosexuality. Their work would forever change the social and cultural norms that depicted homosexuality as a mental illness.

The early investigations into homosexuality were performed on a skewed sample of people who visited gay bars, patients in psychiatric hospital, and prison inmates. Not surprisingly, these studies confirmed the societal beliefs and stereotypes that homosexuals were alcoholics, crazed, and criminal. In the mid-1950s, Dr. Evelyn Hooker (1963) at UCLA carried out the first rigorous studies using nonclinical gays and discovered that psychiatrists could not identify lesbians and gay men using psychological testing. Psychiatrists who made money "curing" allegedly insane gays now could not even identify them (Hooker 1963). Evelyn Hooker (who was heterosexual) and other respected academic researchers showed every antigay stereotype to be incorrect. With this evidence, the American Psychiatric

Association (APA) dropped homosexuality as a mental illness from the *Diagnostic and Statistical Manual of Mental Disorders (DSM)* in 1973 (Bayer 1981).

The Stonewall Riots and Gay Liberation

There are junctions in history at which many forces come together to mark the creation of a major shift in the social paradigm. The riot at Stonewall Inn in New York's Greenwich Village was such an event.

On the night of June 27, 1969, officers from the Public Morals Section of the New York City Police Department attempted to shut down the Stonewall Inn—a small local gay bar. The bar was a favorite place to meet for drag queens, street kids, dope heads, speed freaks, and other marginal people. As people were dismissed by the police and allowed to leave, they gathered across the street. Each time someone appeared in the doorway that the crowd knew, they applauded, which encouraged the brassy individual to pose and make some flippant remark. This infuriated the police even more. When the paddy wagon came to take away the drag queens, bar owner, and bartender, a cry went up from the crowd to overturn the paddy wagon. The wagon drove off, but then the crowd exploded by throwing bottles and stones at the police. The police had to retreat into the bar. A battle cry was heard through the Village and hundreds came out to participate. A small fire began in the window of the Stonewall. Soon after, more police arrived and the crowd scattered.

For the next couple of nights, there were street demonstrations that were more political in nature. Groups of people milled around the streets yelling "gay power," holding hands, and kissing in public. A group of gay cheerleaders were heard singing "We are the Stonewall girls/We wear our hair in curls/We have no underwear/ We show our pubic hairs" (Marotta 1981, 75). After the first two days of disturbances, the Mattachine Society of New York handed out flyers in the Village capitalizing on the "Christopher Street Riots" as the "Hairpin Drop Heard around the World" (Marotta 1981, 77).

Michael Brown was a New Left homosexual who was thrilled to see homosexuals fight against the police. Days after the riots, he met with Dick Leitsch of MSNY to discuss sponsoring more demonstrations. When Leitsch adamantly insisted that MSNY could not engage in such activity, Michael Brown set up an independent action committee that became the Gay Liberation Front (GLF).

Before Stonewall, about a dozen gay organizations existed. Within three months after the riot, more than 50 lesbian and gay organizations formed throughout the United States. These organizations have become more radical with many cities hosting marches and festivals in June to commemorate the anniversary of the Stonewall Riots. It is these events, more than any other, that helped bring unity to the gay community and influenced political and legal progress.

GLF was composed of a series of small groups in the United States and other Western countries. It never became a formal organization. GLF represented an important transitional phase for the homophile movement. It built coalitions with other disenfranchised groups and attempted to dismantle oppressive economic, political, and social structures. Many of its participants had been members of the New Left, such as the Students for a Democratic Society (SDS), and others who rejected strict social norms such as pacifists and "hippies." GLF was responsible for the beginnings of many college lesbian and gay student groups. It believed that a total transformation of society was needed to obtain equality and freedom for all marginalized people. Primarily, they engaged in consciousness-raising sessions in people's living rooms, church basements, and storefronts. These groups were nonhierarchical in structure and often did not have a leader. They built upon the belief that the "personal is the political" and launched a number of small newsletters and engaged in demonstrations.

The ideological differences between the revolutionaries, social radicals, and reformers were too great to maintain, and GLF soon broke apart. Many, if not most of the reformers, felt alienated by the radical politics of GLF. Although they had outgrown the conservative homophile groups, they did not want to overthrow the entire political and social system as advocated by radicals and revolutionaries. Instead they sought a more activist organization that would bring about political change to eliminate discrimination against homosexuals. It was these GLF reformers who created the Gay Activists Alliance (GAA).

GAA engaged in petition drives, political "zaps," and street theater. "Zaps" are demonstrations in which politicians are directly confronted in public and asked pointed questions or chastised for antigay statements. Street theater included "gay-in" or "kiss-in" in which members of the same sex would hold hands or kiss in public, something that heterosexuals are able to do but was (and still is) "shocking" when done by same-sex couples. GAA was successful at obtaining media attention and brought gay issues to the forefront of public discussion. In New York, these actions informed Mayor Lindsay and the city council, all of whom were heterosexual, about gay issues. Seeing how government was unfair toward gay people they ended entrapment, police harassment, and public employment discrimination. GAA was able to educate those in power about homophobia, and it was heterosexuals who changed the power structure.

Many groups formed in the early 1970s. They reflected the identity of their members. Separatism was advocated by some as the solution to heterosexual oppression. The National Organization of Women (NOW) was challenged by lesbian feminist over women's fears of being identified as dykes. Bisexuals made their needs known and became a voice within the lesbian and gay liberation movement. The 1969 Eastern Regional Conference of Homophile Organizations (ERCHO) proposed a national celebration each June 28 to commemorate the Stonewall Riots. Now, most major cities and many smaller ones hold Gay Pride festivals and parades to which tens of thousands, and sometimes hundreds of thousands, people attend and participate.

The Stonewall Riot in 1969 is considered by many as the beginning of the modern gay rights movement. For the next decade, the fledgling gay community focused mostly on community building. Gay student groups formed at many large colleges, community services centers were opened, cities and counties granted money for developing health service centers to serve the historically underserved

LGBT community, theaters mounted more gay-themed plays, gay pride parades and festivals sprang up in most major cities, and more.

Equal Rights and Community Building

There was a decline in radical activism in the decade following Stonewall. Gay reformers aimed at community building and political activism. They worked to educate and overcome oppressive laws, not to overthrow the system. There were over 1,100 organizations nationwide devoted to lesbian and gay concerns by 1973. This number would more than double by the 1980s and again more than double by the 1990s. There are support organizations for every conceivable group—businesses, students, schools, scientist, lawyers, academics, artists, religious organizations, racial and ethnic minorities, recreation, and more. There was also a flood of publications, media, and more devoted to lesbian and gay concerns.

Government agencies were made aware that homosexuals underutilized their social services. Many cities developed entire centers providing services for lesbians and gay men. Some of the services included mental and physical health clinics, vocational services, counseling, lesbian advocacy, telephone hotlines, roommate referral, rap groups, medical services, legal help, and more. Often these centers provided professional advice to cities and governmental agencies about the needs, opinions, and concerns of the gay community.

One of the most influential political groups formed in the United States is the National Gay and Lesbian Task Force (NGLTF). Founded in 1973 as the National Gay Task Force (NGTF), it blended the old homophile movement with the newer reformist strategies of GAA. Lambda is a national organization that promotes the civil rights of lesbians, gay men, bisexuals, transgendered, and AIDS sufferers through litigation, education, and public policy work. When the secretary of state rejected its application for incorporation, Lambda took the case to the New York Supreme Court where the decision was overturned.

Again, we see the process of a handful of gay activists educating heterosexuals to overcome their homophobia. Lambda argued that the U.S. Constitution explicitly allows people to come together to advocate for legal change (otherwise known as the right of assembly guaranteed in the First Amendment); and this was Lambda's goal concerning gay rights. The New York Supreme Court agreed and rejected the unfairness inherent in denying its application for incorporation. It was heterosexual judges who changed the prohibition against gay groups forming in the state of New York.

Later in 1974, similar arguments were made at the U.S. Supreme Court level in *Gay Students Organization v. Bonner*. Here, gay activists educated the Court about the right of lesbians and gay men to come together and form organizations qualifying for federal tax-exempt status. Again, heterosexual judges found the arguments convincing and ruled that homosexual groups were to receive the same treatment by the IRS as any other qualifying group.

One of the most significant policy changes came from the American Psychiatric Association (APA) in 1973–1974. The APA formed a committee in the early 1970s to review the research on homosexuality as related to its classification as a mental illness. It reviewed the works of Dr. Evelyn Hooker and many other researchers, along with the 1969 recommendations by the National Institute of Mental Health (NIMH) Task Force on Homosexuality, to repeal sodomy laws and educate the public about homosexuality (Thompson 1994, 69). The committee, along with the APA's Council on Research and Development, Reference Committee, and Assembly, made recommendations to remove homosexuality from its list of mental illness. The APA Board unanimously passed a resolution removing homosexuality from the *DSM*. A group of psychoanalysts filed a petition against the resolution. A referendum was held during which more than 58 percent of the 10,000 voting members supported (with 37.8 percent against) the Board action. Future challenges to the resolution were rejected by even larger margins.

Conservatives and members of the Religious Right often considered that this change in the *DSM* was accomplished by a band of scheming gay activists who pushed through their agenda. This is not true. It was a multiyear review of academic and government research combined with a clear presentation of the findings to the members that convinced the APA to change its position. The membership of the APA reflects society and is mostly heterosexual. It was primarily heterosexuals who reviewed the research and agreed that the change was needed. It was heterosexuals who overcame their bias and homophobia and made a rational decision based on objective research. In the intervening 30 years, no academic research has found any evidence suggesting that homosexuality is a mental illness. If anything, the research has affirmed that there are no differences in psychosocial measures related to sexual orientation.

Gay rights grew nationwide during the 1970s with individual cities and counties (but no states) adopting antidiscrimination statutes. However, there was a conservative backlash. For example, in 1977 the Miami-Dade County Commission passed an ordinance making it illegal to discriminate on the basis of sexual orientation. This came about because local gay groups brought their concerns about employment and housing discrimination to the Commission. The Commission, which was comprised of heterosexuals, understood the need for such an ordinance. It understood that it was not giving homosexuals additional rights, but rather was providing the city with the legal power to enforce rights already enjoyed by all Americans but denied homosexuals due to historical and social reasons.

Upset by this development, singer and Florida Citrus Commission representative Anita Bryant organized a group called "Save Our Children." It used scare tactics claiming homosexuals molest children and are mentally ill. It obtained sufficient signatures to place a referendum on the ballot to overturn the ordinance. The county citizens passed it overwhelmingly. The "Save Our Children" campaign is an example of emotional hysteria caused by religious conservatives and based on false information and stereotypes that overruled decisions made by heterosexuals who were educated on the issue. Twenty years later, Dade County passed the same ordinance and, this time, religious conservatives were unsuccessful at overturning it.

The very next year, 1978, a similar battle occurred in California. Senator Briggs collected signatures and placed Proposition 6 on the ballot. It would have barred homosexuals from teaching in public schools. The "Save Our Children" slogan and methodology were used to promote the proposition. Despite this, every teacher and labor union, Democrats, many Republicans, and many others including Governor Ronald Reagan came out against the proposition. It failed to pass.

It seems that many Americans were not ready to give antidiscrimination protection to lesbians and gay men (as we saw in Dade County), but were not ready to outright discriminate against them (as in California's Briggs Initiative).

Tragedy hit in 1978. Dan White gunned down the mayor of San Francisco and Supervisor Harvey Milk in city hall. White was a conservative supervisor on the San Francisco city council who held much animosity toward openly gay supervisor Harvey Milk. In November 1978, White resigned his position on the council. He changed his mind and asked the mayor for his position back. The mayor refused. A week later, White entered city hall and shot Harvey Milk and Mayor George Moscone to death. The murder of the two men resulted in one of the most impressive memorial services ever seen in San Francisco in which more than 40,000 men, women, and children marched by candlelight to city hall.

At the trial, White's lawyers claimed that White was addicted to junk food and the sugar affected his judgment (what has since become known as the "Twinkie Defense"). White was not convicted of first-degree murder but, rather, voluntary manslaughter and was sentenced to seven years in prison. The gay community exploded at the lenient sentence and took to the streets of San Francisco. That night in 1979, in what is referred to as "White Night," police cars were overturned, fires set, and thousands of people marched to city hall. More than 150 people were injured and property damages in excess of $1 million resulted. White was released after serving just five years of his sentence. He committed suicide in 1985.

Anita Bryant's crusade, Briggs effort, and the murder of Harvey Milk and George Moscone galvanized the gay movement. But it also galvanized conservative religious groups into what is today known as the Religious Right. In 1979, Rev. Jerry Falwell launched the Moral Majority (renamed the Liberty Federation in 1989). In the same year, Beverly LaHaye founded Concern Women for America. Pat Robertson, who began the Christian Broadcast Network (CBN) in 1961 and has hosted *The 700 Club* since 1968, opened CBN University in 1977, making his operation one of the best-financed conservative religious organizations in the nation. These three groups would become, and are, the most power antigay organizations in the United States.

As disco receded in the late 1970s, a new scourge swept the gay community in the 1980s forever changing the face of gay liberation. The cause was AIDS. Unknown and unnamed in the 1970s, AIDS would kill tens of thousands of young men in the coming decade. Gay rights organizations, political parties, and cultural groups saw major shifts in their membership as young men died from the mysterious disease. Many gay men faced their greatest fears with the AIDS epidemic—that antigay moralizing was right and that God was judging gay men.

Much of the LGBT rights progress came to a halt with the advent of AIDS. The 1980s saw a tragic loss in life and leadership in the LGBT community from mounting AIDS deaths. But from this holocaust came discourse. Average Americans, politicians, the media, and religious organizations had to talk about homosexuality in ways they never faced before. With illness and death affecting so many, no one could claim not knowing someone who was LGBT. From this discourse developed policies to protect those with HIV from discrimination in the workplace, housing, and elsewhere. Realizing the overt discrimination LGBT people faced on a daily basis naturally led politicians to develop antidiscrimination laws to provide some level of protection.

1980s and 1990s—AIDS and Discrimination

Seeing the need to coordinate pro-gay political efforts, the Human Rights Campaign (HRC) was founded in 1980. It focused on fighting antigay ballot initiatives and supported candidates who promote antidiscrimination policies based on sexual orientation. Its political action committee (PAC) provides financial support for candidates and typically raises and donates more than $1 million a year to candidates at the federal level. For example, by 1998, of the 200 political candidates to whom it contributed money, 91 percent won their respective races.

The 1980s saw a continuation in the trend toward greater recognition and equality for lesbians and gay men. For example, over 200,000 people participated in the first March on Washington in 1979. In 1981, a court case in Dallas banned police from discriminating against lesbians and gays in employment as police officers (*Childers v. Dallas Police Department*). In 1982, Wisconsin became the first state to pass a wide-reaching law prohibiting discrimination against lesbians and gay men. A high school support program for lesbian and gay children was established in 1984 (Project 10, Los Angeles). In 1987, the second March on Washington took place with over 600,000 people attending. The National Education Association in 1988 adopted a resolution calling for every school district to provide counseling for students struggling with their sexual orientation.

The U.S. Supreme Court handed down a significant antigay ruling in 1986. Michael Hardwick was charged with engaging in sodomy in Georgia. Hardwick sued, and the case reached the U.S. Supreme Court. The Court ruled against Hardwick in a 5–4 decision stating that claims for "homosexual sodomy" as a protected right to privacy are "facetious, at best." The Court established that lesbians and gay men have no right to sexual expression under the federal constitutional. This ruling would hinder the civil rights gains by lesbians and gay men for decades. Interestingly, soon after his retirement, Supreme Court justice Lewis Powell conceded that he "had made a mistake" and should have voted to strike down Georgia's sex statute (Marcus 1990).

AIDS

The 1980s also marked the advent of AIDS. The first cases were reported in 1981 in the United States and exclusively involved gay men. Doctors were unsure what caused this "Gay Plague" and initially called it gay-related immune deficiency (GRID). As more nongays came down with the disease (Haitians, intravenous drug users, hemophiliacs, and heterosexuals), it became obvious that it was not related to being gay, but rather was an immune deficiency caused by a virus spread through bodily fluids. Bruce Voller, a biological researcher, coined the terms *acquired immune deficiency syndrome* (AIDS) to better reflect the nature of the disease.

There was much hysteria about AIDS. People who developed AIDS were often fired from their jobs, forced out of their apartments and housing, lost their health insurance, and more. Children who were asymptomatic but infected with human immunodeficiency virus (HIV) were expelled from schools. Public swimming pools were emptied, scrubbed, disinfected, and refilled after a person with AIDS used the pool. Mortuaries refused to handle the bodies of people who died from AIDS. Airlines refused to allow people with AIDS to fly. And even health professionals sometime refused to care for those with AIDS. Massive discrimination resulted, and the government initially ignored the severity of the problem.

The Religious Right used AIDS to reignite its antigay crusades. They claimed AIDS was "God's punishment" for the "immoral" gay "lifestyle." They called for a general quarantine of people with AIDS, the firing of lesbian and gay teachers, and more draconian measures. Even the mainstream media refused to cover the AIDS epidemic until the first heterosexuals were reported to be infected (Shilts 1987). It was seven years into the epidemic before President Ronald Reagan publicly spoke the word AIDS. Yet Patrick Buchanan, Reagan's Chief of Communications, was very outspoken, claiming that AIDS was "God's awful retribution" for homosexual behavior and that AIDS patients did not deserve help ("Buchanan Calls AIDS 'Retribution'" 1992). AIDS, unfortunately, is still tied to antigay sentiments in many people's minds even though it was never a gay disease.

President Reagan appointed a 13-member AIDS panel in July 1987. Although there was much in-fighting between the members, the panel made remarkably progressive recommendations including the call for massive governmental funding for research and care. The panel also recommended legislation to prevent discrimination against people with AIDS (PWA) and people infected with the virus. These recommendations impacted the 1990 adoption by Congress of the American with Disabilities Act (ADA).

The frustration in the gay community over overt discrimination and government inaction compelled Larry Kramer and other activists to form AIDS Coalition to Unleash Power (ACT UP) in 1987. ACT UP was a group of individuals united in anger and committed to ending the AIDS crisis through direct action. The slogan "Silence = Death" originated with ACT UP. It engaged in a number of high-profile demonstrations that brought significant media attention to the problem. For example, in 1989, over 5,000 ACT UP members demonstrated in front of and inside New York's St. Patrick's Cathedral rallying against the Catholic Church's antigay stance and policies on AIDS.

There was one "good" that came from the AIDS crisis—it compelled the media, government, and average citizen to talk about homosexuality and gay issues in ways they never did before. For example, *The New York Times* used the word *gay* in reference to homosexuality for the first time in 1987. AIDS brought more attention to gay rights than the previous 30 years of educational efforts and public demonstrations.

By 1993, the "cocktail" was developed to treat AIDS. Various drugs had been created using different biological strategies in the 1980s to combat HIV. It was discovered that blending the drugs together proved to be effective at reducing viral infection to undetectable levels at the same time reducing side effects from taking the drugs and reducing viral resistance. The highly active antiretroviral therapy (HAART) methodology was quickly adopted by most physicians, resulting in a dramatic drop in deaths caused by opportunistic infections. By the 2010s, insurance companies began underwriting a similar cocktail of medications to prevent infection. This is known as pre-exposure prophylaxis (or PrEP) or, if exposure has taken place then taking HIV medication immediately after exposure (known as PEP: post-exposure prophylaxis) for a few days. PrEP/PEP has proven to be effective at reducing the spread of HIV.

Antigay Backlash

To counter the political progress lesbian and gay rights were making and the successes of the Human Rights Campaign (HRC), Pat Robertson formed the Christian Coalition in 1989. It was a political organization that worked to elect conservative Christians to political office. Formed as a nonprofit religious organization, it violated its tax-exempt status by issuing voters guides and engaging in other direct political action. By 1999, the IRS revoked its tax exemption.

Many other antigay groups were formed in the 1980s and 1990s. These included the Family Research Council, Focus on the Family, Moral Majority, Traditional Values Coalition, Truth in Action Ministries, Exodus International, Westboro Baptist Church, National Association for Research & Therapy of Homosexuality (NARTH), MassResistance, and others. Many of these organizations have been racked by internal scandal when leaders were found in same-sex sexual relationships or were in violation of their nonprofit status. A few of the organizations crossed the line into advocating violence and have earned a listing with the Southern Poverty Law Center and the Anti-Defamation League as a recognized hate group. These hate groups included the Family Research Institute, Family Research Council, Traditional Values Coalition, MassResistance, and Westboro Baptist Church. Westboro Baptist Church, led by the late Reverend Fred Phelps, is infamous for picketing funerals of American military personnel or other high-profile deaths with slogans such as "God Hates Fags," "Thank God for Dead Soldiers," and similar. The outrageousness of Westboro Baptist Church actions has produced many counter demonstrations and brought divergent groups together in support of their gay and lesbian families and friends.

1990–2010s and Marriage Equality

Lesbians and gay men want their relationships to be safe and stable, and as valued by society as heterosexual relationships. Sodomy laws made the idea of same-sex marriage inconceivable since merely being homosexual classified them as "criminal." Still, some brave gays and lesbians filed for marriage licenses in the 1960s, 1970s, and 1980s without success. Many states updated their criminal codes and revoked or rescinded their sodomy statutes besides including language granting privacy and equality clauses. By 1990, three couples in Hawaii tested their state's constitution's equal protection clause by petitioning to marry. The court sided with the couples in *Baehr v. Lewin*. This sent shock waves through the cultural and political landscape of the United States. The prospect of same-sex couples having the right to marry was incomprehensible for many Americans. For Hawaii, the same-sex marriage case was tossed between lower courts, the legislature, committees, and more for the next nine years only to have it blocked by a constitutional amendment in 1999 defining marriage as the union between one man and one woman.

The prospect of same-sex marriage united conservatives and the Religious Right in efforts to block such marriages. At the federal level, Georgia representative Bob Barr (Republican) introduced the Defense of Marriage Act (DOMA) in 1996. The bill modified the legal code to enable states to: (1) prohibit same-sex marriages, (2) refuse to recognize same-sex marriages legally performed elsewhere, and (3) to make same-sex couples ineligible for a host of state and federal rights and benefits. The bill was fast-tracked through Congress and approved with a veto-proof margin. Although President Bill Clinton was not in favor of same-sex marriage at that time, he did not think the bill was needed since marriage is traditionally a state function. Regardless, he thought the prospect of Congress overruling his veto could set off a call to change the U.S. Constitution to restrict marriage to opposite-sex couples only. The prospect of a constitutional amendment battle would divert the country from more important problems. So, he signed the bill in September 21, 1996, but did not hold a traditional bill signing ceremony nor allow photographs to be taken of his signing. Many states also passed their own versions of DOMA. Four states passed statutes prohibiting same-sex marriages, and 29 states passed amendments to their state constitutions banning same-sex marriages and the recognition of same-sex marriages legally performed elsewhere.

From the very beginning, many legal analyst and government attorneys predicted both federal and state DOMAs would not survive court challenges. At the state level, preventing civil rights based on a characteristic such as sexual orientation would be in conflict with due process and equality clauses. At the federal level, DOMA would violate the Tenth Amendment of the U.S. Constitution since it would be overreaching into state legal territory. Lawsuits were quickly filed against both federal and state DOMAs.

Vermont saw the next legal challenge for same-sex marriage. As with Hawaii, the Vermont court sided with same-sex couples and declared that same-sex couples must have the same rights as opposite-sex couples (*Baker v. Vermont*). The court pushed the problem back to the Vermont legislature to solve. In 2000, Vermont created "civil unions" for same-sex couples that conferred all the rights and responsibility of marriage without the use of the word *marriage*. This was an obvious attempt to placate religious opposition to same-sex marriage. As soon as civil unions were adopted, same-sex couples sued in court for this "separate but equal" approach to balancing the rights of LGBT citizens and religious fundamentalist. California also implemented a statewide domestic partnerships registry—the first in the nation—to provide the benefits of marriage to same-sex couples without calling it *marriage*. This approach, too, was challenged in court.

Finally, in 2004, Massachusetts became the first state in the United States to approve same-sex marriage. The Massachusetts Supreme Judicial Court ruled in 2003 (*Goodridge v. Department of Public Health*) that nothing short of full marriage would fulfill the equality clause of the state constitution.

From the Hawaii case in 1990 and for the next 20 years, many states faced the challenge of same-sex marriage. Gay and lesbian couples sued for the right to marry while legislatures wrestled with ways to either accommodate the relationship without using the word "marriage" or outright blocking them by legally defining marriage in ways to exclude same-sex couples. Many conservatives and religious fundamentalist did not trust their state legislators or courts and successfully amended their state constitutions to exclude same-sex marriage through the use of DOMA.

Importantly, the overturning of state sodomy statutes by the U.S. Supreme Court in 2003 (*Lawrence v. Texas*) effectively made homosexuals equal, under the law, to heterosexuals. By decriminalizing homosexuality, local, state, and federal governments now faced questions of how to fully integrate homosexuals and their relationships into their legal frameworks that often were constructed with a heterosexual bias.

The fight for same-sex marriage in California became an extended struggle between those favoring equal rights for all and those wanting to keep LGBT people as second-class citizens. In 2000, Proposition 22 was passed by the voters to limit marriage to one man and one woman. In 2004, San Francisco mayor Gavin Newsom instructed city employees to grant marriage licenses to same-sex couples. He believed he had the right under the U.S. Constitution. Approximately 4,000 same-sex couples obtained their licenses before the state attorney ordered Newsom to cease and desist from issuing further license. In 2008, the California Supreme Court ruled against Proposition 22 and same-sex marriages resumed in June 16, 2008. Months before the ruling, Proposition 8 gathered sufficient signatures to be placed on the November ballot. Proposition 8 was designed to modify the state constitution to ban same-sex marriages. Between June and November 2008, approximately 18,000 same-sex marriages were performed. Proposition 8 was narrowly approved by the voters, which brought an immediate cessation to same-sex marriages. Proposition 8 was challenged in court, and the California State Supreme Court ruled it to be a valid amendment to the constitution. That put California in the unique position of having thousands of legal marriages that other citizens could no longer obtain the same right. American Foundation for Equal Rights (AFER) took the case to federal court to challenge Proposition 8 under the U.S. Constitution. U.S. District Court for the Northern District of California judge Vaughn R. Walker conducted a full trial and ruled

Proposition 8 unconstitutional in August 12, 2010, because it violated both the due process and equal protection clauses of the U.S. Constitution (*Perry v. Schwarzenegger* renamed *Hollingsworth v. Perry*). Neither the governor nor attorney general wanted to defend the state against the ruling. However, supporters of Proposition 8 appealed the case to the U.S. Supreme Court. On June 26, 2013, the Court ruled that the petitioners did not possess legal standing, which reverted to Judge Walker's ruling. Same-sex marriage resumed in California on June 28, 2013.

Much happened throughout the country during the decade of legal skirmishes in California. In 2008, Connecticut became the second state to approve same-sex marriage. Many more states enacted same-sex marriage laws: Iowa (2009 by judicial decision), Vermont (2009 by legislative action), New Hampshire (2010 by legislative action), District of Columbia (2010 by legislative action), New York (2011 by legislative action), Maine (2012 by ballot initiative), Maryland (2012 by ballot initiative), Washington (2012 by ballot initiative), California (2013 by judicial decision), Delaware (2013 by legislative action), Minnesota (2013 by legislative action; just six months after voters rejected an antigay marriage initiative the legislature passed enabling legislation), Rhode Island (2013 by legislative action), New Jersey (2013 by judicial decision), Illinois (2013 by legislative action taking effect in 2014), Hawaii (2013 by legislative action), a few counties of New Mexico (2013 by judicial action), and Utah (2013 by judicial action). Also, a number of First People nations approved same-sex marriage: Native American nations of Ceara & Little Traverse Bay Bands of Odawa Indians (Michigan), Pokagon Band of Potawatomi Indians (Michigan), Santa Ysabel Tribe (California), and the Confederated Tribes of the Colville Reservation (Washington).

Importantly, in 2013 the U.S. Supreme Court ruled the DOMA to be unconstitutional (*United States v. Windsor*). The Court decided that Section 3 of DOMA violated the due process clause of the Fifth Amendment. The case clearly demonstrated the inequality DOMA imposed on LGBT citizens. Here, Edith "Edie" Windsor and Thea Spyer, residents of New York, married in Toronto, Ontario, where same-sex marriages were legal. The women had been together for 40 years and built up significant assets. Spyer died in 2009, and Windsor was required to pay $363,053 in federal estate taxes on her inheritance of her wife's estate. If they had been an opposite-sex couple, there would have been no inheritance tax. The court agreed that Section 3 of DOMA, which specified that the term "spouse" only applied to opposite-sex marriage, denied due process to same-sex couples.

Finally, in 2015, the U.S. Supreme Court ruled that marriage is a fundamental right that could not be denied same-sex couples. The *Obergefill v. Hodges* decision overturned the *Baker v. Nelson* ruling, claiming that the equal protection clause, due process clause, and Fourteenth Amendment required marriage equality. Of course, there was a major outcry from conservatives and Republicans. Some county clerks refused to sign marriage certificates issued to same-sex couples. Likewise, some judges refused to officiate same-sex marriages. Much of this outcry died down, and same-sex marriages are becoming as mundane and common as are opposite-sex marriages.

Additional Topics

A recurring theme we shall notice is that the advances in gay rights are the result of heterosexuals overcoming their own internalized homophobia and cultural heterosexism. Laws and customs are created by the larger society, and heterosexuals dominate that society. Only by heterosexuals learning and overcoming their own prejudices against those who do not conform to their heterosexual bias are able to change laws and cultural norms. The last 50 years of U.S. history demonstrates how local city councils, state governments, and eventually the federal government have changed due to changes in heterosexuals championing equal rights for all—including LGBTQ people. Without straight allies, the gay rights movement would not advance.

Sodomy

Beginning with the revision of Illinois criminal code in 1961 and the repeal of its statutes against consensual sodomy, the number of states with sodomy laws reduced significantly over the next 50 years. Gay activists and attorneys brought attention to state legislatures and courts about the unfairness of these laws. Sodomy laws are a violation of the modern concept of privacy and result in the unequal application of the law (a violation of the equal protection clause of the U.S. Constitution). Many courts revoked their state's sodomy laws. In 2003, the U.S. Supreme Court revisited the issue of sodomy in *Lawrence v. Texas*. The three-judge panel of the Texas Fourteenth Court of Appeals ruled that the Texas law was unconstitutional and violated the 1972 Equal Rights Amendment to the Texas Constitution. The full Court of Appeals reversed the decision. Ultimately, the case was taken to the U.S. Supreme Court. The Court ruled that the Texas statute was unconstitutional since it violated due process and equal protection guarantees. The net effect of *Lawrence* was to require states to recognize same-sex sexual activity on the same footing as opposite-sex sexual activity. It is important to recognize that it has been predominantly heterosexual judges who came to understand that sodomy laws are discriminatory and invasive and ruled them invalid.

Don't Ask, Don't Tell

In 1983, the Uniform Code of Military Justice (UCMJ) was modified to formally ban homosexuality by classifying all forms of "unnatural carnal copulation" to be "sodomy" and punishable by court-martial. When Bill Clinton became president of the United States in 1992, one of the first issues he took up was the presence of gays in the military. The fierce response by many legislators and the Religious Right resulted in a compromise bill entitled "Don't Ask, Don't Tell" (DADT) being approved in 1993. It did not radically change the UCMJ but rather added words that directed military personnel to not inquire as to a person's sexual orientation, not to share if known, and if rumors were heard to not pursue or harass. Instead of liberating LGBT military personnel, it created a hostile environment of whispers and court-martial. From 1993 through its repeal 17 years later, more than 14,500 service men and women were discharged from the military under DADT (Servicemen Legal Defense Fund n.d.).

When Barack Obama was sworn in as president in 2010, he promised to work with Congress toward the repeal of the law. Under pressure from the court and the White House, the House of Representatives and Senate passed legislation repealing DADT. President Barack Obama signed the policy into law on September 20, 2011.

Restricting Rights

Colorado's Amendment 2 was one of the watershed decisions made by the U.S. Supreme Court concerning gay rights. Early in the 1990s, a number of cities and counties in the state of Colorado enacted antidiscrimination statutes that included sexual orientation. This angered a number of conservative residents. Colorado for Family Values (CFV) was formed and successfully placed an amendment to the Colorado Constitution on the ballot. Amendment 2 sought to repeal any existing law or policy that protected persons with "homosexual, lesbian, or bisexual orientation" from discrimination in the state and to prohibit future adoption or enforcement of any such law or policy. CFV claimed the amendment provided "special rights" to lesbians, gay men, and bisexuals that they neither "deserved" nor "needed." On November 3, 1992, the voters passed the amendment.

In 1995, the U.S. Supreme Court agreed to review the Colorado Supreme Court's decision. The Court ruled (6–1) that Amendment 2 appeared to violate the fundamental right of lesbians, gay men, and bisexuals to participate in the political process on a basis equal to other Coloradans. Justice Kennedy stated, "We conclude that Amendment 2 classifies homosexuals not to further a proper legislative end but to make them unequal to everyone else. This Colorado cannot do. A state cannot so deem a class of persons a stranger to its laws."

A new approach taken by conservatives and Republicans to restrict the rights of LGBTQ citizens is to claim providing services (e.g., wedding cakes to same-sex couples) violates a strongly held religious belief and is protected by the First Amendment. To support that approach, the federal government passed the Religious Freedom Restoration Act (RAFA) in 1993. Many states have implemented similar laws. The political and legislative discussion always centers around discriminating against LGBTQ people. Many of these laws have been overruled by courts only to have legislatures recraft and pass similar laws. It is expected that the RAFA approach will be in challenged in courts for the next couple decades.

Finally, some states have passed or are considering legislation to restrict transgender people from using public bathrooms. "Bathroom bills" require people to use the bathroom that matches the gender on a person's birth certificate. Obviously, this is a direct attack on transgender citizens. It is claimed that such laws are needed to protect women and children from sexual predators, yet no transgender person has ever been arrested for assault in a public bathroom. The public and media outcry against the bills and financial backlash has influenced some states to revoke their discriminatory "bathroom" laws.

Schools and Antibullying Programs

Another major development in the 1990s–2010s occurred in the public schools. Many schools faced having to accept a gay-straight alliance (GSA) student group on campus. A number of schools refused to accept these groups, but courts consistently upheld the Equal Access Act (EAA), which requires schools to accept all noncurricular student groups on an equal footing. This trend should continue with many more, if not most, schools having gay supportive programs on campus.

A number of tragic suicides made the news in late 2000s. Many centered on gay students who experienced extreme bullying about their sexual orientation. School districts around the country began implementing antibullying campaigns. The suicide by 18-year-old Tyler Clementi influenced syndicated columnist Dan Savage to launch the "It Gets Better Project" in 2010. The goal was to compile 100 or so videos from individual contributors to post on YouTube that would convey the message to gay and lesbian children that life would get better as an adult and to 'hang in there.' By February 2011, more than 10,000 people had submitted videos that were watched more than 30 million times. The "It Gets Better Project" gained overwhelming support from politicians, school districts, and LGBT support organizations like GLSEN and Trevor Project.

Public Access

The 1990s also brought to the forefront the potential conflict between antidiscrimination statutes and the desires of private organizations. Two U.S. Supreme Court decisions illustrate this problem.

Each year the Boston St. Patrick's Day Parade is sponsored by the South Boston Allied War Veterans Councils. They refused to allow a gay marching group to participate. The gay group sued, and the court initially sided with the gay group. The parade organizers canceled the event and appealed to the U.S. Supreme Court. In *Hurley v. Irish-American Gay, Lesbian and Bisexual Group of Boston* (1995), the Court upheld the First Amendment right of the organizers to exclude gays from their event, not because they were gay but rather because the "private" organizers of the event had the right to control the message of the event. The Court said parades are a "form of expression" and private sponsors cannot be forced to include groups that "impart a message the organizers do not wish to convey." Eventually, Boston St. Patrick's Day Parade organizers allowed a gay Irish veterans group march in the parade in 2015.

Similarly, the U.S. Supreme Court upheld the right of the Boy Scouts (BSA) to exclude openly gay men from serving as troop leaders or participating as members (*Boy Scouts of America v. Dale*, 2000). They held that requiring the Boy Scouts to include Mr. Dale in their ranks would violate the organization's First Amendment right of "expressive association." The Court said, "We are not, as we must not be, guided by our views of whether the Boy Scouts' teachings with respect to homosexual conduct are right or wrong. Public or judicial disapproval of a tenet of an organization's expression does not justify the state's effort to compel the organization to accept members where such acceptance would derogate from the organization's expressive message." Years later, BSA modified its policy to allow gay youths to participate (2013), gay adult to work as leaders (2015), and transgender youths to participate (2017).

Sexual Orientation Change Efforts (and Exodus International Apology)

By the late 1990s, there was a shift in the tactics of the Religious Right. Claiming that homosexuals are child molesters and mentally ill just did not have the impact that it used to have. Likewise, "No Special Rights" slogan is still used but, it too, is losing its impact. Too many people, courts, and politicians know these stereotypes and slogans are completely untrue. A new tactic was used to raise funds from conservatives and the Religious Right. It was claimed that homosexuals could change their sexual orientation. Their logic was that since they believed homosexuality was a sin, then not changing his or her sexual orientation was proof that LGBT persons were choosing to sin and not deserving of equal rights.

From the earliest days of the gay rights movement, there have been organizations and persons who claimed sexual orientation could be changed. One of the earliest organizations called Love in Action was founded in 1973 in San Francisco. It was an "ex-gay" ministry that provided spiritual counseling for gay men wishing to reduce their homosexual feelings and become heterosexual. Often referred to as "reparative" therapy (i.e., to "repair" their "broken" sexual orientation), an international organization formed to help coordinate worldwide change efforts. Exodus International would grow to include over 270 ministries. Various psychological techniques were used to attempt the change including shock therapy, talk therapy, behavioral modification, aversion therapy, and prayer (often humorously referred to as "pray away the gay").

Many religious leaders and some academic researchers jumped on the sexual orientation change effort (SOCE) bandwagon. Paul Cameron, a discredited psychologist and sex researcher, founded the Institute for Scientific Investigation of Sexuality (renamed the Family Research Institute [FRI] in 1982) to promote his materials. The academic materials produced by FRI are used extensively by the Religious Right to support their antigay beliefs. FRI is identified as a hate group by the Southern Poverty Law Center. Similarly, the National Association for Research & Therapy of Homosexuality (NARTH) was founded in 1992 to provide clinically based sexual orientation conversion therapies. They too produced academic (but fraudulent) materials used by the Religious Right.

Regardless that most of these ex-gay programs experienced major scandals (e.g., leaders found preying on their homosexual clients, use of same-sex prostitutes, and more), the money poured in during the 1980s and 1990s. In July 1998, full-page paid advertisements were placed in major national newspapers promoting the "ex-gay" movement. The ads were purchased through a coalition of 15 Christian Right organizations. They condemned homosexuality as a sin but emphasized curing homosexuality as an act of prolife. They hoped to plant the idea that homosexuality is a chosen lifestyle and is alterable. Logically this would imply that homosexuals have chosen a lifestyle that is stigmatized and "criminal" with legal restrictions, discrimination, and pain. They claimed that all homosexuals need to do is choose heterosexuality to receive full rights. Accepting the ex-gay movement's position would undermine lesbian and gay men's claim to civil rights. "The ex-gay movement poses a significant new threat to efforts to secure civil rights legal protections for gay/lesbian/bisexual/transgender people. Potentially, it is the most damaging manifestation of an ongoing backlash against this community. . . . The long-term goal of the Christian Right in using the ex-gay movement to convince people that lesbian, gay, and bisexual people can become heterosexual is to create a restrictive legal environment in which equal rights are only accorded to heterosexual men and women" (Khan 1998, 17–18).

In 2003, Dr. Robert Spitzer published an article that claimed: "highly motivated" homosexuals could change their sexual orientation. This was significant because Dr. Spitzer was a highly regarded expert and considered "unbiased" since he participated in the 1973 effort to have the American Psychological Association declassify homosexuality as a mental disorder. Immediately the Religious Right held up his work as proof that homosexuals could change if they really wanted to. However, therapists were hearing more and more horror stories about SOCE therapy from their clients. For example, a friend of John Evans (one of the founders of Love in Action) committed suicide due to his inability to change. Evans stated in a 1993 interview with *The Wall Street Journal* that SOCE destroyed people lives and proponents are living in a fantasy world. Every major psychology organization came out against SOCE, claiming that it not only didn't work but that it caused emotional harm in those attempting to change. Between 2012 and 2013, the SOCE industry collapsed. Alan Chambers, president of Exodus International, told the Gay Christian Network in 2012 that all efforts to change sexual orientation were failures and potentially harmful. Exodus International publicly apologized for all the harm it caused and disbanded. Similarly, Dr. Spitzer published a letter in *Archives of Sexual Behavior* in 2012 apologizing to the gay community. He acknowledged that his 2003 research was flawed, that sexual orientation cannot be changed, and SOCE harm clients.

California senator Ted Lieu became concerned about the terrible toll SOCE were taking on their citizens and, in particular, teenagers. He authored a bill to prohibit the use of reparative therapy on children under age 18. It passed and was signed into law in 2013 by Governor Jerry Brown who stated, "These practices have no basis in science or medicine, and they will now be relegated to the dustbin of quackery" (Shapiro 2013). The law was challenged, but the court concluded that the state has the right to regulate specific industries and create standards. SOCE were proven to not work and harm clients and, thus, the state could require licensed therapist to not engage in such activity or risk losing their license. New Jersey and other states have passed similar laws, and many other states are considering the same. The National Center for Lesbian Rights is the primary organization spearheading the national effort to ban SOCE.

Theocratic State

It is important to remember the Religious Right's goal is to create a theocratic state, a "nation whose laws are based on fundamentalist's interpretation of the Bible" ("We've Come a Long Way . . . Maybe" 2000). Founder and director of the Christian Coalition, Pat Robertson, stated, "The country was founded by Christians. It was founded as a Christian nation. They're trying to sell us this nonsense about separation of church and state. And that's what it is, it's a fanatical interpretation of the First Amendment. . . . We're going to win this battle but we've got to stand together, all the Christians in America need to join hands together and say we've had enough of this utter nonsense" (White 1997). Similarly, Dean Wycoff, director of the Moral Majority of Santa Clara County, California, stated, "I agree with capital punishment and I believe that homosexuality . . . could be coupled with murder. . . . It would be the government that sits upon this land who will be executing the homosexuals" (Young 1982, 77). The agenda of the Religious Right is to take control of the United States and use state power to discriminate, incarcerate, and kill those who do not agree with them—particularly homosexuals.

Separate but Equal

The LGBTQ rights movement parallels the civil rights movement. The process of overcoming prejudice is the process of deconstructing a social bias. For example, African Americans have move from being nonpersons and property when slavery was legal to gaining citizenship through the adoption of the Fourteenth Amendment to the U.S. Constitution. But there was a backlash by Christian conservatives who influenced state and local authorities to enact Jim Crow laws that kept the races separate. For almost 100 years, separate-but-equal was the law of the land, and terror perpetrated by white supremacists was used to keep blacks in their place. Then, in 1954, the U.S. Supreme Court ruled that separate-but-equal was inherently unequal. Only then was America faced with fully integrating African Americans into the society. Still, the Civil Rights Act of 1964 and other legislative acts were required to ensure the equal participation of people of different races. This process deconstructed the allocation of rights and privileges associated with race.

LGBTQ people are entering the second phase of overcoming the stigmatization associated with their sexual orientation and gender differences. Until the beginning of the civil rights movement, homosexual behavior was illegal, and lesbians and gays were often arrested, prosecuted, imprisoned, and killed, and were constantly at risk of losing their jobs, homes, and children. Slowly, cities and states removed antigay laws and replaced them with antidiscrimination laws aimed at providing some protection in the areas of employment and housing. Although marriage equality has been achieved, some states are trying to deny equal rights to same-sex marriages. Also, the Religious Freedom Restoration Acts at both the federal and state levels are opening the door to outright discrimination against LGBTQ people.

It is expected that the courts will eventually rule that any scheme that attempts to allow discrimination against LGBTQ people in the public sphere is inherently unequal. Ultimately, gay liberation will deconstruct sexual orientation and gender presentation much as African American liberation deconstructed race and the women's movement deconstructed gender roles.

The major impediment to African Americans gaining equal rights has been white supremacists and Christian fundamentalists. The major impediment to women's rights has been male supremacists and Christian fundamentalists. The major impediment to gay rights has been heterosexist people and Christian fundamentalists. In each case, the arguments used by bigots and Christian fundamentalists—such as blacks and women are naturally inferior, a position they support by quoting scientists of the time and scripture from the Bible—have been shown to be false. The stereotypes used against homosexuals have all been proven false. More than anything, this demonstrates that discrimination against a class of people is never justified and that the real issue is not science or scripture, but a *culture war* involving those in power and those who are stigmatized. The way a culture is changed is through education. As more people, courts, and politicians learned homosexuals are virtually indistinguishable from heterosexuals, bias and discrimination are reduced. Heterosexuals overcame their homophobia and heterosexism and changed society to make it safe for people of differing sexual orientations and gender presentation to exist together. Heterosexuals are an important and necessary ally for lesbians, gay men, bisexuals, transgender, transsexuals, and intersex people.

References

Baehr v. Lewin, 74 Haw. 530, 852 P.2d 44 (1993), reconsideration and clarification granted in part, 74 Haw. 645, 852 P.2d 74 (1993).

Baker v. Vermont, 744 A.2d 864 (Vt. 1999).

Bayer, R. 1981. *Homosexuality and American Psychiatry*. New York: Basic Books.

Berlet, C. 1998. Who Is Mediating the Storm? Right-Wing Alternative Information Networks. In L. Kintz & J. Lesage (Eds.), *Media, Culture, and the Religious Right* (pp. 249–274). Minneapolis, MN: University of Minnesota Press.

Blumenfeld, W. J., & Raymond, D. (Eds.). 1993. *Looking at Gay and Lesbian Life* (Rev. ed.). Boston, MA: Beacon Press.

Boy Scouts of America v. Dale, No. 99–699 U.S. (2000).

Buchanan Calls AIDS "Retribution." 1992, February 28. *Boston Globe*.

Childers v. Dallas Police Dept., 513 F. Supp. 134 (N.D. Tex. 1981).

D'Emilio, J., & Freedman, E. B. 1988. *Intimate Matters: A History of Sexuality in America*. New York: Harper & Row.

Gay Students Org. v. Bonner, 367 F. Supp. 1088 (D.N.H.), aff'd, 509 F.2d 652 (1st Cir. 1974).

Goodridge v. Dept. of Public Health, 798 N.E.2d 941 (Mass. 2003).

Hollingsworth v. Perry (formerly *Perry v. Brown* and *Perry v. Schwarzenegger*), 570 U.S. ___ (2013) (Docket No. 12–144).

Hooker, E. 1963. The Adjustment of the Male Overt Homosexual. In H. M. Ruitenbeed (Ed.), *The Problem of Homosexuality* (pp. 141–61). New York: Dutton. (Reprinted from *Journal of Projective Techniques, 21,* 18–31, 1959.)

Hurley v. Irish-American Gay, Lesbian and Bisexual Group of Boston, No. 94–749, (1995, June 19).

Katz, J. 1976. *Gay American History: Lesbians and Gay Men in the U.S.A.* New York: Thomas Y. Crowell.

Khan, S. 1998, October. *Calculated Compassion: How the Ex-Gay Movement Serves the Right's Attack on Democracy.* A report from Political Research Associates, the Policy Institute of the National Gay and Lesbian Task Force, and Equal Partners in Faith.

Lawrence v. Texas, 539 U.S. 558 (2003).

Letter from Hall Call to Dwight Huggins, Sam Morford, Tony Segura, et al., August 30, 1956; appended to Segura's letter to Huggins in MSNY files. Reported in Marotta, T. (1981). *The Politics of Homosexuality* (p. 15). Boston: Houghton Mifflin Company.

Marcus, R. 1990, October 26. Powell Regrets Backing Sodomy Law. *Washington Post,* (325), A3.

Marotta, T. 1981. *The Politics of Homosexuality.* Boston: Houghton Mifflin Company.

One, Inc. v. Olesen, 355 U.S. 371 (1958).

Plant, R. 1988. *The Pink Triangle.* New York: New Republic Books/Henry Holt.

Servicemen Legal Defense Fund. (n.d.). About Don't Ask Don't Tell. Retrieved September 13, 2013, from http://www.sldn.org/pages/about-dadt

Shapiro, Lila. 2013, June 25. Straight Talk: How Mathew Shurka and His Conversion Therapist Renounced the "Gay Cure." *Huffington Post.* Retrieved January 1, 2014, from http://www.huffingtonpost.com/2013/06/25/mathew-shurka-conversion-therapy_n_3466943.html

Shilts, R. 1987. *And the Band Played On: Politics, People, and the AIDS Epidemic.* New York: St. Martin's Press.

Thompson, M. (Ed.). 1994. *Long Road to Freedom: The Advocate History of the Gay and Lesbian Movement.* New York: St. Martin's Press.

United States v. Windsor, 570 U.S. ___ (2013) (Docket No. 12–307).

We've Come a Long Way . . . Maybe. 2000, March 3. *Frontiers, 18*(22), 12.

White, M. 1997. *The Justice Report* (Special Edition). Selected quotes from the *700 Club.* Soulforce, P.O. Box 4467, Laguna Beach, CA 92652, journey@soulforce.org.

Young, P. D. 1982. *God's Bullies: Native Reflections on Preachers and Politics.* New York: Holt, Rinehart, & Winston.

Chronology

First People (Native Americans), Polynesians, Indians, Asiatic Eskimos	Before the influence of Christianity, many of these indigenous societies saw sex as a gift from the spirit world. In general, it was unimportant whom you had sex with and homosexual behavior was accepted. Also accepted were transgendered people who adopted the behaviors and clothing of both men and women. *Two-spirited* people (previously termed *Berdaches* and also known as *yirka-la ul, mahu, hijras*) were thought to have two spirits and often held the position of teacher and shaman in these societies.
United States	The expansion westward of white Europeans brought with them various legal codes that included sodomy provisions. As territories and then states formed, these codes were adopted into state charters and constitutions. Sodomy provisions were based on English or Spanish legal codes that were, originally, based on religious tenets formed during the many Catholic Inquisitions that swept Europe in the twelfth through fourteenth centuries. Sodomy was not clearly defined and used as a catch-all phrase to punish people for sexual transgressions (real or perceived). Often the penalty for committing sodomy was death.
1610	The Virginia Colony passes the first sodomy law in America. It requires the death penalty for "sodomites."
1625	The first known death sentence related to sodomy is carried out in the American colonies when Richard Cornish, master of the ship *Ambrose*, is hanged in Virginia Colony.
1778	Baron Frederich von Steuben is the first soldier known to be dismissed from the U.S. military for engaging in homosexuality.

The Homophile Movement

The homophile movement is marked by the medicalization of homosexuality and an increase in public discourse on the topic.

1869	Karoly Maria Benkert (who used the pseudonym K. M. Kertbeny) is a Hungarian physician who coins the word *homosexual*. It would be another 10 years before the word *heterosexual* is defined. Heterosexuality initially is used to denote a sexual perversion.
1919	The Institute for Sex Research is established by Magnus Hirschfeld in Berlin, Germany. It is one of the world's first organizations to explore sexual topics from a scientific standpoint. Hirschfeld becomes aware of

the need to formally organize to help reform attitudes and laws concerning homosexuality.

1920 to 1935   The "Harlem Renaissance" is an unprecedented time in which African American culture flourished. Many lesbian and gay writers, artists, and musicians are central to this cultural explosion. These included Claude McKay, Bessie Smith, Langston Hughes, Countee Cullen, Ma Rainey, Bruce Nugent, Alain Locke, Ethel Waters, and others.

1925   Henry Gerber and others found the Society for Human Rights in Chicago. It is the first gay rights group in the United States and survives only a short time. The members of the Society are arrested and imprisoned.

1933   Hirschfeld's Institute for Sex Research is ransacked by Nazi students and destroyed. Vast collections of library and artistic works are burned. Two of the three famous photos used in history books showing Nazi book burnings are photos of the destruction of Hirschfeld's collection.

The Modern Gay Movement

1941 to 1945   World War II dislocates millions of people and brings large numbers of lesbians and gay men to the city. There, they organize, reject the medical deviancy label, and create the modern gay movement.

Almost 10,000 enlisted personnel in the U.S. military received dishonorable discharges for homosexuality. They were called "blue discharges" because the orders were typed on blue paper.

1948   The first U.S. lesbian magazine, *Vice Versa*, begins publishing in Los Angeles. From her desk at RKO Studios, Lisa Ben (anagram for "lesbian") typed each issue twice using four carbons, then circulated it among her friends who then circulated it to their friends.

Alfred Kinsey and the Kinsey Institute publishes its groundbreaking study of sexual behavior in American men—*Sexual Behavior in the Human Male*.

1948 to 1953   McCarthyism purges homosexuals from federal government and thousands lose their jobs. More homosexuals lose their jobs than those accused of being Communists. Ironically, Roy Cohn, McCarthy's right-hand man, is known to be gay and later becomes President Donald Trump's legal mentor.

1951   The Mattachine Society is founded by Harry Hay, Bob Hull, and Chuck Rowland in Los Angeles. It evolves into the ONE Institute and Archives located near the campus of the University of Southern California and becomes the most celebrated and long-lived gay rights organization in the United States.

1953   The Kinsey Institute publishes *Sexual Behavior in the Human Female*.

ONE, the nation's first gay male magazine, begins publishing in Los Angeles as an adjunct to the Mattachine Society.

Dr. Evelyn Hooker begins studying male homosexual personalities. It is this research that leads to her findings that there are no discernible psychosocial differences between homosexual and heterosexual men.

1954   Copies of *ONE* magazine are seized by the Los Angeles postmaster who refuses to distribute them on the grounds they are "obscene, lewd, lascivious and filthy." *ONE* editors sue, are ruled against by two lower courts, but eventually prevail in 1958 in the U.S. Supreme Court decision (*One, Inc. v. Olesen*). Without this favorable decision, the gay rights movement would have been severely hampered for decades.

1955   The Daughters of Bilitis is founded by Del Martin and Phyllis Lyon in San Francisco. This is the first national lesbian organization in the United States and soon begins publication of *The Ladder*.

1961   Illinois becomes the first state to decriminalize consensual homosexual sex conducted in private and repeal its sodomy statutes.

1967   The first protest demonstration by gay activists against any police department in the world is held in front of the Black Cat and New Faces bars in Silver Lake, California (a community within Los Angeles).

The Birth of Gay Liberation

1969   New York City police raid the Stonewall Inn on June 27. The bar patrons, including transvestites, butch lesbians, and gay teenagers, violently resist. This event is considered the birth of the modern gay liberation movement and is commemorated by parades and festivals around the United States and world.

1973   The American Psychiatric Association removes homosexuality from its list of mental disorders.

Arson at the Louisiana UpStairs Lounge kills 32 gay people. This would be the worst mass killing of gay people until the massacre at Pulse gay nightclub in Orlando Florida in 2016.

1977   Fundamentalist singer Anita Bryant and the "Save Our Children" campaign are successful at convincing voters in Dade County, Florida, to repeal a gay rights law.

1978   Supervisor Harvey Milk and Mayor George Moscone of the city of San Francisco are shot to death at the city hall by ex-supervisor Dan White. White is later convicted of involuntary manslaughter, sentenced to seven years in prison (of which he serves only five), and commits suicide in 1985. The announcement of his conviction for involuntary manslaughter in 1979 triggers mass riots in the streets of San Francisco in what is known as "White Night" riots.

1979   The Moral Majority is founded by Jerry Falwell and his associates. It will become one of the major opponents to gay rights in United States.

The First National March on Washington for Lesbian and Gay rights draws over 100,000 marchers.

1981 A cluster of men contract rare diseases associated with impaired immune system yet for no known reason. The only common characteristic between the men was that they were either intravenous drug users or homosexual or both. There is no known mechanism to explain the problem. Initially, the general press referred to the mysterious disease as gay-related immune deficiency (GRID).

Wisconsin becomes the first state to pass antidiscrimination laws based on sexual orientation in the areas of employment, housing, and public accommodation.

1982 Bruce Voeller suggests that gay-related immune disorder (GRID) be renamed Acquired Immune Deficiency Syndrome (AIDS) as a better reflection of the characteristics of the disease. The medical community adopts the terminology.

1986 The U.S. Supreme Court, in the Georgia *Bowers vs. Hardwick* case, upholds the right of states to enforce sodomy laws.

The experimental drug zidovudine (AZT) is released by the U.S. Public Health Services for people with pneumocystis carninii pneumonia (PCP).

1987 AZT is approved in the United States and elsewhere for the treatment of AIDS.

The New York Times, for the first time in its history, uses the word *gay* in reference to homosexuality.

Larry Kramer, along with other activists, begins the AIDS Coalition to Unleash Power (ACT UP). Its goal is to bring public and government attention to the need for AIDS funding and research.

1988 October 11 is designated as the National Coming Out Day in honor of the historic 1987 lesbian and gay march on Washington.

1989 Over 5,000 ACT UP members demonstrate in front of and inside New York's St. Patrick's Cathedral. They rally against the Catholic Church's antigay stance and policies on AIDS.

1990 The Americans with Disability Act (ADA) is signed into law. It explicitly prohibits AIDS-based discrimination.

Queer Nation is founded in New York City as a direct action, in-your-face, group with the rallying cry, "We're here, we're queer, get used to it!"

1992 Voters in the state of Colorado approve Amendment 2 to the state constitution prohibiting gay rights legislation. Supreme Court late rules the law unconstitutional in 1996.

1993 Soon after taking office as president of the United States, Bill Clinton directs the secretary of defense to look into overturning the 1981 ban on gays in the military. Fierce opposition from conservative members of Congress and fundamental religious groups throughout the nation force Clinton to settle for the "don't ask, don't tell" (DADT) compromise. It is revoked in 2011.

1995 Protease inhibitors, a new generation of AIDS drugs, show considerable success and receive approval from the Food and Drug Administration. When combined with other HIV medications, the "cocktail" is effective at keeping the virus under control.

1996 President Clinton signs the federal Defense of Marriage Act (DOMA) in which marriage is defined as the union of one man and one woman. Interestingly, no local, state, or federal law defines "man" or "woman."

1998   In a gay murder that shocked the nation, University of Wyoming freshman Matthew Shepard is found hanging spread-eagle on a fence post in subzero weather beside a remote road in Laramie, Wyoming. He had been abducted, beaten, burned with a cigarette, and left to die. His death a few days later became the springboard for many organizations to push for hate crime laws in their states. His funeral is picketed by Westboro Baptist Church members carrying signs that read "Matthew burns in Hell."

1999   A coalition of 18 Religious Right organizations launches Phase Two of its "Truth in Love" ad campaign, which urges gay men and lesbians to enter therapy to convert to heterosexuality.

2000   The U.S. Supreme Court rules the Boy Scouts of America, as a private organization, has the right to ban gays from its ranks.

2001   In April, the Netherlands becomes the first country in the modern world to legally recognize same-sex marriage.

2003   U.S. Supreme Court in *Lawrence et al v. Texas* reverses Texas court support for sodomy and explicitly overrules the 1986 Georgia *Bowers v. Hardwick* decision. As such, sodomy laws as commonly constructed are struck down throughout the nation.

2004   Massachusetts, by judicial decision, becomes the first state in the United States to approve gay marriage.

2012   Dr. Robert L. Spitzer recants his position that homosexuality can be "cured" stating that his research was flawed. He officially apologizes to the gay community.

2013   Exodus International announces that it is closing its doors and ceasing all worldwide activities. After three decades of operation trying to change people's sexual orientation through spiritual counseling, the board of directors apologized to the gay community for all the pain and suffering it caused.

   U.S. Supreme Court rules in *United States v. Windsor* that the Defense of Marriage Act (DOMA) is unconstitutional.

   Sexual orientation change effort (SOCE) SB1172, a California bill passed in 2012 prohibiting licensed mental health providers from attempting to change the sexual orientation of children and young adults under the age of 18, is upheld in court.

2014   Arizona state legislature passes a "religious freedom" bill that allows businesses and business employees to discriminate against classes of people required by their strongly held religious beliefs. The bills are sponsored and supported by antigay legislators. The governor vetoes the bill after national media threaten financial boycott of Arizona.

   President Obama signs an executive order to modify existing antidiscrimination federal law to include sexual orientation and gender identity covering federal contractors.

   California becomes the first state to officially ban "gay panic" and "trans panic" legal defense.

2015   U.S. Supreme Court in *Obergefell v. Hodges* declares marriage as a fundamental right that cannot be denied same-sex couples, thereby legalizing same-sex marriage in all states of the union.

   Legalizing same-sex marriage sets off a firestorm of resistance from conservative and fundamentalists. Kentucky county clerk Kim Davis refuses to sign marriage certificates for same-sex couples. She is sued, fails to comply, held in contempt of court, jailed for five days, and released upon her promise not to interfere with other clerks signing the documents.

Mormon Church issues new guidelines for lay leaders requiring children of same-sex couples to leave the family after age 18 if they want to continue being part of the church.

2016 Alabama's chief justice Roy Moore directs the state's probate judges to refuse marriage licenses to same-sex couples in defiance to the U.S. Supreme Court approval of same-sex marriage. Later in the year he is charged with ethics violations and effectively removed from office.

North Carolina passes a "bathroom bill" requiring people to use the bathroom that correspond to the sex of the person listed on their birth certificate. This is a direct discrimination against transgender people. The public outcry results in the legislature issuing a partial repeal.

A lone gunman enters the Pulse gay nightclub in Orlando Florida and kills 49 people and wounds an additional 53. This is the worst antigay hate crime and massacre in U.S. history.

The pope blames the Roman Catholic Church for being "very negative about gay people" throughout its history and stated, "I believe that the church not only should apologize to the person who is gay whom it has offended but has to apologize to the poor, to exploited women, to children exploited for labor; it has to ask forgiveness for having blessed many weapons" (Dwyer 2016).

2017 The Seventh District Court of Appeals clarifies the meaning of "sex" in Title VII of the 1964 Civil Rights Act to include sexual orientation and transgender.

Texas Supreme Court upholds the right of cities to deny spousal benefits to married same-sex couples. This is in direct violation of the U.S. Supreme Court determination approving same-sex marriage in *Obergefell v. Hodges*.

Reference

Dwyer, Colin. 2016, June 26. "Pope Francis: Church Should Apologize to Gays and Other Marginalized Groups. *NPR*. http://www.npr.org/sections/thetwo-way/2016/06/26/483630582/pope-francis-church-should-apologize-to-gays-and-other-marginalized-groups

Chapter 1

Early America

For thousands of years, the First People inhabited the Americas from the northern reaches of what is now known as Canada to the tip of South America. Their cultural practices and religious beliefs were very different from the invading Europeans. Identity around sexual practices was unknown. Gender roles, although, were strictly prescribed. But who held a "female" gender role, or "male" gender role, or mixed gender role was fluid. For many tribes, it was believed that each person had an innate spirit that could be expressed as female, male, or mixed and that expressing one's spirit should not be challenged. When the first white Europeans settled the Americas, they often found men and women not conforming to European gender standards. Some of the Europeans wrote about their experiences of meeting transgendered First People (which they called "berdache" and are now termed "two-spirited"). Homosexual behaviors and same-sex coupling seem to be very prevalent and open in the New World and that offended the Europeans.

Many of the original colonies were comprised of exclusively or mostly men. There were considerable same-sex sexual behaviors, and there are surviving reports detailing the punishments handed out for these transgressions. By the early 1600s, men were being executed for engaging in masturbation and sodomy, and application of English moral beliefs was codified in settlement compacts. With the arrival of women to the settlements, lesbianism became an issue and included in sodomy codes.

Document 1
NAVAJO SACREDNESS FOR NADLEEH

The largest Native American ethnic group in the United States is the Navajo. Their creation myth centers on Turquoise Boy and White Shell Girl. These characters were androgynous persons who dressed in the clothing of the other sex. Their cleverness helped save humans from the great flood and further helped invent many useful tools, including axes, hoes, and baskets. Turquoise Boy and White Shell Girl are viewed as the first Nadleeh—a term meaning "changing one" or "one who is transformed" and includes transsexuals, transvestites, intersex, and other gender nonconforming people. The message of the creation myth for the Navajo is that their existence benefits from the inclusion of Nadleeh. By including such people in their mythology, having gender nonconforming people in the tribe was never questioned but, in fact, considered a blessing. Providing a spiritual explanation provides a special place for transvestites, hermaphrodites, and

androgynous persons presenting them as part of the natural order with positive contribu-
tions to the success of the tribe. Contrast this with Christianity's description of homosexu-
ality and homosexuals as inherently sinful, sometimes even worthy of death. The core
spiritual beliefs of a culture can mean the difference of life or death for LGBT people.

The family which counted a transvestite among its members or had a hermaphrodite child born to them was considered by themselves and everyone else as very
fortunate. The success and wealth of such a family was believed to be assured.
Special care was taken in the raising of such children and they were afforded favor-
itism not shown to other children of the family. As they grew older and assumed
the character of *nadle* [sic], this solicitude and respect increased. . . . This respect
verges almost on reverence in many cases. . . .

   They know everything. They can do both the work of a man and a woman.
I think when all the nadle are gone, that it will be the end of the Navaho.

   If there were no nadle, the country would change. They are responsible for
all the wealth in the country. If there were no more left, the horses, sheep, and
Navaho would all go [disappear]. They are leaders just like President Roosevelt.
A nadle around the hogan will bring good luck and riches. They have charge of all
the riches. It does a great deal for the country if you have nadle around.

   You must respect a nadle. They are, somehow, sacred and holy.

Source: W. W. Hill. "The Status of the Hermaphrodite and Transvestite in Navaho
Culture." *American Anthropologist* 37 (1935): 274–278.

Document 2

INDIAN SODOMY IN FLORIDA (1528 AND 1702 REPORTS)

Similar to Jacques Marquette's observations in the Illinois Valley, French explorer Pierre
Liette reported on his experience living with Miami Indians in 1702.

Sodomy prevails more among them than in any other nation, although there are
four women to one man. It is true that the women, although debauched, retain
some moderation, which prevents the young men from satisfying their passions as
much as they would like. There are [homosexual] men who are bred for this purpose from their childhood. When they are seen frequently picking up [women's
tools . . .] but making no use of the bow and arrow, as all the other small boys
do, they are girt with a piece of leather or cloth . . . a thing all the women wear.
Their hair is allowed to grow and is fastened behind the head. . . . They imitate
[women's] accent, which is different from that of the men. They omit nothing
that can make them like the women. There are men sufficiently embruted to have
[homosexual] dealings with them.

Source: Pierre Liette. "Memoir of Pierre Liette on the Illinois Country." *The Western Country in the 17th Century.* Edited by Milo Quaife. New York: Citadel, 1962, 112–113. Used by permission of Kensington Press.

Document 3

VIRGINIA SODOMY LAW (1610)

The London Company attempted to establish the first English settlement in the New World in 1607 at Jamestown, Virginia. Although there was no official legal code for the colony at first, being an English settlement meant that English law would be adopted. Almost 100 years earlier under King Henry VIII, sodomy or "buggery" (meaning all nonprocreative sex) was made illegal and punishable by death in England. Finally, in 1610, Virginia created its own legal code using much of the English common code. Instead of using the legal term sodomy *they used the religious term* sodomie *indicating the influence religion had on the creation of antisodomy statutes. Similar laws were adopted by later English colonies.*

No man shall commit the horrible, detestable sins of Sodomie upon pain of death; & he or she that can be lawfully convict[ed] of Adultery shall be punished with death. No man shall ravish or force any woman, maid or Indian, or other, upon pain of death.

Source: May 24, 1610, Virginia law. William Strachey. *For The Colony in Virginea Britannia: Lawes Divine, Morall and Martiall, &c.* London: Walter Barre, 1612.

Document 4

THE EXECUTION OF RICHARD CORNISH (1624–1625)

The "Minutes of the Council and General Court of Colonial Virginia" records the testimony and trial of Captain Richard Cornish in 1624 who was accused, convicted, and executed for having sex with one of his ship's crewmen. He would be the first man put to death for sodomy under colonial law. Some Virginia settlers disagreed with the conviction and execution. Thomas Hatch was tried in 1625 for criticizing the court's decision. His punishment included having one of his ears cut off, being whipped at the pillory, and being sold into seven years of indentured servitude. Three witnesses stated the following about Thomas Hatch:

. . . [he] said that in his conscience he thought the said Cornish was put to death wrongfully, whereupon this depondent [witness] said, "You were best take heed what you say, you have a precedent before your eyes the other day, and it will cost you your ears if you say such words." To which Thomas Hatch replied, "I care not for my ears, let them hang me if they will. . . ."

[The Court's decision reads:] It is ordered that Thomas Hatch for his offence shall be whipped from the fort to the gallows and from thence be whipped back again; and be set upon the pillory and there to lose one of his ears, and that his [indentured] service to Sir George Yardly for seven years shall begin from the present day.

Source: H. R. McIlwaine, ed. *Minutes of the Council and General Court of Colonial Virginia, 1622–1632.* Richmond, VA: Colonial Press: 1924, 34, 42, 78, 81, 83.

Document 5

WILLIAM PLAINE EXECUTED IN NEW ENGLAND FOR TEACHING MASTURBATION (1646)

Another man, William Plaine, was executed in the New England town of Guilford after he confessed under torture to have engaged in sodomy with two men in England before migrating to America. Governor John Winthrop of the Massachusetts Bay Colony wrote the following about the case:

. . . masturbations, which he had committed, and provoked others to the like above a hundred times; and to some who questioned the lawfulness of such filthy practice, he did insinuate seeds of atheism, questioning whether there was a God, etc. The magistrates and elders (so many as were at hand) did all agree that he ought to die, and gave divers reasons from the word of God. And indeed it was *horrendum facinus* [horrible crime], and he a monster in human shape, exceeding all human rules and examples that ever had been heard of, and it tended to the frustrating of the ordinance of marriage and hindering the generation [reproduction] of mankind.

Source: John Winthrop. *History of New England from 1630 to 1649.* Edited by James Savage. Boston: Little, Brown, 1853, vol. 2, 324.

Document 6

AFRICAN AMERICAN JAN CREOLI KILLED AND BURNED IN DUTCH COLONY (1646)

In 1646, an African slave named Jan Creoli was accused and executed by Dutch officials for engaging in sodomy with a young boy in the New Netherland colony (later renamed New York). The boy, also a slave, was forced to watch the execution. Initially the boy was tied to a stake and faggots (kindling wood) piled around him to give the impression that he, too, was to be executed. Instead the boy was not killed (in deference to his age) but rather whipped with the intention to scare him to never engage in sodomy again. It is thought the use of faggots to burn sodomites at the stake is the origin of the pejorative term, faggot.

Jan Creoli, a negro, sodomy, second offense; this crime being condemned of God (Genesis c. 19; Leviticus c. 18:22, 29) as an abomination, the prisoner is sentenced to be conveyed to the place of public execution, and there choked to death, and then burnt to ashes. . . .

Manuel Congo, a lad ten years old, on whom the above abominable crime was committed, to be carried to the place where Creoli is to be executed, tied to a stake, and faggots piled around him, for justice sake, and to be flogged. Sentence executed.

Source: E. B. O'Cakkaghan, ed. *Calendar of Historical Manuscripts in the Office of the Secretary of State, Albany, N.Y.* Albany, NY: Weed and Parsons, 1865, 103.

Document 7

SARA NORMAN AND MARY HAMMON ACCUSED OF LEWD BEHAVIOR (1649)

Sodomy laws rarely included women. The first record of two women being charged for illegal sexual intimacy occurred in Plymouth Colony in 1649. Sara Norman, a married woman, was charged with engaging in sodomy with 15-year-old Mary Hammon. Because the sodomy laws applied only to men, Sara Norman was convicted on the charges of "unchaste behavior" and forced to publicly acknowledge her behavior. Mary Hammon was cleared of the charges—perhaps because of her young age.

Whereas the wife of Hugh Norman, of Yarmouth, hath stood presented [in] divers Courts for misdemeanor and lewd behavior with Mary Hammon upon a bed, with divers lascivious speeches by her also spoken, but she could not appear by reason of some hindrances unto this Court, the said Court have therefore sentenced her, the said wife of Hugh Norman, for her wild behavior in the aforesaid particulars, to make a public acknowledgment, so far as conveniently may be, of her unchaste behavior, and have also warned her to take heed of such carriages for the future, lest her former carriage come in remembrance against her to make her punishment the greater.

Source: Nathaniel Shurtleff and David Pulsifer, eds. *Records of the Colony of New Plymouth.* Boston: William White, 1855, vol. 2, 137, 148, 163.

Document 8

NEW HAVEN LAW PROHIBITS LESBIANISM (1655)

The New Haven colony approved a comprehensive law in 1655 that contains specific provisions including prohibitions against woman-on-woman sexual relations. This law was unique and remarkable for its thoroughness. It included statements on anal sex, bestiality, and masturbation in its list of illegal lesbian behavior.

If any man layeth with mankinde, as a man lyeth with a woman, both of them have committed abomination, they both shall surely be put to death. Levit. 20.13. And if any woman change the naturall use into that which is against nature, as Rom. I.26 she shall be liable to the same sentence, and punishment, or if any person, or persons, shall commit any other kinde of unnaturall and shamefull filthines, called in Scripture the going after strange flesh, or other flesh than God alloweth, by carnall knowledge of another vessel than God in nature have appointed to become one flesh, whether by abusing the contrary part of a grown woman, or child of either sex, or unripe vessel of a girle, wherein the natural use of the woman is left, which God hath ordained for the propagation of posterity, and Sodomiticall filthinesse is committed by a kind of rape, nature being forced, through the will were inticed, every such person shall be put to death.

Source: J. Hammond Trumbull. *The True-Blue Laws of Connecticut and New-Haven.* Hartford, CT: American Publishing Co., 1879, 201.

Document 9

PURITAN SERMON ON THE CRY OF SODOM (1674)

A sermon given by the Reverend Samuel Danforth of Duxbury was published in Cambridge, Massachusetts, in 1674. The Puritans in New England had executed a young man for having sex with an animal. The sermon was to answer people who challenged the execution. Danforth claimed that if the boy had not been executed, then God would have destroyed the Massachusetts colony just as he had destroyed Sodom. The sermon condemns all nonprocreative and nonmarried sex including masturbation ("self-pollution"), bestiality, fornication, homosexuality, and adultery.

The sins of Sodom were many and great . . . [but the] most grievous of all [was] abominable filthiness in all manner of Uncleanness. . . . [Such] wickedness cried unto Heaven for vengeance . . . with Fire and Brimstone. . . . Not only whoredom and Self-pollution, but also Adultery. . . . Going after strange flesh: Sodomy and Bestiality. . . . Filthiness with his own body alone [was the] sin of Onan [who] abhorred the lawful use of the Marriage-bed, and most impurely defiled himself. . . . [which was] so detestable in the sight of God. . . . Sodomy [is] filthiness committed between parties of the same Sex—when Males with Males, and Females with Females work wickedness.

If a man lieth with mankind, as he lieth with a woman, both of them have committed an abomination: they shall surely be put to death, their blood shall be upon them, Leviticus 20:13. This sin raged amongst the Sodomites, and to their perpetual Infamy, it is called Sodomy. Against this wickedness, no indignation is sufficient. . . .

Some among us stand astonished . . . [that God would allow] a Youth . . . [a] Child of Religious Parents . . . [to be executed in a] Dreadful Example of Divine Vengeance. You pity his Youth and tender years . . . [but] I pray, pity the holy Law of God, which is shamefully violated . . ., pity the Land, which is fearfully polluted and defiled. . . . The execution of Justice upon such a notorious Malefactor, is the only way to turn away the wrath of God from us. . . . Divine Wrath . . . strikes a holy fear and dread . . . [into] Our cursed Natures. . . . [The] holiest man hath as vile and filthy a Nature, as the Sodomites. . . . [This boy's execution is God's] Instruction and Astonishment to all New England . . . [making people] afraid to go on impenitently in the same sins. . . . Go to now, ye wanton and lascivious persons, go on in your Frolicks and mad Pranks. . . . He that is a Sodomite, let him be a Sodomite still; he that is a Beast, let him be a Beast still. . . . Justify this poor Condemned Wretch in all his Villainy. . . . Justify Sodom in all her Abomination. . . .

The Wrath of God [is the only thing powerful enough to] restrain the rest of our Youth, and all others. . . . [God] hath cut off this rotten and putrid Member [to] prevent the spreading of the Infection. . . . Detest and abominate the sin of Sodomy . . . [and those who] abuse themselves with mankind. . . . [Sodomy] makes men despise the Ordinance of Marriage . . . [which is the] remedy [for] boiling and burning lusts. . . . Repent . . . unclean Speculations, vile affections, unchaste fire . . . [through the] help of Christ to mortify thy lusts and crucify the flesh. . . . Take the Sword of the Spirit, and thrust it into the bowels of thy lusts. . . . If once thou has escaped out of Sodom, tremble to think of returning. . . . Let the fear of God . . . stop thine Ears at filthy Jests, amorous Songs. . . . Abhor all lascivious Touches, unchaste Embracings. . . .

Let us carefully Watch over our Children, Servants, and all that are under our Care and Charge, lest they be stained and defiled. . . . [Every man should] charge his Children and Family to beware of the wickedness. Arise, and depart out of Sodom.

Source: S. Danforth. *The Cry of Sodom Enquired Into . . . With a Solemn Exhortation to Tremble at God's Judgements and to Abandon Youthful Lusts.* Cambridge, MA: Marmaduke Johnson, 1674.

Document 10

ILLINOIS INDIAN TRANSGENDER (1677)

The earliest explorers of North America were often confused and mystified by the First People they encountered. French explorers roamed the region of the Great Lakes and upper Mississippi Valley. They met many tribes where women were highly respected and some men dressed in women's clothing and served as spiritual leaders. Jesuit Father

Jacques Marquette conducted his first voyage in the area between 1673 and 1677. He was mystified by the male two-spirit persons mixing both men's and women's roles found among the Illinois and nearby tribes. He reported the following:

I know not through what superstition some Illinois, as well as some Nadouessi, while still young, assume the garb of women, and retain it throughout their lives. There is some mystery in this, for they never marry and glory in demeaning themselves to do everything that the women do. They go to war, however, but can use only clubs, and not bows and arrows, which are the weapons proper to men. They are present at all the juggleries [village events], and at the solemn dances in honor of the Calumet [spirit]; at these they sing, but must not dance. They are summoned to the [government] Councils, and nothing can be decided without their advice. Finally, through their profession of leading an Extraordinary life, they pass for Manitous—that is to say, for Spirits—or persons of Consequence.

Source: Jacques Marquette. "Of the First Voyage Made." *The Jesuit Relations.* Edited by Reuben Gold Thwaites. Cleveland, OH: Burrows, 1896–1901, vol. 59, 129.

Document 11

PIRATES IN THE CARIBBEAN (1724)

There have always been all-male and all-female societies. The buccaneer culture found between Carolina and Trinidad from the late 1500s to the early 1700s was one such all-male society. The competing interests by English, Dutch, Spanish, and Portuguese governments over this region resulted in confusion and outright anarchy. The lawlessness provided the opportunity for groups of pirates to plunder other ships of the gold and wealth stolen from First People of Mexico, Central, and South America. But who were these "buccaneers" (as pirates of this period and geographic location would be called) that worked independently of any government?

Many men found their way to the pirate life. As best as we can tell, many buccaneers came from lower English class families. It is hard for modern people to imagine, but England and elsewhere in the 1500s was a brutal life, particularly for children. There was no child protective service agency, or child welfare, or orphanages, or even centralized police. If parents died or were incapacitated for any reason and there were no other adults to take care of them, children were often abandoned (or pushed out) of homes. For survival, boys often formed roving gangs that camped in forest and stole from travelers. Being outside the reach of law and living in all-male groups with little or no contact with females, it would be safe to assume that the boys had sex with each other. The problem was so acute in England and other European countries that one solution was to draft the boys into the military. English constables routinely rounded up these boys and young men and pressed them into service with the navy. There, the young men learned valuable skills, and they continued to live in all-male societies—very much like their youth. However, the English navy was extremely brutal and classist at that time (recount the Mutiny on the Bounty) with little chance of advancement for the uneducated lads. When pirates boarded ships, often the sailors were given the choice of joining the pirates. For many sailors, the democratic life and freedom of pirating seemed the better choice than staying with the brutal English navy. Sailors joining the pirate life entered into a world that was already known to them—an all-male community of lower-class English men like themselves for whom homosexual behavior was not just an "option" but rather their sole sexual and relationship outlet.

It has been well documented that colonial officials reported that pirate harbors like Port Royal, Jamaica, were filled with "sodomites" and that when navy sailors were prosecuted for sodomy they often claimed to not know it was illegal. These and other reports indicate how widespread same-sex male sexual behaviors and relationships were. Pirates often paired up, and there are many stories of one pirate dying while trying to save his mate. Some relationships were as permanent as marriage. (See B. R. Burg. 1983. Sodomy and the Perception of Evil: English Sea Rovers in the Seventeenth Century Caribbean. New York: New York University Press.)

Some women also became pirates. Mary Read and Anne Bonny are probably the two most famous women pirates. Mary Read was an Englishwoman who cross-dressed as a man to become a sailor. When her ship was captured, she joined the pirates and ended up in the Bahamas. There, she met Anne Bonny a South Carolina female pirate. The two became a couple about whom historian Rictor Norton wrote:

[It] is more than likely, and equally significant that Anne Bonny and Mary Read were lesbian pirates. Our historical knowledge of these two women is based mainly upon the account written by Captain Charles Johnson (probably a pseudonym for Daniel Defoe) in *A General History of the Robberies and Murders of the Most Notorious Pirates*, published in 1724 shortly after Anne and Mary were brought to trial for piracy on the high seas.

We first hear of Anne Bonny, born Anne Cormac, in 1710—as a thirteen-year-old tomboy in the port of Charleston, South Carolina. . . . Although the daughter of a wealthy lawyer and plantation owner, her red hair was cut short, her face was dirty, and her habits were rowdy. As one historian notes, Anne grew up into a strapping, boisterous girl, of a fierce and courageous temper. . . . [After her father disinherited her] she burnt down the plantation, then fled to the British-controlled port of New Providence (on modern Nassau in the Bahamas), a haven for such pirates as Blackbeard and Captain Kidd. . . .

[After Anne met and joined up with Mary Read, they] remained inseparable, and both alternately donned male and female clothing. In due course they took command of another ship, and Men-of-War were sent out to capture "those infamous women." They abandoned all caution and raided numerous other ships. . . . [The] obvious enjoyment of their cross-dressing, and the fact that they acted together as a couple and obviously loved one another . . . suggests that they must be relevant to any history of lesbian experience.

Source: Rictor Norton. 2008. "Lesbian Pirates: Anne Bonny and Mary Read." *Lesbian History*, updated June 14. http://rictornorton.co.uk/pirates.htm.

Document 12

COMMENTARIES ON THE LAWS OF ENGLAND (1765)

The English common law was codified in print in 1765 by Sir William Blackstone in Commentaries on the Laws of England. *Judges in both the American colonies and England quickly adopted it as their primary reference. Even after the American colonies declared their independence from England, they carried over the English common law into their state and federal criminal code. American judges continued to refer to Blackstone's* Commentaries *well into the twentieth century. For example, in the U.S. Supreme Court decision on* Bowers v. Hardwick *1986 sodomy case, Chief Justice Warren Burger cited Blackstone in his opinion. Blackstone considered homosexual behavior so detestable that he wrote the most offending descriptions in Latin and referred to sodomy as a "crime not fit to be named." The* Commentaries *show the close connection between Christian religious teachings on sexuality and the impact with Anglo-American law.*

The crime is more detestable . . . of a still deeper malignity; the infamous crime against nature, committed either with man or beast. Acrime, which ought to be strictly and impartially proved, and then strictly and impartially punished. But it is an offense of so dark a nature, so easily charged, and the negative so difficult to be proved, that the accusation should be clearly made out: for, if false, it deserves punishment inferior only to that of the crime itself.

I will not act so disagreeable part, to my readers as well as myself, as to dwell any longer upon a subject, the very mention of which is a disgrace to human nature. It will be more eligible to imitate in this respect the delicacy of our English law, which treats it, in it's [sic] very indictments, as a crime not fit to be named; "peccatum illud horribile, inter christianos non numinandum." [that horrible sin not to be named among Christians]. . . .

A word concerning it's [sic] punishment. This is the voice of nature and of reason, and the express law of God, determined to be capital [i.e., punished by death]. Of which we have a signal instance, long [ago], by the destruction of two cities [the Bible story of Sodom and Gommorah] by fire from heaven; so that this is an universal, not merely a provincial, precept.

And our antient law in some degree initiated this punishment, by commanding such miscreants to be burnt to death; though Fleta says they should be buried alive; either of which punishments was indifferently used for this crime among the antient Goths. But now the general punishment of all felonies is the same, namely, by hanging: and this offense . . . was made single felony by the statute 25 Henry VIII, c. 6.

Source: William Blackstone. *Commentaries on the Laws of England.* London: 1765, Book IV, Chapter 15, section IV.

Document 13

SPANISH COLONIAL SUPPRESSION OF SODOMITES IN CALIFORNIA (1775–1777)

In 1775, the second military governor of California, Pedro Fages, observed Indian men who dressed and acted as women and, surprisingly, were held in high esteem. He reported to the Crown:

I have substantial evidence that those Indian men who both here and farther inland, are observed in the dress, clothing, and character of women—there being two or three such in each village—pass as sodomites by profession (it being confirmed that all these Indians are much addicted to this abominable vice) and permit the heathen to practice the execrable, unnatural abuse of their bodies. They are called *joyas* [jewels], and are held in great esteem.

Source: Pedro Faxes. "Supplemento Noticia del Misiones de Monterey y California por Pedro Faxes." Papers of Pedro Fages, Library of the California Historical Society: 1775.

Document 14

SPANISH PRIESTS CONDEMN TRANSGENDERED YUMA INDIANS (1775)

Jesuit Father Pedro Font visited the Yuma Indians of the lower Colorado River valley in 1775. This was part of an expedition headed by Juan Bautista de Anza to explore the area and make reports back to the Spanish government about the prospects of expanding Spanish rule to the area. In his report, Father Pedro Font reported encountering some transgendered males.

Among the women I saw some men dressed like women, with whom they go about regularly, never joining the men. The commander called them *amaricados*, perhaps because the Yumas call effeminate men *maricas*. I asked who these men were, and they replied that they were not men like the rest, and for this reason they went around covered this way. From this I inferred they must be hermaphrodites, but from what I learned later I understood that they were sodomites, dedicated to nefarious practices. From all the foregoing I conclude that in this matter of incontinence there will be much to do when the Holy Faith and the Christian religion are established among them.

Source: Pedro Font. *Font's Complete Diary of the Second Anza Expedition.* Translated by Herbert Eugene Bolton, *Anza's California Expeditions.* Berkeley: University of California Press, 1930–1931, vol. 4, 105.

Further Reading

Arguelles, Lourdes, and B. Ruby Rich. 1984. "Homosexuality, Homophobia, and Revolution." *Signs* 9:4.

Binhammer, Katherine. 1996. "The Sex Panic of the 1790s." *Journal of the History of Sexuality* 6:3.

Faderman, Lilian. 1981. *Surpassing the Love of Men*. New York: William Morrow.

Gilley, Brian Joseph. 2006. *Becoming Two-Spirit: Gay Identity and Social Acceptance in Indian Country*. Lincoln: University of Nebraska Press.

Hill, W. W. 1935. "The Status of the Hermaphrodite and Transvestite in Navaho Culture." *American Anthropologist* 37: 274–278.

Liette, Pierre. 1962. "Memoir of Pierre Liette on the Illinois Country," in *The Western Country in the 17th Century*. Edited by Milo Quaife. New York: Citadel, 112–113.

Norton, Rictor. 2008. "Lesbian Pirates: Anne Bonny and Mary Read." *Lesbian History*, updated June 14. http://rictornorton.co.uk/pirates.htm.

Roscoe, Will. 1991. *The Zuni Man-Woman*. Albuquerque: University of New Mexico Press.

Chapter 2

Early United States of America

The founders of the United States witnessed the terrible problems that originate from religion. They created a secular framework for governing the diverse populations making up the new nation that did not rely on a king or dictator but rather a collaboration between people. As such, a new era of freedom was ushered in for some people. Still, there was widespread systemic discrimination against entire classes of people (slaves, women, immigrants, atheists, homosexuals, and others). Resistance movements called for the end of slavery, women's rights, and more. The Fourteenth Amendment clearly ended institutional slavery. Women were still demanding to be treated equally as men and win the right to vote. A handful of authors were able to discretely speak about homosexuality in veiled terms. By the late 1800s, some of the pro-gay research and writings originating in Germany were distributed in the United States bringing language and hope to a secret underclass.

Document 15
U.S. DECLARATION OF INDEPENDENCE (1776)

The founders of the United States seriously considered the role of government. For thousands of years, the right to rule came from ancestry and power often justified by religion. When Thomas Jefferson penned the words to the Declaration of Independence, he proclaimed that government authority derived from the people and that its purpose was to secure "life, liberty, and the pursuit of happiness" for its people. This was a radical idea and challenged the king of England authority and the idea that kings ruled through the grace of God—a God whose laws were written in the Bible. Considering slavery was common throughout the history of the world, to declare that all men are created equal was radical. This idea of equality would drive many civil rights issues, including the abolitionist movement, women's right to vote, racial civil rights, and, most recently, the equal rights for LGBT people, including the right to marry.

We hold these truths to be self-evident: That all men are created equal; that they are endowed by their Creator with certain unalienable rights; that among these are life, liberty, and the pursuit of happiness; that, to secure these rights, governments are instituted among men, deriving their just powers from the consent of the governed; that whenever any form of government becomes destructive of these ends, it is the right of the people to alter or to abolish it, and to institute new government, laying its foundations on such principles, and organizing its powers in such form, as to them shall seem most likely to effect their safety and happiness.

Source: National Archives.

Document 16

U.S. CONSTITUTION AND BILL OF RIGHTS (1791)

The original U.S. Articles of Confederation lacked a strong central authority. When the new Constitution was drafted, it was clear that specific rights were being overlooked. The English authority routinely violated people's rights and property, and it was decided a Bill of Rights needed to be added to clearly limit government authority. These eight amendments listed here have the most influence on civil rights.

The early colonies were hotbed of religious dissent. Although it is often said the immigrants from Europe coming to America were seeking religious freedom, that does not mean they wanted to set up communities that respected all religions. Instead, they came to set up colonies of like-minded people of one religion whereupon they discriminated and prosecuted all those who did not believe as they did. They wanted the ability to discriminate and set up their regional law to support their theocratic state. Many Americans were tired of the ongoing religious conflict in the states and insisted a separation between church and state. The First Amendment was the first step toward quelling religiosity enforced by the state.

The English frequently entered people's homes, searched through their possessions, arrested "suspects," and sometimes conducted trials without a jury. Americans wanted greater control over their lives and property, and protections from an incursive government. The Fourth and Eighth Amendments limited government power to act arbitrarily.

For marginalized groups, each amendment provided the legal groundwork for challenging laws that kept them oppressed. For LGBT people, it has been a long struggle. Religious tenets influenced the creation of sodomy laws in virtually every state. These laws made the very existence of homosexuals illegal and open to prosecution and discrimination. As each state overcame its sodomy laws, LGBT people demanded the rights affirmed by the other amendments. It would take until 2003 in Lawrence v. Texas for the last vestiges of religious condemnation to be expelled from American legal system and with it the justification for denying the other rights guaranteed by the Constitution and Bill of Rights.

> Amendment 1: Congress shall make no law respecting an establishment of religion, or prohibiting the free exercise thereof; or abridging the freedom of speech, or of the press; or the right of the people peaceably to assemble, and to petition the government for a redress of grievances.

Amendment 4: The right of the people to be secure in their persons, houses, papers, and effects, against unreasonable searches and seizures, shall not be violated. . . .

Amendment 5: No person shall be held to answer for a capital, or otherwise infamous crime, unless on a presentment or indictment of a grand jury . . . nor shall be compelled in any criminal case to be a witness against himself, nor be deprived of life, liberty, or property, without due process of law. . . .

Amendment 6: In all criminal prosecutions, the accused shall enjoy the right to a speedy and public trial, by an impartial jury. . . .

Amendment 7: In suits . . . the right to trial by jury shall be preserved. . . .

Amendment 8: Excessive bail shall not be required, nor excessive fines imposed, nor cruel and unusual punishments inflicted.

Amendment 9: The enumeration in the Constitution, of certain rights, shall not be construed to deny or disparage others retained by the people.

Amendment 10: The powers not delegated to the United States by the Constitution, nor prohibited by it to the States, are reserved to the States, or to the people.

Source: National Archives.

Document 17

BACHELOR FRIENDSHIPS OF THE NINETEENTH CENTURY (1840)

The concept of "confirmed bachelor" has been around a long time. Victorian England and Philadelphia of the early 1800s and probably any large city of the time had networks of unmarried men who would socialize and eat at certain taverns and restaurants. Because these cultures at this time were highly sexually repressive and polite conversation did not allow for the discussion of sex, these men could avoid marriage and socially navigate gossip by being labeled "confirmed bachelor." Although the men were considered "odd," speculation of their sexuality was avoided, and their carefully constructed covers were supported by the lack of public discussion of sex.

A number of examples illustrate the process. James Buchanan was a political leader of the Democratic Party and was elected president of the United States in 1856. As a confirmed bachelor, he is the only man ever to be president who was not married. His niece, Harriet Lane whom Buchanan adopted, served as the official White House hostess. Although a "confirmed bachelor," speculation about his sexual orientation was limited. Buchanan had a close relationship with William Rufus King (who became vice president under Franklin Pierce). The two of them lived together for 10 years until King left for an assignment in France. They attended social functions together. Andrew Jackson called them "Miss Nancy" whereas Aaron V. Brown (governor of Tennessee) referred to King as Buchanan's "better half." Buchanan wrote to Cornelia Roosevelt in May 1844, "I am now 'solitary and alone,' having no companion in the house with me. I have gone a wooing to several gentlemen, but have not succeeded with any one of them. I feel that it is not good for man to be alone, and [I] should not be astonished to find myself married to some old maid who can nurse me when I am sick, provide good dinners for me when I am well, and not expect from me any very ardent or romantic affection" (Watson 2012). Regardless of these few comments, the president's sexual affairs were considered his private business and not part of the public discourse.

Abraham Lincoln is another politician whose sexual affairs had been speculated about and debated in the late twentieth century and continues today. As a young man he was a member of the Society of Bachelors in Springfield, Illinois. He lived and shared a bed with Joshua Fry Speed for four years. The men often bragged about sharing the same bed. Lincoln was thrown into deep depression when Speed had to leave the area due to family business. While away, Speed was pressured to marry. Lincoln was also pressured to marry and found a suitable woman in Mary Todd. On their wedding day, Lincoln failed to show up and left Mary Todd at the altar. Only after spending the summer with Speed was Lincoln able to follow through with his commitment to marry Mary Todd. Lincoln never forgot Speed and wanted to name his first born after Speed (to which Mary Todd objected). Mary Todd would visit New York for days and weeks leaving Lincoln at the White House. During those respites from Mary Todd, he often slept with his bodyguards (known as the Bucktail Brigade). Considering how open Lincoln was of his love for men, there was surprisingly very little gossip, and the lack of public discourse on homosexuality helped shield him from accusations of sodomy.

The nineteenth-century American society's acceptance of the category of "confirmed bachelor" and the lack of public discourse on sexuality allowed these men to have same-sex relationships without political repercussions—as long as they were not caught in a public situation and convicted of sodomy. Similar acceptance was available to unmarried women. Single unmarried women of financial means could live alone or with another woman. Public female-female households were so common in New England that the term Boston marriages was coined.

Confirmed bachelor, Boston marriages, and spinster were convenient terms to cover for loving same-sex relationships. Writers were careful to not mention homosexuality but rather strong friendships. New England poet and essayist Henry David Thoreau (1817–1862) illustrates this in his 1838 poem titled "Friendship." Although he refers to the men as "mates," he states that their love cannot speak but "without the help of Greek" (a veiled reference to Greek homosexuality). In an 1840 entry in his personal journal, Thoreau writes about a dream he had and his desire to live with a male partner in a same-sex community:

Why should not we put to shame those old reserved worthies by a community of such. . . . Constantly, as it were through a remote skylight, I have glimpses of a serene friendship land [where] I would live henceforth with some gentle soul such a life as may be conceived, double for variety, single for harmony,—two, only that we might admire our oneness,—one, because indivisible.

Sources: Entry for January 26, 1840. *The Journal of Henry David Thoreau.* Boston: Houghton Mifflin Co., 1906, 113–114; Watson, Robert P. *Affairs of State: The Untold History of Presidential Love, Sex, and Scandal, 1789–1900.* New York: Rowman & Littlefield Publishers, Inc., 2012.

Document 18

NATIONAL WOMEN'S RIGHTS CONVENTION (1852)

Lesbians faced many hurdles in establishing same-sex households in early America. The culture forced women to be married, have children, and be at home under the control of their husband or father. Christian clergy used the writings of Paul to support the belief that women had to subjugate themselves to men and be submissive to their husband. Women wanting to live alone needed not only the financial resources to support their household but also political and legal independence from men. Women faced fighting a system that gave men special rights. Similarly, the LGBT rights movement faces a system that gives heterosexuals special rights.

At the National Women's Rights Convention held in Syracuse, New York, in 1852, we see how similar the struggle for women's rights parallels the struggle for LGBT rights. The first speakers at the convention spoke on how the Bible could be reinterpreted so as to not be so antiwomen. Finally, Ernestine Rose spoke up and made the point that women's rights would not be won by appealing to the Bible but rather appealing to the American Revolutionary idea of justice, equality, and freedom. Her speech was a major shift away from Judeo-Christian rationalization and more toward the concept of democracy. The future women's rights movement would take that approach. Rose said:

For my part, I see no need to appeal to any [biblical] written authority, particularly when it is so obscure and indefinite as to admit of different interpretations. When the inhabitants of Boston converted their harbor into a teapot rather than submit to unjust taxes, they did not go to the Bible for their authority; for if they had, they would have been told from the same authority to "give unto Caesar what belonged to Caesar." Had the people, when they rose in the might of their right to throw off the British yoke, appealed to the Bible for authority, it would have answered them, "Submit to the powers that be, for they are from God." No! On Human Rights and Freedom, on a subject that is as self evident as that two and two make four, there is no need of any written authority. . . .

We ask not for our rights as a gift of charity, but as an act of justice. For it is in accordance with the principles of republicanism that, as woman has to pay taxes to maintain government, she has a right to participate in the formation and administration of it. That as she is amenable to the laws of her country, she is entitled to a voice in their enactment, and to all the protective advantages they can bestow; and as she is as liable as man to all the vicissitudes of life, she ought to enjoy the same social rights and privileges. And any difference, therefore, in political, civil, and social rights, on account of sex, is in direct violation of the principles of justice and humanity, and as such ought to be held up to the contempt and derision of every lover of human freedom.

Source: Elizabeth Cady Stanton, Susan B. Anthony, and Matilda Joslyn Gage. *History of Woman Suffrage.* New York: Fowler and Wells, 1881, vol. 1, 537.

Document 19

WALT WHITMAN AND THE HOMOEROTIC POETRY OF DEMOCRACY (1860)

Walt Whitman sought a breakdown in class differences. He was inspired by Ralph Waldo Emerson's 1841 poem "Friendship" to develop his philosophy of male love. Whitman was attracted to working-class men and envisioned a time when love between men would become the basis for democratic equality. Whitman saw male relationships as being more than just based on sexual acts but rather a new way of uniting a profound psychic and spiritual bond.

In the 1876 edition of "Leave of Grass," Whitman expanded upon his concept of male-to-male love and clearly speaks of the need for society to encourage loving same-sex relationships.

The special meaning of the Calamus cluster of "LEAVES OF GRASS" . . . mainly resides in its political significance. In my opinion it is by a fervent, accepted, development of comradeship, the beautiful and sane affection of man for man, latent in all the young fellows, north and south, east and west—it is by this, I say, and by what goes directly and indirectly along with it, that the United States of the future, (I cannot too often repeat,) are to be most effectually welded together, intercalated, anneal'd into a living union.

Then, for enclosing clue of all, it is imperatively and ever to be borne in mind that "LEAVES OF GRASS" entire is not to be construed as an intellectual or scholastic effort or poem mainly, but more as a radical utterance out of the Emotions and the Physique—an utterance adjusted to, perhaps born of, Democracy and the Modern, in its very nature regardless of the old conventions, and, under the great laws, following only its own impulses.

Source: Walt Whitman. *Complete Prose Works.* Philadelphia, PA: David McKay, 1892, 285.

Document 20

FOURTEENTH AMENDMENT TO THE CONSTITUTION (1868)

The founders of United States constructed the Constitution such that it could be amended. They did not consider the document that they wrote to be a "perfect" construct and recognized that there could be occasion when future societies would want to amend it. After the terrible destruction caused by the Civil War and the passage of the Thirteenth Amendment abolishing slavery, it became obvious that many Southern racists states were still violating the rights of African American freed slaves. Congress passed the Fourteenth Amendment to the Constitution guaranteeing equal protection for all citizens by extending federal protection to all levels of government. This empowered the federal government to act when states and local governments interfered with citizens' civil rights. As such, this extended the concept of individual rights and has been used by every civil rights effort.

All persons born or naturalized in the United States, and subject to the jurisdiction thereof, are citizens of the United States and of the state wherein they reside. No state shall make or enforce any law which shall abridge the privileges or immunities of citizens of the United States; nor shall any state deprive any person of life, liberty, or property, without due process of law; nor deny to any person within its jurisdiction the equal protection of the laws.

Source: National Archives.

Document 21

WALT WHITMAN'S *DEMOCRATIC VISTAS* (1870)

In Democratic Vistas, Walt Whitman describes his concept of democracy. Whitman was disappointed by the materialistic and vulgar democracy he found in America and sought a spiritualization of the general politics that paralleled loving, pure, sweet, strong manly friendships. He warned against the religious fanaticism that so often led to wars, persecutions, and murders. But he did not advocate the elimination of religion but rather a balance between religion and reason, science, and free will. He proposed a new morality not based upon the Bible but rather based on democracy and freedom.

It is to the development, identification, and general prevalence of that fervid comradeship (the adhesive love, at least rivaling the amative love hitherto possessing imaginative literature, if not going beyond it), that I look for the counterbalance and offset of our materialistic and vulgar American democracy, and for the spiritualization thereof. Many will say it is a dream, and will not follow my inferences: but I confidently expect a time when there will be seen, running like a half-hid warp through all the myriad audible and visible worldly interests of America, threads of manly friendship, fond and loving, pure and sweet, strong and life-long, carried to degrees hitherto unknown—not only giving tone to individual character, and making it unprecedently emotional, muscular, heroic, and refined, but having the deepest relations to general politics. I say democracy infers such loving comradeship, as its most inevitable twin or counterpart, without which it will be incomplete, in vain, and incapable of perpetuating itself.

This very conscience, or idea of conscience, of intense moral right, and in its name and strain'd construction, the worst fanaticisms, wars, persecutions, murders, etc., have yet, in all lands, in the past, been broach'd, and have come to their devilish fruition. Much is to be said—but I may say here, and in response, that side by side with the unflagging stimulation of the elements of religion and conscience must henceforth move with equal sway, science, absolute reason, and the general proportionate development of the whole man. These scientific facts, deductions, are divine too—precious counted parts of moral civilization, and, with physical health, indispensable to it, to prevent fanaticism. For abstract religion, I perceive, is easily led astray, ever credulous, and is capable of devouring remorseless, like fire and flame. . . . We want, for these States, for the general character, a cheerful, religious fervor, endued with the ever-present modifications of the human emotions, friendship, benevolence, with a fair field for scientific inquiry, the right of individual judgment, and always the cooling influences of material Nature.

Source: Walt Whitman. *Complete Prose Works*. Philadelphia, PA: David McKay, 1892, Notes 2 and 3.

Document 22
FEMALES PASSING AS MEN (1894)

One way that same-sex couples have been able to live their lives in relative ease is for one of the partners to assume the appearance of the other gender. By "passing" as the other gender, the couple would be perceived to be a heterosexual couple, and no one would give it a second thought. In days before driver's licenses, credit cards, passports, and more, it was fairly easy to pass as someone else, even a different gender.

These arrangements were fairly common. This is known by numerous nineteenth-century newspaper accounts of discovering someone who was passing as the other gender. Typically this occurred when someone died, was incarcerated, or was in the hospital. One such case happened in Black River Falls, Wisconsin, in 1894. A man everyone knew as Frank Blunt was jailed for theft. The sheriff discovered he was female. Her female wife, Gertrude Field, came forward to seek an attorney to defend him in court. The newspaper reported how emotional Field became when visiting him in jail.

Anna Morris, alias Frank Blunt, the woman who has tried to be a man for the last fifteen years, was sentenced to the penitentiary for one year by Judge Gilson at Fond du Lac. She was arrested several months ago in Milwaukee charged with stealing $175 in Fond du Lac. It was then discovered that the prisoner was a woman, although she had worn masculine attire nearly all her life. A jury convicted her of larceny and a motion for a new trial was overruled. After the sentence had been passed Gertrude Field, a woman who claimed to have married the prisoner in Eau Claire, fell upon the neck of the prisoner and wept for half an hour. The woman has furnished all the money for Blunt's defense, and now proposes to carry the case to the Supreme Court.

Source: "Anna Morris Given One Year." *The Badger State Banner*, January 18, 1894, 3.

Further Reading

Adam, Barry D. 1987. *The Rise of a Gay and Lesbian Movement*, 2nd ed. (1995). Boston: Twayne.

Katz, Jonathan Ned. 1976. *Gay American History*. New York: Thomas Crowell.

Plummer, Ken (ed.). 1993. *Modern Homosexualities: Fragments of Lesbian and Gay Experiences*. New York: Routledge.

Watson, Robert. 2012. *Affairs of State: The Untold Story of Presidential Love Sex and Scandal, 1789–1900*. Lanham, MD: Rowman & Littlefield Publishers, Inc.

Chapter 3

Turn of the Twentieth Century through World War I

The Industrial Revolution not only provided new technology but also uprooted thousands of years of agrarian society. Industrial jobs, located mostly in cities, drew young men and women off the farm to earn wages. Concentrating so many single people in city centers led to a boom in restaurants, bars, rooming houses, and more, where single people could mingle and engage in surreptitious relationships away from the prying eyes of their families and provincial community. Self-righteous leaders viewed the "decline" in morals with distain and advocated laws to stem the tide of vice. Many anti-vice campaigns were launched leading to a crackdown on "inverts" (the term given to describe homosexuals).

WWI and later WWI hastened the move of single people off the farm. Military personnel were exposed to new cultures and lands, and mixed together people with different experiences and beliefs forcing many to reconsider their upbringing and prejudices. After the war, the military conducted witch hunts and sting operations to ferret out homosexuals. The pro-homosexual information coming from Germany and the Scientific Humanitarian Committee headed by Dr. Magnus Hirschfeld influenced some gay people to form their own pro-homosexual organization. The Society for Human Rights was formed in 1924 to promote dignity and acceptance of homosexuals. The nascent organization was quickly squashed and the founders placed in prison, but it was an important first step toward the Gay Civil Rights Movement. Regardless of the oppression, more and more pro-gay literature was published—although often in coded language—that would influence future generations.

Document 23
ANTHONY COMSTOCK SEEKS TO IMPRISON INVERTS (1900)

Anthony Comstock was the founder and director of the New York Society for the Suppression of Vice. The organization's goal was to suppress all information on sexual behaviors outside of heterosexual sex within marriage. That included all discussion and pictures of sex in general, masturbation, same-sex love, birth control, and abortion. The activities of the Society led to Congress passing the 1873 Act for the Suppression of Trade in, and Circulation of, Obscene Literature and Articles of Immoral Use. The act became commonly known as the Comstock Law and not only suppressed erotic writings and illustrations but also limited the use of such information in medical journals. In 1900, Earl Lind wrote to Comstock to suggest that the sodomy laws should be repealed, especially since they proscribed a 20-year prison term. Comstock wrote back (and not knowing that Lind was a homosexual) recommending that all "inverts" (the term he used for homosexuals) should be imprisoned for life. Here is Comstock's reply.

Inverts are not fit to live with the rest of mankind. They ought to have branded in their foreheads the word "Unclean." . . . Instead of the law making twenty years' imprisonment the penalty for their crime, it ought to be imprisonment for life. . . . They are willfully bad, and glory and gloat in their perversion. Their habit is acquired and not inborn. Why propose to have the law against them now on the statute books repealed? If this happened, there would be no way of getting at them. It would be wrong to make life more tolerable for them. Their lives ought to be made so intolerable as to drive them to abandon their vices.

Source: Anthony Comstock, quoted in Earl Lind. *Autobiography of an Androgyne.* New York: Medico-legal Journal, 1918, 24–25.

Document 24

U.S. NAVY ENTRAPS HOMOSEXUALS (1919)

The Communist Revolution of 1917 in Russia disturbed many Americans and instigated many investigations. People suspected of being a Communist or "subversive" were arrested, tried, and deported. These police actions were perceived not only as political acts but also as attempts to protect the moral fabric of America. In this climate of fear and suspicion, the first federal investigation into homosexuality was conducted and published by the U.S. Senate. Report of the Committee on Naval Affairs, Sixty-Seventh Congress, First Session, Relative to Alleged Immoral Conditions and Practices at the Naval Training Station, Newport, R.I. (Washington: Government Printing Office 1921) was issued after a two-year investigation that began in 1919. A captain at the U.S. Naval Training Station in Rhode Island heard rumors of homosexual behaviors occurring between local men and sailors at the Newport YMCA. A sting operation was conducted with volunteer sailors offering themselves sexually to men at the YMCA. The year-long operation netted several sailors, a couple of civilians, and Samuel Kent, an Episcopal chaplain.

Kent was an exemplary clergyman who volunteered for the armed forces in World War 1, and as medical support during the influenza epidemic of 1918. The chief of the investigation team dismissed Kent's national service, claiming that he could spot a "queer" by the way he walked and talked. Although a couple of the undercover sailors testified that Kent engaged in sex with them to the point of orgasm, the Episcopal Church stepped in to defend Kent. A skillful defense attorney got a split jury, and a verdict of not guilty was declared. A number of ministers, including Episcopal bishop James Perry, sent a protest letter to President Woodrow Wilson on January 10, 1920. They did not defend homosexuality but complained about the entrapment strategies used by the navy.

Those of us who have been associated in social and religious work among both army and navy call your attention to certain deleterious and vicious methods employed by the Navy Department. . . . [Naval officials who claimed] the unusual power of detecting sexual degeneracy at sight [ordered] over a score of sailors and instructed them in the details of a nameless vice and sent them through the community to practice the same in general and in particular to entrap certain designated individuals. . . .

It must be evident to every thoughtful mind that the use of such vile methods cannot fail to undermine the character and ruin the morals of the unfortunate youths detailed for this duty, render no citizen of the community safe from suspicion and calumny, bring the city into unwarranted reproach, and shake the faith of the people in the wisdom and integrity of the naval administration. . . .

At the earliest moment [we call upon you to] eliminate from the navy all officials, however highly placed, who are responsible for the employment of such execrable methods. . . . The people of the United States are entitled to the assurance that hereafter nobody who enlisted in the navy will be consigned to a career of vice. . . .

[On January 22, 1920, these ministers sent another letter to U.S. senator Carroll Page, chairman of the Senate Naval Affairs Committee, to complain about the entrapment proceedings authorized by naval officers, which]

. . . constituted an indignity [to the] people of Newport. . . . What are we to think of such proceedings? What recourse have we? What recourse has any innocent citizen accused by these depraved persons?

Source: William Safford Jones et al. to Woodrow Wilson, January 10, 1920, 26283–2591:11, Josephus Daniels papers, container 464, Library of Congress.

Document 25
SOCIETY FOR HUMAN RIGHTS (1924)

The Scientific Humanitarian Committee was founded in Germany by Dr. Magnus Hirschfeld in 1897. It became the world's first and foremost organization for researching and publishing on same-sex love found throughout history and in different cultures. Two directors from one of its divisions, the Institute for Sexual Research (based in Berlin), toured the United States in 1906/1907 giving lectures before scientific and medical organizations. As such, some Americans became familiar with the work of the Committee and Institute. The tireless work of Dr. Hirschfeld helped organize the German homosexual emancipation movement with a call to rescind Paragraph 175 of German law, which outlawed homosexuals and sodomy.

Henry Gerber, a young American soldier stationed in Germany from 1920 to 1923, visited Berlin and the Institute for Sexual Research. He subscribed to publications published by the German homosexual rights movement. He was impressed at how well organized the movement was and despaired at the severe antigay climate of America. When he returned to the United States, he took a job with the U.S. Post Office in Chicago and eventually began the first homosexual rights organization in the United States. He recounted his experience for ONE Magazine (1962).

I bitterly felt the injustice with which my own American society accused the homosexual of "immoral acts." I hated this society which allowed the majority, frequently corrupt itself, to persecute those who deviated from the established norms in sexual matters. What could be done about it, I thought. Unlike Germany, where the homosexual was partially organized and where sex legislation was uniform for the whole country, the United States was in a condition of chaos and misunderstanding concerning its sex laws, and no one was trying to unravel the tangle and bring relief to the abused. . . . I realized at once that homosexuals themselves needed nearly as much attention as the laws pertaining to their acts. How could one go about such a difficult task? The prospect of going to jail did not bother me. I had a vague idea that I wanted to help solve the problem. I had not yet read the opinion of Clarence Darrow that "no other offence has ever been visited with such severe penalties as seeking to help the oppressed." All my friends to whom I spoke about my plans advised against my doing anything so rash and futile. I thought to myself that if I succeeded I might become known to history as deliverer of the downtrodden, even as Lincoln. But I am not sure my thoughts were entirely upon fame. If I succeeded in freeing the homosexual, I too would benefit.

Source: Henry Gerber. "The Society for Human Rights—1925." *ONE Magazine,* v. 10: 9, September 1962: 5–10. ONE National Gay and Lesbian Archives at the USC Libraries, Los Angeles, California.

Using his experience in Germany, Gerber convinced six of his friends to be on the board of the first homosexual rights organization in the United States. The "Society for Human Rights" was charted by the state of Illinois on December 10, 1924, and was incorporated as a nonprofit society. Its stated purpose was:

to promote and to protect the interests of people who by reasons of mental and physical abnormalities [sic] are abused and hindered in the legal pursuit of happiness which is guaranteed them by the Declaration of Independence, and to combat the public prejudices against them.

Source: State of Illinois, Cook County, Incorporation of the Society for Human Rights, Chicago, December 10, 1924.

The vague nature of the purpose for the Society did not raise any concerns by the Illinois secretary of state. Gerber wanted to replicate what he experienced in Germany.

He wanted to educate homosexuals, help them network, publish a magazine, and ulti-mately lobby legislators to educate them about the issues to rescind sodomy laws. Gerber recounted the organizing difficulties:

The first difficulty was in rounding up enough members and contributors so the work could go forward. The average homosexual, I found, was ignorant concern-ing himself. Others were fearful. Still others were frantic or depraved. Some were blasé. . . . We wondered how we could accomplish anything with such resistance from our own people . . .

As secretary of the new organization I wrote to many prominent persons solicit-ing their support. . . . I then set about putting out the first issue of *Friendship and Freedom* and worked hard on the second issue. It soon became apparent that my friends were illiterate and penniless. I had to both write and finance. Two issues, alas, were all we could publish. The most difficult task was to get men of good reputation to back up the Society. I needed noted medical authorities to endorse us. But they usually refused to endanger their reputations. The only support I got was from poor people. . . . I realized this start was dead wrong, but after all, move-ments always start small and only by organizing first and correcting mistakes later could we expect to go on at all. The Society was bound to become a success, we felt, considering the modest but honest plan of operation. It would probably take long years to develop into anything worth while. Yet I was willing to slave and suf-fer and risk losing my job and savings and even my liberty for the ideal.

One of our greatest handicaps was the knowledge that homosexuals don't orga-nize. Being thoroughly cowed, they seldom get together. Most feel that as long as some homosexual acts are against the law, they should not let their names be on any homosexual organization's mailing list any more than notorious bandits would join a thieves' union. . . .

Source: Henry Gerber. "The Society for Human Rights—1925." *ONE Magazine* 10, n. 9 (September 1962), 5–10. ONE National Gay and Lesbian Archives at the USC Libraries, Los Angeles, California.

Although the six men who formed the Society's board had the best of intentions, the vice president, Al Meininger, was married and had a child, something unknown to the other five board members. The wife became suspicious that her husband was having affairs with men and reported him to a social worker and to the police. Meininger was forced to confess both about being bisexual and his involvement with Society. The police arrested all six directors. Gerber recounted the night the police and newspaper reporter for The Chicago Examiner *forced their way into his home:*

He told me he had orders from his precinct captain to bring me to the police sta-tion. He took my typewriter, my notary public diploma, and all the literature of the Society and also personal diaries as well as my bookkeeping accounts. At no time did he show a warrant for my arrest. At the police station I was locked up in a cell but no charges were made against me. . . . [The next morning I saw] a copy of the *Examiner*. There right on the front page I found this incredible story: "Strange Sex Cult Exposed." The article mentioned Al who had brought his male friends home. . . . A raid of the flat, the report continued, had turned up . . . a pamphlet of this "strange sex cult" which "urged men to leave their wives and children."

What an outright untruth; what a perversion of facts. . . . The police, I suppose, had hoped or expected to find us in bed. They could not imagine homosexuals in any other way. My property was taken without excuse. This . . . with the Constitution [supposed] to protect the people from unreasonable arrest and search. Shades of the Holy Inquisition. . . .

In the Chicago Avenue Police Court, the detective triumphantly produced a powder puff which he claimed he found in my room. That was the sole evidence of my crime. It was admitted as evidence of my effeminacy. I have never in my life used rouge or powder. The young social worker, a hatchet-faced female, read from my diary, out of context: "I love Karl." The detective and the judge shuddered over such depravity. To the already prejudiced court we were obviously guilty. We were guilty just by being homosexual. This was the court's conception of our "strange cult."

The judge spoke little to us and adjourned court with the remark he thought ours was a violation of the federal law against sending obscene matter through the mails. Nothing in our first issue of *Friendship and Freedom* could be considered "obscene" of course. . . . The following Thursday the four of us were taken before the same judge. This time two post office inspectors were also present. Before the judge appeared in court, one of the inspectors promised that he would see to it that we got heavy prison sentences for infecting God's own country.

As the trial began, our attorney demanded that we be set free since no stitch of evidence existed to hold us. The judge became angry and ordered our attorney to shut up or be cited for contempt. The post office inspectors said that the federal commissioner would take the case under advisement from the obscenity angle. . . . [After being released on bail] I went down to the post office to report for work. But I was told that I had been suspended—more of the dirty work of the post office inspectors. Next I called upon the managing editor of the *Examiner*. I confronted him with the article in the paper. He told me he would look into the matter and make corrections, but nothing was ever done. I had no means to sue the paper, and that was the end of that. . . .

The experience generally convinced me that we were up against a solid wall of ignorance, hypocrisy, meanness and corruption. The wall had won. . . . After a few weeks a letter from Washington arrived advising me that I had been officially dismissed from the Post Office Department for "conduct unbecoming a postal worker."

Source: Henry Gerber. "The Society for Human Rights—1925." *ONE Magazine* 10, n. 9 (September 1962), 5–10. ONE National Gay and Lesbian Archives at the USC Libraries, Los Angeles, California.

Document 26
THE WELL OF LONELINESS (1929)

Female novelist Radclyffe Hall published The Well of Loneliness *in 1928. Hall was at the height of her writing career with the resounding success of* Adam's Breed. *She decided to tackle a plot concerning a "sexual invert" (homosexual). She knew this was highly controversial and that no one had, by this time, written a novel concerning a lesbian loving other women. The book presents "inversion" as a natural, God-given state, but at the same time reinforced the shame and self-hatred many homosexuals felt at this time. There was no explicit sexuality in the book other than a brief statement, "and that night, they were not divided."*

The book became an instant best seller. Hall, a very mannish woman who would be considered butch or transgendered by today's standards, came under severe attacks by British newspapers and her book judged obscene by the British courts. The book was equally attacked in the United States while also becoming a best seller in the states. The Society for the Suppression of Vice filed a complaint with the New York City magistrate's court. It claimed the book violated the New York State Penal Code for indecent literature. The police seized over 800 copies of the book, and the publisher was brought to trial. Judge Hyman Bushel ruled the book obscene on February 21, 1929, not because of explicit writings on sexuality but because it argued for the acceptance of same-sex love. He wrote the following in his decision:

The book here involved is a novel dealing with the childhood and early womanhood of a female invert. . . . The book culminates with an extended elaboration upon her intimate relations with a normal young girl, who becomes a helpless subject of her perverted influence and passion, and pictures the struggle for this girl's affections between this invert and a man from whose normal advances she herself had previously recoiled, because of her own perverted nature. . . .

The author has treated these incidents not without some restraint; nor is it disputed that the book has literary merit. To quote the people's brief: "It is a well written, carefully constructed piece of fiction, and contains no unclean words." Yet the narrative does not veer from its central theme. . . . The unnatural and depraved relationships portrayed are sought to be idealized and extolled. The characters in the book who indulge in these vices are described in attractive terms, and it is maintained throughout that they be accepted on the same plane as persons normally constituted, and that their perverse and inverted love is as worthy as the affection between normal beings and should be considered just as sacred by society.

The book can have no moral value, since it seeks to justify the right of a pervert to prey upon normal members of a community, and to uphold such relationship as noble and lofty. Although it pleads for tolerance . . . it does not argue for repression or moderation of insidious impulses. An idea of the moral tone which the book assumes may be gained from the attitude taken by its principal character [who complains about those who] "try and make me ashamed of my love. I'm not ashamed of it; there's no shame in me."

The theme of the novel is not only antisocial and offensive to public morals and decency, but the method in which it is developed, in its highly emotional way attracting and focusing attention upon perverted ideas and unnatural vices, and seeking to justify and idealize them, is strongly calculated to corrupt and debase those members of the community who would be susceptible to its immoral influence. . . . The courts [have] the duty of protecting the weaker members of society from corrupt, depraving, and lecherous influences, although exerted through the guise and medium of literature, drama or art. The public policy so declared was reaffirmed by the Legislature by its recent amendment to the Penal Law, making it a misdemeanor to prepare, advertise, or present any drama, play, etc., dealing with the subject of sex degeneracy or sex perversion. . . . I am convinced that "The Well of Loneliness" tends to debauch public morals, that its subject matter is offensive to public decency, and that it is calculated to deprave and corrupt minds open to its immoral influences.

Source: People v. Friede, City Magistrate Hyman Bushel's Court of New York City, February 21, 1929. For background information on this case, see Jonathan Ned Katz, *Gay American History*. New York: Thomas Crowell, 1976, 397–405.

The decision was appealed. The three men on the New York City appellate court unanimously reversed the decision on April 19, 1929, and ruled The Well of Loneliness *not obscene. This case was important not only because it opened the way for more homosexual-themed materials to be published and distributed, but it also created a public space where homosexuality and the rights of homosexuals could be discussed.*

Further Reading

Chauncey, George. 1994. *Gay New York: Gender, Urban Culture, and the Making of the Gay Male World*, 1890–1940. New York: Basic Books.

Garber, Eric. 1989. "A Spectacle in Color: The Lesbian and Gay Subculture of Jazz Age Harlem," in *Hidden from History*. Edited by Martin Bauml Duberman, Martha Vicinus, and George Chauncey, Jr. New York: NAL Books, 318–331.

Katz, Jonathan, 1983. *The Gay/Lesbian Almanac*. New York: Morrow.

Nardi, Peter. 1994. *Growing Up before Stonewall: Life Stories of Some Gay Men*. New York: Routledge.

Weeks, Jeffrey. 1981. *Sex, Politics and Society*. London: Longman.

Chapter 4

World War II to 1950

The size of WWII was unparalleled in history. The number of people involved and geographic locations touched by the war forced greater mixing of different people with differing beliefs and cultures. The world recoiled from learning about the atrocities committed in the Nazi concentration camps which included the murder of homosexuals. At the same time, Sigmund Freud and Alfred Kinsey began to medicalize human sexuality that provided a platform to discuss homosexuality in public settings. Similar to what happened after WWI, personnel wasn't needed by the military at the conclusion of WWII, and an effort was made to discharge excess personnel. "Blue slip" discharges were given to homosexuals who dishonored their service to their country and affected future employment in the public sphere. Still, efforts were made by a handful of forward-thinking homosexuals to disseminate information about homosexuality and the plight of homosexuals.

Document 27
THE GERMAN CRIMINAL CODE, PARAGRAPH 175 (1935)

Soon after the unification of Germany, Kaiser Wilhelm I adopted Paragraph 175 in 1871 into the legal code, criminalizing sexual acts between males. Various attempts were made to either rescind the law or broaden it to include lesbians. Those efforts failed and the law was mostly ignored.

Ernst Roehm was Hitler's right-hand man during the early development of the Nazi Party in the 1920s and was openly homosexual. Roehm headed the dreaded SA (Sturmabteilung, otherwise known as storm-troopers or the Brownshirts) for Hitler and was primarily responsible for the acts of terror used to raise Hitler to power. In 1929, the German Constitution was modified, and Paragraph 175 was temporarily removed. It was a hollow victory. In 1934, a power struggle occurred within the Nazi Party, and Roehm was ousted. He, along with his supporters, was killed during what has been named "The Night of the Long Knives." On June 28, 1935, the German government amended its constitution to prohibit homosexuality by the reinstatement of Paragraph 175. This started the systematic extermination of "undesirables," including homosexuals. Paragraph 175 was used to send gay men and lesbians to the concentration camps where most of them died. It is estimated that 5,000 to 15,000 gay men were sent to the concentration camps. Year-by-year, the law and punishment against male homosexuals increased as part of the "racial" purity programs. Eventually, the death penalty was applied to any male homosexual activity, including masturbation. Although female homosexual activity was not specified under Nazi law, lesbians were rounded up along with prostitutes and gypsies and accused of being "decadent." After the war, legal-minded Allied commanders returned homosexual prisoners back to prison to serve out their sentence. Paragraph 175 was completely rescinded in March 1994. Approximately 140,000 men were convicted under the law.

§ 175 *Lewdness between men*

- A man who engages as the active or passive partner in lewdness with another man is to be punished by imprisonment.
- With an involved party who at the time of the act had not yet reached the age of twenty-one years, the Court can refrain from punishment in mild cases.

§ 175a *Severe lewdness* (Schwere Unzucht) A punishment of up to ten years in the penitentiary, and even with mitigating circumstances no less than three months imprisonment for:

- a man, who by force or by threat of harm to life and limb forces another man to engage in such an act as either the active or passive partner;
- a man, who by abusing a dependency founded in a service-, work-, or employment-based relationship coerces another man into engaging in such an act as either the active or passive partner;
- a man over twenty-one years old who entices a male under twenty-one years old to engage in such an act as either the active or passive partner;
- a man who professionally offers himself for such an act as either the active or passive partner.

§ 175b *Bestiality* Unnatural fornication of a man with a beast is to be punished by imprisonment; a sentence of loss of civil rights may also be passed.

Source: German Criminal Code, §175 StGB, revised June 28, 1935.

Document 28

SIGMUND FREUD ON HOMOSEXUALITY (1935)

An American mother wrote to the famous Austrian psychiatrist Sigmund Freud concerning her homosexual son. Surprisingly, Freud wrote back in English claiming that the boy's desires could not be changed and that the best the mother could do is to help her son to accept who he was and live life productively as a well-adjusted homosexual. Perhaps Freud had been influenced by the homosexual rights movement in Germany promoted by Magnus Hirschfeld. Freud wrote:

I gather from your letter that your son is a homosexual. . . . Homosexuality is assuredly no advantage but it is nothing to be ashamed of, no vice, no degradation, it cannot be classified as an illness; we consider it to be a variation of the sexual function produced by a certain arrest of sexual development. Many highly respectable individuals of ancient and modern times have been homosexuals, several of the greatest men among them (Plato, Michelangelo, Leonardo da Vinci, etc.). It is a great injustice to persecute homosexuality as a crime and a cruelty too. If you do not believe me, read the books of Havelock Ellis.

By asking me if I can help, you mean, I suppose, if I can abolish homosexuality and make normal heterosexuality take its place. The answer is, in a general way, we cannot promise to achieve it. In a certain number of cases we succeed in developing the blighted germs of heterosexual tendencies which are present in every homosexual, [but] in the majority of cases it is no more possible. It is a question of the quality and the age of the individual. The result of treatment cannot be predicted.

What [psychiatric] analysis can do for your son, runs in a different line. If he is unhappy, neurotic, torn by conflicts, inhibited in his social life, analysis may bring him harmony, peace of mind, full efficiency, whether he remains a homosexual or gets changed. If you make up your mind he should have analysis with me—I don't expect you will—he has to come over to Vienna. I have no intention of leaving here. However, don't neglect to give me your answer.

Sincerely yours with kind wishes,

S. Freud

Source: Sigmund Freud. "Letter to an American Mother." *International Journal of Psychoanalysis* 32 (1951): 331.

Document 29

LESBIAN CHALLENGES GEORGIA'S SODOMY LAW (1939)

The language in sodomy laws varied significantly from state to state. Rarely did they mention sexual behaviors between women. Ella Thompson was arrested for having oral sex with another woman and convicted of violating Georgia's sodomy law. Thompson's attorney appealed the conviction while she languished in jail because the Georgia law did not specify sex between women. The Georgia Supreme Court ruled in her favor on January 12, 1939, stating that the law could not be applied to two women. This is the first known case in the United States of a woman challenging a sodomy conviction. Although the case did not challenge the sodomy statute, it demonstrated lesbian resistance to oppression.

This record presents the question whether the crime of sodomy, as defined by our law, can be accomplished between two women. By Code . . . sodomy is defined as "the carnal knowledge and connection against the order of nature, by man with man, or in the same unnatural manner with woman." Wharton, in his Criminal

Law . . . lays down the rule that "the crime of sodomy proper can not be accomplished between two women, though the crime of bestiality may be." We have no reason to believe that our lawmakers in defining the crime of sodomy intended to give it any different meaning. Indeed the language of the Code above quoted seems to us to deliberately exclude the idea that this particular crime may be accomplished by two women, although it may be committed by two men, or a man and a woman. That the act here alleged to have been committed is just as loathsome when participated in by two women does not justify us in reading into the definition of the crime something which the lawmakers omitted.

The petitioner's conviction was a nullity and she is entitled to be discharged.

Source: Thompson v. Aldredge, 200 S.E. 799: 187 Ga. 467. South Eastern Reporter, vol. 200 (Jan.–March 1939) (St. Paul, MN: West, 1939), 799–800.

Document 30

LESBIANS IN THE WOMEN'S ARMY CORPS (1945)

Because of the need for soldiers during war, militaries typically welcome and accommodate many who otherwise would not be considered during peacetime. During both World War I and World War II, the U.S. military accepted and pretty much ignored lesbian and gay soldiers. As long as they did not cause an issue of their homosexuality, they could serve openly and form relationships with other same-sex military personnel. President Franklin Roosevelt did not direct the military to enforce antigay policies against gay or lesbian military personnel during the war. This may be related to tolerance for his wife's alleged lesbianism. Through letter correspondence, strong evidence suggests that Eleanor Roosevelt was openly involved with newspaperwoman Lorena Hitchcock, but there is no evidence Franklin condemned it. He took a hands-off policy concerning homosexuality and prioritized winning the war over persecuting homosexuals.

The military was primarily a single-sex environment during the war. The newly formed Women's Army Corps (WAC) attracted many women who sought to live independent lives in relatively nondiscriminatory environments. WAC rules forbade married women from serving and sought to keep men and women separate so as to reduce the chances for pregnancies. As such, the WAC was overly populated by lesbians who often paired up in same-sex couples.

Once the war was over in 1945, the military quickly downsized its operation and severely reduced its personnel. One approach was to ride itself of "sex perverts." General Dwight Eisenhower, future president of the United States, actively tried to remove lesbians under his command. One of his assistants was Nell "Johnnie" Phelps (1922–1997) who protested against the discharges and became informally known as the WAC who stood up to the general. As a civilian, she became active in the women's and lesbian rights movement. She died in 1997, and her ashes were buried with full honor in the U.S. Veterans Cemetery in Los Angeles.

[During World War II Johnnie] enlisted in the newly created Women's Army Corps. She was sent to the South Pacific to work as a medic and lost her first [female] lover when their boat was bombed as they landed on Leyte, Philippines, in 1944. Later during that tour of duty, Johnnie was wounded and received a Purple Heart [commendation medal]. When her tour was over she reenlisted and was sent to Germany as part of the Post-WWII "Occupation" forces. . . .

Later, Johnnie was assigned to head the motor pool for General Eisenhower's battalion. One day he asked her to prepare a list of lesbians in the units. She gave her now-famous answer: "If the general pleases, I'll be happy to do this, but you have to know that the first name on the list will be mine." At that point Eisenhower's secretary added that Sergeant Phelps's name would be second on the list and hers would be first, since she was going to type it. Johnnie estimated that 97% of the women in the units were lesbian and told the general that he would basically lose most of the battalion. She also reminded the general that the group of approximately 900 women had had no "illegal pregnancies, AWOLS or misconducts," and that every six months while under his command, they had received commendations for meritorious service. Eisenhower told them to forget the order, but later when he was President and the McCarthy witch-hunts ruined the lives of many Gays and Lesbians, Eisenhower did not intervene.

Source: Yolanda Retter. "Her/Story: Johnnie Phelps, The WAC Who Stood Up to General Eisenhower." *ONE-IGLA Bulletin* n. 5 (Summer 1998): 4–5. ONE National Gay and Lesbian Archives at the USC Libraries, Los Angeles, California.

Document 31

PSYCHIATRISTS OPPOSE HOMOSEXUAL RIGHTS LAWS (1945)

Not all psychiatrists were as enlightened as Sigmund Freud concerning homosexuality. Freud believed homosexuality was completely natural and that families, friends, and health professionals should have the goal of helping homosexuals to accept themselves as homosexuals and lead productive lives. Professor Thomas Moore of the Catholic University of America wrote an article in 1945 that mixes his religious views with his psychiatric knowledge to advocate that homosexuals needed either to become heterosexual or to be celibate and cut off all ties to members of the same sex. Moore advocated that every human had the duty to be heterosexually married and produce children.

Various movements have been started in a number of nations to do away with penal laws against homosexuality. Before one lends support to such a movement, he should consider something more than the problem whether or not the homosexual is a sick man or a criminal. Homosexuality is to a very large extent an acquired abnormality and propagates itself as a morally contagious disease. It tends to build up a society with even a kind of language of its own, and certainly with practices foreign to those of normal society. It tends to bring about more and more unfruitful unions that withdraw men and women from normal family life, the development of homes, and the procreation of children. The growth of a homosexual society in any country is a menace, more or less serious, to the welfare of the state. . . . Granted that some homosexuality may have a biological factor, it is still a matter of importance to control the spread of homosexuality due to psychological causes. Furthermore, it is not evident that homosexuals in whom there is perhaps a biological trend to homosexuality cannot with some effort make a normal heterosexual adjustment. Laws that would countenance the supposed biological rights of homosexuals would therefore rest on false foundations. . . .

It would be malpractice for a psychiatrist to help the [homosexual] patient to remain in his pathological condition and feel more comfortable in its perpetuation. . . . If we examine the matter objectively, trying to rise above the clouds of passion and desire, we will admit that a human being comes into the world to use his powers and functions in the service of God and the social order. . . . Sex pleasure is associated with genital function in married life that children may be sought and brought into the world.

Source: Thomas V. Moore. "The Pathogenesis and Treatment of Homosexual Disorders: A Digest of Some Pertinent Evidence." *Journal of Personality* (Durham, N.C.) 14 (1945): 57.

Document 32
VICE VERSA PREDICTIONS (1947)

Oftentimes just one person can make difference in ways that cannot be predicted. Edythe Eyde was inspired to write and produce a lesbian-focused publication in 1947. Working as a secretary for a movie production company in Burbank, California, she was knowledgeable about the printing industry. She was aware that commercial printers would refuse to print her newsletter. She resorted to typing multiple copies of her newsletter using carbon paper on a manual typewriter (this is in the days before photocopy machines). Although she had not met any other lesbians at the time she launched the newsletter, she was aware of her attraction to other women and surmised, correctly, that other women living at the same Los Angeles rooming house where she lived were also lesbian.

One of her first articles predicted the future changes for the gay community with uncanny accuracy.

Whether the unsympathetic majority approves or not, it looks as though the third sex is here to stay. With the advancement of psychiatry and related subjects, the world is becoming more and more aware that there are those in our midst who feel no attraction for the opposite sex. . . . [Lesbian themed] books such as *Diana* and *The Well of Loneliness* are available in inexpensive editions at book marts and even the corner drugstores. With such knowledge being disseminated through fact and fiction to the public in general, homosexuality is becoming less and less a taboo subject, and although still considered by the general public as contemptible or treated with derision, I venture to predict that there will be a time in the future when gay folk will be accepted as part of regular society. . . .

Perhaps even *Vice Versa* might be the forerunner of better magazines dedicated to the third sex, which in some future time might take their rightful place on the newsstands beside other publications, to be available openly and without restriction to those who wish to read them. . . .

In days gone by, when woman's domain was restricted to the fireside, marriage and a family was her only prospect, the home was the little world around which life revolved, and in which, unless wives were fortunate enough to have help, they had to perform innumerable household chores besides assuming the responsibility of bearing children. But in these days of frozen foods, motion picture palaces, compact apartments, modern innovations, and female independence, there is no reason why a woman should have to look to a man for food and shelter in return for raising his children and keeping his house in order unless she really wants to. Today, a woman may live independently from man if she so chooses and carve out her own career. Never before have circumstances and conditions been so suitable for those of lesbian tendencies.

Source: Edythe Eyde. "Here to Stay." *Vice Versa—America's Gayest Magazine* 1, n. 4 (September 1947): 1. ONE National Gay and Lesbian Archives at the USC Libraries, Los Angeles, California.

Document 33

EMPLOYMENT OF HOMOSEXUALS AND OTHER SEX PERVERTS (1950)

During World War II, the Soviet Union was an ally of the United States in its efforts to defeat Nazi Germany. The Soviet Union was a Communist country, whereas the United States was staunchly anti-Communist. Those conflicting political views were ignored during wartime. Once the war ended, a number of events triggered the witch hunts that consumed Congress in the early 1950s. The Soviet Union absorbed all the eastern bloc countries, including half of Germany and split Berlin into two. Mao Zedong Communist government took control of China. The Soviet Union exploded its own nuclear bomb. Julius and Ethel Rosenberg were arrested, tried, and executed for stealing atomic bomb secrets to give the Soviets. Alger Hiss, a high-level State Department official, was convicted of perjury (in relationship to espionage). And, the United States launched war in North Korea over its Communist government. For many conservative Americans, it seemed that Communists were attempting to take over the planet.

American conservatives had a long history of painting anything they disagreed with to be either "Socialist" or "Communist" since, what is termed, the First Red Scare of 1917–1920. Many progressive reforms such as child labor laws or women suffrage were reported by conservative commentators to be "Communist plots." Conservatives were primed to believe the U.S. government was being overrun by Communists.

In 1950, the U.S. Congress was almost balanced between Republicans and Democrats. Republicans had not been in power since 1933 and latched onto any scandal to unseat Democrats. Undersecretary of State John Peurifoy testified to a Senate committee investigating government worker loyalty that 91 State Department employees had resigned since 1947 during investigations into their security risk. Peurifoy assured the senators that the employees were not Communists but rather homosexuals. Instead of calming the situation it only encouraged Republicans to begin new investigations into the "infiltration" of government by homosexuals. In one fell swoop, homosexuality became a hot political topic.

At the same Senate hearing, police lieutenant Roy E. Blick of the Washington, D.C., vice squad estimated that there were 5,000 homosexual "perverts" in the city and that 3,700 of them worked for the federal government. Having such clear, concise numbers shocked the committee who immediately ordered an investigation. Senator Kenneth Wherry, Republican floor leader, offered to chair the subcommittee claiming that homosexuals should not be allowed to work for the government because they could be blackmailed as Communist spies. Wherry did not provide any evidence to support his claim.

A few months later, the Senate Investigations Subcommittee of the Committee on Expenditures reported back to the Senate on its findings. The report was based on testimony from psychiatrists and law enforcement agencies but not from any open homosexuals. It focused on ways to identify and terminate the employment of homosexuals. It did not question the core idea that homosexuality and federal employment were not compatible. It was reported that 1,700 applicants for federal jobs between 1947 and 1950 were denied employment because they had been arrested for homosexual conduct. The committee recommended the FBI and local police to conduct more investigations into the sexuality of all job applicants.

The primary objective of the subcommittee in this inquiry was to determine the extent of the employment of homosexuals and other sex perverts in Government; to consider reasons why their employment by the Government is undesirable; and to examine into the efficacy of the methods used in dealing with the problem. . . . Psychiatric physicians generally agree that indulgence in sexually perverted practices indicates a personality which has failed to reach sexual maturity. . . . Homosexuals and other sex perverts are not proper persons to be employed in Government for two reasons; first, they are generally unsuitable, and second, they constitute security risks. . . .

Persons who commit such acts are law violators. Aside from the criminality and immorality involved in sex perversion such behavior is so contrary to the normal accepted standards of social behavior that persons who engage in such activity are looked upon as outcasts by society generally. The social stigma attached to sex perversion is so great that many perverts go to great lengths to conceal their perverted tendencies. This situation is evidenced by the fact that perverts are frequently victimized by blackmailers who threaten to expose their sexual deviations. . . .

Those who engage in overt acts of perversion lack the emotional stability of normal persons. In addition there is an abundance of evidence to sustain the conclusion that indulgence in acts of sex perversion weakens the moral fiber of an individual to a degree that he is not suitable for a position of responsibility. Most of the authorities agree and our investigation has shown that the presence of a sex pervert in a Government agency tends to have a corrosive influence upon his fellow employees. These perverts will frequently attempt to entice normal individuals to engage in perverted practices. . . . One homosexual can pollute a Government office. . . .

There is no place in the United States Government for persons who violate the laws or the accepted standards of morality, or who otherwise bring disrepute to the Federal service by infamous or scandalous personal conduct. Such persons are not suitable for Government positions and in the case of doubt the American people are entitled to have errors of judgment . . . resolved on the side of caution.

Source: U.S. Senate Investigations Subcommittee of the Committee on Expenditures. *Employment of Homosexuals and Other Sex Perverts in the U.S. Government.* Washington: Government Printing Office, 1950.

Further Reading

Black, Allida. 2001. *Modern American Queer History.* Philadelphia, PA: Temple University Press.

Bronski, Michael. 2011. *A Queer History of the United States.* Boston: Beacon Press.

D'Emilio, John. 1983. *Sexual Politics, Sexual Communities.* Chicago, IL: University of Chicago Press.

Duberman, Martin. 1991. *About Time: Exploring the Gay Past, rev. ed.* New York: Penguin USA/Meridian.

Faderman, Lilian. 1991. *Odd Girls and Twilight Lovers: A History of Lesbian Life in Twentieth-Century America.* New York: Columbia University Press.

Gluckman, Amy and Betsy Reed (eds.). 1997. *Homo Economics: Capitalism, Community and Lesbian and Gay Life.* New York: Routledge.

Plant, Richard. 1986. *The Pink Triangle: The Nazi War against Homosexuals.* New York: Henry Holt and Company.

Chapter 5

1950s

After WWII, many of the young men and women did not return to their family farms but decided to live in the large cities. San Francisco was known for its gay population, and many gay men gravitated to the freedoms provided in the city. Many cities developed their own predominantly gay neighborhoods. As a teenager in Los Angeles, Harry Hay learned about the Society for Human Rights. Years later in 1948 while attending a "beer bust" at the University of Southern California, he organized with some friends the "Bachelors for Wallace" that evolved into the "International Bachelors Fraternal Order for Peace and Society Dignity." The group was renamed the "Mattachine Society" and registered with the California Department of Corporations as a nonprofit organization to promote gay rights.

The Mattachine quickly grew and formed other support organizations focused on research (ONE Inc.) and publishing (*ONE Magazine*). In 1952, one of the board members of ONE was arrested for solicitation. Instead of plea bargaining and hoping the situation would fade away, Dale Jennings decided to fight back against police entrapment. This is probably the first challenge to police authority ever to be tried. Jennings won which inspired many others to fight police corruption. Soon after, the U.S. postmaster denied ONE from distributing its newsletter through the U.S. mail condemning it as "obscene." Before the days of electronic media and the Internet, the only way to disseminate information was through the mail. ONE fought the postmaster, and the U.S. Supreme Court ruled in favor of ONE. This one action probably was the most important victory that enabled the growth in LGBT activism.

Research by Dr. Evelyn Hooker shook the foundation of psychiatry's pathologized model of homosexuality. Homosexuals were deemed to possess a criminal psychology that was prone to alcoholism and mental illness. It was accepted that projective tests were able to spot homosexuals. Her research demonstrated that these stereotypes were not correct. The findings were verified by many other researchers, which had great impact on the field of psychology and professional medical organizations.

The 1950s were still a dangerous period for LGBT people. Police continued to raid gay and lesbian bars, the military discharged homosexuals, the McCarthy witch hunts resulted in thousands of homosexuals being fired from their federal jobs, and more. Within this culture of hate a few brave LGBT people organized and fought back.

Document 34

FORMATION OF THE MATTACHINE SOCIETY (1950)

In 1930, at the early age of 17, Harry Hay enticed older gentlemen for sex at the notorious Pershing Square in downtown Los Angeles. From one of these older men, Hay learned of the Society for Human Rights formed in Chicago many years earlier. The Society represented the earliest gay rights group in the United States but, unfortunately, they were arrested for organizing the group and launching a newsletter. Hay found the idea of men getting together for anything other than sex "an eye opener of an idea."

Hay enrolled in the drama department at Stanford University in 1930. Hay was tired of hiding his sexual orientation and told his friends. Many avoided contact with him, but his closest friends were not perturbed by the information. Hay quickly realized that acting was unlikely to provide a living for him, so he became active in guerrilla theater productions focused on workers' rights and demonstrations. From there he joined the Communist Party as union organizer and developer of cultural projects for the next 15 years. The party was decidedly antihomosexual and, under their pressure, Hay married another party member, Anita Platky. Their marriage lasted for 15 years producing two daughters.

In 1948, during a "beer bust" at the University of Southern California, Hay and a group of gay friends developed the idea of an organization named "Bachelors for Wallace," in support of presidential candidacy Henry Wallace of the Progressive Party. Hay realized that gay men needed to organize themselves to combat the rising tide of Senator Joseph McCarthy's anti-Communist and antihomosexual campaign. Two years later, Bob Hull, Chuck Rowland, and Dale Jennings along with Hay founded the "International Bachelors Fraternal Order for Peace and Social Dignity." Later the organization was renamed the Mattachine Society. In 1950, Hay (writing under the pseudonym Eann MacDonald) wrote:

In order to earn for ourselves any place in the sun, we must . . . [work] for the full class citizenship participation of Minorities everywhere, including ourselves. We, the androgynes of the world, have formed this responsible corporate body to demonstrate by our efforts that our physiological and psychological handicaps need be no deterrent in integrating 10% of the world's population towards the constructive social progress of mankind.

Source: Eann MacDonald [pseudonym for Harry Hay], Preliminary Concepts, International Bachelors Fraternal Orders for Peace and Social Dignity (Los Angeles: privately printed, July 7, 1950). Box 1, Folder 21, Mattachine Society Project Collection, Coll 2008–016, ONE National Gay and Lesbian Archives at the USC Libraries, Los Angeles, California.

Document 35

MATTACHINE SOCIETY MEETINGS (1950)

Fearing arrest by the police, Harry Hay structured the Mattachine Society like a leftist cell used by early organizers of the Communist Party. Only five members knew the details of the many subgroups of Mattachine, thereby keeping most of Mattachine secret from its members.

These were the days of intense police raids on both Gay bars and house parties. Entrapment, blackmail, job firings, financial ruin, wrecked families, violence, vindictive court trials and incarceration in prisons and mental institutions were all too common. Our founding five set up Mattachine along the classic lines of revolutionaries with separate cells, or guilds, whose attending members would remain unknown to each other. We allowed no photographs to be taken, and insisted nothing be put down in writing—no notes, no phone lists, or anything that could be used for blackmail or turned over to the F.B.I.

We decided to call ourselves Mattachine after . . . medieval peasant monks who wore masks. . . . We too were forced to wear masks on the job and elsewhere. Paranoia was such at our early meetings that we had to promise total secrecy. Some newcomers were blindfolded and driven around in circles before taken to a meeting. Others came accompanied by members of the opposite sex as a cover for their safety. . . . We had five such guilds in the Los Angeles area, each operating independent of the others. Those people attending one guild's discussion group were unaware of the activities of another group. . . . In each guild, however, there were one or two members who reported back regularly to the founding group of five. The guild gatherings might have up to 50 people in attendance, crowded into a private residence. . . .

Mattachine was important because it got us to stop thinking of ourselves in negative terms. For years we had been told that we were sick and criminal, perverts and degenerates. Any cop could tell you what a homosexual was. We weren't a separate people, a natural phenomenon, according to them. No, we were heterosexual persons who performed depraved homosexual acts and had been led astray by a choir-master or a scout-master. . . .

It was important, therefore, to establish another word for ourselves, one that would combat the negative images. At Mattachine we decided to call ourselves Homophiles [after the Greek word "homo" (the same) and "philos" (love of)], emphasizing the love aspect of our relationships and de-emphasizing the sexual. Gay was still a coded word used only by those in the scene. . . . By using homophile in our literature, in the courts and elsewhere, we effectively confused and defused our enemies. . . .

We believed that as a special people we had made significant contributions for thousands of years, and we were determined that we continue contributing as openly Gay people in present-day society and for all time. . . . [We] used to talk about the snake pit of despair we all were in before the emergence of Mattachine, how far we've come, and how much further we have yet to travel.

Source: Ernie Potvin. "Harry Hay Remembers Jim Kepner." *ONE-IGLA Bulletin* n. 5 (Summer 1998), 14, 16. ONE National Gay and Lesbian Archives at the USC Libraries, Los Angeles, California.

Document 36

MATTACHINE PROTESTS POLICE ENTRAPMENT (1952)

One of the cofounders of Mattachine Society, Dale Jennings, was arrested in 1952 by vice detectives. Typically people (mostly men) arrested by vice on morals charges would plead guilty and pay the small fine. By doing so the case would be kept out of the paper helping them to keep the charge secret. Being arrested by vice could easily lead to loss of job, loss of family, and disillusionment of marriage. Vice often provided a significant source of income for cities, and homosexual men were an easy target. In this case, Dale Jennings decided, with the help of Mattachine, to fight the charges. The members of Mattachine were resentful of the mistreatment of homosexuals and the "extortion" vice played in their lives. The Mattachine organized a Citizen's Committee to Outlaw Entrapment. They were able to raise the funds necessary to hire an attorney for the defense.

At the arraignment, Jennings surprised the court by demanding a jury trial. Such openness and potential media coverage was unheard of. The case, Los Angeles v. William Dale Jennings, *was held on May 19, 1952. At the trial Jennings openly admitted to being a homosexual (probably the first time that ever happened in a court of law). He argued that the plainclothes policeman entrapped him because he was a single man found in an area known to be frequented by homosexual men and that the officer initiated the contact. At the trial, the attorney had to explain to the jury how entrapment against homosexuals was conducted since the public did not know this. Publicity surrounding the case brought considerable media attention to Mattachine, and membership swelled. Jennings describes the case for* ONE Magazine *as follows:*

The trial was a surprise. The attorney [George Shibley], engaged by the Mattachine Foundation, made a brilliant opening statement to the jury. . . . [saying] the only true pervert in the court room was the arresting officer. . . . The jury deliberated for forty hours and asked to be dismissed when one of their number said he'd hold out for guilty till hell froze over. The rest voted for straight acquittal. Later the city moved for dismissal of the case and it was granted. . . .

Yes, I gave my name and publicly declared myself to be a homosexual, but the moment I was arrested my name was no longer "good" and this incident will stand on record for all to see for the rest of my life. In a situation where to be accused is to be guilty, a person's good name is worthless and meaningless. Further, without the interest of the Citizens' Committee to Outlaw Entrapment and their support which gathered funds from all over the country, I would have been forced to resort to the mild enthusiasm of the Public Defender. Chances are I'd have been found guilty and now be either still gathering funds to pay the fine or writing this in jail.

Yet I am not abjectly grateful. All of the hundreds who helped push this case to a successful conclusion, were not interested in me personally. They were being intelligently practical and helping establish a precedent that will perhaps help themselves if the time comes. In this sense, a bond of brotherhood is not mere blind generosity. It is unification for self-protection. Were all homosexuals and bisexuals to unite militantly, unjust laws and corruption would crumble in short order and we, as a nation, could go on to meet the really important problems which face us. Were heterosexuals to realize that these violations of our rights threaten theirs equally, a vast reform might even come within our lifetime. This is no more a dream than trying to win a case after admitting homosexuality.

Source: Dale Jennings. "To Be Accused, Is to Be Guilty." *ONE Magazine* 1, n. 1 (January 1953): 10. ONE National Gay and Lesbian Archives at the USC Libraries, Los Angeles, California.

Document 37

JIM KEPNER'S FIRST MATTACHINE MEETING (1953)

Early pioneers of the gay rights movement often felt alone and met great resistance from other LGBT people. Jim Kepner attempted to organize homosexuals in San Francisco in the 1940s but without success. On his own, he searched public libraries and other sources for information concerning same-sex love. But, there was none to be found. In 1942, Kepner made the conscience decision to dedicate his life to gathering and preserving as much as he could locate on homosexuality and sexual variance. Using every spare dollar he could scrounge up, he bought rare books and clipped articles from newspapers and magazines that addressed LGBT topics. Decades of effort resulted in a large collection of books, documents, and many personal items from other people recognizing the need to archive the gay movement. The collection formally was known as the International Gay and Lesbian Archives. Eventually, the collection was merged with the ONE Institute on the campus of University of Southern California in the 1990s making the largest library/ archive collection on LGBT materials in the world.

Kepner moved to Los Angeles in 1952 and became involved with the Mattachine Society. However, Mattachine/ONE faced many philosophical challenges between its members and its goals. The Mattachine shifted most of its operations to San Francisco with the move of Harry Hay to the bay area. Meanwhile ONE Inc. built membership in Los Angeles. Kepner wrote about his attendance at a meeting of Mattachine in 1953:

Can you fall in love with a roomful of men? I did. Trying for ten years to find another gay to join in fighting for our rights, here was a roomful. Already committed, already organized, talking of building community, a really handsome intelligent lot. . . . I burst with love and zeal, grateful to be invited into membership. We'd hid in the dark 2,000 years, ignorant of ourselves, afraid, persecuted. No more hiding! No more damned hiding! We were on the move, and I was part of it. I loved that roomful of men.

Source: Jim Kepner. "A Roomful of Men: Los Angeles, January 1953." *ONE-IGLA Bulletin* n. 5 (Summer 1998): 14. ONE National Gay and Lesbian Archives at the USC Libraries, Los Angeles, California.

Document 38

TAMPA LESBIAN BAR RAID (1953)

Flo Fleischman was a student at the University of Tampa in the late 1940s. She was a writer for the school newspaper and hoped to become the editor, but rumors of her lesbianism cost her that position. Discouraged by the discrimination, she dropped out of school and joined the underground gay scene.

Florida, at the time, was extremely antigay, and the gay community suffered continued harassment from politicians, religious leaders, and the police. Gay bars were typically owned by the Mafia who paid protection money to the local police. Still, the police often raided gay bars to exert their power over homosexuals and bar owners. Fleischman was caught in a number of these raids. She decided to leave for Southern California in 1956 hoping for a better life. It would be almost a decade later in 1963 that she became an activist again. She organized a group of lesbians in the South Bay of Los Angeles and eventually had the group formally become part of the Daughters of Bilitis in 1965. However, many of the women members dropped out over fears of being found out and losing their jobs. Later, Fleischman helped to establish the Council on Religion and the Homophile, and joined the Metropolitan Community Church (MCC) in 1971. MCC was the world's first church founded by gays providing spiritual resources for gay people. Fleischman graduated from MCC's Samaritan Theological Seminary and became a pastor. By 1995, she became a board member of the ONE Institute and became its president two years later. Fleischman recounted her history in an interview with ONE:

Coming out publicly in "my day" was unheard of—coming out privately was dangerous enough. "My day" was the 1940s, and as a young lesbian in Florida I was acutely aware of the threats, insults, prejudice and beatings hurled at my kind. Most of all it was the constant hammering in our heads that we were somehow "unworthy to walk this earth." . . . The message was being delivered loudly from virtually every pulpit by strident ministers and priests who ranted and raved on the sins of homosexuality. Addressing any such person who might be in their congregation, they'd tell us we were "going to burn in hell" if we didn't turn to heterosexuality. It was a recurring theme. . . .

At school the greatest stress from being different was the inability to find other people like myself. Organized lesbian and gay groups were unheard of. No matter what social group one joined in "my day," you were obliged to attend their events accompanied by the opposite sex. I rebelled by becoming an introvert with plummeting grades and a lost will to exist. . . . [In 1949, when] I entered the University of Tampa, it was the day I came out, not publicly but privately, to myself and a few intimate friends. Coming out publicly would mean being ostracized with attacks from many directions. It happened anyway. I had been feature editor of the university newspaper and nominated for editor when I was reported to the Dean's office [in 1950]. This resulted in loss of my position and removal from the paper's staff. By the end of the semester I was forced to leave college entirely for being "too overt a homosexual." The greatest blow came the next day from my girlfriend who left me a "Dear Flo" letter telling me we were through. She couldn't withstand the stigma of being known as a "woman lover."

In "my day" Tampa had mostly mixed lesbian/gay bars, all sleazy. One called Charlie's was for women only and a real dump. One afternoon [in 1953] I strolled in looking for a buddy. . . . I had put my hand on the barmaid's shoulder and asked if she had seen my friend when, from out of nowhere, I was whirled around and heard [from an undercover vice policewoman] "let's go, you lesbian, you're under arrest for lewd and lascivious conduct." All of us were hauled off to jail.

Unwarranted random bar raids were just another part of the times during "my day." And this day, like many others, the cops were showing pocket-size porno books to all the lesbians, promising to let them off if they would have sex with them. No one took up their offer and instead spent the rest of the night in jail. I faced up to them threatening to sue and they let me off. . . .

In years to follow, I witnessed other degrading incidents in which vice squads jostled innocent lesbians and gays out of bars and violated their human rights in a number of different ways. Later, as a pastor for several Metropolitan Community Churches, these experiences were to help me in ministering to others. Although "my day" for coming out may have occurred in Florida during the '40s, the '90s are "my day" to serve with pride on the board of ONE Institute where my story and countless numbers of others are being preserved for generations to come.

[The Mattachine Society grew and became the longest-lived homophile organization in the United States. It has been at the forefront of freedom of the press and archiving gay history. Evolving from the Mattachine Society, the One Inc. is currently located on campus at the University of Southern California and contains more than 1 million archived books and items, making it the largest collection of gay and lesbian items in the world.]

Source: Rev. Flo Fleischman. "Lesbian Reflections on the Frightening Forties." *ONEIGLA Bulletin* n. 2 (Spring/Summer 1996): 10. ONE National Gay and Lesbian Archives at the USC Libraries, Los Angeles, California.

Document 39

THE CRITTENDEN REPORT ON HOMOSEXUALITY IN THE U.S. NAVY (1957)

Senator Joseph McCarthy caused considerable turmoil in the Senate with his public investigations into the issue of Communists and homosexuals employed by the federal government. One claim made over and over was that homosexuals could be blackmailed and, thus, were open to being used as spies against the United States. A 1950 report by the Investigations Subcommittee of the Senate Committee on Expenditure in Executive Departments concluded that all government agencies "are in complete agreement that sex perverts in Government constitute security risks" (Johnson 2004, pp. 114–15).

The U.S. Navy Board of Inquiry appointed a panel to review the navy's policies regarding homosexuality and to make recommendations as needed. Naval Captain S. H. Crittenden Jr. was assigned as chairman of the panel in 1956. The panel heard from many experts including personnel officers, psychiatrists, and the director of Naval Intelligence—the same agency responsible for discovering homosexuals and discharging them from the military. The Crittenden Board made its report on March 15, 1957. However, the report was never publicly released and buried by the Pentagon for many decades. President Lyndon Johnson signed the Freedom of Information Act in 1966. When asked, the navy reported there was no such study of homosexuality. Eventually, in 1976, it became known that such a report existed and through many requests through the Freedom of Information Act, the report was released in 1981. Still, many parts of the report are missing, and some sections have not been released because of the unidentified "confidential" nature of the testimony. The report summary conclusion stated there was "no sound basis for the belief that homosexuals posed a security risk."

The Board noted that in the area of sexual perversion, only homosexuality is covered by specific directives, although other categories are equally violative of moral codes, laws, and accepted standards of conduct. . . . The homosexuals disclosed represent only a very small proportion of homosexuals in the Navy, and that homosexual behavior by persons who are not exclusively homosexual is even more common. . . . A concept which persists without sound basis in fact is the idea that homosexuals necessarily pose a security risk. It is difficult to determine just how this idea developed, but it seems that it first appeared in governmental directives in 1950, in the report of the Hoey Committee. This Committee, however, based its recommendation on "the *opinions* of those best qualified to know, namely, the intelligence agencies of the Government." However, no intelligence agency, as far as can be learned, adduced any factual data before that Committee with which to support these opinions. . . . Some intelligence officers consider a senior officer having illicit heterosexual relations with the wife of a junior officer or enlisted man much more of a security risk than the ordinary homosexual. The matter of indiscretion would appear to be of more importance than the question of the nature of any sexual activity. There is some information to indicate that at least some homosexuals are quite good security risks. . . . Many exclusively homosexual persons have served honorably in all branches of the military service without detection. . . . Based on testimony of record, the practice of the other services and its own experience, the Board has little difficulty in reaching the conclusion that mandatory discharge of all one-time, non-habitual offenders is not in the best interest of the naval services. . . . The ineffectiveness as a deterrent of the policy of court-martial and *confinement* for *all* homosexual offenders has . . . been illustrated. . . . The other than honorable discharge should not be *mandatory* for any class of offender. . . . . . . The exclusion from service of all persons who, on the basis of their personality structure, could conceivably engage in homosexual acts is totally unfeasible in view of the large proportion of the young adult male population which falls in this category. . . . *Recommendations*: a. Maintain in great part the present service approach to the problem of homosexual behavior. b. Be alert to keep abreast of any widely accepted changes in the attitude of society at large toward the overall problem. c. The service should not move ahead of civilian society nor attempt to set substantially different standards in attitude toward or action with respect to homosexual offenders.

Source: S. H. Crittenden. "Report on Homosexuality in the United States Navy." Papers of the Secretary of the Navy, March 15, 1957, 2, 4, 5, 6, 7, 11, 15, 22, 24, 25, 38, 56.

Document 40

EVELYN HOOKER'S PSYCHOLOGICAL RESEARCH (1957)

Evelyn Hooker accepted a position in the Psychology Department of the University California, Los Angeles where she remained until 1970. Some of her students and associates suggested that she conduct research with homosexuals. Many of the homosexuals she met were members of ONE and the Mattachine Society and had no interest in repressing their homosexuality. That was a revolutionary idea. She delayed the research due to personal issues of a divorce and beginning a second marriage.

Since Hooker had no interest in "curing" homosexuals (which was how many counselors made money), she needed to fund her research with grants. In 1953, Hooker applied to the National Institute of Mental Health (NIMH) for a six-month grant to study the adjustments of nonclinical homosexual men and to compare them to a similar group of heterosexual men. This research had never been done before. All previous research included only homosexuals who were either in prison, or mental patients, or were in therapy to change their sexual orientation. John Eberhart, chief of the grants division of NIMH, explained that her application was quite extraordinary considering this was the height of the McCarthy witch hunt era. Even so, she received the grant, which was continually renewed until 1961. In her 1957 research, Hooker found that expert clinical judges could not distinguish the projective tests protocols of nonclinical homosexual men from a comparable group of heterosexual men, nor were there differences in adjustment ratings. Other academic investigators soon validated her findings. Research by Hooker and others directly led to the American Psychiatric Association deleting homosexuality from the DSM in 1973. Hooker gained great satisfaction from contributing to the freedom and lifting of stigma from this marginalized group.

Hooker entered private practice in the 1970s and was appointed chair of the National Institute of Mental Health Task Force on Homosexuals. She won many awards and acclaim. She died at her home in Santa Monica, California, November 19, 1996, at the age of 89. In a 1997 obituary, Hooker's influence as a heterosexual woman helping to establish the intellectual basis for lesbian and gay rights was outlined.

Few Gays today know that 30 years ago we were virtual wards of the psychiatric profession. They had power to explain us to the world, to pronounce us sick, and to subject those of us who fell into their hands to any treatments then fashionable: "therapy," imprisonment, castration, shock treatment, etc. While many of them sincerely wished to help, and a few of them did, they mostly labeled us as neurotic or psychotic, unstable and fixated at an infantile level of sexuality—and raged at us when we rejected their judgment.

Two persons did the most to revolutionize that: Dr. Alfred C. Kinsey . . . and Dr. Evelyn Gentry Hooker. . . . While teaching psychology at UCLA and living in gay Santa Monica Canyon, it hadn't occurred to her that the derogatory textbook paragraphs about homosexuals would apply to friends and neighbors [like] . . . philosopher Gerald Heard and novelist Christopher Isherwood. Her pioneering research was urged on her by a particularly bright student, Sam From, who, impressed by her tremendous energy and humanity, challenged her to get acquainted with his Gay friends and their lives, to study them and put to the test what psychiatrists were saying about them. . . .

She applied for and received a National Institute of Mental Health grant (the man in charge flew out to make sure she was not Lesbian, then recommended funding her study). She set up a controlled experiment to test the accepted view that Gays were by definition neurotic, unstable, infantile, and identifiable. "Projective tests" in wide use were assumed to be able to identify homosexual leanings, even in persons who didn't know they had them, and to prove that homosexuals were neurotic. Thousands had lost government and private jobs for seeing the "wrong" thing in the eight Rorschach inkblots . . . or for giving "wrong" responses to the Thematic Apperception Test (TAT). . . . Certain answers were interpreted as showing the testee was homosexual and mentally disturbed.

In 1953, the pioneer homophile groups Mattachine and ONE helped her recruit 74 exclusively Gay men who'd never been in therapy or in trouble with the law. . . . She gave the matched pairs the Rorschach, TAT and other tests, and took the results blind to top experts who were sure they could identify homosexuals from the test results alone. Asked to evaluate the responses, they could not tell which were by homosexuals. They "knew" that all homosexuals were maladjusted, but rated more than half of the Gays as better adjusted than the heteros! This astonished even Hooker. The tests showed no difference between the Gay and non-Gay groups. Her study disproved many homophobic assumptions made universally by psychologists at the time and proved that these tests, taken alone, could not identify homosexuals. . . .

She published her then highly controversial results in two careful articles, "The Adjustment of the Male Overt Homosexual," in the *Journal of Projective Techniques*, 1957 and 1958, and kept in touch for years with those she'd interviewed, becoming intimate with Gay life, combining scientific objectivity with warmth, commitment and humor. She spoke widely, infuriating professional homophobes. . . . [and] became convinced that the subject would better be approached from a sociological viewpoint. In the *Journal of Psychology* 1956, her "Preliminary Analysis of Group Behavior of Homosexuals" looked at how the Gay community gives support for those who didn't find it in their early background. . . .

Dr. Stanley Yolles, Director of the U.S. Public Health Service's National Institute of Mental Health, appointed her in September 1967 to head a Task Force on Homosexuality. . . . [In] 1969 the Task Force recommended, with minor dissents, additional research and education, intensive research on possible prevention and treatment factors, repeal of legal penalties on private adult consensual homosexual acts, and the ending of employment discrimination. The Nixon Administration buried the report and fired Dr. Yolles. . . .

In 1992 David Haughland made the moving documentary [film] "Changing Minds: The Story of Dr. Evelyn Hooker" [which] was nominated for an Academy Award. . . . She denied being a hero, as many called her, saying that curiosity and empathy rather than courage had impelled her research, but she added that even as a child, she knew she would do something to better the lot of mankind. She'd demolished the prevailing dogma that homosexuals were inherently abnormal and helped legitimize homosexuality.

Source: Jim Kepner. "A Memory of Dr. Evelyn Hooker." *ONE-IGLA Bulletin* no. 3 (1997): 10–11. ONE National Gay and Lesbian Archives at the USC Libraries, Los Angeles, California.

Document 41

SUPREME COURT RULES *ONE* IS NOT OBSCENE (1958)

When the ONE Magazine *began publishing in 1953, the editors were very careful not to be sexually explicit. At the time, it was illegal to publish and distribute materials that were "obscene." Of course, there was wide interpretation as to what was obscene, and each issue of* ONE Magazine *was reviewed by attorneys to assure the material would not jeopardize* ONE Magazine, *its staff, or supporters. All the writers used aliases to avoid potential legal repercussions. For example, Irma Corky Wolf wrote under the name "Ann Carll Reid," William Door Legg wrote using the name "Bill Lambert" or "Hollister Barnes," and even the art director, Joan Corbin, used the name "Eve Elloree."*

Regardless of the efforts made to avoid legal controversy, Otto Olesen, Los Angeles postmaster, seized the October 1954 issue of ONE Magazine *and refused to allow the magazine to be distributed to subscribers through the U.S. postal system. Olesen charged the magazine to be "obscene." These were serious charges that could lead to the arrest, conviction, payment of fines, and imprisonment for the magazine's staff. ONE's leaders saw themselves as a persecuted minority needing to convey their message of equal rights for all and decided to sue the U.S. Post Office. Doing so made ONE the first homophile organization to sue the government on constitutional grounds. They lost their first case, and the federal judge ruled the magazine obscene (One, Inc. v. Olesen, 1958). They appealed to the Ninth Circuit Court of Appeals and lost again. The court ruled (241, F. 2d. 771) that ONE was "lewd, obscene, lascivious and filthy."*

ONE didn't give up and appealed the case to the U.S. Supreme Court. Luckily, the Supreme Court had just considered a similar case in January 1958 that changed the landscape on obscenity. In Roth v. U.S. *(354 U.S. 476), the Court clarified that for a published work to be considered "obscene" it must, on a whole, appeal to the average person's "prurient interest." Furthermore, the nonprurient discussion of sexual behaviors, politics, history, and problems is an important topic of human interest and cannot abridge protection under the Constitution. General discussions of sexuality could be made without censorship from government officials. Because of this decision, the Court ruled the* Roth *decision applied equally to discussions about homosexuality. Without hearing any oral arguments, the Court ruled that ONE Magazine was not obscene, overturned the Court of Appeals ruling, and ordered the postmaster to allow distribution of the magazine through the mail. This ruling is probably the most important legal victory achieved by the gay rights movement. Although future rulings on constitutional rights including same-sex marriage and overturning Colorado Amendment 2 are deeply important, none of these would not have been possible if basic education and communication about homosexuality was blocked by the government. The gay rights movement owes a great debt to the small group of ONE activists that took on this fight in the 1950s.*

ONE cofounder Dorr Legg wrote a provocative essay in the 1958 ONE Magazine declaring that "I Am Glad I Am a Homosexual" and shows that the victory at the Supreme Court was achieved by daring activists not willing to accede to second-class citizenship.

"I am proud of being a homosexual." This powerfully affirmative statement, made by a speaker at the Constitutional Convention of the Mattachine Society, in April 1953, acted as an electrifying catalyst. Some few applauded its forthrightness. Others, whether consciously or not, [agreed] with popular opinion—that homosexuality is wrong: that it is sinful; that it is shameful. . . .

The admitted homosexuals are a smaller group, comprised mainly of those claiming to be more intellectually sophisticated, and of the flaming queens. This group, in whatever terms, expresses pride in its homosexuality, finding nothing either sinful or shameful in it. They feel that homosexual men and women should be in every way as free to practice their sexual preferences as are other segments of the population; that they should enjoy the same legal and social privileges as others, no more, but also, no less. They feel themselves under no obligations whatever to conform to the particular social standards of any particular community; that instead of their adjusting to popular mores, the mores should be adjusted to their own wishes. . . .

This rugged individualism has an almost anarchistic quality that is yet as American as the "hot dog." It is in the spirit of that old Colonial flag, emblazoned with a rattlesnake and the motto, "Don't tread on me." This is the individualism of the queen, flaunting makeup and a bracelet or two in the face of an amused or embarrassed public, and of the intellectual. . . . [challenging] the unhealthy manifestations of a society so sick, a culture so unsure of itself that it shrinks in horror from some of the greatest and basically elemental forces of man and nature, while striving feverishly at an impossible repression. . . . Some of the most shining stars in the human firmament have been homosexual.

Without these great men and women the world in which we live today would indeed be a sad, drab place—less moral. Who doubts this knows neither religion, history, nor art.

Like other homosexuals who have self-respect and a natural pride, I am proud of being a human being, quite as capable as any of my fellows of doing good work, to the extent of my individual abilities. In addition, I feel sure that my particular way of life has given me certain insights into human problems and character that most heterosexuals apparently lack. . . .

Do these concepts seem shocking, or startling? If so, the reader should prepare himself to continue being shocked, for ideas such as these are present today in the minds of many homosexuals. They will be expressing them more and more vigorously as time goes on. Their day is on the march. They are actively, resiliently proud of their homosexuality, glad for it. Society is going to have to accustom itself to many new pressures, new demands from the homosexual. A large and vigorous group of citizens, millions of them, are refusing to put up any longer with outworn shibboleths, contumely and social degradation.

Like the rest of my brothers and sisters I am glad to be a homosexual, proud of it. Let no one think we don't mean business, or intend to enforce our rights.

Source: Hollister Barnes (pseudonym for Dorr Legg). "I Am Glad I Am a Homosexual." *ONE Magazine* (August 1958): 6–9. ONE National Gay and Lesbian Archives at the USC Libraries, Los Angeles, California.

Document 42

MATTACHINE NATIONAL CONVENTION (1959)

The Mattachine Society came to a major turning point in 1953. At the general membership meeting held at the First Unitarian Universalist Church in Los Angeles, several hundred members attended. Many of the original founders of the organization, including Harry Hay, resigned from the board in protest over the new direction the officers wanted to take the organization. Harold (Hal) Call was a masculine anti-Communist businessman and journalist who wanted the Mattachine to shift more toward political action and education to change heterosexuals' prejudicial attitudes. In contrast, Harry Hay and many other members believed that homosexuals (often called androgynes) were fundamentally different in their essential self when compared to heterosexuals and that the homophile movement required self-reflection for personal growth to overcome years of internalized self-hatred, thereby building self-esteem. Call criticized Hay and his supporters as being ineffective at creating a civil rights movement. Call wanted more homosexuals to open businesses to become economically viable in the community. Call believed that through economic power gays and lesbians could better control, and change, society's antigay prejudices and stereotypes.

Call also wanted the Mattachine to be a more democratic and open organization. The secret structure of the Old Left only reinforced feelings of marginalization. Call advocated a sexual revolution where same-sex behavior was as accepted as opposite-sex behaviors. Call was a tireless activist in San Francisco giving newspaper interviews, inviting theologians, newspaper editors, psychiatrists, and other authorities to speak at Mattachine meetings—even if the speaker did not completely agree with Mattachine on the topic. He made the first documentary film about homosexuals and showed it often. His message was that homosexuals were just like everyone else except for what they did in bed. He launched The Mattachine Review *to spread his thoughts across the nation.*

The spread of Mattachine and the Daughters of Bilitis led to national conventions of homosexuals. In 1959, the largest ever meeting was held at a major hotel in Denver, Colorado, over a Labor Day weekend. The four-day event attracted members from 12 states and generated significant favorable press. Prominent leaders such as Del Martin and Jim Kepner gave keynote speeches. Surprisingly even one Colorado politician spoke about the need to repeal the state's sodomy laws. Hall Call gave an interview in the September 5 issue of The Denver Post *explaining the convention's theme, "New Frontiers in Acceptance of the Homophile."*

The idea is to talk frankly about what homosexuality really is, and the intelligent attitude to take in facing the problems it poses for society. . . . Among those you love most deeply there is likely to be at least one homosexual: a son or daughter, brother or sister. Most homosexuals are NOT insane, stupid, willfully perverted, unnatural or socially incompetent as is often believed. . . . Most can and do lead useful and productive lives. . . . But homosexuals as such have only limited social and civil rights. . . . This is why a group of responsible, socially conscious citizens, including many who are not themselves homosexual, has formed the Mattachine Society . . . to encourage medical and social research pertaining to socio-sexual behavior and to publish the results of such research. It sponsors educational programs to aid social and emotional variants and seeks to promote among the general public an understanding of the problems of such persons.

Source: "Tangents." *ONE Magazine* 7, no. 10 (October 1959): 14–15. ONE National Gay and Lesbian Archives at the USC Libraries, Los Angeles, California.

Further Reading

Abelove, Henry, Michele Aina Barale, and David Halperin (eds.). 1993. *The Lesbian and Gay Studies Reader.* New York: Routledge.

Bullough Vern, Dorr Legg, Barry Elcano et al. (eds.). 1976. *An Annotated Bibliography of Homosexuality and Other Stigmatized Behavior*. New York: Garland.

Chauncey, George, Jr. 1982–1983. "From Sexual Inversion to Homosexuality." *Salmagundi* 58–59: 114–146.

Dynes, Wayne. 1987. *Homosexuality: A Research Guide*. New York and London: Garland.

Herdt, Gilbert (ed.). 1997. *Same Sex, Different Cultures: Gays and Lesbians across Cultures*. Boulder, CO: Westview Press.

Johnson, David K. 2004. *The Lavender Scare: The Cold War Persecution of Gays and Lesbians in the Federal Government*. Chicago, IL: University of Chicago Press.

Sears, James T. 1997. *Lonely Hunters: An Oral History of Lesbian and Gay Southern Life, 1948–1968*. Boulder, CO: Westview.

Weeks, Jeffrey. 1981. *Sex, Politics and Society*. London: Longman.

Chapter 6

1960s

The 1960s was the decade when the civil rights movement made its greatest achievements. Passage of the Civil Rights Act (1964) gave hope for a Great Society promised by President John. F. Kennedy and President Lyndon Johnson. However, the rights for homosexuals were pretty much lost in the rhetoric. Surprising to most, Martin Luther King's most trusted advisor was an openly gay African American named Bayard Rustin. Rustin possessed great organizing skills and was responsible for organizing the 1963 March on Washington.

There were efforts here and there to gain visibility and garner support. The first openly gay man to run for public office was Jose Sarria in San Francisco. The Mattachine Society picketed the White House in 1965, lesbians began their own publication (*The Ladder*), and other activisms. As with any steps forward in civil rights, there are a few steps back. The U.S. Supreme Court upheld deporting homosexual immigrants, police continued raids on the gay bars, workers were being discharged from jobs for being homosexual, and worst. Yet, a few select court cases began to challenge the automatic discharge of homosexuals from their federal or state jobs. In 1969, a raid on the Stonewall Inn in New York would become the event for rallying the LGBT community and organizing LGBT people in colleges and community centers. The Stonewall Riots would become the turning point for the modern gay rights movement.

Document 43
JOSE SARRIA RUNS FOR SAN FRANCISCO CITY COUNCIL (1961)

Jose Sarria was the first openly gay person to run for a public office in the United States. In many ways it is fitting that the first gay person with enough guts to run for public office made his living as a drag queen.

The 1950s were a dangerous time for LGBT people, even in San Francisco. The growth in the number of gay bars alarmed many citizens of San Francisco who pressured politicians to take action. The California Department of Alcoholic Beverage Control (ABC) was instructed to close down as many gay bars as possible under the guise of them being "disorderly houses." ABC would send in an undercover spy to investigate the bars looking for effeminate men or masculine women. The spy would call the police who would raid the bar, close it down, and levy a large fine against the owner of the bar dissuading him or her from reopening. ABC raided the Black Cat bar in 1948. This time, the bar fought back and sued the ABC for violating the rights of the patrons and the rights of the business owner. Surprisingly, when the case was appealed and heard by the California State Supreme Court, the judges sided with the Black Cat and ruled in favor of the owner.

Still, San Francisco police were arresting three to four hundred LGBT people each week in the early 1950s on charges of lewd behavior or solicitation. Besides raiding bars, police would conduct undercover sting operations. Here, police would train one of their younger good-looking officers to solicit a suspected homosexual for sex. Once the man (usually men) agreed, he would be arrested (what we would classify as police entrapment today). Another tactic was for police to arrest men or women who cross-dressed for Halloween. The law at the time made it illegal to cross-dress if there was an "intent to deceive." The usual routine was for the person who was arrested to plead no contest and pay a small fine to get it over without any fanfare or publicity. In a way, the cost of harassment was a fine paid for being part of the gay community.

Jose Sarria gave up his dreams of being a school teacher when he was caught in one of these sting operations at the St. Francis Hotel. Having a "morals" conviction precluded him from earning a state teaching credential. To support himself, he began performing in drag at the Black Cat. Fed up with the extortion used by heterosexuals against homosexuals, Jose Sarria advised every gay person who was arrested to plead not guilty and demand a jury trial. Soon, the backlog of court cases influenced judges to order the police to back off on the excessive number of arrests.

Sarria was known for his inventive drag shows and had a large following. Often during the show he would mix in politics and encourage the audience to be proud of who they were and not accept the condemnation and harassment from heterosexuals. At the end of the show he would sometimes lead a group from the audience to the doors of the city jail with the crowd singing "God save us Nellie queens" to the homosexuals awaiting arraignment. He also launched the Imperial Court system (drag kings and drag queens who put on drag shows and also raise money for charity). Sarria created a flyer for drag queens to carry proclaiming they were "a boy" if stopped by the police. This nullified the "intent to deceive" law and eventually led to the chief of police ordering the Halloween harassment of cross-dressing to cease.

The supposed leniency toward homosexuals became a political issue in 1959. Politicians were trying to outdo themselves in condemning homosexuality. Sarria had had enough of homophobic politicians characterizing homosexuals as a "threat of sexual perversion" and decided to do what no other openly gay person had done before in the United States; he decided to run for public office with the platform of freedom for homosexuals. He had no delusions of winning a seat on the San Francisco Board of Supervisors. In an interview conducted by the Bay Area Reporter about the election, Sarria summarized what happened.

In 1960—to the delight of some and the dismay of many in the emerging gay community—the Sunday afternoon opera queen decided to run for San Francisco Supervisor. "I said in 1960 that we have 10,000 votes in this town and we could win an election," Jose said. "They told me I was full of shit."

The one thing you never tell Jose is that he can't accomplish something. With the determination of the spurned, Jose set about to prove his point. "I needed $25 and 35 signatures [to file as a candidate]. The $25 was easy. But I couldn't get the signatures. Many told me they were behind me, but that they just could not sign. Nobody wanted to endorse a known homosexual. . . ."

[After finally collecting the signatures, Jose filed with the city clerk as a candidate.] To say that the political establishment was horrified by the prospect of a queen in City Hall would be an understatement. Both Republicans and the Democrats refused to list Jose—a tactic to keep him off the ballot. "I went in to the Democrats and told them I had been a Democrat all my life and you cannot deny me the right to run. And if you do I will sue your ass and take you all the way to the Supreme Court," Jose said. Since the Black Cat case was by this time headed for the Supreme Court, it was not an idle threat.

The Democrats listed Jose—but city leaders packed the ballot. . . . Jose didn't win—"If I would have won, I would have died!" he said—but his 7,000 votes shocked the city. In an era when most Americans still would not utter the word "homosexual," a barmaid opera queen whose best Sunday suit was a red dress had won 7,000 votes for public office. San Francisco would never be the same. . . .

[After losing the election] Jose took the next natural step: declared himself ruling monarch of the gay community. . . . Many in the emerging gay community saw Jose's camp as a potential embarrassment to them—even though Jose had by now written the book on gay lib in San Francisco. The biggest gay meetings ever were held—all to argue over whether a drag queen should be allowed to represent the gay community. . . . "Here is the problem," the Empress Jose told the audience. "You don't want a man dressed up as a woman running around town representing you. So let me tell you . . . if you don't agree, I'll do it anyway. . . ." Few can doubt that the Empress I Jose reigns still. He is the Queen Mother of the gay community.

Source: Brian Jones. "Empress I Jose." *Bay Area Reporter* (October 10, 1985): 12–13. Used by permission of the *Bay Area Reporter*.

Document 44

ACLU BEGINS GAY RIGHTS CASES (1963)

The American Civil Liberties Union (ACLU) has been a significant legal force in the United States to challenge various kinds of infringement on individual rights. Often attorneys for the ACLU work for free (pro bono) and have represented clients in some of the most important civil rights cases in recent times. Currently, the executive director of the ACLU is Anthony D. Romero, the first openly gay Latino man to run the organization.

In the 1950s, the ACLU refused to represent federal cases involving homosexuals— including employment discrimination, security clearances, entrapment, and more. Cases at the local levels in New York, Los Angeles, Washington, D.C., and San Francisco encouraged the national-level board to reconsider. By 1963, the national board for the ACLU agreed to begin accepting and representing these cases. Matt Coles, director of the

ACLU Lesbian and Gay Rights Project, reported in 1963 that that decision was a pivotal point in the fight for LGBT civil rights.

In that year it brought its first important challenge to federal civil service rules which allowed lesbians and gay men to be fired on the basis of sexual orientation [*Scott* v. *Macy*]. It took twelve years, but the U.S. Civil Service Commission eventually changed those rules in response to another ACLU sponsored case. Also in 1963, the ACLU brought its first challenge to a state sodomy law [*Enslin* v. *Walford*, followed by *Delany* v. *Florida* in 1967]. . . .

The ACLU dockets of the '60s read like primers on just how bad things were only thirty years ago. . . . Police didn't just raid gay bars. They shuttered them, particularly if they allowed people to dance or, god forbid, hold hands. They also sat outside bars and took down license plate numbers to intimidate people into staying away. . . . [vice squads conducted] "sting" operations designed to entrap gay men into making passes at police officers. It would be years before those operations would cease in some parts of the U.S. [though police in many locales continue to do such stings today]. Throughout the '60s the ACLU fought government attempts to deport lesbians and gay men. Those efforts culminated in the [ACLU's] first U.S. Supreme Court case on gay rights, *Boutillier* v. *The Immigration and Naturalization Service*. We lost. . . .

By the early 1970s, the issues were changing. Employment discrimination cases became more common. The ACLU brought its first challenge to an antigay military policy in 1970 [*Schlegel* v. *U.S.*, which also lost]. Even more interesting, issues that are still hotly contested today started appearing on ACLU dockets in the '70s. In 1972, well ahead of its time, the ACLU brought the first challenge to a ban on same-sex marriage . . . [*Baker* v. *Nelson* and *McConnell* v. *University of Minnesota* where the ACLU defended a] librarian fired because he attempted to marry his partner. . . . In 1973 the ACLU took on the defense of a much honored teacher in Washington who lost his job for being gay. Although we lost the [*Gaylord* v. *Tacoma*] case, we forced a university in Mississippi in 1977 to recognize a lesbian and gay student group [*Mississippi Gay Alliance* v. *Mississippi State University*]. . . . In 1976 *Voeller* v. *Voeller* [the ACLU mounted a] defense of a gay father denied visitation with his children. . . .

In 1980 Wisconsin passed the first statewide law against employment discrimination based on sexual orientation. In the '70s and early '80s, twenty one states got rid of sodomy laws, and in a 1980 ACLU case [*People* v. *Onofre*], New York's highest court struck down its sodomy law as a violation of the right to privacy. . . . [Other prominent ACLU cases included] a 1982 case in which the ACLU brought a suit [*Brinkin* v. *Southern Pacific*] for funeral leave for a gay man whose lover died. . . . [In 1984 *National Gay and Lesbian Task Force* v. *Oklahoma* was a great victory when the United States] Supreme Court strikes down a law targeting teachers who support gay rights.

Source: Matt Coles. "Looking Back: Lesbian and Gay Rights, AIDS, and the ACLU." *Lesbian & Gay Rights, AIDS/HIV, 2000: An ACLU Report.* New York: American Civil Liberties Union, 2000, 5–7. Used by permission of the American Civil Liberties Union.

Document 45

MOHAVE INDIAN TWO-SPIRIT PERSON (1964)

Americans began to be aware about Native Americans (now also referred to as First People) in the 1960s. The movies brought First People to the film and TV as never before. Albeit mostly as a stereotype, it got Americans to consider the rights of First People and include their study in anthropological or ethnic studies. ONE Institute sent a reporter in 1964 to interview Elmer Gage. He was a 35-year-old Mohave Indian living on the Colorado River Reservation. He was considered a homosexual who was open and proud of his status. Although some of his tribe members would make fun of him, in general, he was respected as the best Mohave beadworker and craftsman of his generation besides being a traditional Bird Dancer. He lived with, and took care of, his elderly grandmother. He was open about having had sexual relations with a few Mohave men. ONE Magazine was most interested in his story because he modeled self-acceptance in ways many homosexuals lacked at the time.

E: I can't say if it's a disadvantage being gay because I've been this way so long. Who knows? It's a disadvantage being a lot of things. It's a disadvantage not money, a lot of things. . . . Do I like being made fun of? I don't like it much. When they start to talk about me I just go along with it. I'm not crazy about it. But, for the most part, we all get along. They don't mean any harm by it.

Q: How did you learn about sex?

E: From other boys my age. Of course, it took me awhile to get it all straight in my mind. But we played around a lot and I enjoyed it. Now most of those kids are married and have children of their own. . . . But some of the boys run around with me. We have a good time. Oh, I don't mean like sex all the time. I mean we have a good time like friends—singing Mohave songs and dancing. . . . Being gay has its disadvantages. But I don't think I would like to change. I guess I'm on my own personal little warpath—not against whites but against heterosexuals who think everyone should be like them. I'm not always happy, but I am always me. And they can like it or lump it. Life's too short to spend your time being something you don't want to be. Like the old saying, "To thine own self be true." I'm true to myself and my own nature. I think that's all anyone has a right to ask of me.

Source: Bob Waltrip. "Elmer Gage: American Indian." *ONE Magazine* 13 (March 1965): 6–10. ONE National Gay and Lesbian Archives at the USC Libraries, Los Angeles, California.

Document 46

MATTACHINE PICKETS THE WHITE HOUSE (1965)

The Mattachine Society of Washington decided it was time that the organization brings public awareness to homosexual issues. At this time, there had not been any public demonstration for gay rights in the United States. It was decided to picket in front of the White

House in 1965 holding signs that protested Fidel Castro's discrimination and treatment of homosexuals and similar signs aimed at the mistreatment by the U.S. government. The attempt was to bring public awareness to the similarities in the discrimination against homosexuals by dissimilar governments and to show their support for the United States against the Communist regime. The picket attracted television coverage, probably the first time a group of homosexuals (13 members attended) were shown as regular people on television. The success of the event encouraged Mattachine to conduct a similar protest at Independence Hall and the Liberty Bell in Philadelphia on July 4 of that year. In The Ladder, *Frank Kameny outlined his strategy for lesbian and gay rights.*

There was, and is, a feeling that given any fair chance to undertake dialogue with our opponents, we would be able to impress them with the basic rightness of our position. Unfortunately, by this approach alone we will not prevail because most people operate not rationally, but emotionally, on questions of sex in general, and homosexuality in particular.

It is thus necessary for us to adopt a strongly positive approach, a militant one. It is for us to take the initiative—the offensive, not the defensive—in matters affecting us. It is time that we begin to move from endless talk (directed in the last analysis by us to ourselves) to firm, vigorous action.

We are right; those who oppose us are both factually and morally wrong. We are the true authorities on homosexuality, whether we are accepted as such or not. We must demand our rights, boldly, not beg cringingly for mere privileges, and not be satisfied with crumbs tossed to us.

The question of homosexuality as a sickness is probably the most important single issue facing our movement today. There are some who say that we will not be accepted as authorities, regardless of what evidence we present, and therefore we must take no positions on this matter but must wait for the accepted authorities to come around to our position—if they do. This makes us a mere passive battlefield across which conflicting "authorities" fight their intellectual battles. I, for one, am not prepared to let others dispose of me as they see fit. I intend to play an active role in the determination of my own fate.

Source: Frank Kameny. *The Ladder* 9, no. 8 (May 1965): 14–20. Courtesy of the Gay, Lesbian, Bisexual, Transgender Historical Society.

Document 47

SAN FRANCISCO ACTIVISM (1965)

In the 1960s, gay activism was on the rise in San Francisco. Both the Mattachine Society and the Daughters of Bilitis (DOB) were headquartered in San Francisco. Years of harassment by police against the gay bars encouraged bar owners in San Francisco to form the Tavern Guild in 1962, which later launched the Society for Individual Rights (SIR). The surprising support for Jose Sarria's campaign of the San Francisco Board of

Supervisors led to the formation of the League for Civil Education and the publication of LCE News. *Voter registration drives were made throughout the community to increase political power for LGBT residents. Jim Foster, a soldier discharged from the U.S. Army in 1959 because of his homosexuality, combined social and political events, and became a force within the Democratic Party. Foster was convinced that the way to equality was to increase the support by heterosexuals for LGBT rights and launched the first gay and lesbian Democratic Club within the San Francisco Democratic Party. A number of local Christian ministers also rose to the call for equal rights. The Reverend Cecil Williams, an African American minister, saw the parallels between the racial civil rights movement and the call for gay civil rights.*

These disconnected forces came together in the mid-1960s. Representatives from the DOB, the Council on Religion and the Homosexual, the Mattachine Society, SIR, the Tavern Guild, and others decided to hold a joint costume ball on New Year's Eve in 1965 to bring the groups together and as a fund-raiser for these groups. Many leaders of the community would report that what happened at this dance was a turning point for the movement. The police surrounded the event (more than 600 people attended) and arrested many people and carted them away in paddy wagons. Some of the attendees were prominent ministers of the area and their congregations. Finally, heterosexuals experienced the police harassment homosexuals had put up for decades in San Francisco. The Ladder reported,

Dozens of police swarmed in and around California Hall in San Francisco on New Year's Day, invading a benefit costume ball organized by the Council on Religion and the Homosexual. A line-up of police cars, one paddy wagon, plainclothes and uniformed officers, and police photographers greeted over 600 patrons at this supposedly gala event. Attending the ball were prominent ministers in the San Francisco area, as well as many members of their congregations. . . .

Arrested were three attorneys and a housewife who challenged inspectors from the sex-crimes detail by insisting the police needed either a warrant, or information that a crime was being committed, in order to enter the hall. The four were charged with obstructing police officers. A clergyman was threatened with arrest. . . .

"Angry Ministers Rip Police" said one newspaper headline over a report of a press conference held by the ministers on January 2. The clergymen accused the police of "intimidation, broken promises, and obvious hostility. . . ." San Francisco newspapers carried a stream of letters and articles about the ball. Wire service reports were picked up by newspapers around the country. Radio and TV (including BBC) discussed the repercussions from the ball and also took up the subject of homosexuality in general. . . .

Del Martin, DOB treasurer and a member of the Council, commented that "this is the type of police activity that homosexuals know well, but heretofore the police had never played their hand before Mr. Average Citizen. . . . It was always the testimony of the police officer versus the homosexual, and the homosexual, fearing publicity and knowing the odds were against him, succumbed. But in this instance the police overplayed their part. . . . Police action in this affair will be contested in court to establish the right of homosexuals and all adults to assemble lawfully without invasion of privacy."

The homosexual-dance cause célèbre (see "After the Ball" in the February/March LADDER) closed on a technicality in court. . . .

Source: Kay Tobin. "After the Ball . . ." *The Ladder,* February–March: 4–5, and June 1965, 16. Courtesy of the Gay, Lesbian, Bisexual, Transgender Historical Society.

Document 48

LESBIAN ACTIVISM AND *THE LADDER* (1966)

As with any civil rights movement, there are many different approaches to activism. There are those who are more conservative in nature and want organizations to focus on education and legal strategies, whereas there are those who favor direct confrontation through street demonstration and more. The LGBT movement reflected those varying approaches. Especially in the early years of the Mattachine and Daughters of Bilitis (DOB), the organizations took a more conservative approach while some members advocated for demonstrations in the street.

Barbara Gittings felt very isolated in the 1950s as a closeted college student. She sought out others like herself and eventually learned about ONE Inc. and the Mattachine Society in California. She flew to California and met with Del Martin and Phyllis Lyon— founders of the DOB. Soon after, Gittings launched the New York Chapter of the DOB. In 1963 Gittings, along with her photographer lover Kay Tobin Lahusen, launched the DOB's publication The Ladder—the first lesbian publication available nationwide. The Ladder made it a priority to have photographs of real lesbians on the front cover of the publication so as to encourage others to be open about their sexual orientation.

Gittings soon met Frank Kameny. She related to his activist approach and Gittings and Tobin participated in the picketing of the White House, Independence Hall in Philadelphia, and the Pentagon in Washington in 1965. The Ladder often highlighted these activities. To gain greater distribution of the publication, Gittings was able to persuade bookstores to carry the magazine. At the time there was no such thing as a gay and lesbian bookstore. In keeping with the belief that success with the movement would come about by massive numbers of LGBT people coming out, the magazine included a section "A Lesbian Review" to interview "out" lesbians and tell their stories. One such interview was of the then vice president of DOB New York who was African American. A photo of her was on the front and back cover. The back cover showed the woman picketing at the White House carrying a placard reading "Denial of Equality of Opportunity Is Immoral." This document is an interview with Ernestine Eckstein, showing her militant beliefs yet at the same time revealing her own dislike for antigay stereotypes.

Picketing I regard as almost a conservative activity now. The homosexual has to call attention to the fact that he's been unjustly acted upon. This is what the Negro did. . . . I do regard picketing as a form of education! But one thing that disturbs me a lot is that there seems to be some sort of premium placed on psychologists and therapists by the homophile movement. I personally don't understand why that should be. So far as I'm concerned, homosexuality per se is not a sickness. When our groups seek out the therapists and psychologists, to me this is admitting we are ill by the very nature of our preference. And this disturbs me very much. . . .

Homosexuals are invisible, except for the stereotypes, and I feel homosexuals have to become visible and to assert themselves politically. Once homosexuals do this, society will start to give more and more. . . . Any movement needs a certain number of courageous people, there's no getting around it. They have to come out on behalf of the cause and accept whatever consequences come. . . .

I don't find in the homophile movement enough stress on courtroom action. I would like to see more test cases in courts, so that our grievances can be brought out into the open. That's one of the ways for a movement to gain exposure, a way that's completely acceptable to everybody. . . . We should concentrate on the discrimination by the government in employment and military service, the laws used against homosexuals, the rejection by the churches. . . .

Source: Barbara Gittings and Kay Tobin. "Interview with Ernestine Eckstein." *The Ladder* (June 1966): 4–11. Courtesy of the Gay, Lesbian, Bisexual, Transgender Historical Society.

Document 49

SUPREME COURT EXCLUDES AND DEPORTS HOMOSEXUAL IMMIGRANTS (1967)

People classified as homosexuals were regularly arrested, tried, and deported from the United States by the U.S. Immigration and Naturalization Service (INS). Persons "afflicted with psychopathic personality, or sexual deviation, or mental defect" as defined under Sections 1182 and 1251 of Title 8 of the U.S. Code were excluded from the United States. The American Civil Liberties Union (ACLU) helped a gay immigrant challenge the law to the highest level. Unfortunately, the U.S. Supreme Court ruled against the immigrant in 1967 (Boutilier v. INS) and ordered him deported. The ruling had deep consequences. INS used the ruling for over a decade to aggressively arrest and deport homosexual immigrants. Even after the American Psychiatric Association and the American Psychological Association declassified being homosexual in 1973 as no longer a mental disorder, the INS refused to modify or rescind its policy. The ACLU requested the INS to change its policy and halt deportation of homosexuals. On August 8, 1974, Sam Bernsen, acting INS general counsel, denied the request stating that the phrase "psychopathic personality" was not used in a clinical sense but that rather the law applied to all homosexuals since they do not possess the "good moral" character needed to be a citizen of the United States.

Petitioner, a Canadian national, was first admitted to this country on June 22, 1955, at the age of 21. His last entry was in 1959, at which time he was returning from a short trip to Canada. His mother and stepfather and three of his brothers and sisters live in the United States. In 1963, he applied for citizenship and submitted to the Naturalization Examiner an affidavit in which he admitted that he was arrested in New York in October 1959, on a charge of sodomy, which was later reduced to simple assault and thereafter dismissed on default of the complainant. In 1964, petitioner, at the request of the Government, submitted another affidavit which revealed the full history of his sexual deviate behavior. It stated that his first homosexual experience occurred when he was 14 years of age, some seven years before his entry into the United States. Petitioner was evidently a passive participant in this encounter. His next episode was at age 16, and occurred in a public park in Halifax, Nova Scotia. . . .

. . . . The Public Health Service issued a certificate in 1964 stating that, in the opinion of the subscribing physicians, petitioner "was afflicted with a class A condition, namely, psychopathic personality, sexual deviate" at the time of his admission. Deportation proceedings were then instituted. "No serious question," the Special Inquiry Officer found, "has been raised either by the respondent [petitioner here], his counsel or the psychiatrists [employed by petitioner] who have submitted reports on the respondent as to his sexual deviation."

. . . . The legislative history of the Act indicates beyond a shadow of a doubt that the Congress intended the phrase "psychopathic personality" to include homosexuals such as petitioner. . . . [and] that term "persons afflicted with psychopathic personality," and that the classes of mentally defectives should be enlarged to include homosexuals.

Likewise, a House bill, H.R. 5678, adopted the position of the Public Health Service that the phrase "psychopathic personality" excluded from entry homosexuals and sex perverts.

Affirmed.

Source: Boutilier v. INS, 387 U.S. 118 (1967).

Document 50

HOMOPHILE ACTION LEAGUE (1968)

The 1960s saw the formation of a number of groups that bridged the homophile organizations of the 1950s (e.g., Mattachine, Daughters of Bilitis [DOB]) and the direct political action groups of the 1970s. The Homophile Action League (HAL) in Philadelphia and Society for Individual Rights (SIR) in San Francisco were typical of these "bridge" groups. HAL was founded by former members of the Philadelphia division of the DOB in 1968. HAL stated that it was less interested in "fitting in" and was going to take political action to bring attention to LGBT issues. During its few short years of existence, it fought against discrimination, brought attention to police entrapment and raids, and pressured the media to stop portraying gay people by negative stereotypes. HAL's first newsletter made this editorial.

This newly formed group, open to both men and women, has adopted the name "Homophile Action League," and has as its main purpose "to strive to change society's legal, social and scientific attitudes toward the homosexual in order to achieve justified recognition of the homosexual as a first-class citizen and a first-class human being."

This far-reaching goal will be sought through a variety of means. A major emphasis will be placed on informing and enlightening the public, through the utilization of the mass media and diverse publications. Another focus will be on assisting homosexuals in the battle to secure their constitutional rights and to deal effectively with all manner of publicly-sanctioned discrimination against them. Still another vehicle for implementing our purpose will be the initiation of and participation in social action projects, such as organizing a boycott of business firms whose personal policies discriminate against homosexuals.

We wish to emphasize that word "ACTION" in our name. There is much work to be done and it is our intention to do it. We are *not* a social group. We do *not* intend to concentrate energies on "uplifting" the homosexual community, for such efforts would be badly misplaced. It is our firm conviction that it is the heterosexual community which is sadly in need of uplifting and it is in that direction that our action will be focussed [*sic*].

Source: Homophile Action League Newsletter (1968), 1. ONE National Gay and Lesbian Archives at the USC Libraries, Los Angeles, California.

Document 51

EMPLOYMENT RIGHTS: *NORTON V. MACY* (1969)

The issue of homosexuality and federal employment came to court in 1969. Clifford Norton was employed by the National Aeronautics and Space Administration. He was arrested by officers of the District of Columbia Police Department's morals squad in Lafayette Square (directly across from the White House) for a traffic violation after they saw him attempt to make the acquaintance of another man. He was fired from his job. He sued and the Washington, D.C., circuit court agreed that the government had failed to show a specific connection between the employee's potentially embarrassing conduct and any reduction in the efficiency of the department for which he worked. On the basis of this and related decisions, the Civil Service Commission issued a directive to federal supervisors in December 1973 that stated that "you may not find a person unsuitable for Federal employment merely because the person is a homosexual or has engaged in homosexual acts" (Civil Service Bulletin 1973). Later this concept was expanded by the enactment of the Civil Service Reform Act of 1978. Supervisors were directed not to discriminate against employees on the basis of conduct that does not adversely affect the performance of others. Finally, in 1998 President Bill Clinton signed an executive order specifically banning discrimination based on sexual orientation in the federal civilian workforce.

9 Fair Empl.Prac.Cas. 1382, 135 U.S.App.D.C. 214 Clifford L. NORTON, Appellant, v.
John MACY et al., Appellees.
No. 21625.
United States Court of Appeals District of Columbia Circuit.
Argued Jan. 13, 1969.

Appellant, a former GS-14 budget analyst in the National Aeronautics and Space
Administration (NASA), seeks review of his discharge for "immoral conduct" and
for possessing personality traits which render him "unsuitable for further Government employment.". . . .

Appellant's dismissal grew out of his arrest for a traffic violation. In the early
morning of October 22, 1963, he was driving his car in the vicinity of Lafayette Square. He pulled over to the curb, picked up one Madison Monroe Procter,
drove him once around the Square, and dropped him off at the starting point.
The two men then drove off in separate cars. Two Morals Squad officers, having observed this sequence of events, gave chase, traveling at speeds of up to
45 miles per hour. In the parking lot of appellant's Southwest Washington apartment building, Procter told the police that appellant had felt his leg during their
brief circuit of Lafayette Square and had then invited him to appellant's apartment
for a drink. The officers arrested both men and took them "to the Morals Office to
issue a traffic violation notice."

. . . . Accordingly, this court has previously examined the merits of a dismissal
involving a statutorily protected employee charged with off-duty homosexual conduct. In other cases, we have recognized that, besides complying with statutory pro-
cedural requirements, the employer agency must demonstrate some "rational basis"
for its conclusion that a discharge "will promote the efficiency of the service." "The
ultimate criterion (is) whether the employer acted reasonably. . . ." As we summarized in Leonard v. Douglas, Congress did not attempt a definition of "cause," providing only that it must be one that would promote the efficiency of the service.

. . . . The homosexual conduct of an employee might bear on the efficiency of the
service in a number of ways. Because of the potential for blackmail, it might jeopardize
the security of classified communications. As we acknowledged in Dew v. Halaby,
it may in some circumstances be evidence of an unstable personality unsuited for
certain kinds of work. If an employee makes offensive overtures while on the job,
or if his conduct is notorious, the reactions of other employees and of the public
with whom he comes in contact in the performance of his official functions may
be taken into account. Whether or not such potential consequences would justify
removal, they are at least broadly relevant to "the efficiency of the service."

. . . . Lest there be any doubt, we emphasize that we do not hold that homosexual
conduct may never be cause for dismissal of a protected federal employee. Nor do
we even conclude that potential embarrassment from an employee's private conduct may in no circumstances affect the efficiency of the service. What we do say is
that, if the statute is to have any force, an agency cannot support a dismissal as promoting the efficiency of the service merely by turning its head and crying "shame."

Source: Norton v. Macy, 417 F.2d 1161 (D.C. Cir. 1969).

Document 52

TEACHERS' RIGHTS: *MORRISON V. STATE BOARD OF EDUCATION* (1969)

A teacher, Marc Morrison, engaged in noncriminal same-sex conduct. The school board deemed his behavior "immoral" and revoked his teaching credential. The California Supreme Court held that teaching credentials cannot be revoked because of homosexual conduct unless school authorities demonstrate an "unfitness to teach." Importantly, the court required factual evidence of fitness rather than mere speculation about immorality.

Nov. 20, 1969

MARC S. MORRISON, Plaintiff and Appellant, v. STATE BOARD OF EDUCATION, Defendant and Respondent.

For a number of years prior to 1965 petitioner held a General Secondary Life Diploma and a Life Diploma to Teach Exceptional Children, issued by the State Board of Education, which qualified petitioner for employment as a teacher in the public secondary schools of California. (Ed. Code, §§ 12905, 13251.) On August 5, 1965, an accusation was filed with the State Board of Education charging that petitioner's life diplomas should be revoked for cause. On March 11, 1966, following a hearing, and pursuant to the recommendations of a hearing examiner, the board revoked petitioner's life diplomas because of immoral and unprofessional conduct and acts involving moral turpitude as authorized by section 13202 of the Education Code. This revocation rendered petitioner ineligible for [1 Cal.3d 218] employment as a teacher in any public school in the state. On February 14, 1967, petitioner sought a writ of mandate from the Superior Court of Los Angeles County to compel the board to set aside its decision and restore his life diplomas. After a hearing the superior court denied the writ, and this appeal followed.

For the reasons hereinafter set forth we conclude (a) that section 13202 authorizes disciplinary measures only for conduct indicating unfitness to teach, (b) that properly interpreted to this effect section 13202 is constitutional on its face and as here applied, and (c) that the record contains no evidence to support the conclusion that petitioner's conduct indicated his unfitness to teach. The judgment of the superior court must therefore be reversed.

Source: Morrison v. State Board of Education, 1 Cal.3d 214 (1969).

Document 53

STONEWALL INN RIOTS AND THE BEGINNING OF THE MODERN GAY RIGHTS MOVEMENT (1969)

Early on the morning of June 28, 1969, police raided the Stonewall Inn on Christopher Street in New York City. Although there had been many police raids against gay bars in

New York, the raid on Stonewall expanded into a full riot lasting a couple of days. A cry went out to the gay community who came out in droves to protest the police harassment. The riot was appropriated by some of the local gay organizations who took the battle cry nationwide. From this action grew the thousands of gay rights groups formed on college campuses, community centers, and, now, the gay pride events found in most major cities.

Police Raid on N.Y. Club Sets off First Gay Riot
    By Dick Leitsch, Reprinted from New York Mattachine Newsletter
    The first gay riots in history took place during the pre-dawn hours of Saturday and Sunday, June 28–29 in New York's Greenwich Village. The demonstrations were touched off by a police raid on the popular Stonewall Club, 53 Christopher Street. This was the last (to date) in a series of harassments which plagued the Village area for the last several weeks.
    Plainclothes officers entered the club at about 2 a.m., armed with a warrant, and closed the place on grounds of illegal selling of alcohol. Employees were arrested and the customers told to leave. The patrons gathered on the street outside and were joined by other Village residents and visitors to the area.
    The police behaved, as is usually the case when they deal with homosexuals, with bad grace, and were reproached by "straight" onlookers. Pennies were thrown at the cops by the crowd, then beer cans, rocks, and even parking meters. The cops retreated inside the bar, which was set afire by the crowd.
    A hose from the bar was employed by the trapped cops to douse the flames, and reinforcements were summoned. A melee ensued, with nearly a thousand persons participating, as well as several hundred cops. Nearly two hours later the cops had "secured" the area.

Even Waiters' Tips

The next day, the Stonewall management sent in a crew to repair the premises, and found that the cops had taken all the money from the cigarette machine, the jukebox, the cash register, and the safe, and had even robbed the waiters' tips!
    Since they had been charged with selling liquor without a license, the club was reopened as a "free store," open to all and with everything being given away, rather than sold.
    A crowd filled the place and the street in front. Singing and chanting filled Sheridan Square Park, and the crowds grew quickly.
    At first, the crowd was all gay, but as the weekend tourists poured into the area, they joined the crowds. They'd begin by asking what was happening. When they were told that homosexuals were protesting the closing of a gay club, they'd become very sympathetic, and stayed to watch or to join in.
    . . . . .
    The crowds were orderly, and limited themselves to singing and shouting slogans such as "Gay Power," "We Want Freedom Now," and "Equality for Homosexuals." As the mob grew, it spilled off the sidewalk, overflowed Sheridan Square

Park, and began to fill the roadway. One of the six cops who were there to keep order began to get smart and cause hostility.

A bus driver blew his horn at the meeting, and someone shouted, "Stop the Bus!" The crowd surged onto the street and blocked the progress of the bus. As the driver inched ahead, someone ripped off an advertising card and blocked the windshield with it. The crowd beat on the sides of the (empty) bus and shouted, "Christopher Street belongs to the queens!" and "Liberate the street."

Source: Dick Leitsch. *"Police Raid on N.Y. Club Sets Off First Gay Riot."* New York Mattachine Newsletter, 1969. Reprinted in *The Advocate* (September 1969). Available at: https://www.advocate.com/society/activism/2012/06/29/our-archives-1969-advocate-article-stonewall-riots

Further Reading

Faderman, Lillian. 2015. *The Gay Revolution: The Story of the Struggle.* New York: Simon & Schuster.

Rupp, Leila and Susan Freeman (eds.). 2014. *Understanding and Teaching: U.S. Lesbian, Gay, Bisexual, and Transgender History.* Madison: University of Wisconsin Press.

Shilts, Randy. 1993. *Conduct Unbecoming: Gays & Lesbians in the U.S. Military Vietnam to the Persian Gulf.* New York: St. Martin's Press.

Chapter 7

1970s

The Stonewall Riot sparked the modern gay rights movement. From that event influenced the development of thousands of gay rights organizations on college campuses, community centers, supportive religious organizations, and more. With the greater organizing came greater visibility for LGBT people and issues—sometimes in very controversial ways. As more LGBT people stood up against discrimination in the workplace, housing, family structure, the military, politics, and more, greater media attention was garnered for the LGBT civil rights movement. With greater visibility came backlash from conservatives, fundamentalist Christians, and others.

Homosexuality has a long history of being attacked through sodomy laws. Activists stood up to local and state restrictions, and sodomy laws were struck down in state after state during the 1970s. One of the major contributors to the marginalization of LGBT people stemmed from the medical field of psychology pathologizing homosexuality as a mental disease. Activists directly challenged the American Psychological Association's classification of homosexuality as a mental disorder leading to a rewriting of the *DSM* to eliminate homosexuality from its classifications.

Also, it became apparent in the 1970s that public perception of the gay community was restricted to images of white men. As such, the gay community began to recognize the needs of women, bisexuals, transgender, and others, and formed ever more focused groups to address their individual concerns. The 1970s were a time of creating political organizations to agitate for gay rights and to advocate for equality in political rights. Unfortunately, tragedy hit the LGBT community when Mayor George Mascone and Supervisor Harvey Milk were gunned down in San Francisco City Hall in 1978 by Dan White. Pent-up rage in the gay community led to major demonstrations and conflict.

Document 54
GAY LIBERATION FRONT AND THE GAY ACTIVISTS ALLIANCE (1970)

The LGBT community has come to mark the beginning of the modern gay liberation movement by the riots that took place at the Stonewall Inn, New York on June 28,

1969. Many protests took place that summer in New York City by LGBT people tired of the constant harassment from police. Within weeks, the Gay Liberation Front (GLF) was formed to use direct confrontation against anyone or any organization that limited gay rights. Unlike older, more established organizations that often begged for acceptance, the radicalized gays demanded equality and not feeling the need to gain the approval of heterosexuals. Many wanted to "blow people's minds" by demanding liberty in all aspects of life.

At the time, New York law prohibited same-sex couples from dancing together. As such, GLF organized a number of dances, some at public universities. New York University denied a request to hold a gay and lesbian dance on campus. More than 2,000 people rioted on campus and a weeklong sit-in ensued. The success of the action encouraged students across the nation to launch their own GLF at their colleges. Initially, GLF meetings were revolutionary in tone and paid attention to issues of capitalism, racism, and exploitation of the labor classes and poor. However, the traditional leftist organizations focused on racial issues such as Black Power often demeaned their gay brothers and refused to include LGBT issues in their agenda. As such, GLF and many LGBT organizations withdrew from collaborating with leftist organization and focused solely on gay and lesbian rights. These leftist radicals broke away to form the Gay Activist Alliance (GAA).

The GAA perfected the "zap." This is an action directed at a particular individual or organization designed to embarrass homophobes while at the same time garnering media attention. For example, at the time, the New York credit bureau included a person's sexual orientation in credit reports supplied to banks. Often this led to a denial of credit. When confronted with the practice, the president of the company said, "If one looks like a duck, walks like a duck, associated only with ducks, and quacks like a duck, he is probably a duck." GAA conducted a demonstration in front of the company dressed as ducks loudly making quacking sounds. The company promised to stop the practice when the protestors left. Zapping would be a technique used by ACT-UP and Queer Nation decades later.

The notoriety caused by GLF and GAA spread to all major cities and other LGBT groups. Confrontational tactics resulted in news media often seeking out spokespersons for interviews. In many ways, the radicalization of the gay movement as demonstrated by the GLF and GAA eclipsed the older, more conservative, gay rights organizations.

In 1970, many cities like Los Angeles, Chicago, and New York decided to commemorate the Stonewall Riot. In Los Angeles, 1,200 people marched down Hollywood Boulevard. Chicago had several hundred marchers turn out. New York had approximately 10,000 to 20,000 people march from Greenwich Village to the center of the city. The New York Times *gave front page coverage for the march while barely mentioning the riots of the year before. The* Village Voice *captured the excitement of the event as follows:*

Thousands and thousands and thousands, chanting, waving, screaming—the outrageous and the outraged, splendid in their flaming colors, splendid in their delirious up-front birthday celebration of liberation. . . . They swept up Sixth Avenue, from Sheridan Square to Central Park, astonishing everything in their way. No one could quite believe it, eyes rolled back in heads, Sunday tourists traded incredulous looks, wondrous faces poked out of air-conditioned cars. My God, are those really homosexuals? Marching? Up Sixth Avenue?

Source: Jonathan Black. 1970. "A Happy Birthday for Gay Liberation." *Village Voice,* July 2: 1.

Document 55
"GAY LIB ZAPS PSYCHOLOGISTS" (1970)

Homosexuality was classified as a mental disorder by the medical profession until 1973. Until that time, many psychiatrists and psychologists attempted to change sexual orientation through radical behaviorism. One technique to try and change sexual orientation was to induce pain while someone looked at same-sex pornographic photos or movie clips. The idea of operant conditioning was to train homosexuals to associate pain with their same-sex desires. Then, it was believed, the person would no longer desire homosexuality but rather live as a heterosexual.

Early on, gay activists knew that they needed the medical profession to reevaluate their pathologic perspective on homosexuality. As long as gays were perceived to be inherently "ill," they could not gain respect or rights. In 1970, a Behavioral Modification Conference met at the Los Angeles Biltmore Hotel to show a film and discuss ways that electric shocks could be used to reduce male homosexual same-sex attraction. The Los Angeles Gay Liberation Front learned about the conference, and about 40 of its members infiltrated the event. While the film and slides were shown, GLF members yelled out "Barbarism!" Medieval torture!" and "This is disgusting!" The leaders of the action—Don Kilhefner, Morris Kight, and Del Whan—turned on the lights, took away the microphone, and took over the event. Kight told the audience that their actions were barbaric even if the client asked for such technique. Kight further emphasized that each therapist in the room must assume responsibility for their actions and stop such barbaric practices. Kilhefener refused to give up the microphone stating that small discussion groups would be held, each headed by a GLF member. About 20 of the therapists left, but the rest remained and engaged in the discussions. Kilhefner, who would later earn his PhD in psychology and become a gay-affirming therapists, had this to say:

I'm a firm believer in free speech. But what you people out there call free speech in fact has been a monologue for over a half century. And we would like to start a dialogue. Right now the GLF is suggesting that this morning be reconstituted. If a dialogue is to begin, let it begin now. You have been our oppressor for too long, and we will take this no longer. We are going to reconstitute this session into small groups, with equal numbers of GLF members and members of your profession. We're going to be talking about what you as psychologists are going to do to clear up your own f***ed minds. . . . This is what we're going to be doing. Anybody who can't dig it, we ask you to leave.

Source: Originally appeared in *The Advocate* in 1970.

Document 56

CONGRESS TO UNITE WOMEN (1970)

Since the very beginnings of the National Organization for Women (NOW) in 1966, people who were threatened by the increase in power by women have tried to claim that the organization was a front for lesbians. Being labeled a lesbian caught many NOW members unprepared. Betty Friedan, founder of NOW, responded poorly to the claims and initially sided with the homophobes and said she believed there was a lesbian plot—a "lavender menace"—trying to take over NOW. Many of the lesbian members who helped build the New York chapter of NOW felt betrayed by the heterosexual members of NOW.

NOW organized a Congress to Unite Women in November 1969. The press release failed to list the Daughters of Bilitis as one of the supporting groups. Slighted by the oversight, the lesbians decided to fight back. On the very first night of the Congress, 17 women interrupted the proceedings and took control of the stage. They wore T-shirts labeled "lavender menace" and forced the members to address the lesbian issue. The women shared their stories of what it was like to be a lesbian and why lesbians wanted to participate in the women's movement. By the end of the Congress, a set of resolutions were adopted that confronted the issues of women and lesbian rights. The resolution stated:

A. Be it resolved that Women's Liberation is a Lesbian plot.

B. Resolved that whenever the label "Lesbian" is used against the movement collectively, or against women individually, it is to be affirmed, not denied.

C. In all discussions on birth control, homosexuality must be included as a legitimate method of contraception.

D. All sex education curricula must include Lesbianism as a valid, legitimate form of sexual expression of love.

Source: Daughters of Bilitis at the Congress to Unite Women, New York City, November 1969.

Document 57

DEMOCRATIC PARTY CONVENTION (1972)

Jim Foster helped guide the Society for Individual Rights (SIR) through much of the police turmoil in San Francisco in the 1960s. As police harassment reduced, SIR was transformed into the Alice B Toklas Memorial Democratic Club in 1971. Its purpose was to help support the Democratic Party in San Francisco. U.S. senator George McGovern of South Dakota ran for the Democratic presidential nomination in 1972. He was a liberal politician who came out in favor of gay rights. Foster immediately organized a campaign to support McGovern's candidacy and gathered more than one-third the signatures needed to place McGovern on the California Democratic primary ballot.

At the Democratic National Convention in Miami of that year, McGovern won his party's nomination. McGovern gave thanks to Jim Foster and lesbian activist Madeline Davis and offered them the opportunity to speak to the convention and national television. This was a first—to have openly gay and lesbian speakers who spoke about gay rights. Foster began his speech as follows:

We do not come to you pleading your understanding or begging your tolerance. We come to you affirming our pride in our lifestyle, affirming the validity to seek and maintain meaningful emotional relationships and affirming our right to participate in the life of this country on an equal basis with every citizen.

Source: James M. Foster papers, #7439. Division of Rare and Manuscript Collections, Cornell University Library. Used by permission.

Document 58

MASS MURDER AT THE UPSTAIRS LOUNGE (1973)

On June 24, 1973, arson at the Louisiana UpStairs Lounge killed 32 gay people. The stairwell leading to the gay bar was doused with flammable liquid that created a fire bomb and engulfed the upstairs room. Some men escaped, but many died a terrible death being burned alive. No suspect was ever charged for the crime. The event received very little news coverage although some talk show radio hosts made snide comments about the killing of gay people. This would be the worst mass killing of LGBT people until the terrible tragedy at Pulse gay nightclub in Orlando Florida in June 2016.

Remembering the UpStairs Lounge: The U.S.A.'s Largest LGBT Massacre Happened 40 Years Ago Today

By Terry Firma June 24, 2013

That Sunday, dozens of members of the Metropolitan Community Church (MCC), the nation's first gay church, founded in Los Angeles in 1969, got together there for drinks and conversation. It seems to have been an amiable group. The atmosphere was welcoming enough that two gay brothers, Eddie and Jim Warren, even brought their mom, Inez, and proudly introduced her to the other patrons. Beer flowed. Laughter filled the room.

Just before 8:00PM, the doorbell rang insistently. To answer it, you had to unlock a steel door that opened onto a flight of stairs leading down to the ground floor. Bartender Buddy Rasmussen, expecting a taxi driver, asked his friend Luther Boggs to let the man in. Perhaps Boggs, after he pulled the door open, had just enough time to smell the Ronsonol lighter fluid that the attacker of the UpStairs Lounge had sprayed on the steps. In the next instant, he found himself in unimaginable pain as the fireball exploded, pushing upward and into the bar.

The ensuing 15 minutes were the most horrific that any of the 65 or so customers had ever endured—full of flames, smoke, panic, breaking glass, and screams.

MCC assistant pastor George "Mitch" Mitchell escaped, but soon returned to try to rescue his boyfriend, Louis Broussard. Both died in the fire, their bodies clinging together in death, like a scene from the aftermath of Pompeii.

Metal bars on the UpStairs Lounge windows, meant to keep people from falling out, were just 14 inches apart; while some managed to squeeze through and jump, others got stuck. That's how the MCC's pastor, Rev. Bill Larson, died, screaming, "Oh, God, no!" as the flames charred his flesh. When police and firefighters surveyed and began clearing the scene, they left Larson fused to the window frame until the next morning.

Thirty-two people lost their lives that Sunday 40 years ago—Luther Boggs, Inez Warren, and Warren's sons among them.

Homophobia being what it was, several families declined to claim the bodies and one church after another refused to bury or memorialize the dead. Three victims were never identified or claimed, and were interred at the local potter's field.

When the Rev. William Richardson, of St. George's Episcopal Church, agreed to hold a small prayer service for the victims, about 80 people attended, but many more complained about Richardson to Iveson Noland, the Episcopalian bishop of New Orleans. Noland reportedly rebuked Richardson for his kindness, and the latter received volumes of hate mail.

The UpStairs Lounge arson was the deadliest fire in New Orleans history and the largest massacre of gay people ever in the U.S. Yet it didn't make much of an impact news-wise. The few respectable news organizations that deigned to cover the tragedy made little of the fact that the majority of the victims had been gay, while talk-radio hosts tended to take a jocular or sneering tone: What do we bury them in? Fruit jars, sniggered one, on the air, only a day after the massacre.

. . . .

Source: Terry Firma. "Remembering the UpStairs Lounge: The U.S.A.'s Largest LGBT Massacre Happened 40 Years Ago Today." *Patheos*, June 24, 2013. http://www.patheos.com/blogs/friendlyatheist/2013/06/24/remembering-the-upstairs-lounge-the-u-s-a-s-largest-lgbt-massacre-happened-40-years-ago-today/#disqus_thread

Document 59

MULTIPLE STRUGGLES FOR LESBIAN WOMEN OF COLOR (1973)

Although major strides were made with the civil rights movement and the women's movement in the 1960s and 1970s toward overcoming injustice, there was little progress made concerning the racism found in the mostly white-dominated gay and lesbian rights movement. Lesbians of color were acutely aware of their multiple struggles against racism in the lesbian community while at the same time supporting the broad goals of lesbian rights. Decades of effort to bridge the gap between gender, race, and ethnicity seemed to fail. Although many dialogues and antiracism workshops were held, little progress could be seen. At the historic West Coast Lesbian Conference held in Los Angeles 1973, a group of lesbians of color made this statement:

The workshop on racism began by trying to define racism and by giving examples from our lives, as to how racism functions. Because of the magnitude of the problem we got bogged down. So we dealt with each other instead. . . . We decided to make proposals to make the next conference better with regard to the problem of racism. . . . Racism is here. We don't like it and we don't want to see it any more [sic], particularly from our lesbian sisters. . . . Del Martin [a white activist] pointed out that in her travels across the country she has not seen one lesbian organization that has successfully dealt with the issue of racism. Racism is an issue that we have yet to come to terms with. We must, for there is no greater oppression than that which comes from a sister.

Source: "Report from the Racism Workshop." *The Lesbian Tide*, June 1973: 19. Used by permission of Jeanne Cordova.

Document 60

PARENTS AND FRIENDS OF LESBIANS AND GAYS (1973)

Being a lesbian, gay, bisexuals, or transgendered (LGBT) youth can be very frightening and lonely experience. Probably the greatest fear LGBT youth have is rejection from the family. Beginning in 1973, a group of mostly parents with LGBT children came together to offer support to other parents with LGBT children. The group was named the Parents and Friends of Lesbians and Gays (PFLAG) and was established first in New York and Los Angeles, and eventually expanded to over 350 chapters with 200,000 members and supporters representing all states. Oftentimes small communities will have a PFLAG chapter and no other resources for LGBT teens and their families. The story of how PFLAG was founded is simple.

It started simply, almost accidentally. In 1972 the *New York Post* published a letter from Jeanne Manford, whose gay son had been beaten badly at a protest, while police stood by. . . . Two months later, Manford and her son Marty marched in New York's gay pride parade together. Manford carried a sign which read, "Parents of Gays: Unite in Support for Our Children." The crowd screamed, yelled and cried as Manford approached. . . . In March 1973, New York City Parents of Gays held its first meeting. Nearly 20 people gathered in a Methodist church in Greenwich Village to share their stories and support each other. . . . [In 1976, Adele and Larry Starr] launched the Los Angeles group, the first parent's group to apply for non-profit, tax exempt status. . . . [In 1981] 30 people met at the Starr's home in Los Angeles to write bylaws for a national organization. . . .

[Today] we've taken our place at the national table. . . . Ten years ago we were an afterthought. Now people call us to testify before Congress. We all did what we did because of the love [for] our children.

Source: Carolyn Wagner. n.d. "PFLAG's Rich Past Provides Solid Foundation for Future." PFLAG Web site (http://www.pflag.org/about/history.html). Used by permission of PFLAG.

Document 61

GAY RIGHTS TO ORGANIZE: *GAY STUDENTS ORG. V. BONNER* (1974)

Students at the University of New Hampshire formed a Gay Students Organization (GSO) in 1973. They attempted to hold a number of social events such as dances and plays on campus. Although the events were held without incident, the governor of New Hampshire got wind of the events and complained to the University Board of Trustees. The Board issued a position statement on November 10, 1973, against the GSO and ordered them to schedule no further social functions. The GSO filed suit, and the court ruled in their favor—one of the first and most influential cases legitimizing the rights of LGBT students on college campuses.

GAY STUDENTS ORGANIZATION OF the UNIVERSITY OF NEW HAMPSHIRE, et al. v. Thomas N. BONNER, Individually and as President of the University of New Hampshire, et al.

. . . . [The Governor wrote an] open letter to the Board of Trustees, wherein he stated:

> Therefore, after very careful consideration, I must inform you the trustees and administration that indecency and moral filth will no longer be allowed on our campuses. I am not interested in legalistic hairsplitting that begs these important issues. Either you take firm, fair and positive action to rid your campuses of socially abhorrent activities or I, as governor, will stand solidly against the expenditure of one more cent of taxpayers' money for your institutions. Pl.'s Ex. E dated December 15, 1973.

[The Board of Trustees declared a] declaration tightened the restrictions on the GSO's activities, specifically indicating that the ban on social functions would henceforth be interpreted more expansively than it had in the past.

VI. Summary

In essence, this case is quite simple. The First Amendment guarantees all individuals, including university students, the right to organize and associate "to further their personal beliefs." Healy v. James, *supra*, 408 U.S. at 181, 92 S.Ct. 2338. Absent the attendance of well-defined circumstances, a university must recognize any bona fide student organization and grant to that organization the rights and privileges which normally flow from such recognition—those rights and privileges which are necessary to the maintenance and growth of the organization. Moreover, although a university may reasonably regulate the activities of student organizations, once it grants a particular privilege to one or more organizations, the Fourteenth Amendment requires that that privilege be available to all organizations on an equal basis. From this, it follows that the GSO has the same right to be recognized, to use campus facilities, and to hold functions, social or otherwise, as every other organization on the University of New Hampshire campus.

. . . . Minority groups, as well as majority groups, must be given an opportunity to express themselves; for only in this way can our system of peaceful social change be maintained.

By this, I do not mean that the University must stand by while the GSO and its members incite violence, disrupt school activities, or commit crime. As the University must respect the rights of the GSO, so must the GSO respect the rights of the rest of the University community. This, in essence, is what the Constitution requires.

For the foregoing reasons, the defendants are herewith enjoined from prohibiting or restricting the sponsorship of social functions or use of University facilities for such functions by the Gay Students Organization. Defendants are further enjoined from treating the Gay Students Organization differently than other University student organizations.

Source: Gay Students Organization of University of New Hampshire v. Bonner, 367 F.Supp. 1088 (D.N.H.1974).

Document 62
THE NATIONAL FEDERATION OF PRIESTS' COUNCILS (NFPC) (1974)

At a 1974 meeting, the National Federation of Priests' Councils (NFPC), an organization of Roman Catholic priests and bishops, adopted a pro-gay rights resolution.

BE IT RESOLVED that the NFPC hereby declares its opposition to all civil laws which make consensual homosexual acts between adults a crime and thus urge their repeal: and BE IT FURTHER RESOLVED that the NFPC also express [sic] its opposition to homosexuality as such being the basis of discrimination against homosexuals in employment, governmental services, housing and child rearing involving natural or adoptive parents.

Source: NFPC Resolution 74–20 "Civil Rights of Homosexual Persons." Used by permission of the National Federation of Priests' Councils.

Document 63

LESBIAN CHILD CUSTODY RIGHTS (1974)

Lesbians and gay men often don't come out until after being married and having children. If they divorce, what should be a straightforward legal process often becomes a legal quagmire for the homosexual partner. Gay men rarely gained custody of their children. Historically, courts have favored the mother with custody of the children, an advantage lesbians should benefit from. Instead, once the sexual orientation of the lesbian mother is mentioned in custody court battles, obtaining custody of the child was near-impossible. That changed in 1974 when Cheryl Bratman filed a request on behalf of a lesbian mother in Los Angeles who wanted custody of her children. Surprisingly, the court sided with the lesbian mother and awarded her custody of her children. This was one of the first victories for lesbian mothers. Jeanne Cordova wrote about this in an issue of Lesbian Tide:

In order to win custody of her child in court, a lesbian mother needs a special lawyer, the right judge, social workers, psychiatrists, an alcoholic or absent husband, in-laws who don't contest, money, great commitment and energy, an impeccable background, community and political support and a state which has passed laws favorable to gay rights. . . . In child custody cases the burden of proof (that the child should be taken) rests with the state, in-laws, or relatives, not with the biological parent. . . . [But] the moment the word lesbian is mentioned in a court room, the burden of proof shifts. . . .

It is not enough for the defending mother to call upon her opposition (husband, in-laws, state) to "prove it." Ignorance and prejudice are so rampant in the minds of most judges that "inference" alone is often more than enough to swing the decision. . . . The question of whether or not the mother's sexual orientation negatively affects her children is sometimes not even considered. . . . The lesbian parent's battle is never really over. Opposing parties can contend for the child until she/he reaches the age of 18. . . .

[Often] the husband is so upset that his wife left him for another woman that he will use the custody as a battle of revenge. The lesbian mother must, therefore, assess the time, money and vengeance her ex-husband is prepared to invest in the struggle. Similarly, she must evaluate her own resources of money, energy and stamina. In making this decision, the gay parent must also realize publicity and/or subpoena might also cost her her job, her career, her friends and alienation from family.

Source: Jeanne Cordova. "How to Win a Lesbian Custody Case." *Lesbian Tide,* July–August 1974: 20–21. Used by permission of Jeanne Cordova.

Document 64

LESBIANS AS THE VANGUARD OF FEMINISM (1975)

In the early days of the lesbian feminist movement, a philosophy claiming lesbianism was a natural outgrowth from feminist theory developed. It was assumed that all women had the capacity to develop same-sex feelings toward other women and that women would be emotionally fulfilled in an egalitarian relationship. It was further assumed that men formed dominant-submissive relationships, whereas women formed egalitarian relationships. In the following document, Rita Mae Brown develops these ideas. At the time, she was a member of the "Furies"—a collective of angry white lesbians living together in Washington, D.C. Brown would later become a best-selling lesbian novelist with Rubyfruit Jungle.

Lesbianism, politically organized, is the greatest threat that exists to male supremacy. How can men remain supreme, how can they oppress women if women reject them and fight the entire world men have built to contain us? The beginning rejection is to put women first. . . . Committing yourself to women is the first concrete step toward ending that common oppression. If you cannot find it in yourself to love another woman, and that includes physical love, then how can you truly say you care about women's liberation? . . . Relationships between men and women involve power, dominance, role play, and oppression. A man has the entire system of male privilege to back him up. Another woman has nothing but her own self. Which relationship is better for you? It's obvious.

If women still give primary commitment and energy to the oppressors how can we build a strong movement to free ourselves? Did the Chinese love and support the capitalists? Do the Viet Cong cook supper for the Yankees? Are Blacks supposed to disperse their communities and each live in a white home? The answer, again, is obvious. Only if women give their time to women, to a women's movement, will they be free. You do not free yourself by polishing your chains. . . .

[Lesbianism] offers you potential equal relationships with your sisters. It offers escape from the silly, stupid, harmful games that men and women play, having the nerve to call them "relationships." It offers change. . . . As you change yourself, you will begin to change your society also. A free, strong self cannot live in the muck that men have made. . . . You will discover the thousand subtle ways that heterosexuality destroyed your true power; you will discover how male supremacy destroys all women. . . . You will find love and that you are beautiful [and] strong.

Source: The Shape of Things to Come by Rita Mae Brown. Copyright ©1972 by Rita Mae Brown. Used by permission of Brandt and Hochman Literary Agents, Inc. All rights reserved.

Document 65

THE AMERICAN PSYCHOLOGICAL ASSOCIATION REMOVES HOMOSEXUALITY FROM *DSM* (1975)

One of the most significant decisions came from the American Psychiatric Association (APA) in 1973–1974. The APA formed the APA Task Force on Nomenclature and

Statistics committee in the early 1970s to review the research on homosexuality as related to its classification as a mental illness. Dr. Robert Spitzer and other members of the committee reviewed the data and recommended homosexuality to be eliminated from the DSM. It reviewed the works of Dr. Evelyn Hooker and many other researchers, along with the 1969 recommendations by the National Institute of Mental Health (NIMH) Task Force on Homosexuality, to repeal sodomy laws and educate the public about homosexuality. The committee, along with the APA's Council on Research and Development, Reference Committee, and Assembly, made recommendations to remove homosexuality from its list of mental illness. The APA Board unanimously passed a resolution removing homosexuality from the DSM. A group of psychoanalysts filed a petition against the resolution. A referendum was held during which more than 58 percent of the 10,000 voting members supported (with 37.8 percent against) the Board action. Future challenges to the resolution were rejected by even larger margins.

Conservatives and members of the Religious Right often considered this change in the DSM was accomplished by a band of scheming gay activists that pushed through their agenda. This is not true. It was a multiyear review of academic and government research combined with a clear presentation of the findings to the members that convinced the APA to change its position. The membership of the APA reflects society and is mostly heterosexual. It was primarily heterosexuals who reviewed the research and agreed that the change was needed. It was heterosexuals who overcame their bias and homophobia and made a rational decision based on objective research. In the intervening 30 years, no academic research has found any evidence suggesting that homosexuality is a mental illness. If anything, the research has affirmed that there are no differences in psychosocial measures related to sexual orientation.

Resolution Passed January 1975, by American Psychological Association the Council of Representatives

The American Psychological Association supports the action taken on December 15, 1973 by the American Psychiatric Association, removing homosexuality from that Association's official list of mental disorders. The American Psychological Association therefore adopts the following resolution:

> Homosexuality, per se, implies no impairment in judgment, stability, reliability, or general social or vocational capabilities: Further, the American Psychological Association urges all mental health professionals to take the lead in removing the stigma of mental illness that has long been associated with homosexual orientations.

Regarding discrimination against homosexuals, the American Psychological Association adopts the following resolution concerning their civil and legal rights:

The American Psychological Association deplores all public and private discrimination in such areas as employment, housing, public accommodation, and licensing against those who engage in or who have engaged in homosexual activities and declares that no burden of such judgment, capacity, or reliability shall be placed upon these individuals greater than that imposed on any other persons. Further, the American Psychological Association supports and urges the enactment of civil rights legislation at the local, state, and federal level that would offer citizens who engage in acts of homosexuality the same protections now guaranteed to others on the basis of race, creed, color, etc. Further, the American Psychological Association supports and urges the repeal of all discriminatory legislation singling out homosexual acts by consenting adults in private.

Source: J. J. Conger. "Proceedings of the American Psychological Association, Incorporated, for the year 1974: Minutes of the Annual Meeting of the Council of Representatives." *American Psychologist* 30 (1975): 620–651. Available at: http://www.apa.org/about/policy/discrimination.aspx

Document 66

MILITARY SERVICE: *MATLOVICH V. SECRETARY OF THE AIR FORCE* (1976)

In this celebrated 1975 case, Leonard Matlovich sued the air force to be reinstated after being dismissed for homosexuality. His story made the cover of Time *magazine (September 8, 1975) and was later made into an NBC TV movie, starring Brad Dourif* (Seargent Matlovich vs. the U.S. Air Force *originally shown August 21, 1978). His suit dragged on to 1980 when a federal judge ordered Matlovich reinstated. Instead of reentering the air force, he settled for financial restitution and became a gay rights activist. He died in 1988 of complications from HIV/AIDS. His tombstone reads "When I Was in the Military, They Gave Me a Medal for Killing Two Men and a Discharge for Loving One."*

18 Fair Empl.Prac.Cas. 1061, 18 Empl. Prac.
  Dec. P 8710,
  192 U.S.App.D.C. 243
  Leonard P. MATLOVICH, Appellant, v.
  SECRETARY OF THE AIR FORCE and Colonel Alton J. Thogersen, Appellees.
  Decided Dec. 6, 1978.
  1 In March 1975, appellant Leonard P. Matlovich, after some twelve years of excellent service in the military, wrote to the Secretary of the Air Force, through his commanding officers, that he had concluded that his "sexual preferences are homosexual as opposed to heterosexual." He added that in his view his sexual preferences would in no way interfere with his Air Force duties and that he considered himself fully qualified for further military service. He asked that the provision in AFM 39–12 (Change 4) Oct. 21, 1970, para. 2–103, relating

to the discharge of homosexuals be waived in his case. At that time Matlovich was a Technical Sergeant assigned to the 4510th Support Squadron, Tactical Air Command, Langley Air Force Base, Virginia. His letter triggered an investigation by the Air Force Office of Special Investigation during which appellant provided information concerning his homosexual experiences since 1973; he stated that these were all consensual and occurred in private, while he was off duty and off-base, with males over twenty-one. He also said that he had had such relations with two other members of the Air Force (one of whom had been discharged by that time), neither of whom had worked for him (he added that "as any responsible NCO (non-commissioned officer) I would always refrain from such a relationship").

3 Matlovich's commanding officer at Langley Air Force Base accepted the Board's recommendation of discharge but determined that the discharge should be honorable. The Secretary of the Air Force then declined to waive the provisions of AFM 39–12, Supra, and directed that the honorable discharge be executed.

4 Appellant immediately applied to the Air Force Board for the Correction of Military Records (AFBCMR) to overturn his discharge and also amended his complaint below . . . to seek reinstatement, as well as a declaratory judgment that the discharge was invalid.

15. . . . the Air Force cannot justify appellant's discharge. What we say is that the Air Force should explicate more fully its reasons for refusing to retain appellant as its regulation provides that it may do and its practice shows that it has done in other cases so that the court can decide if it was arbitrary, capricious, or unlawful in exercising its discretion whether or not to retain Matlovich.

28 Accordingly, the decision granting summary judgment to the Government is vacated and remanded with instructions to remand to the Air Force for further proceedings consistent with this opinion. Appellant can of course seek judicial relief from any adverse determination made on this remand.

Source: Matlovich v. Secretary of the Air Force, 591 F.2d 852 858 (D.C. Cir. 1978).

Document 67

UNION OF AMERICAN HEBREW CONGREGATIONS RESOLUTION (1977)

In 1977, the Union of American Hebrew Congregations passed a pro-gay rights resolution. Now known as the Union for Reform Judaism, this organization supports 900 congregations in the Reform Judaism faith in America and Canada and founded the Hebrew Union College in 1875.

Homosexual persons are entitled to equal protection under the law. We oppose discrimination against homosexuals in areas of opportunity, including employment and housing. . . . We affirm our belief that private sexual acts between consenting adults are not the proper province of government and law enforcement agencies.

Source: Used by permission of the Union for Reform Judaism, http://urj.org.

Document 68

TEACHERS' RIGHTS: *GAYLORD V. TACOMA SCHOOL DIST. NO. 10* (1977)

A Tacoma, Washington, school district discovered in 1972 that James Gaylord was a homosexual. The officials believed that being known as a "gay teacher" would automatically impair his efficiency as a teacher. He sued when he was fired. The Washington Supreme Court agreed with the Tacoma School District that a "gay teacher" could not effectively teach. During the trial, the Washington State Supreme Court resorted to encyclopedias, including the New Catholic Encyclopedia, to conclude that homosexuality was implicitly immoral. As such, the court surmised that Gaylord could not be trusted to teach students about morality, and his presence was considered disruptive even though he had been a successful teacher for the previous 12 years. This court's opinion about the immorality of homosexuality was contradictory to the conclusions reached by the state, which had repealed its sodomy law by the time of the trial.

JAMES M. GAYLORD, Appellant, v. TACOMA SCHOOL DISTRICT No. 10 et al,
  Respondents.
The Supreme Court of Washington, En Banc.
May 15, 1975.
. . . . Mr. Gaylord contends he was an excellent teacher up until the day he was discharged despite the alleged public knowledge of his status as a homosexual. He stresses the trial court's finding of fact that "There is no allegation or evidence that James Gaylord has ever committed any overt acts of homosexuality. The sole basis for his discharge is James Gaylord's status as a homosexual." He argues to this court that expert testimony showed overwhelmingly that, even if knowledge of his status as a homosexual became public, he would be able to function efficiently as a teacher without risk of harm to the school or to the pupils. The school district, on the other hand, presented testimony at trial by its administrative staff that when knowledge of appellant's status as a homosexual became known to the students and their parents, the resulting complaints would affect appellant's teaching efficiency and injure the school.

This crucial question of fact was resolved in favor of the school district by the trial judge. He found the public knowledge of Gaylord's status would "impair the optimum learning atmosphere in the classroom.". . . .

The trial court's finding that the teacher's status would "impair the optimum learning atmosphere in the classroom" is basic to an affirmance of the district's action. . . .

There is no allegation or evidence that James Gaylord has ever committed any overt acts of homosexuality. The sole basis for his discharge is James Gaylord's status as a homosexual.

VI.

Jack Beer, Wilson High School Vice-Principal, Maynard Ponko, Wilson High School Principal, and Trygve Blix, former Tacoma School District personnel director, all testified that in their opinion, the knowledge of James Gaylord's homosexuality would cause some students, teachers, and parents to object to James Gaylord's continued presence in the classroom, and that these types of objections would impair said administrators' ability to administer the school and would therefore damage the educational process.

Yet, opposite positions were given by expert witnesses:

VII.

Drs. S. Harvard Kauffman and Jerman Rose, psychiatrists specializing in child and adolescent psychiatry, testified that in their opinion James Gaylord's presence in the classroom did not pose any threat of harm to the personal or educational development of the students at Wilson High School, and that in their opinion James Gaylord would be able to function well as a teacher even if his students had knowledge of his homosexuality. . . .

VIII.

Dr. Stephen Sulzbacher, an educational psychologist from the University of Washington, testified that he had consulted with virtually every school district in Western Washington, was personally aware of the professional competence of homosexuals teaching in said public schools, and that, in his opinion, James Gaylord would be able to continue teaching effectively in the classroom, even if students, teachers and parents knew of his homosexuality. . . .

Source: Gaylord v. Tacoma School Dist., 85 Wn2d 348 (WA. 1975).

Document 69

CIVIL SERVICE REFORM ACT (1978)

On the basis of Norton v. Macy *and related decisions, the Civil Service Commission issued a directive to federal supervisors in December 1973 that stated that "you many not find a person unsuitable for Federal employment merely because the person is a homosexual or has engaged in homosexual acts" (Civil Service Bulletin 1973). Later this concept was expanded by the enactment of the Civil Service Reform Act of 1978. Supervisors were directed not to discriminate against employees on the basis of conduct that does not adversely affect the performance of others.*

§ 2302. Prohibited personnel practices

(b) Any employee who has authority to take, direct others to take, recommend, or approve any personnel action, shall not, with respect to such authority—

(10) discriminate for or against any employee or applicant for employment on the basis of conduct which does not adversely affect the performance of the employee or applicant or the performance of others; except that nothing in this paragraph shall prohibit an agency from taking into account in determining suitability or fitness any conviction of the employee or applicant for any crime under the laws of any State, of the District of Columbia, or of the United States;. . . .

Source: 5 U.S.C. §2302(b)(10).

Document 70

HARVEY MILK ON THE SAN FRANCISCO BOARD OF SUPERVISORS (1978)

Harvey Milk arrived in San Francisco in 1972 and used his savings to open a camera shop in the Castro District. At the time, the Castro District was comprised of working-class Irish, but gay men were slowly moving in to fix up the dilapidated Victorian houses. Instead of joining the established gay rights organizations, Milk decided to run for the city's Board of Supervisors. Against the advice of Jim Foster and others, Milk ran for the office and came in 10th out of a field of 32 candidates. For the next two years, Milk helped develop the Castro District and labor unions (he was informally called the "Mayor of Castro Street"). His second run for the Board of Supervisors had him come in second. That was a remarkable achievement for an openly gay man running for political office. Recognizing the gaining political influence by the gay community, Mayor George Moscone appointed Milk to the city permits board besides naming lesbian activists Phyllis Lyon and Jo Daley to the city's Human Rights Commission. Del Martin was also appointed to the Commission on the Status of Women.

Milk ran for Board of Supervisors a third time and won. As an openly gay politician Milk was aware of the power he wielded. He was effectively the leader of the gay community and used the opportunity to exert his influence on a national level. He gave speeches inviting all persecuted LGBT people to move, or, at least visit San Francisco. Milk spearheaded many progressive and gay rights measures on the Board. As such, he received many death threats. Milk sponsored a gay rights city ordinance that the only conservative on the Board, Dan White, voted against. Dan White was a former police-man who was very conservative and Catholic. By the fall of 1978, White realized that he was outnumbered on the Board and gave a letter of resignation to Mayor Moscone. Ten days later after attending a Police Officer's Association, White decided to ask for his position back. Moscone had already chosen someone to fill the vacancy and refused his request. On November 27, 1978, Dan White snuck into City Hall with his police pistol and shot and killed both Mayor George Moscone and Supervisor Harvey Milk. The city was in shock. Dan White was tried for murder six months later. The all-white hetero-sexual Catholic jury returned a verdict of voluntary manslaughter and not murder. Dan White would be eligible for release within five years. The light conviction for not one, but two murders, infuriated the gay community. That night thousands of gays and lesbians marched through the street to city hall, turning over police cars and torching many. The police retaliated by bursting into gay bars in the Castro District bludgeoning everyone in sight.

The riot has become known as "White Night Riot" and resulted in 100 gay people and 61 police officers being hospitalized and millions of dollars in property damage. But the crisis represented a turning point in gay politics and history. The new mayor, Diane Feinstein, and Board of Supervisor sympathized with the gay community over the lenient sentence. A new police commissioner was appointed. Over the next few years, the San Francisco police made major efforts to hire nonwhite, and gay and lesbian officers. Many bigoted police officers resigned. Raids on gay bars stopped. At long last, the simmering animosities between the city, police, and gay community resided.

An example of Milk's influence can be seen in the following document. This is a speech he gave following the Gay Freedom Day Parade on June 25, 1978. More than a quarter million people marched in the parade making it the largest such event in the nation at that time. Milk's inspirational voice against right-wing zealots can be heard.

My name is Harvey Milk—and I want to recruit you. I want to recruit you for the fight to preserve your democracy from the John Briggs and the Anita Bryants who are trying to constitutionalize bigotry. We are not going to allow that to happen. We are not going to sit back in silence as 300,000 of our gay brothers and sisters did in Nazi Germany. We are not going to allow our rights to be taken away and then march with bowed heads into the gas chambers. On this anniversary of Stonewall I ask my gay sisters and brothers to make the commitment to fight. For themselves, for their freedom, for their country. . . .

Blacks did not win their rights by sitting quietly in the back of the bus. They got off! . . . We are coming out to fight the lies, the myths, the distortions! We are coming out to tell the truth about gays!

For I'm tired of the conspiracy of silence. I'm tired of listening to the Anita Bryants twist the language and the meaning of the Bible to fit their own distorted outlook. But I'm even more tired of the silence from the religious leaders of the nation who know that she is playing fast and loose with the true meaning of the Bible. I'm tired of their silence more than of her biblical gymnastics!

And I'm tired of John Briggs talking about false role models. He's lying in his teeth and he knows it. But I'm even more tired of the silence from educators and psychologists who know that Briggs is lying and yet say nothing. . . . I'm tired of the silence, so I'm going to talk about it. And I want you to talk about it.

Gay people, we are painted as child molesters. I want to talk about that. I want to talk about the *myth* of child molestations by gays. I want to talk about the *fact* that in this state some 95 percent of child molestations are heterosexual. . . . I want to talk about the *fact* that some 98 percent of the six million rapes committed annually are heterosexual. I want to talk about the *fact* that one out of every three women who will be murdered in this state this year will be murdered by their husbands. I want to talk about the *fact* that some 30 percent of all marriages contain domestic violence. . . . Today I'm talking about the *facts* of heterosexual violence and what the hell are you going to do about that??? Clean up your own house before you start telling lies about gays. . . .

I'm tired of our so-called friends who tell us we must set standards.

What standards?

The standards of the rapists? The wife beaters? The child abusers? The people who ordered the bomb to be built? . . . The people who built the concentration camps—right here in California, and then herded all the Japanese-Americans into them during World War II. . . . What standards do *you* want *us* to set? Clean up your act, clean up your violence before you criticize lesbians and gay men because of their sexuality. . . . It is madness to glorify killing and violence on one hand and be ashamed of the sexual act, the act that conceived you, on the other. . . .

There is a difference between morality and murder. The *fact* is that more people have been slaughtered in the name of religion than for any other single reason. That, that, my friends, that is the true perversion! . . .

What are you going to do about it? You must come out . . . to your relatives. I know that that is hard and will upset them but think of how they will upset you in the voting booth. Come out to your friends, if indeed they are your friends. Come out to your neighbors, to your fellow workers, to the people who work where you eat and shop. . . . Once and for all, break down the myths, destroy the lies and distortions. For your sake. For their sake. For the sake of the youngsters who are becoming scared by the votes from Dade to Eugene.

If Briggs wins he will not stop. They never do. Like all mad people, they are forced to go on, to prove they were right! There will be no safe "closet" for any gay person. So break out of yours today—tear the damn thing down once and for all! . . .

I call upon lesbians and gay men from all over the nation, your nation, to gather in Washington one year from now. . . . And we will tell you about America and what it really stands for. . . . Let me remind you what America is. Listen carefully.

On the Statue of Liberty it says: "Give me your tired, your poor, your huddled masses yearning to breathe free." In the Declaration of Independence it is written: "All men are created equal and they are endowed with certain inalienable rights." And in our National Anthem it says: "Oh, say does that star-spangled banner yet wave o'er the land of the free."

For Mr. Briggs and Mrs. Bryant . . . and *all* the bigots out there: That's what America is. No matter how hard you try, you cannot erase those words from the Declaration of Independence. No matter how hard you try, you cannot chip those words from off the base of the Statue of Liberty. And no matter how hard you try you cannot sing the "Star Spangled Banner" without those words.

That's what America is. Love it or leave it.

Source: Harvey Milk. "That's What America Is." June 25, 1978, speech. Harvey Milk Archives-Scott Smith Collection, San Francisco Public Library. Used by permission.

Document 71

COMING OUT AS FREE SPEECH: *GAY LAW STUDENTS ASS'N V. PACIFIC TELE. AND TEL. CO.* (1979)

Coming out, in some states, is considered a political act protected by the First Amendment and the due process clause of the Fourteenth Amendment. In 1979, the California Supreme Court ruled in this case that a person's affirmation of homosexuality was analogous to expressing a political view and as such was protected under the state labor code.

Over 60 years ago the California Legislature, recognizing that employers could misuse their economic power to interfere with the political activities of their employees, enacted Labor Code sections 1101 and 1102 to protect the employees' rights. Labor Code section 1101 provides that "No employer shall make, adopt, or enforce any rule, regulation, or policy: (a) Forbidding or preventing employees from engaging or participating in politics. . . . (b) Controlling or directing, or tending to control or direct the political activities of affiliations of employees." Similarly, section 1102 states that "No employer shall coerce or influence or attempt to coerce or influence his employees through or by means of threat of discharge or loss of employment to adopt or follow or refrain from adopting or following any particular course or line of political action or political activity." These sections serve to protect "the fundamental right of employees in general to engage in political activity without interference by employers."

. . . .

A principal barrier to homosexual equality is the common feeling that homosexuality is an affliction which the homosexual worker must conceal from his employer and his fellow workers. Consequently one important aspect of the struggle for equal rights is to induce homosexual individuals to "come out of the closet," acknowledge their sexual preferences, and to associate with others in working for equal rights.

In light of this factor in the movement for homosexual rights, the allegations of plaintiffs' complaint assume a special significance. Plaintiffs allege that PT&T discriminates against "manifest" homosexuals and against persons who make "an issue of their homosexuality.". . the allegations charge that PT&T has adopted a "policy . . . tending to control or direct the political activities or affiliations of employees" in violation of section 1101, and has "[attempted] to coerce or influence . . . employees . . . to . . . refrain from adopting [a] particular course or line of political . . . activity" in violation of section 1102.

Source: DeSantis v. Pacific Telephone and Telegraph Co., Inc. 608 F.2d 327 (9th Cir., 1979).

Further Reading

Downs, Jim. 2016. *Stand By Me: The Forgotten History of Gay Liberation.* New York: Basic Books.

Escoffier, Jeffrey. 1998. *American Homo: Community and Perversity.* Berkeley: University of California Press.

Licata, Salvatore and Robert Petersen (eds.). 1985. *The Gay Past: A Collection of Historical Essays.* New York: Routledge.

Chapter 8

1980s

More than anything, AIDS dominated the LGBT landscape in the 1980s. Beginning as a mysterious illness in the late 1970s and early 1980s striking mostly young, healthy gay men, scientific research came to understand that a retrovirus was responsible for the wasting disease. Although the disease makes no distinction between heterosexuals or homosexuals because it began in the homosexual community in the United States, it became known as the gay plague.

HIV is contracted from bodily fluids (e.g., blood or semen) or by the sharing of hypodermic needles from infected partners. HIV has an incubation period of a few years and, at the time, was fatal for most people since there was no treatment for the disease. Great fear swept the United States and world, and blame was assigned to gay men. Homophobia and outright antigay hate slowed governmental involvement in the research and treatment of AIDS patients. The Religious Right seized upon AIDS to fundraise and denounce gay rights. Many politicians and religious leaders claimed that AIDS was God's retribution against all things gay; and that gay men (and, to some extent, lesbians) deserved their plight because they sinned against God's word.

The inaction by government encouraged many lesbians to organize and provide care for gay men infected with HIV. AIDS activists took to the street, corporate boardrooms, and government offices to demand action. AIDS eventually became classified as a disability and, as such, protected under the Americans with Disability Act and other regulations. AIDS forced many Americans to think about gay rights and homosexuality for the first time.

Document 72
ANITA BRYANT'S STARTLING REVERSAL (1980)

Anita Bryant is a beauty pageant winner (a second runner-up in the 1959 Miss America contest) and singer, who traveled with comedian Bob Hope to entertain military troops in the 1960s and 1970s. After that, she became a spokesperson for the Florida Citrus Commission. In 1977, she started a campaign against gay and lesbian rights in Miami-Dade County, called Save Our Children, in order to repeal an ordinance that made it illegal to discriminate on the basis of sexual orientation. She gained much publicity, and a referendum was placed on the ballot. The antidiscrimination ordinance was repealed. As a result, she became known for her anti-LGBT rights views and her conservative religious and political values. In the following interview with The Ladies Home Journal *in 1980, she talks about rethinking her strict, black-and white beliefs about marriage and divorce, feminism, and softening her stance against gay rights.*

Divorce was what I feared most. . . . When I was growing up in the Bible Belt, the kind of sermon I always heard was—wife submit to your husband, even if he's wrong. . . . [When I married Bob] I had such doubts about getting married and I was depressed all through the honeymoon. Our problems never ended after that. It was obvious to anyone around us by the way we cut each other verbally and embarrassed each other. . . . He saw me as a meal ticket. . . . I felt like a caged animal, smothered, stymied, and I saw that he was miserable too. . . . I hit bottom enough I wanted to [commit suicide]. . . . [In early 1980, when Anita filed for divorce, her church threatened] that if I did not submit to my husband they would have me excommunicated. . . . I've about given up on the fundamentalists, who have become so legalistic and letter-bound to the Bible. . . . Fundamentalists have their head in the sand. The church is sick right now and I have to say I'm even part of that sickness. . . . There are some valid reasons why militant feminists are doing what they're doing. Having experienced a form of male chauvinism among Christians that was devastating, I can see how women are controlled in a very ungodly un-Christian way. . . .

[I can also see how fundamentalists have] a personal vendetta about gays. They harbored hatreds. . . . I guess I can better understand the gays' and the feminists' anger and frustration. As for the gays, the church needs to be more loving, unconditionally, and willing to see these people as human beings, to minister to them and try to understand. . . . [Now days] I'm more inclined to say live and let live. . . . I know now there are no easy answers. I'm learning every day, growing and changing. . . . The answers don't seem quite so simple now.

Source: Cliff Jahr. "Anita Bryant's Startling Reversal." *Ladies' Home Journal* 97, no. 12 (December 1980): 60–68.

Document 73

DEMOCRATIC PARTY AND GAY RIGHTS (1980)

Throughout the 1960s and 1970s, the Democratic Party became the party to champion social justice. Embracing racial equality and then women's rights naturally led to supporting LGBT rights by 1980. At the Democratic National Convention held in 1980, an unprecedented 77 elected delegates were openly gay and lesbian. The Democratic Party made it part of their plank to support LGBT rights and to establish strong ties with LGBT organizations. During the proceedings, 400 delegates signed a petition to place Mel Boozer, an African American gay man, on the nomination ballot for vice president of the United States. Although he removed his name from consideration, Boozer gave an electrifying speech in which he outlined the parallels between the gay rights movement with the black civil rights movement.

I rise in anguished recognition of more than twenty million Americans who love this country, and who long to serve this country in the freedom that others take for granted. Twenty million Lesbian and Gay Americans whose lives are blighted by a veil of ignorance and misunderstanding. . . . Now more than ever, fairness, equal justice, and compassion are under attack by the forces of the extreme right. But we also believe that the ideals embedded in our Constitution by the founders of the Republic are alive and well in the Democratic Party. . . . We are pleased that the platform of our party calls for an end to this kind of discrimination. . . . Is this not the same party which has championed the causes of every minority which has come before us? . . . Is this not the same party that has sought to include women on an equal basis? Is this not the same party which has led the battle for civil rights in Black America?

Would you ask me how I dare to compare the civil rights struggle with the struggle for Lesbian and Gay rights? I can compare them and I do compare them, because I know what it means to be called a nigger and I know what it means to be called a faggot, and I understand the difference, in the marrow of my bones. And I can sum up that difference in one word: NONE. Bigotry is bigotry.

Source: "Text of Mel Boozer's Speech." *Washington Blade,* August 21, 1980: 6.

Document 74

GAY STUDENTS' RIGHTS: *FRICKE V. LYNCH* (1980)

In this celebrated case, Aaron Fricke wanted to bring his friend Paul Guilbert to the Cumberland High School (Rhode Island) senior prom. The principal denied the request, saying that there was a "real and present threat of physical harm" toward the two boys. Fricke sued. At the trial, the judge acknowledged that the principal's fears were real but said that the school should have looked into ways of increasing security and instituting other safety measures rather than denying the couple the right to attend. The court recognized that attendance at a prom is "symbolic speech," much like marching in a parade, and thus merits First Amendment protection. Aaron and his friend Paul were allowed to attend the prom.

Aaron FRICKE v. Richard B. LYNCH, in his official capacity as Principal of Cumberland High School.
Civ. A. No. 80–214.
United States District Court, D. Rhode Island.
May 28, 1980.
OPINION
PETTINE, Chief Judge.
. . . . The senior reception at Cumberland High School is a formal dinner dance sponsored and run by the senior class. It is held shortly before graduation but is not a part of the graduation ceremonies. This year the students have decided to hold the dance at the Pleasant Valley Country Club in Sutton, Massachusetts on

Friday, May 30. All seniors except those on suspension are eligible to attend the dance; no one is required to go. All students who attend must bring an escort, although their dates need not be seniors or even Cumberland High School students. Each student is asked the name of his date at the time he buys the tickets.

The principal testified that school dances are chaperoned by him, two assistant principals, and one or two class advisers. They are sometimes joined by other teachers who volunteer to help chaperone; such teachers are not paid. Often these teachers will drop in for part of the dance. Additionally, police officers are on duty at the dance. Usually two officers attend; last year three plainclothes officers were at the junior prom.

The seeds of the present conflict were planted a year ago when Paul Guilbert, then a junior at Cumberland High School, sought permission to bring a male escort to the junior prom. The principal, Richard Lynch (the defendant here), denied the request, fearing that student reaction could lead to a disruption at the dance and possibly to physical harm to Guilbert. The request and its denial were widely publicized and led to widespread community and student reaction adverse to Paul. Some students taunted and spit at him, and once someone slapped him; in response, principal Lynch arranged an escort system, in which Lynch or an assistant principal accompanied Paul as he went from one class to the next. No other incidents or violence occurred. Paul did not attend the prom. At that time Aaron Fricke (plaintiff here) was a friend of Paul's and supported his position regarding the dance.

This year, during or after an assembly in April in which senior class events were discussed, Aaron Fricke, a senior at Cumberland High School, decided that he wanted to attend the senior reception with a male companion. Aaron considers himself a homosexual, and has never dated girls, although he does socialize with female friends. He has never taken a girl to a school dance. Until this April, he had not "come out of the closet" by publicly acknowledging his sexual orientation.

Aaron asked principal Lynch for permission to bring a male escort, which Lynch denied. A week later (during vacation), Aaron asked Paul Guilbert—who now lives in New York—to be his escort (if allowed), and Paul accepted. Aaron met again with Lynch, at which time they discussed Aaron's commitment to homosexuality; Aaron indicated that although it was possible he might someday be bisexual, at the present he is exclusively homosexual and could not conscientiously date girls. Lynch gave Aaron written reasons for his action; his prime concern was the fear that a disruption would occur and Aaron or, especially, Paul would be hurt. He indicated in court that he would allow Aaron to bring a male escort if there were no threat of violence.

After Aaron filed suit in this Court, an event reported by the Rhode Island and Boston papers, a student shoved and, the next day, punched Aaron. The unprovoked, surprise assault necessitated five stitches under Aaron's right eye. The assailant was suspended for nine days. After this, Aaron was given a special parking space closer to the school doors and has been provided with an escort (principal or assistant principal) between classes. No further incidents have occurred.

This necessarily brief account does not convey the obvious concern and good faith Lynch has displayed in his handling of the matter. Lynch sincerely believes that there is a significant possibility that some students will attempt to injure Aaron and Paul if they attend the dance. Moreover, Lynch's actions in school have displayed a concern for Aaron's safety while at school. Perhaps—one cannot be at all sure—a totally different approach by Lynch might have kept the matter from reaching its present proportions, but I am convinced that Lynch's actions have stemmed—in significant part—from a concern for disruption.

Aaron contends that the school's action violates his first amendment right of association, his first amendment right to free speech, and his fourteenth amendment right to equal protection of the laws.

. . . .

The present case is so difficult because the Court is keenly sensitive to the testimony regarding the concerns of a possible disturbance, and of physical harm to Aaron or Paul. However, I am convinced that meaningful security measures are possible, and the first amendment requires that such steps be taken to protect— rather than to stifle—free expression. Some may feel that Aaron's attendance at the reception and the message he will thereby convey is trivial compared to other social debates, but to engage in this kind of a weighing in process is to make the content-based evaluation forbidden by the first amendment. . . . Because the free speech claim is dispositive, I find it unnecessary to reach the plaintiff's right of association argument or to deal at length with his equal protection claim.

Source: Aaron Fricke v. Richard B. Lynch, 491 F. Supp. 381 (1980) U.S. Dist.

Document 75

WISCONSIN ANTIDISCRIMINATION LAW (1981)

The progress in gay and lesbian rights has always been the process of a few steps forward and then a few steps back, often with support coming from unexpected sources. By the early 1980s, the debate for gay rights raged at all levels of government and very little progress being made at the national level. The local level was a very different story. Individual cities and some states saw the wisdom in extending protection in employment and housing based on sexual orientation. Surprisingly, Wisconsin became the first state to enact an antidiscrimination statute that included sexual orientation. Wisconsin's legislation would become a model for many other states to draft similar legislation in the future.

Section 12: It is the declared policy of this state that all persons shall have an equal opportunity for housing regardless of sex, race, color, sexual orientation, handicap, religion, national origin, sex or marital status of the person maintaining the household, lawful source of income, age or ancestry. . . . This section shall be deemed an exercise of the police powers of the state for the protection of the welfare, health, peace, dignity, and human rights of the people of this state.

Section 13: The equal rights council shall . . . educate the people of the state to a greater understanding, appreciation and practice of human rights for all people, of whatever race, creed, color, sexual orientation, national origin, to the end that this state will be a better place in which to live.

Section 14: The practice of denying employment and other opportunities to, and discriminating against, properly qualified persons by reasons of their age, race, creed, color, handicap, sex, national origin, ancestry, sexual orientation, arrest record or conviction record, is likely to foment domestic strife and unrest, and substantially and adversely affect the general welfare of a state by depriving it of the fullest utilization of its capacities for production. The denial by some employers, licensing agencies and labor unions of employment opportunities to such persons solely because of their age, race, creed, color, handicap, sex, national origin, ancestry, sexual orientation, arrest record or conviction record, and discrimination against them in employment tends to deprive the victims of the earnings which are necessary to maintain a just and decent standard of living, thereby committing grave injury to them. . . .

Except where permitted by law, a person shall not: Deny an individual the full and equal enjoyment of the goods, services, facilities, privileges, advantages, or accommodations of a place of public accommodation or public service because of religion, race, color, national origin, age, height, weight, handicap, marital status, sexual orientation, student status, or because of the use by an individual of adaptive devices.

Source: Wisconsin State Laws of 1981, Chapter 12, sections 12–14, and (3)(b)(i).

Document 76

VIOLENCE AGAINST LESBIANS (1982)

Kathleen Sarris represented Justice Inc. a gay and lesbian rights group in Indianapolis, at a 1980 press conference. She spoke about the needs of the LGBT community for safety and acceptance. Christian ministers were also present and gave extremely antigay comments. The press conference received wide media coverage on local television. Immediately after the press conference, she received threatening phone calls and letters. Soon after she was viciously beaten and raped. She testified before Congress about her experience.

Within 24 hours of the press conference, I began receiving threatening telephone calls and letters. The phone calls and letters were religious in nature; they spoke of acting in the name of God or Jesus and exacting retribution. They also spoke of my leading people to become sodomites, and that this person would put an end to my work. My initial response was that it was an annoying hoax, and it would die down and go away. Instead, the letters and telephone calls continued with systematic regularity. I decided to move out of my home. . . . Within days, the letters and phone calls resumed. It was very apparent that I was being tracked. . . . [I] went to talk with the Indianapolis police. Their response was there was nothing they could do, and if I couldn't stand the heat, I should get out of the kitchen! After a couple of weeks the letters and phone calls stopped. I assumed the person got tired of playing the game.

Then, approximately two weeks after the letters stopped, I was leaving my office and as I turned to lock the door, I felt the barrel of a gun in the back of my head. He pushed me back into the reception area. For the next three hours, he beat me with his fists, his gun, and his belt. I was sexually molested and, ultimately, I was raped. Throughout the assault, he talked about how he was acting for God; that what he was doing to me was God's revenge on me because I was a "queer" and getting rid of me would save children and put an end to the [gay] movement in Indiana.

At the end of his torture, he had me stand up; I was facing the desk in the reception area, and he again put his gun to the back of my head. I heard him draw back the hammer, and the chamber clicked into position. It was at that point it occurred to me that I had nothing to lose, I picked up an object from the desk and swung around and hit him in the head. While he was stunned, I kicked him and he lost the gun. We struggled for about ten minutes until he finally knocked me unconscious. When I regained consciousness, about an hour later, he was gone. . . .

[After calling a hospital ambulance] I was in the Emergency room for eight hours; I suffered a concussion, hair line fracture of my right cheek bone, dislocation of my jaw, and damage to my left knee. While I was in the Emergency room, the detectives were able to piece together the whole scenario of the past few months. It was then that I learned the Indianapolis Police department could have attempted to get fingerprints and conducted a paper and ink analysis on the letters; also, they could have ordered a tracer on my telephone. The Indianapolis police chose not to give me any help. . . .

It has been four years since the assault, and the pain is still very real. . . . I live with constant fear that it will happen again. I also live with the knowledge that because of my orientation, because I chose to exercise what I believe are my constitutional rights, my life has no value to certain people.

Source: Kathleen Sarris testimony, Hearing before the Subcommittee on Criminal Justice of the Committee on the Judiciary, House of Representatives, 99th Congress, Second Session on Anti-Gay Violence; October 9, 1986, pp. 164–165. Washington: Government Printing Office, Serial No. 132.

Document 77

LESBIANS OF COLOR CONFERENCE (1983)

The gay rights movement has always been split between two perspectives for achieving political change—those who prefer personal change and growth versus those

*who advocate mass political mobilization. Discussions on these perspectives perme-
ate many conferences, workshops, and meetings of LGBT organizations. With the
inroads made by conservatives dominated by the leadership of President Ronald Reagan national politics in the 1980s, a sense of defeat consigned many activists to look
inward and focus on community building over direct political action. In this vein, the
Lesbians of Color Conference was held for the first time in 1983 in Malibu, California.
More than 200 women attended. There were many discussions over politics and race
that were emotionally difficult. Nancy Reiko Kato attended and was disappointed at
the lack of political focus. As a progressive socialist, she wanted to see women of various sexualities and races unite to overcome discrimination and persecution toward
equality for all. Ultimately she wanted to see the division over sexuality and skin color
abandoned.*

Los Angeles Lesbians of Color organized the conference so that "we may begin to
know each other, reach out, touch and trust, to form lasting alliances and friendship." Unfortunately, what they had in mind were primarily personal and social,
rather than political, alliances.

There is nothing at all wrong with getting to know each other. But at a time
when lesbians of color desperately need to mount national strategies to fight
against everything from anti-abortion attacks to gaybashing to social service cuts
to repressive immigration legislation to union busting, getting to know each other
is not enough.

This conference had great potential as a starting point for strategizing and organizing against rightwing reaction. But it shortchanged those women who came for
serious political discussion and active proposals for fighting back that they could
take home to their communities. Most of the workshops were aimed . . . to retreat
from political commitment.

But there is no real retreat from politics, or from the racism, sexism, and class
oppression that permeate capitalist society, including the movements for social
change. The anti-political atmosphere at the conference actually gave rise to two very
definite brands of political ideology, lesbian separatism and cultural nationalism,
both of which express capitulation to racist and sexist divisiveness and thrive in an
atmosphere of political retreat.

Separatism and cultural nationalism are exclusionary by nature. Separatists see
men—and straight women—as the enemy. Cultural nationalists see culture and
color as the only bases for interaction and alliance. Both attack all those who do
not look, think, or act like they do. . . . Some lesbians of color are looking for
a safe space, thinking safety is where we are all the same. But in reality, safety
is where we can unite with others to defeat the right wing, capitalism, and the
patriarchy.

Source: Nancy Reiko Kato. "Lesbians of Color Conference: The Politics of 'Sister-
hood.'" *Voices of Color.* Edited by Yolanda Alaniz and Nellie Wong. Seattle: Red
Letter Press, 1999, 30–34. Used by permission of Red Letter Press.

Document 78

TEACHERS' RIGHTS: *NATIONAL GAY TASK FORCE V. BOARD OF EDUCATION OF OKLAHOMA CITY* (1985)

Lesbian and gay teachers in the Oklahoma City school system brought suit against the state to rescind a state law permitting punishment of teachers for "public homosexual conduct." This conduct was defined as advocating, soliciting, imposing, encouraging, or promoting public or private homosexual activity in a manner that may bring it to the attention of schoolchildren or school employees. "Advocacy," the court ruled, is squarely within the protection of the First Amendment. Thus, teachers have the right to take political action, including advocating for lesbian and gay rights.

The NATIONAL GAY TASK FORCE and on behalf of all teachers and principals prospectively and presently employed by the Board of Education of the City of Oklahoma City, State of Oklahoma, and who are similarly situated, Plaintiff-Appellant, v. The BOARD OF EDUCATION OF the CITY OF OKLAHOMA CITY, State of Oklahoma, Defendant-Appellee.

United States Court of Appeals, Tenth Circuit. March 14, 1984.

The National Gay Task Force (NGTF), whose membership includes teachers in the Oklahoma public school system, filed this action in the district court challenging the facial constitutional validity of Okla.Stat. tit. 70, § 6–103.15. The district court held that the statute was constitutionally valid. On appeal NGTF contends that the statute violates plaintiff's members' rights to privacy and equal protection, that it is void for vagueness, that it violates the Establishment Clause, and, finally, that it is overbroad. . . . The trial court held that the statute reaches protected speech but upheld the constitutionality of the statute by reading a "material and substantial disruption" test into it. We disagree. The statute proscribes protected speech and is thus facially overbroad, and we cannot read into the statute a "material and substantial disruption" test. Therefore, we reverse the judgment of the trial court.

I—We see no constitutional problem in the statute's permitting a teacher to be fired for engaging in "public homosexual activity." . . . The part of § 6–103.15 that allows punishment of teachers for "public homosexual conduct" does present constitutional problems.

. . . . Dissent: Any teacher who advocates, solicits, encourages or promotes the practice of *sodomy* "in a manner that creates a substantial risk that such conduct will come to the attention of school children or school employees" is in fact and in truth *inciting* school children to participate in the abominable and detestable crime against nature. . . . . does not merit any constitutional protection.

Source: National Gay Task Force v. Board of Education of the City of Oklahoma City, Oklahoma, 729 F.2d 1270 (10th Cir. 1984).

Document 79

PRIVATE CONSENSUAL SEXUAL BEHAVIOR: *BOWERS V. HARDWICK* (1986)

Until 1961 the laws of all American states viewed same-sex relations as against the law and subject to varying criminal penalties. In 1961 Illinois became the first state of the union to embrace legal reform, removing private consensual homosexual behavior from the interfering regulation of the law. By 1986, the year that the U.S. Supreme Court issued its landmark ruling in Bowers v. Hardwick, *24 states had removed the sanction of the criminal law against such relationships.*

The prime example of how sodomy laws impact sexual minorities in areas far removed from sexual behavior is the case of Bowers v. Hardwick, 478 U.S. 186 (1986). *That case has affected in ways big and small many other legal cases.*

Michael Hardwick was an Atlanta bartender at a local gay bar. His only prior brush with the law came when he was given a citation for drinking an alcoholic beverage in the street. Unfortunately for him, he failed to pay the fine. In circumstances that to this day are unclear, an Atlanta policeman came to his house in regard to that citation. Hardwick's housemate led the policeman to Hardwick's bedroom, where Hardwick was engaging in consensual sexual activity in the privacy of his bedroom with another man. The police officer proceeded to arrest Hardwick, charging him under a Georgia law that provided that "a person convicted of the offense of sodomy shall be punished by imprisonment for not less than one nor more than 20 years" (Ga. Code Ann. § 16–6–2 [1984]).

After much hesitation about challenging the arrest (because of the inevitable public exposure that it would bring), Hardwick opted to fight, feeling that both his personal constitutional rights and those of other gay people in Georgia were at stake. After the Eleventh Circuit Court of Appeals ruled in favor of Hardwick, declaring the Georgia statute unconstitutional because it violated the right to privacy found in the U.S. Constitution, the U.S. Supreme Court agreed to hear the case. The results of this case were disappointing to Hardwick, the wider gay and lesbian community, and advocates for a robust right to privacy. The Supreme Court viewed the matter as a "gay case," even though the Georgia statute was neutral on its face with respect to the sexual orientation of those who engaged in the practice of sodomy. Moreover, as we would learn years later, the outcome of the case hinged on the fateful decision of one justice to change his vote from striking down to upholding the statute, a decision reached because he believed that the impact of sodomy laws was symbolic and because Hardwick was never actually imprisoned for the offense.

Justice Lewis Powell had originally voted to declare the Georgia statute unconstitutional, but, under intense lobbying by Justice Warren Burger and because of his own discomfort with homosexuality, later changed his vote and decided to uphold the statute. In yet another irony, note Deb Price and Joyce Murdoch in their behind-the-scenes look at gay issues and the Supreme Court, Courting Justice, *Justice Powell had hired a string of gay clerks over the years, including the year that Hardwick came before the Court, although he was apparently unaware of his clerks' sexual orientation, at least outwardly. Several years later, apparently shocked by the wave of condemnation of the Hardwick decision, Justice Powell admitted that his concurring opinion had been in error, although he claimed that the impact of the decision was minor.*

The Supreme Court, however, did not unanimously hold against Michael Hardwick; in fact, the Court only mustered a bare majority for its opinion upholding the Georgia sodomy law. The dissent adopted by Justices Blackmun, Brennan, Marshall, and Stevens was stinging.

Bowers v. Hardwick Sodomy Law Case (1986)

Justice White delivered the opinion of the Court.

The issue presented is whether the Federal Constitution confers a fundamental right upon homosexuals to engage in sodomy and hence invalidates the laws of the many states that still make such conduct illegal and have done so for a very long time. . . . Respondent would have us announce, as the Court of Appeals did, a fundamental right to engage in homosexual sodomy. This we are quite unwilling to do. It is true that despite the language of the Due Process Clauses of the Fifth and Fourteenth Amendments, which appears to focus only on the processes by which life, liberty, or property is taken, the cases are legion in which those Clauses have been interpreted to have substantive content, subsuming rights that to a great extent are immune from federal or state regulation or proscription. Among such cases are those recognizing rights that have little or no textual support in the constitutional language. . . .

This category includes those fundamental liberties that are "implicit in the concept of ordered liberty," such that "neither liberty nor justice would exist if [they] were sacrificed" . . . [or] are "deeply rooted in this Nation's history and tradition." It is obvious to us that neither of these formulations would extend a fundamental right to homosexuals to engage in acts of consensual sodomy. Proscriptions against that conduct have ancient roots. Sodomy was a criminal offense at [English] common law and was forbidden by the laws of the original states. . . . In fact, until 1961, all fifty states outlawed sodomy, and today, twenty-four states and the District of Columbia continue to provide criminal penalties for sodomy performed in private and between consenting adults. Against this background, to claim that a right to engage in such conduct is "deeply rooted in this nation's history and tradition" or "implicit in the concept of ordered liberty" is, at best, facetious.

Nor are we inclined to take a more expansive view of our authority to discover new fundamental rights imbedded in the Due Process Clause. . . . Respondent asserts that there must be a rational basis for the law and that there is none in this case other than . . . that homosexual sodomy is immoral and unacceptable. This is said to be an inadequate rationale to support the law. The law, however, is constantly based on notions of morality, and if all laws representing essentially moral choices are to be invalidated under the Due Process Clause, the courts will be very busy indeed. Even respondent makes no such claim, but insists that majority sentiments about the morality of homosexuality should be declared inadequate. We do not agree.

* * *

Justice Blackmun, with whom Justice Brennan, Justice Marshall, and Justice Stevens join, dissenting:

This case is no more about "a fundamental right to engage in homosexual sodomy," as the Court purports to declare, than Stanley v. Georgia was about a fundamental right to watch obscene movies. . . . Rather, this case is about the most comprehensive of rights and the right most valued by civilized men, namely, "the right to be let alone." The statute at issue denies individuals the right to decide for themselves whether to engage in particular forms of private, consensual sexual activity. . . . Like Justice Holmes, I believe that "it is revolting to have no better reason for a rule of law than that it was laid down in the time of Henry IV. It is still more revolting if the grounds upon which it was laid down have vanished long since, and the rule simply persists from blind imitation of the past." I believe we must analyze Hardwick's claim in the light of the values that underlie the constitutional right to privacy. . . .

The Constitution embodies a promise that a certain private sphere of individual liberty will be kept largely beyond the reach of government. . . . Only the most willful blindness could obscure the fact that sexual intimacy is a sensitive, key relationship of human existence, central to family life, community welfare, and the development of human personality. The fact that individuals define themselves in a significant way through their intimate sexual relationships with others suggests, in a Nation as diverse as ours, that there may be many "right" ways of conducting those relationships, and that much of the richness of a relationship will come from the freedom an individual has to choose the form and nature of these intensely personal bonds.

In a variety of circumstances we have recognized that a necessary corollary of giving individuals freedom to choose how to conduct their lives is acceptance of the fact that different individuals will make different choices. . . . The Court claims that its decision today merely refuses to recognize a fundamental right to engage in homosexual sodomy; what the Court really has refused to recognize is the fundamental interest all individuals have in controlling the nature of their intimate associations with others.

The behavior for which Hardwick faces prosecution occurred in his own home, a place to which the Fourth Amendment attaches special significance. . . . The right of an individual to conduct intimate relationships in the intimacy of his or her own home seems to me to be the heart of the Constitution's right to privacy.

Source: Michael Bowers, Attorney General of *Georgia v. Michael Hardwick.* United States Supreme Court 478 U.S. 186 (Decided June 30, 1986).

Document 80

DIGNITY USA'S RESPONSE TO THE "CONGREGATION FOR THE DOCTRINE OF THE FAITH—ON THE PASTORAL CARE OF HOMOSEXUAL PERSONS . . ." (1986)

Dignity USA is a religious organization serving lesbian and gay Catholics. According to the Catholic Church, homosexuals must be chaste in order to be moral in the eyes of God. This was outlined in the Vatican's document "Congregation for the Doctrine of the Faith—On the Pastoral Care of Homosexual Persons: Letter to the Bishops of the Catholic Church," October 1, 1986, and signed by Joseph Cardinal Ratzinger, who later became Pope Benedict XVI.

Dignity USA responded to this letter by a document that was approved by the DignityUSA House of Delegates in Miami, July, 1987. Later, coming from that document were frequently asked questions (FAQs) about Catholicism and homosexuality, which appeared on the Dignity USA Web site, and which are excerpted here.

FAQs: Catholicism, Homosexuality, and Dignity

2. What is the official Catholic teaching about homosexuality?

The Catholic Church holds that, as a state beyond a person's choice, being homosexual is not wrong or sinful in itself. But just as it is objectively wrong for unmarried heterosexuals to engage in sex, so too are homosexual acts considered to be wrong. . . .

8. What options are open to a person who is homosexual and Catholic?

Official Catholic teaching requires that homosexual people abstain from sex. . . . many gay and lesbian Catholics have formed consciences that differ from official Church teaching and have entered into homosexual relationships. In this respect they are exactly like the many married Catholic couples who cannot accept the official teaching on contraception. . . .

10. How could someone do what (the Church says) is wrong and not be living in sin?

As the Catholic Church understands it, wrong and sin are not the same thing. Wrong is harm, disorder, destruction; it is in the objective or external world. Sin is self-distancing from God; it is in the heart. . . . The Church teaches right and wrong but never says who is a sinner. Only God knows our hearts. Many homosexual people simply cannot believe that gay sex as such is wrong. So they do what for them is "the best they can do," though Church teaching says that homogenital acts are wrong. Still, according to the same Church's teaching on conscience, they do not sin in their hearts nor before God. Then they need not confess what is not sin, and they may participate in the Sacraments of the Church.

Source: Used by permission of DignityUSA.

Document 81
AIDS AS GOD'S PUNISHMENT (1987)

Rev. Billy James Hargis was the founder of the Christian Crusade organization in 1950 that grew to become one of the largest fundamentalist Christian radio programs bringing in millions of dollars a year in revenue. He was a member of the John Birch Society and favored segregation. He promoted the idea that the civil rights movement itself was a *"godless communist plot." He founded American Christian College in 1971 but was forced to resign three years later when he was accused of having sex with both female and male students. Still, he continued to preach and write until his death in 2004. He wrote an article for* Christian Crusade *magazine in 1987 preaching that God creates and spreads diseases like AIDS to teach people to maintain a monogamous heterosexual marriage.*

AIDS, as well as herpes, is a result of the judgment of God on a nation which has despised His stern commandments regarding sex. . . . This AIDS plague is a shout from heaven, saying "You've gone too far." As the Lord speaks in judgment, the guilty must suffer, and many innocent along with the guilty. AIDS is undoubtedly one of the last plagues. The end of our age is near. . . . Authorities want $2 billion a year to fight AIDS. What is needed, beyond everything else, is to repent and get right with God. . . .

Some disagree with this conclusion that herpes and AIDS is [sic] the judgment of God upon unrepentant sinners, by saying that many non-homosexuals have also contracted AIDS although they are not guilty of any wrongdoing. . . . The sins of a few compared to the whole [population] can cause an epidemic among the masses who become their innocent victims. This is not the fault of God. Instead it is the fault of those who sinned, and who inflicted their fellow human beings with this awful plague. . . . Don't blame God because a little child somewhere is dying of AIDS that he got from a needle during treatment or surgery in a hospital. If anyone is to blame, it is the person who spread the disease. . . . These innocent children are not guilty. Then someone says, "What about the woman whose husband has infected her with AIDS?" The sin is of the man who infected her. The sin is not hers. But, it rains on the just and the unjust. All of this debate about an unmerciful God is not going to change that. . . . If we cannot check our ungodly sexual lusts, then not only should we expect the consequences, but others will also suffer, and perhaps die, because of our sin.

Source: Billy James Hargis. "AIDS: Sign of the Times!" Billy James Hargis Papers (MC 1412). Used by permission of Special Collections, University of Arkansas Libraries.

Document 82

ACT UP (AIDS COALITION TO UNLEASH POWER) (1987)

ACT UP was formed at the Lesbian and Gay Community Service Center in New York City in 1987. Years of inaction by the government to address the impending pandemic frustrated many people infected with HIV. ACT UP motto was "United in anger and committed to direct action to end the AIDS crisis." To that end it conducted many demonstrations that were unabashedly confrontational by being rude, brash, and impolite. Its first action involved over 250 people who descended on Wall Street to bring attention to the obscene profits being made by American pharmaceutical companies. Ironically, the first medications that showed promise against HIV was developed and financed through government research. Even though AZT was basically a free gift to the pharmaceutical companies, they charged exorbitant prices for these life-sustaining drugs. The anger in the LGBT community led to many chapters of ACT UP being formed across the nation. Many of the actions were designed to shock opponents of gay and lesbian rights while also bringing attention to the overwhelming plight of people with AIDS.

Lesbians have the lowest infection rates for AIDS. Yet, many lesbians were right there from the very beginnings of ACT UP. Some lesbians questioned the need to be involved, whereas other lesbians felt it was their duty as homosexuals to support their gay brothers in need considering that many homophobes do not distinguish between lesbians and gay men in their hate. Maxine Wolfe provided an interview in 1995 where she recounts her activism in New York and involvement with ACT UP.

The people who came to the first meeting of ACT UP included individuals from GMHC (Gay Men's Health Crisis) who had become totally disaffected by [GMHC's] unwillingness to do any political stuff. There were people from the PWA[People With AIDs] Coalition who wanted to get out on the streets. . . . There was also the SILENCE = DEATH Project, which . . . [placed posters] on the streets, to get the message out to people: "Why aren't you doing something?" So they created the SILENCE = DEATH logo well before ACT UP ever existed, and the posters at the bottom said. . . . "Turn anger, fear, grief into action." . . .

When Larry Kramer came to speak, in March 1987 . . . there was a very particular audience in that room. . . . He had been screaming for years and nobody had done anything. From my point of view, there was a whole group of people there ready to do something. . . . At some point [Larry] yelled, "What are you gonna do?" . . . Soon after, [ACT UP] did their first Wall Street action. They did not have a lot of people come to their meetings until after [New York City's] Gay Pride that June. . . . I had marched behind them at the Gay Pride March and saw this incredible "thing," which was a [representation of] a concentration camp with wire all around and people inside. There were people outside the wire dressed in masks and military gear and handing out flyers. . . .

If you can imagine, there is always this tension in the Gay Pride March in New York because the majority come to it for a celebration and they do not want it to be anything political at all. . . . ACT UP took that leadership role in that Gay Pride march and marched in the middle of a "space" that is apolitical and often commercial. . . . The New York ACT UP style was wonderful . . . writing leaflets that you could read and I think more importantly, not relying only on the written word but also [on] visual media. . . . We focused on what would stand out, what would show up. . . . We would [also] pretend to be almost anything if we could get in somewhere. . . . ACT UP was about organizing the unorganized . . . it was about mobilizing a community that had not been organized to do this kind of direct action in the last twelve or fourteen years. Secondly, ACT UP was about people doing stuff for themselves.

Source: Laraine Sommella and Maxine Wolfe. "This Is about People Dying: The Tactics of Early ACT UP and Lesbian Avengers in New York City." *Queers in*

Space: Communities, Public Places and Sites of Resistance. Edited by Gordon Brent Ingram, Anne-Marie Bouthillette, and Yolanda Retter. Seattle: Bay Press, 1997, 407–437. Used by permission of Maxine Wolfe.

Document 83

OLD LESBIANS ORGANIZING FOR CHANGE (OLOC) MISSION STATEMENT (1987)

By the late 1980s and early 1990s, a generation of LGBT activists entered into their senior years. Many faced retirement and senior living. Being lifelong activists they were not willing to go quietly into the night but rather continue with their activism. In some ways retirement freed up additional time that could be devoted to social activism. In 1987, a group of older women hosted the first old lesbian conference in Los Angeles, California. From here, some went on to form a national organization named Old Lesbian Organizing for Change (OLOC). It was open to women over 60 years of age with the mission to raise awareness about ageism including the common conception that everything young is better. OLOC purposefully chose the name "Old" to appropriate the pejorative into their identity, similar to how the LGBT rights movement has appropriated the term queer. Old is used to scorn and ignore entire classes of people. By using the term in OLOC, they hope to bring awareness to the challenges and discrimination faced by old lesbians from the youth-oriented, mass-marketed gay media.

Who We Are

Old Lesbians Organizing for Change is a national organization for Old Lesbians age 60 and over.

OLOC Mission Statement

We are committed to:

- addressing what it means to be Old and to be Lesbian
- finding ways to gather groups of Old Lesbians together for ongoing support
- working against all oppressions that affect Old Lesbians
- standing in solidarity with allies for racial, economic and social justice

OLOC Vision Statement

OLOC will be a cooperative community of Old Lesbian activists from many backgrounds working for justice and the well-being of all Old Lesbians.

Why We Call Ourselves Old

Society calls us Old behind our backs while calling us "Older" to our faces. "Old" has become a term of insult and shame. To be "Old" means to be ignored and scorned, to be made invisible and expendable.

We refute the lie that it is shameful to be an "Old" woman. We name ourselves "Old Lesbians" because we will no longer accommodate ourselves to language that implies in any way that "Old" means inferior.

We call ourselves OLD with pride. In doing so, we challenge the stereotypes directly. Thus, we empower and change ourselves, each other, and the world.

What Is Ageism?

Ageism is a social disease.

Are You Ageist?

Do you consider "young" a compliment and "old" a derogatory synonym for ugly, decrepit, out-of-date ("You don't look your age.")?

Do you speak/do for an Old Lesbian instead of letting her speak/do for herself and assume she needs help?

Do you view an Old Lesbian either as a burden or an icon, rather than as an equal with whom a reciprocal relationship is desirable?

Do you patronize a courageous Old Lesbian by trivializing her anger as "feistiness?" (Would you call Superman "feisty"?)

Do you categorize an outspoken Old Lesbian as "complaining," "difficult," or "crotchety?"

Do you assume that an Old Lesbian is asexual?

Are you unsupportive of an Old Lesbian looking for a partner, or disrespectful of an Old Lesbian's choice to be single?

Do you refrain from confronting ageist remarks because they are "not really meant that way?"

Source: Old Lesbians Organizing for Change Web site. http://www.oloc.org/. Accessed April 11, 2104. Used by permission of the OLOC National Steering Committee.

Document 84

NATIONAL COMING OUT DAY (1988)

The National Gay Rights Advocates coordinated a National Coming Out Day (NCOD) in 1988. As a legal reform organization, it was aware of academic research showing that when heterosexuals know even one gay or lesbian coworker, friend, or relative, they tend to have less antigay prejudice and feelings. The goal of NCOD was to encourage more LGBT people to "come out of the closet" to their family, friends, coworkers, church members, and more. The event was such a success that it continues to this day and has expanded into a full week of events throughout the nation. In recent years, NCOD has been administered by the Human Rights Campaign and takes place on college campuses, in the workplace, and elsewhere. The following document is from the Los Angeles maga-zine Lesbian News *commenting on the impact of NCOD.*

This day will be celebrated by people from coast to coast. . . . Last year's October 11th March on Washington energized the Gay community across the country, as it took our strength and spirit to the nation's capitol. This year the strength comes home, to the local grassroots organizations that are the backbone of the Gay movement. Coordinated by National Gay Rights Advocates (NGRA) and co-sponsored by The Experience Weekend, the event is a reminder to all Gay men and Lesbians that the time has come to go forward in the campaign for civil rights, the time has come for them to "take their next step."

To excite Gay and Lesbian organizations in local communities, the organizing body of NCOD has begun a large scale campaign of its own. The national media has been put on alert, three full time staff members have been hired by NGRA to work exclusively on the event and "Coming Out Kits" have been mailed to thou-sands of grassroots Gay organizations nationwide. The kits, which include dozens of different ideas for "coming out" . . . [such as] dances, dinners, seminars, letter writing campaigns and celebrations that are in the works. NCOD is making avail-able a wide variety of support materials . . . about obtaining media support as well as an informational circular on how to start a Gay support group. . . .

Says Jean O'Leary, Executive Director of NGRA and co-chair of NCOD . . . "Last year's march clearly showed that, even in the face of the deadly AIDS epidemic, our community is vibrant and growing. We need, more than ever, an annual event to celebrate life, one that will help us renew our commitments to one another. Ours is a community that is coming out of the closet forever."

Source: "A Tribute to Coming Out." *Lesbian News,* Los Angeles, 14, no. 3, October: 1. Used by permission of *Lesbian News.*

Document 85

CONGRESSMAN WILLIAM DANNEMEYER OPPOSES GAY RIGHTS (1989)

William Dannemeyer was a Republican congressman from Orange County, California, in the 1980s. He was first elected to Congress in 1979 from the conservative 39th Dis-trict where he remained until 1993. He has been an ardent foe of gay rights. In 1989, he published Shadow in the Land: Homosexuality in America. *In the book he claims that homosexuals were taking over the country, which would cause a vast epidemic and death due to AIDS and other sexually transmitted diseases. He also claims the epidemic would be so severe that it would cause the collapse of Western civilization as a whole. He advocated the repeal of all gay rights laws and a reinstatement of sodomy laws throughout the country. Since leaving Congress, he and his wife maintained Web sites that claimed Jews are trying to take over the world and that the Holocaust was a plan by Jews to destroy all nations and reduce earth's population to the status of slaves.*

America is surrendering to this growing army of [gay rights] revolutionaries without firing a shot, indeed, without more than a word or two of protest. The homosexual blitzkrieg has been better planned and executed than Hitler's. . . . When they can march down our main thoroughfares, with our official permission and the protection of the police, they have become not a klatch of sexual deviates but a "movement. . . ." [Homosexuals'] demands endanger the very survival of the family as we know it, and the only way to make certain that such recommendations are not put into practice is to reinstitute laws against sodomy in all states. By so doing we would settle the question of rights and prerogatives now in dispute, saying emphatically that homosexuals per se have no rights other than those they enjoy by virtue of being citizens of the United States.

In passing such laws, we would also affirm a normative way of life for all Americans: that they are born and nurtured in traditional families where children have both mothers and fathers and hence learn to understand the marvelous union of man and woman that continually leads to the rebirth of life and love and hope on earth. . . .

We must reinstate traditional prohibitions against homosexuality in order to establish a sense of order and decency in our society, to reconnect us with our normative past. . . . The choice we make will determine whether or not we survive as a people. . . . We have the capacity to make the wrong choice and plunge our people, and indeed the entire West, into a dark night of the soul that could last hundreds of years before the flame is again lit. It has happened before. It can happen again. It is in full knowledge of such a grim possibility that I have written this book.

Source: William Dannemeyer. *Shadow in the Land: Homosexuality in America.* San Francisco: Ignatius Press, 1989, 121–122, 217–219, 221, 228. Used by permission of Ignatius Press.

Document 86

A JEWISH RABBI'S ACCEPTANCE OF GAY AND LESBIAN RIGHTS (1989)

Oftentimes minority groups that have experienced hate are not accepting of others unlike themselves. The Jewish people have reacted to the march toward gay and lesbian rights with mixed actions. Beginning in 1973, the Reform branch of Judaism accepted lesbian and gay Jews into the Union of American Hebrew Congregations. The Orthodox and Conservative branches have been much less accepting.

Beth Chayim Chadashim (BCC) became the first modern Jewish congregation to serve gay and lesbian members. Located in Los Angeles, BCC needed to secure a rabbi to serve as spiritual leader. In 1972, the selection committee interviewed Janet Marder (a heterosexual) for the position. Although she was qualified and liberal, she was unknowledgeable about lesbian and gay sentiments and issues. She was warned by other professionals not to take the position, as it would impact her future as a rabbi. The BCC interview committee had their reservations but did not want to discriminate against her for being heterosexual. Regardless, she was hired and served as rabbi for five years. She later wrote about her experience:

Today, after many trials and many more errors, I hardly recognize myself. My beliefs have changed slowly, but in profound ways that affect my entire outlook on life. . . . My attitude toward homosexuality has moved from uncertain tolerance to full acceptance. I see it now as a sexual orientation offering the same opportunities for love, fulfillment, spiritual growth and ethical action as heterosexuality. . . . [At first] I could find no published rabbinic statements declaring homosexuality an acceptable Jewish way of life. And so I had to decide how much did it matter to me that the voice of my tradition, without exception, ran counter to the evidence of my experience and the deepest promptings of my conscience?

In fact, the Jewish values and principles I regard as eternal, transcendent and divinely ordained do *not* condemn homosexuality. The Judaism I cherish and affirm teaches love of humanity, respect for the spark of divinity in every person, and the human right to live with dignity. . . . There is no Jewish *legal* basis for this belief; my personal faith simply tells me that the duty to love my neighbor as myself is a compelling mitzvah [duty] while the duty to condemn and to kill homosexuals for committing "abominations" most certainly is not. . . .

I know that prejudice against lesbians and gays is deeply rooted, but I also know from my own experience that it is possible to become educated and to change profoundly. . . . There is simply no substitute for an open mind and direct contact with gay people. . . . Lesbians and gay men are all around, and all it takes to bring them out is a friendly, sensitive and respectful manner.

Source: Janet Marder. "Getting to Know the Gay and Lesbian Shul: A Rabbi Moves from Tolerance to Acceptance." *Twice Blessed: On Being Lesbian or Gay and Jewish.* Edited by Christie Balka and Andy Rose. Boston: Beacon Press, 21989, 9–217. Used by permission of the Frances Goldin Agency.

Document 87

EMPLOYMENT RIGHTS:
PRICE WATERHOUSE V. HOPKINS (1989)

Ann Hopkins was a successful senior manager and a candidate for partnership at Price Waterhouse, a nationwide accounting firm. When her nomination came up, many partners at Price Waterhouse reacted negatively and accused her of being "macho," of "overcompensat[ing] for being a woman" (see the document). They suggested she needed to take a "course in charm school" and that to improve her chances of becoming a partner, she should "walk more femininely, talk more femininely, dress more femininely, wear make-up, have her hair styled, and wear jewelry." Hopkins sued and prevailed, with the court stating:

> An employer who objects to aggressiveness in women but whose positions require this trait places women in an intolerable and impermissible Catch 22: out of a job if they behave aggressively and out of a job if they do not. Title VII lifts women out of this bind. . . . She had proved discriminatory input into the decisional process, and had proved that participants in the process considered her failure to conform to the stereotypes credited by a number of decision makers had been a substantial factor in the decision.

BRENNAN, J., Opinion of the Court SUPREME COURT OF THE UNITED STATES
Price Waterhouse v. Hopkins
CERTIORARI TO THE UNITED STATES COURT OF APPEALS FOR THE DISTRICT OF COLUMBIA CIRCUIT
No. 87–1167 Argued: October 31, 1988–Decided: May 1, 1989

On too many occasions, however, Hopkins' aggressiveness apparently spilled over into abrasiveness. Staff members seem to have borne the brunt of Hopkins' brusqueness. Long before her bid for partnership, partners evaluating her work had counseled her to improve her relations with staff members. Although later evaluations indicate an improvement, Hopkins' perceived shortcomings in this important area eventually doomed her bid for partnership. Virtually all of the partners' negative remarks about Hopkins—even those of partners supporting her—had to do with her "interpersonal [p235] skills." Both "[s]upporters and opponents of her candidacy," stressed Judge Gesell, "indicated that she was sometimes overly aggressive, unduly harsh, difficult to work with, and impatient with staff." *Id.* at 1113.

There were clear signs, though, that some of the partners reacted negatively to Hopkins' personality because she was a woman. One partner described her as "macho" (Defendant's Exh. 30); another suggested that she "overcompensated for being a woman" (Defendant's Exh. 31); a third advised her to take "a course at charm school" (Defendant's Exh. 27). Several partners criticized her use of profanity; in response, one partner suggested that those partners objected to her swearing only "because it's a lady using foul language." Tr. 321.

But it was the man who, as Judge Gesell found, bore responsibility for explaining to Hopkins the reasons for the Policy Board's decision to place her candidacy on hold who delivered the coup de grace: in order to improve her chances for partnership, Thomas Beyer advised, Hopkins should "walk more femininely, talk more femininely, dress more femininely, wear make-up, have her hair styled, and wear jewelry." 618 F.Supp. at 1117.

The judge. . . . held that Price Waterhouse had unlawfully discriminated against Hopkins on the basis of sex by consciously giving credence and effect to partners' comments that resulted from sex stereotyping. . . .

We hold that, when a plaintiff in a Title VII case proves that her gender played a motivating part in an employment decision. . . .

Source: Price Waterhouse v. Hopkins, 490 U.S. 228 (1989).

Document 88
FAMILY ISSUES: *BRASCHI V. STAHL ASSOCIATES CO.* (1989)

A New York City gay man was faced with eviction from his apartment when his lover of 11 years died from AIDS. The survivor's name did not appear on the lease. Rent control provisions precluded landlords from evicting "either the surviving spouse of the deceased tenant or some other member of the deceased tenant's family who has been living with the tenant." The man argued that he was "family," and the New York Court of Appeals agreed with that position. The court's precedent-setting decision helped establish the idea that lesbians and gay men can form legitimate families.

Braschi v. Stahl Associates Company
New York Court of Appeals July 6, 1989
OPINION OF THE COURT

Appellant, Miguel Braschi, was living with Leslie Blanchard in a rent-controlled apartment located at 405 East 54th Street from the summer of 1975 until Blanchard's death in September of 1986. In November of 1986, respondent, Stahl Associates Company, the owner of the apartment building, served a notice to cure on appellant contending that he was a mere licensee with no right to occupy the apartment since only Blanchard was the tenant of record. In December of 1986 respondent served appellant with a notice to terminate informing appellant that he had one month to vacate the apartment and that, if the apartment was not vacated, respondent would commence summary proceedings to evict him.

. . . .

The present dispute arises because the term "family" is not defined in the rent-control code. . . .

. . . . We conclude that the term family, as used in [the rent-control regulations], should not be rigidly restricted to those people who have formalized their relationship by obtaining, for instance, a marriage certificate or an adoption order.

. . . . Appellant Braschi should therefore be afforded the opportunity to prove that he and Blanchard had such a household.

. . . . Appellant and Blanchard lived together as permanent life partners for more than 10 years. They regarded one another, and were regarded by friends and family, as spouses.

. . . . Financially, the two men shared all obligations including a household budget. The two were authorized signatories of three safe-deposit boxes, they maintained joint checking and savings accounts, and joint credit cards. In fact, rent was often paid with a check from their joint checking account. Additionally, Blanchard executed a power of attorney in appellant's favor so that appellant could make necessary decisions—financial, medical and personal—for him during his illness. Finally, appellant was the named beneficiary of Blanchard's life insurance policy, as well as the primary legatee and coexecutor of Blanchard's estate. Hence, a court examining these facts could reasonably conclude that these men were much more than mere roommates.

Source: Braschi v. Stahl Associates Company. New York Court of Appeals. 74 N.Y.2d 201, 544 N.Y.S.2d 784, 543 N.E.2d 49. July 6, 1989.

Further Reading

Dannemeyer, William. 1989. *Shadow in the Land: Homosexuality in America*. San Francisco, CA: Ignatius Press.

Deaderick, Sam and Tamara Turner. 1997. *Gay Resistance: The Hidden History*. Seattle, WA: Red Letter Press.

Haggerty, George (eds.). 2000. *Gay Histories and Cultures: An Encyclopedia*. New York: Garland Publishing, Ind.

Moore, Patrick. 2004. *Beyond Shame: Reclaiming the Abandoned History of Radical Gay Sexuality*. Boston: Beacon Press.

Chapter 9

1990s

AIDS activism and direct political activism grew in the 1990s. Achieving protection through the Americans and Disability Act (1990) was important for those with AIDS and helped foster dialogue between LGBT people and their employers, families, religious organizations, and more. There were difficult political battles, and groups such as Queer Nation helped bring ideas of equality to a head. Slowly, sodomy laws were rescinded, antidiscrimination statutes were enacted by local cities and state governments, and private businesses began to include same-sex partners in employee benefits. Issues such as openly LGBT people serving in the military, same-sex marriage, employment and housing protections, same-sex couple adopting children, and more made it into the media and the national dialogue. Gay rights was battered left and right sometimes gaining a few steps forward and other times going back a few steps. For example, with the possibility of same-sex marriage being approved in Hawaii, many states and the federal government made extreme effort to make such marriage either unenforceable or impossible with the passage of so-called Defense of Marriage Acts (DOMA). Sometimes there were work-arounds such as Vermont creating a "domestic partnership" to avoid using the term *marriage* when granting legal status to same-sex unions. Still, the 1990s saw a steady march toward full equality for LGBT people.

Document 89
QUEER NATION (1990)

Similar to the dynamics that founded ACT UP, many LGBT people were frustrated and angry at the decades of antigay politics in the United States. Often activists felt that as progress was made with rights for lesbians and gay men, there was a backlash that pushed the movement even further back. Four gay men in New York City in 1990 formed a group to combat hate crimes and homophobia against lesbians and gays. The group, Queer Nation, was designed to be a direct action organization (like ACT UP) staging kiss-ins, and many other protests at very public activities. This included demonstrating at the 1992 Academy Awards, protesting in front of businesses, and outing closeted media personalities (only those who were publicly antigay). Queer is a pejorative; it is meant to be fighting words. Many oppressed people adopt the language of their oppressor so as to deflate the value of the terms. Queer, like faggot, have been used extensively to smear homosexuals. By adopting the name—Queer Nation—it was asserting that the term queer *could no longer hurt and* nation *to show it was of one community. The Queer Nation Manifesto stated:*

Why Queer?

Queer!

Ah, do we really have to use that word? It's trouble. Every gay person has his or her own take on it. For some it means strange and eccentric and kind of mysterious. That's okay; we like that. But some gay girls and boys don't. They think they're more normal than strange. And for others "queer" conjures up those awful memories of adolescent suffering. Queer. It's forcibly bittersweet and quaint at best—weakening and painful at worst. Couldn't we just use "gay" instead? It's a much brighter word. And isn't it synonymous with "happy"? When will you militants grow up and get over the novelty of being different?

Why Queer . . .

Well, yes, "gay" is great. It has its place. But when a lot of lesbians and gay men wake up in the morning we feel angry and disgusted, not gay. So we've chosen to call ourselves queer. Using "queer" is a way of reminding us how we are perceived by the rest of the world. It's a way of telling ourselves we don't have to be witty and charming people who keep our lives discreet and marginalized in the straight world. We use queer as gay men loving lesbians and lesbians loving being queer. Queer, unlike *gay*, doesn't mean *male*.

Source: Anonymous. "Queer Nation Manifesto" at Web site: http://userwww.service .emory. edu/_lderose/docs/politics/qnation/qnation.html#Twelve

Document 90

ASYLUM FROM TORTURE: *MATTER OF TOBOSO-ALFONSO* (1990)

In the first case of a gay male refugee to be considered for asylum, Judge Robert Brown of the Court of Immigration agreed in 1986 not to return Fidel Armando-Alfonso to Cuba because of the documented mistreatment of homosexuals by the Communist government ("Gay Refugees Tell of Torture" "Gay Refugees Tell of Torture, Oppression in Cuba" 1980. The Advocate, November 27, 15). The Board of Immigration Appeals upheld the decision in 1990, and Attorney General Janet Reno in 1994 designated this decision as precedent for all other requests for asylum by homosexual applicants. As such, lesbians and gay men who are persecuted by their governments may be eligible to remain in the United States. To date, only a few lesbians and gay men have secured asylum in the United States because meeting the criteria for asylum is extremely difficult.

MATTER OF TOBOSO-ALFONSO
In Exclusion Proceedings A-23220644
Decided by Board March 12, 1990D 3

An applicant, who had the status of being a homosexual, both established his membership in a particular social group in Cuba and demonstrated that his freedom was threatened. . . . The applicant is a 40-year-old native and citizen of Cuba who was paroled into the United States in June of 1980, as part of the Mariel boat lift. In 1985 his parole was terminated. He was placed in exclusion proceedings and appeared before an immigration judge in Houston, Texas. The applicant conceded his excludability and applied for asylum and withholding of deportation to Cuba.

. . . . An alien who seeks withholding of deportation from any country must show that his "life or freedom would be threatened in such a country on account of race, religion, nationality, membership in a particular social group, or political opinion." Section 243(h)(1) of the Act. In order to make such a showing, the alien must establish a "clear probability" of persecution on account of one of the enumerated grounds.

. . . . The applicant testified that there is a municipal office within the Cuban Government which registers and maintains files on all homosexuals. He stated that his file was opened in 1967, and every 2 or 3 months for 13 years he received a notice to appear for a hearing. The notice, the applicant explained, was a sheet of paper, "it says Fidel Armando Toboso, homosexual and the date I have to appear." Each hearing consisted of a physical examination followed by questions concerning the applicant's sex life and sexual partners. While he indicated the "examination" was "primarily a health examination," he stated that on many occasions he would be detained in the police station for 3 or 4 days without being charged, and for no apparent reason. He testified that it was a criminal offense in Cuba simply to be a homosexual. The government's actions against him were not in response to specific conduct on his part (e.g., for engaging in homosexual acts); rather, they resulted simply from his status as a homosexual.

. . . . The immigration judge found the "applicant's testimony to be credible and worthy of belief, and, if anything, perceive[d] that he was restrained in his testimony as to the difficulty of his life during the years that he lived in Cuba." The immigration judge further concluded that the applicant had been persecuted in Cuba and that he has a well-founded fear of continued persecution in that country. He found that this persecution resulted from the applicant's membership in a particular social group, namely homosexuals.

. . . . In view of the mandatory nature of section 243(h), the immigration judge's grant of withholding of deportation to Cuba to the applicant will stand and the following order will be entered.

Source: Matter of Toboso-Alfonso. In Exclusion Proceedings. A-23220644. Decided by Board March 12, 1990.

Document 91

CHILD CUSTODY BY DE FACTO PARENTS: *ALISON D. V. VIRGINIA M.* (1991)

The nonbiological mother, Alison D., sued to have visitation rights with the child carried by her lover, Virginia M. Although she was not the legal parent and had not adopted the child, she argued that she was a de facto parent. The New York Supreme Court said that she may, in fact, be a de facto parent, but that such a category had no legal claims, including visitation rights, to the child. Alison lost her right to visit the child.

IN THE MATTER OF ALISON D. (ANONYMOUS), APPELLANT, v. VIRGINIA M. (ANONYMOUS), RESPONDENT.
May 2, 1991

Petitioner Alison D. and respondent Virginia M. established a relationship in September 1977 and began living together in March 1978. In March 1980, they decided to have a child and agreed that respondent would be artificially inseminated. Together, they planned for the conception and birth of the child and agreed to share jointly all rights and responsibilities of child-rearing. In July 1981, respondent gave birth to a baby boy, A.D.M., who was given petitioner's last name as his middle name and respondent's last name became his last name. Respondent shared in all birthing expenses and, after A.D.M.'s birth, continued to provide for his support. During A.D.M.'s first two years, petitioner and respondent jointly cared for and made decisions regarding the child.

In November 1983, when the child was 2 years and 4 months old, petitioner and respondent terminated their relationship and petitioner moved out of the home they jointly owned. Petitioner and respondent agreed to a visitation schedule whereby petitioner continued to see the child a few times a week. Petitioner also agreed to continue to pay one-half of the mortgage and major household expenses. By this time, the child had referred to both respondent and petitioner as "mommy". Petitioner's visitation with the child continued until 1986, at which time respondent bought out petitioner's interest in the house and then began to restrict petitioner's visitation with the child. In 1987 petitioner moved to Ireland to pursue career opportunities, but continued her attempts to communicate with the child. Thereafter, respondent terminated all contact between respondent and the child, returning all of petitioner's gifts and letters. No dispute exists that respondent is a fit parent.

. . . . Although the court is mindful of petitioner's understandable concern for and interest in the child and of her expectation and desire that her contact with the child would continue, she has no right under Domestic Relations Law § 70 to seek visitation and, thereby, limit or diminish the right of the concededly fit biological parent to choose with whom her child associates. She is not a "parent" within the meaning of section 70.

Source: 77 N.Y.2d 651, 572 N.E.2d 27, 569 N.Y.S.2d 586 (1991).

Document 92
BISEXUALS AND GAY RIGHTS (1991)

Bisexuals often feel like the forgotten step-child of the gay rights movement. Too often gay people are dismissive of bisexuals surmising that it is just a "phase" they are going through until they fully realize their homosexuality. Loraine Hutchins and Lani Ka'ahumanu wrote Bi Any Other Name: Bisexual People Speak *(Boston: Alyson Publications, 1991) to help clarify the experiences, issues, and language of bisexuality. The greatest challenge the bisexual movement has faced is getting the message out that human sexuality is much more complex than the common belief in the bipolar heterosexual/homosexual norm. Bisexuals, along with transgendered, transsexual, and intersex people, are demanding a greater awareness to help transform the gay rights movement into a movement recognizing the rights of all sexual minorities. Hutchins and Ka'ahumanu stated in* The Advocate *interview that the real enemy to the gay rights movement is sexual intolerance.*

Bisexuals are here, we're queer, get used to it. Bisexuals are part of the gay movement. We always have been, and we always will be. In fact, many gay men and lesbians behave bisexually. Many bisexuals behave and/or identify as lesbian or gay. Some are also transgender or transsexual people. Some identify primarily with the straight community. We all share the experience of bisexuality.

The real question is: Why do some gays and lesbians have trouble admitting bisexuals are part of the movement? The truth is that bisexuality, or for that matter heterosexuality, is not the enemy. The enemy is sexual intolerance. The enemy is any cultural or political worldview that defines a certain group as "other," inferior, sick, or criminal. Those who invent an "other" are the real enemy.

The gay movement has been diminishing its own strength and breadth by acting exclusively. Whenever people refuse to add the word *bisexual* to titles of gay organizations (as happened a decade before when lesbians demanded that the word *lesbian* be included), whenever AIDS educators include bisexual in the title but not in the body of a brochure or workshop, whenever a truly bisexual hero or heroine is appropriated as supposedly really gay, whenever we ape straight expectations rather than standing tall for sexual diversity as a whole, we betray the larger goals of sexual and human liberation. This not only ostracizes a whole class of supporters and members but also perpetuates the illusion that we can appease the larger society and win concessions from it without radically transforming how it deals with sex. . . .

Source: Loraine Hutchins and Lani Ka'ahumanu. "Do Bisexuals Have a Place in the Gay Movement?" *The Advocate* June 4, 1991, 94. Used by permission.

Document 93

GAYS IN THE REPUBLICAN PARTY (1991)

The Republican Party has been at the forefront of antigay sentiments, laws, and political action in the United States. Patrick Buchanan, conservative political commentator, often attacked gay rights issues in his speeches and newspaper articles. In 1999, he wrote about his condemnation of lesbian and gay Irish Americans desires to march in the New York Saint Patrick's Day Parade. His article clearly states his "visceral" dislike of homosexuals and defended his prejudice and discrimination against LGBT people.

To discriminate is to choose. We all discriminate in our choice of associates and friends. And prejudice simply means prejudgment. Not all prejudgments are rooted in ignorance; most are rooted in the inherited wisdom of the race. A visceral recoil from homosexuality is the natural reaction of a healthy society wishing to protect itself.

Homosexuality is not a civil right. Its rise almost always is accompanied, as in the Weimar Republic, with a decay of society and a collapse of its basic cinder block, the family.

Source: "The Other Minority." *The New Republic,* March 30, 1992: 7. Used by permission of *The New Republic.*

Document 94

REMOVING PROHIBITIONS ON SAME-SEX BEHAVIOR: *KENTUCKY V. WASSON* (1992)

Jeffrey Wasson was a 23-year-old nursing student arrested for solicitation in 1986. The Lexington, Kentucky, police conducted an undercover sting operation around the local gay bar, The Bar Complex. An undercover police officer engaged Wasson in conversation in the parking lot of the bar for about 20 minutes. After that time, Wasson invited the man back to his place. When prodded, Wasson described some of the activities they would engage once back to his place. The police taped the entire conversation. The sexual activities described by Wasson violated a number of Kentucky statutes prohibiting homosexual activity. At that point, Wasson was arrested and charged with solicitation. Twenty-nine other men were arrested that evening through this one sting operation.

The initial trial court dismissed the charges holding the state's sodomy laws unconstitutional. The decision was appealed, and the Fayette Circuit Court agreed with the trial court. The case was taken to the Kentucky Supreme Court, which also upheld the lower court decision thereby throwing out the sodomy laws in effect since 1860. All the courts found that the antisodomy and antisolicitation laws violated the right to privacy and the right to equal protection under the law. Four previous cases in other states had come to the same conclusion—New York in New York v. Onofre, Pennsylvania in Commonwealth v. Bonadio, and two lower appellate courts in Texas v. Morales and Michigan Organization for Human Rights v. Kelley.

Since these decisions were made by state courts in Kentucky, the findings applied only in Kentucky. However, when similar cases came up in other states, the legal logic from Wasson could be applied. Eventually, the U.S. Supreme Court reconsidered the prohibitions on same-sex sodomy in Lawrence v. Texas in 2003 when, here too, the Court decided that such laws violated the Constitution. The legal rationale and language of Wasson was critical in Lawrence v. Texas.

Opinion of the Court by Justice Leibson.

i Right of Privacy

Kentucky has a rich and compelling tradition of recognizing and protecting individual rights . . . upholding the right of privacy against the intrusive police power of the state. . . . Immorality in private which does not operate to the detriment of others is placed beyond the reach of state action by the guarantees of liberty in the Kentucky Constitution. . . . We view the United States Supreme Court decision in *Bowers v. Hardwick* as a misdirected application of the theory of original intent. To illustrate: as a theory of majoritarian morality, miscegenation [interracial sex] was an offense with ancient roots. It is highly unlikely that protecting the rights of persons of different races to copulate was one of the considerations behind the Fourteenth Amendment. Nevertheless in *Loving v. Virginia* (1967), the United States Supreme Court recognized that a contemporary, enlightened interpretation of a liberty interest involved in the sexual act made its punishment constitutionally impermissible.

ii Equal Protection

Certainly, the practice of deviate sexual intercourse violates traditional morality. But so does the same act between heterosexuals, which activity is decriminalized. Going one step further, *all* sexual activity between consenting adults outside of marriage violates our traditional morality. The issue here is not whether sexual activity traditionally viewed as immoral can be punished by society, but whether it can be punished solely on the basis of sexual preference. . . . In the final analysis we can attribute no legislative purpose to this statute except to single out homosexuals for different treatment for indulging their sexual preference by engaging in the same activity heterosexuals are now at liberty to perform. . . . Simply because the majority . . . finds one type of extramarital intercourse more offensive than another, does not provide a rational basis for criminalizing the sexual preferences of homosexuals.

Source: Commonwealth v. Wasson 1992 Ky. LEXIS 140 (Sept. 24, 1992).

Document 95
COLORADO AMENDMENT 2 (1992)

Attempts have been made to limit gay and lesbian rights. A chilling example is the passage of Amendment 2 in the state of Colorado in 1992. This amendment rescinded all existing antidiscrimination laws based on sexual orientation in the state of Colorado and precluded the adoption of future laws that would provide protections against discrimination based on sexual orientation. Ultimately, the U.S. Supreme Court ruled that Amendment

2 violated the fundamental right of lesbians, gay men, and bisexuals to participate in the political process on an equal basis with other Coloradans.

Will Perkins was responsible for placing Amendment 2 on the Colorado ballot in 1991. Born in Montrose, Colorado, on August 22, 1928, Perkins received his BA degree in business from Colorado College in 1950. While in college, he was a respected athlete and was head baseball coach at Colorado College during the 1951–1952 season. Later he played professional baseball for the Chicago White Sox for one year. He married his wife, Bess, with whom he had three daughters and one son.

Perkins worked for many years as a car salesman and eventually became chairman of the board of the Perkins Chrysler Plymouth Company in Colorado Springs. Frustrated with what he perceived as the antifamily gay agenda that was gaining support in many cities throughout the state of Colorado, he became chairman of the Colorado for Family Values (CFV) in 1991. He was able to convince a number of city councils to refuse to adopt or rescind antigay discrimination ordinances. Perkins was successful at obtaining wide support for his efforts and was responsible for placing Amendment 2 on the 1992 statewide ballot. The initiative passed in November 1992 and was immediately challenged in courts. It was eventually ruled unconstitutional (Romer vs. Evans). Perkins continued as chairman of the board of CFV and provides expert advice to other conservative organizations battling gay right ordinances.

This was an important ruling because similar attacks were being mounted in other states against antidiscrimination laws designed to protect lesbians and gay men. What was most revealing from the entire process was the deeper understanding gained about the motivation and strategies used by the Religious Right in mounting the campaigns. Correspondence between the lawyers and leaders of the Religious Right showed that they understood that antidiscrimination laws are meant to help stigmatized groups attain equal status with the dominant group. Yet they purposely chose the motto "no special rights" because of its impact on the minds of voters and its ability to raise money. The Religious Right's mantra "no special rights" is a deception to which they are fully aware. Because of its effectiveness, it is expected that "no special rights" will be used in future attempts to keep lesbians and gay men from gaining equality with heterosexuals.

Neither the State of Colorado, through any of its branches or departments, nor any of its agencies, political subdivisions, municipalities or school districts, shall enact, adopt or enforce any statute, regulation, ordinance or policy whereby homosexual, lesbian or bisexual orientation, conduct, practices or relationships shall constitute or otherwise be the basis of, or entitle any person or class of persons to have or claim any minority status, quota preferences, protected status or claim of discrimination.

Source: Article 2, Section 30, of the Colorado State Constitution, as amended in 1992.

Document 96
SAME-SEX MARRIAGE IN HAWAII:
BAEHR V. LEWIN (1993)

In December 1990, the Hawaii Department of Health denied marriage licenses to three gay couples. The three gay couples sued the department. In September 1991, circuit court judge Robert Klein threw out the case, ruling that homosexual marriage was not a fundamental right. The ruling was appealed. In May 1993, the Hawaii Supreme Court reinstated the lawsuit and ruled that the state's denial of marriage licenses to the three couples violated their rights as a form of sex discrimination. Sex has suspect class status in the Hawaii Constitution and thus requires the highest scrutiny in legal review. The state was required to show a compelling reason to justify the ban. Circuit court judge Kevin Chang ruled in 1996 that prohibiting same-sex couples from marrying violated the state constitution's equal protection clause. However, an amendment to the Hawaii Constitution was passed by the voters in November 1998 that restricted the definition of marriage to opposite-sex couples only. As a result, the state supreme court unanimously overturned Chang's 1996 decision.

Baehr v. Lewin
Hawai'i Supreme Court
May 5, 1993
LEVINSON, Judge, in which Moon, Chief Judge, joins.

On May 1, 1991, the plaintiffs filed a complaint for injunctive and declaratory relief in the Circuit Court of the First Circuit, State of Hawaii, seeking, *inter alia*: (1) a declaration that Hawaii Revised Statutes (HRS) §572–1 (1985)—the section of the Hawaii Marriage Law enumerating the [r]equisites of [a] valid marriage contract"—is unconstitutional insofar as it is construed and applied by the DOH to justify refusing to issue a marriage license on the *sole* basis that the applicant couple is of the same sex; and (2) preliminary and permanent injunctions prohibiting the future withholding of marriage licenses on that sole basis.

. . . . the United States Supreme Court has declared that "the right to marry is part of the fundamental 'right of privacy' implicit in the Fourteenth Amendment's Due Process Clause." *Zablocki v. Redhail*, 434 U.S. 374, 384 (1978). The issue in the present case is, therefore, whether the "right to marry" protected by article I, section 6 of the Hawaii Constitution extends to same-sex couples.

. . . .

Therefore, the precise question facing this court is whether we will extend the *present* boundaries of the fundamental right of marriage to include same-sex couples, or, put another way, whether we will hold that same-sex couples possess a fundamental right to marry.

. . . .

. . . . Accordingly, we hold that sex is a "suspect category" for purposes of equal protection analysis under article I, section 5 of the Hawaii Constitution and that HRS §572–1 is subject to the "strict scrutiny" test. It therefore follows, and we so hold, that (1) HRS §572–1 is presumed to be unconstitutional. . . .

Source: 74 Haw. 645, 852 P.2d 44.

Document 97

LESBIAN ATTORNEY APPOINTED TO HIGH FEDERAL GOVERNMENT POSITION (1993)

In 1993 President Bill Clinton nominated Roberta Achtenberg to be the assistant secretary for Fair Housing in the Department of Housing and Urban Development (HUD). Achtenberg had been a law school dean, elected to the San Francisco Board of Supervisors, and was eminently qualified. She was, however, founder of the Lesbian Rights Project, executive director of the National Center for Lesbian Rights, and her partner Mary Morgan was the nation's first openly lesbian judge. When asked if he would vote to confirm Achtenberg, Senator Jesse Helms opposed her appointment "because she's a damn lesbian. I'm not going to put a lesbian in a position like that. If you want to call me a bigot, fine." In response, Senator Claiborne Pell revealed that his daughter was lesbian, and he said he would not want to see her barred from holding a government job because of her orientation. In spite of the opposition of conservative Republicans, the Senate voted to confirm Ms. Achtenberg on May 25, 1993. The following are excerpts from vote analysis records from the Senate, in favor and against.

Those favoring confirmation contended:

Argument 1: Roberta Achtenberg has a wealth of professional experience as a civil rights attorney and a locally elected official. . . . She has a results-oriented, accommodating approach that will serve her well at HUD. Some of our colleagues do not share our view of her reasonableness. Several charges, all of which we find baseless, have been raised. . . . The most oft-repeated charge is that she has mercilessly attacked the Boy Scouts of America for failing to admit homosexuals. . . . Her vote was just one vote out of a unanimous, 34–0 vote in favor of denying funds. Local law prohibited funding for organizations that discriminate on the basis of sexual orientation, so her vote merely upheld local law. Roberta Achtenberg has assured us that she will not use this post to try to block Federal housing funds for organizations that discriminate on the basis of sexual orientation, because Federal law does not specify that such discrimination is illegal. . . .

Argument 2: We find the lifestyle chosen by this nominee to be morally offensive. . . .

Those opposing confirmation contended:

Argument 1: Ordinarily, we defer to a President's selections . . . [but] when his choices very likely will lead to disastrous public policy consequences, we must exercise our constitutional duty of advice and consent to speak out. . . . Her

expertise is in advancing the legislative agenda of homosexual "rights" groups. . . .
She has actively supported the imposition of her views on others, against their
deeply held religious and personal beliefs. . . . We are very bothered by her will-
ingness to abuse her authority as a public official to wage a campaign against the
Boy Scouts of America. . . .

We fear she intends to do the same at HUD. If confirmed, she will have veto
authority over billions in Federal housing aid. She has stated that she does not
intend to withhold funding based on discrimination against homosexuals, but, in
all candor, we do not trust her. . . .

Argument 2: In choosing this nominee, President Clinton is endorsing a type of
moral relativism which is rejected by the vast majority of Americans, and which
has been repudiated by three decades of failure in social experimentation. . . .
A vote in her favor is a vote in favor of the proposition that we need to accelerate,
not stem, societal collapse.

Source: Senate Record Vote Analysis, Achtenberg Nomination/Confirmation, 103d
Congress, 1st Session, May 24, 1993, 4:29 P.M., page S–6356, Temporary Congressional Record, Vote No. 122.

Document 98

BARRY GOLDWATER ON GAYS
IN THE MILITARY (1993)

*Arizona senator Barry Goldwater was considered the leading conservative politician in
the United States in the mid-1960s. He ran for president in 1964 and chaired the Senate Armed Service Committee besides being an experienced air force plot. He was a
strong supporter of the Department of Defense but took exception to its antigay policy. He
thought the joint chiefs of staff were mistaken to discharge good military personnel simply
because they were homosexual. Goldwater thought the ban on lesbian and gay personnel
was "just plain un-American." In an article published in* The Washington Post National
Weekly, *Goldwater wrote:*

After more than 50 years in the military and politics, I am still amazed to see how
upset people can get over nothing. Lifting the ban on gays in the military isn't
exactly nothing, but it's pretty damn close. . . . When the facts lead to one conclusion, I say it's time to act, not to hide. The country and the military know that eventually the ban will be lifted. The only remaining questions are how much muck
we will all be dragged through, and how many brave Americans like Tom Paniccia
and Col. Margarethe Cammermeyer will have their lives and careers destroyed in
a senseless attempt to stall the inevitable. . . . It's high time to pull the curtains on
this charade of policy.

Source: Barry M. Goldwater. "The Gay Ban: Just Plain Un-American." *Washington
Post National Weekly,* July 21–27, 1993, 28.

Document 99

MARCH ON WASHINGTON (1993)

By early 1990s, the march toward gay rights seemed stalled. Sodomy was still illegal in many states, the military still excluded gays and lesbians from serving openly, only a handful of cities and states provided protection for lesbians and gays against discrimination in employment and housing, AIDS was devastating the gay community, and same-sex marriage was not even on the horizon. President Clinton had just been elected. Part of his campaign promises was to pressure Congress on a number of pro-gay policies. Not wanting to lose that momentum and considering the previous marches on Washington for gay rights happened many years prior in 1987 and 1979, it seemed the right time in 1993 to conduct another massive gathering to remind Clinton of his promise and rouse Congress to take action toward LGBT legal equality.

Public marches are as much about politics as they are to inspire the people. The psychological impact of being in the midst of tens of thousands of like-minded individuals can be inspiring. Minorities often feel ignored or outnumbered, and public demonstrations help overcome the isolation. With the attendance of upward to a million people to the marches on Washington, legislators typically take action in response to the public outpouring. For example, soon after the 1993 March on Washington, the Massachusetts State Legislature passed the nation's first law to protect LGBT students in public schools from discrimination. Massive public marches can spark progressive change.

One of the speakers at the April 25, 1993, March on Washington was Urvashi Vaid. At the time she was the executive director of the National Gay and Lesbian Task Force (NGLTF). Vaid is an American success story. She was born in India, came to the United States with her family while a young child, obtained a law degree, and worked for the Lambda Legal Defense Education Fund as an attorney. Her speech at the march articulated the dangers of right-wing Christians in their efforts to not only restrict the rights of LGBT citizens but their efforts to construct a theocratic state in which homosexuality would be severely punished.

Hello lesbian and gay Americans. I am proud to stand before you as a lesbian today. With hearts full of love and the abiding faith in justice, we have come to Washington to speak to America. We have come to speak the truth of our lives and silence the liars. We have come to challenge the cowardly Congress to end its paralysis and exercise moral leadership. We have come to defend our honor and win our equality. But most of all we have come in peace and with courage to say, "America, this day marks the end of exile of the gay and lesbian people. We are banished no more. We wander the wilderness of despair no more. We are afraid no more. For on this day, with love in our hearts, we have come out, and we have come out across America to build a bridge of understanding, a bridge of progress, a bridge as solid as steel, a bridge to a land where no one suffers prejudice because of their sexual orientation, their race, their gender, their religion, or their human difference."

I have been asked by the March organizers to speak in five minutes about the far right, the far right which threatens the construction of that bridge. The extreme right which has targeted everyone of you and me for extinction. The supremacist right which seeks to redefine the very meaning of democracy. Language itself fails in this task, my friends, for to call our opponents "The Right," states a profound untruth. They are wrong—they are wrong morally, they are wrong spiritually, and they are wrong politically.

The Christian supremacists are wrong spiritually when they demonize us. They are wrong when they reduce the complexity and beauty of our spirit into a freak show. They are wrong spiritually, because, if we are the untouchables of America— if we are the untouchables—then we are, as Mahatma Ghandi said, children of God. And as God's children we know that the gods of our understanding, the gods of goodness and love and righteousness, march right here with us today.

The supremacists who lead the anti-gay crusade are wrong morally. They are wrong because justice is moral, and prejudice is evil; because truth is moral and the lie of the closet is the real sin; because the claim of morality is a subtle sort of subterfuge, a stratagem which hides the real aim which is much more secular. Christian supremacist leaders like Bill Bennett and Pat Robertson, Lou Sheldon and Pat Buchanan, supremacists like Phyllis Schlafley, Ralph Reid, Bill Bristol, R.J. Rushoodie—the supremacists don't care about morality, they care about power. They care about social control. And their goal, my friends, is the reconstruction of American Democracy into American Theocracy.

. . . .

To defeat the Right politically, my friends, is our challenge when we leave this March. How can we do it? We've got to march from Washington into action at home. I challenge everyone of you, straight or gay, who can hear my voice, to join the national gay and lesbian movement. I challenge you to join NGLTF to fight the Right. We have got to match the power of the Christian supremacists, member for member, vote for vote, dollar for dollar. I challenge each of you, not just buy a T-shirt, but get involved your movement. Get involved! Volunteer! Volunteer! Every local organization in this country needs you. Every clinic, every hotline, every youth program needs you, needs your time and your love.

And I also challenge our straight liberal allies, liberals and libertarians, independent and conservative, republican or radical. I challenge and invite you to open your eyes and embrace us without fear. The gay rights movement is not a party. It is not lifestyle. It is not a hair style. It is not a fad or a fringe or a sickness. It is not about sin or salvation. The gay rights movement is an integral part of the American promise of freedom.

. . . .

When all of us who believe in freedom and diversity see this gathering, we see beauty and power. When our enemies see this gathering, they see the millennium. Perhaps the Right is right about something. We call for the end of the world as we know it. We call for the end of racism and sexism and bigotry as we know it. For the end of violence and discrimination and homophobia as we know it. For the end of sexism as we know it. We stand for freedom as we have yet to know it, and we will not be denied.

Source: Urvashi Vaid. "Speech at the 1993 March on Washington for LGBT Rights." http:// urvashivaid.net/wp/?p=97. Used by permission of Urvashi Vaid.

Document 100

DON'T ASK, DON'T TELL (1993)

There have always been and always will be homosexuals in the military. For example, Friedrich Wilhelm August Heinrich Ferdinand von Steuben was a Prussian-born military officer who is credited with creating and teaching essential military tactics, drills, and disciplines during the American Revolutionary War. He is considered one of the "fathers" of the Continental Army and served as General George Washington's chief of staff. Von Steuben was forced to leave Baden (a German state) under threat of prosecution for homosexuality and was openly gay. When he joined Washington's staff at Valley Forge in 1778, two very young European aides, who remained his lovers throughout his life, accompanied him. Later, Colonel Alexander Hamilton (also gay) and General Nathanael Greene assisted Von Steuben in designing the military training program. There is considerable evidence that George Washington had male lovers. Still, there were rules against homosexuals serving in the military at the time but those rules were ignored when needed.

Some periods of time the military is more receptive or repressive than others toward homosexuality, but the need for soldiers during war often mitigates efforts to exclude them from the ranks. For example, during World War II, very few people were discharged from the military. When they were, it was termed a "blue discharge" because the piece of paper the discharge notice came on was blue in color. Once World War II was over, the military stepped up its efforts to discharge homosexuals and mostly lesbians. A 1944 policy change required homosexuals to be committed to military hospitals, medically examined by psychiatrists, and, once confirmed to be homosexual, discharged under Regulation 615–360, section 8.

In 1957, the U.S. Navy Board of Inquiry appointed a panel to review the navy's policies regarding homosexuality. Navel Captain S. H. Crittenden Jr. was appointed as chairman to the panel. The panel issued a report—the Crittenden Report—later that year and concluded that homosexuals pose no security threat to the military. The report was buried for decades until 1976. Only through the Freedom of Information Act has its existence come to light. A number of high-profile cases of dismissals from the military and a number of brutal beatings and murders of gay military members received wide media exposure. In the 1970s and 1980s, a number of gay and lesbian military support groups were formed and actively campaigned to end the antigay policy. During the 1992 U.S. presidential campaign, gays and lesbians serving in the military became a hot issue. Candidate Bill Clinton promised to allow all persons to serve in the military regardless of sexual orientation.

Once Clinton became president, he initiated the process to implement new policy to allow gays and lesbians to serve openly in the military. The media flurry and tidal wave of angry phone calls and letters to the White House and Congress made it impossible for Clinton to proceed. At the same time Congress conservatives rushed to change existing policy into federal law, thereby outflanking Clinton. Eventually, Clinton conceded defeat and issued Defense Directive 1304.26 on December 21, 1993, that codified existing policy with the provision that military personnel were not to ask a recruit or member about their sexual orientation. The policy became known as "Don't Ask, Don't Tell."

SEC. 546. POLICY CONCERNING HOMOSEXUALITY IN THE ARMED FORCES.

1 CODIFICATION.—(1) Chapter 37 of title 10, United States Code, is amended by adding at the end the following new section:

§ 654. Policy concerning homosexuality in the armed forces

(a) FINDINGS.—Congress makes the following findings:

(b)

- . . . .

- Success in combat requires military units that are characterized by high morale, good order and discipline, and unit cohesion.

- One of the most critical elements in combat capability is unit cohesion, that is, the bonds of trust among individual service members that make the combat effectiveness of a military unit greater than the sum of the combat effectiveness of the individual unit members.

- Military life is fundamentally different from civilian life in that—

- the extraordinary responsibilities of the armed forces, the unique conditions of military service, and the critical role of unit cohesion, require that the military community, while subject to civilian control, exist [sic] as a specialized society; and

- the military society is characterized by its own laws, rules, customs, and traditions, including numerous restrictions on personal behavior, that would not be acceptable in civilian society.

- . . . .

- The prohibition against homosexual conduct is a longstanding element of military law that continues to be necessary in the unique circumstances of military service.

- The armed forces must maintain personnel policies that exclude persons whose presence in the armed forces would create an unacceptable risk to the armed forces' high standards of morale, good order and discipline, and unit cohesion that are the essence of military capability.

- The presence in the armed forces of persons who demonstrate a propensity or intent to engage in homosexual acts would create an unacceptable risk to the high standards of morale, good order and discipline, and unit cohesion that are the essence of military capability.

(b) POLICY.—A member of the armed forces shall be separated from the armed forces under regulations prescribed by the Secretary of Defense if one or more of the following findings is made and approved in accordance with procedures set forth in such regulations:

(1) That the member has engaged in, attempted to engage in, or solicited another to engage in a homosexual act or acts unless there are further findings, made and

approved in accordance with procedures set forth in such regulations, that the member has demonstrated that—

(A) such conduct is a departure from the member's usual and customary behavior;

(B) such conduct, under all the circumstances, is unlikely to recur;

(C) such conduct was not accomplished by use of force, coercion, or intimidation;

(D) under the particular circumstances of the case, the member's continued presence in the armed forces is consistent with the interests of the armed forces in proper discipline, good order, and morale; and

(E) the member does not have a propensity or intent to engage in homosexual acts.

(2) That the member has stated that he or she is a homosexual or bisexual, or words to that effect, unless there is a further finding, made and approved in accordance with procedures set forth in the regulations, that the member has demonstrated that he or she is not a person who engages in, attempts to engage in, has a propensity to engage in, or intends to engage in homosexual acts.

(3) That the member has married or attempted to marry a person known to be of the same biological sex.

Source: 103rd Congress, 1st Session, H.R. 2401. (Washington, DC: Government Printing Office), October 6, 1993. Also available online at: http://frwebgate.access .gpo.gov/cgi-bin/ getdoc.cgi?dbname=103_cong_bills&docid = f:h2401eas.txt.pdf

Document 101

CATHOLIC CONDEMNATION OF HOMOSEXUALITY (1994)

Monsignor William B. Smith, professor of moral theology at S. Joseph's Catholic Seminary in Yonkers, New York, issued a public letter in 1994 to Roman Catholics in Oregon concerning Measure 13. The letter intended to sway Catholics to vote in favor of the antigay Measure 13. Measure 13 was a ballot initiative designed to eliminate and prevent antidiscrimination laws aimed at protecting lesbians and gay men. In Monsignor Smith's letter, he referred to homosexuality as a "disorder" and "an intrinsic moral evil"—terms popularized by Pope John Paul II in 1986. Even with this effort, the measure failed to pass with Oregon voters rejecting it by a small margin of 52 percent to 48 percent.

Homosexuality is a behavior to which no one has a moral right and therefore to legislate against it or to deny it privileged and protected status in civil law offends no human nor civil right and is not therefore a form of invidious discrimination. It is of course deplorable that homosexual persons have been or are the object of malice in speech or action. Nevertheless it is improper to accept homosexual behavior as normal in reaction to any crimes committed against homosexual persons or to claim that the homosexual condition is not disordered. It is also wrong to protect behavior to which no one has any conceiveable [sic] right, such as the behavior of homosexuality.

"Sexual orientation" as a condition or inclination does not constitute a quality comparable to race or ethnic background. It is not just inappropriate but positively erroneous and misleading to compare or equate homosexual orientation as the legal or social equivalent of race, color, religion, gender, age or national origin. None of these is ordered toward an intrinsic moral evil; whereas, homosexual orientation is so ordered.

Source: William B. Smith. "To Oregon Catholics." *Voters' Pamphlet*, State of Oregon General Election November 8, 1994, 80.

Document 102

EX-GAYS CONDEMN GAY RIGHTS (1994)

In the 1990s organizations that opposed gay and lesbian rights began to more often use testimony from people who had been actively homosexual, but who later rejected their participation in the gay community. A statement by Richard Weller, who belonged to an organization called Ex-Homosexuals for Truth, was used by the Oregon Citizens Alliance to support its antigay agenda in 1994.

My name is Richard Weller. When I was 17 I was recruited into the gay lifestyle by an older homosexual man. Like so many young people who get drawn into homosexuality I was lonely and naive. Eleven years and six homosexual relationships later I finally sought help. Now I am a normal heterosexual man, dedicated to helping young people avoid the mistakes I made.

For many years I told people I was just born gay to get acceptance. If we were born gay that took away any personal responsibility for our behavior and made people feel sorry for us. All along we knew it was a convenient lie, but it was our word against theirs. Today I am living proof that homosexuals can and do change. I was deep in the lifestyle, spending nine years in one relationship and even thought about getting "married."

Homosexuals put on a good public image, but MANY homosexual men try to recruit young boys and often succeed. All pedophile-rights groups in America are made up of homosexual men. The North American Man/Boy Love Association (NAMBLA) which has advertised in Oregon gay newspapers is just one of several. Most boys who get picked up by homosexuals are not part of the statistics. They are usually older, from 12–17, and they don't have good parental supervision. They usually don't report the sex because they are ashamed or believe they are old enough to decide for themselves.

The problem with "gay rights" is that it makes kids more willing to go along with homosexuality. When the government and teachers tell kids that homosexuality is just another normal lifestyle, they are easier for adult predators to seduce.

I know what I'm talking about. I was one of those kids. I am only one voice against all the pro-gay bias in the media, but mine is the voice of experience.

Source: Richard Weller. "The Voice They Want Silenced." *Voters' Pamphlet*, State of Oregon General Election November 8, 1994, 79.

Document 103

SHARON BOTTOMS CHILD CUSTODY COURT CASE: *BOTTOMS V. BOTTOMS* (1994 AND 1995)

This case demonstrates the power of the sodomy laws. Their existence made all homosexuals criminal by definition. How can a class of citizens argue for equal rights when they are, by definition, criminal? It is one of the reasons the gay rights movement focused on overturning or rescinding all sodomy laws.

Sharon Bottoms divorced her husband in 1991. She was only 18 years old and pregnant at that time. During the divorce process, Sharon gave birth to her son Tyler. The court awarded custody of the infant to Sharon. Sharon gave primary care for Tyler but lived with her mother, Kay, the first few months after Tyler was born. About a year after the divorce, Sharon met April Wade at a picnic and fell in love. Within a few months of their meeting, the two women decided to move in together and raise Tyler as their son. They held a commitment ceremony a month after moving in together. They decided that April would continue her job as a manager of a gift shop providing the sole financial support for the family and that Sharon would be a stay-at-home mom raising the infant boy.

Kay Bottoms was disappointed that Tyler was no longer being shared with her. When she learned that Sharon was emotionally and sexually involved with April, she was "sickened" and sued to gain full custody of her grandson. Courts typically grant custody rights to the biological mother over all other relatives, but Kay claimed that by Sharon becoming a lesbian she was no longer fit to be a parent. During the court proceedings, Sharon admitted to having hit Tyler twice, swore in front of him, and lived on welfare for a year. During the trial, Sharon was honest about her relationship with April, including sharing that she engaged in oral sex with the woman. The prosecution jumped on that admission, as it was a violation of Virginia sodomy law. Technically Sharon was classified as a habitual criminal and a felon simply by admitting to having sex with her lover. On this technicality, the court ruled Sharon immoral and unfit and granted custody of the boy given to the grandmother. Sharon was given limited visitation rights but only if April was not present.

Sharon appealed the decision of the trial court to the Virginia Court of Appeals. It ruled in favor of Sharon and reversed the decision of the lower court.

In this child custody appeal, we find the evidence insufficient to support the trial court's decision to remove custody of a three-year-old child from his natural parent. . . . A child's best interest is presumed to be served by being in the custody of the child's natural parent, rather than a non-parent. A nonparent is granted custody over a parent only when the parent is unfit. . . . The evidence showed that Sharon Bottoms is and has been a fit and nurturing parent who has adequately provided and cared for her son. . . . Bottoms' open lesbian relationship has had no visible or discernible effect on her son. While the child has spent considerable time with his grandmother, Kay Bottoms, the evidence proved that he and his mother, Sharon Bottoms, have had a close, loving mother-child relationship. . . . Unless a parent, by his or her conduct or condition, is unfit or is unable and unwilling to provide or care for a child, a court is not entitled to . . . take custody of a child from his or her parents. . . . In this instance, the open lesbian relationship and illegality of the mother's sexual activity are the only significant factors that the court considered in finding Sharon Bottoms to be an unfit parent. The fact that a parent is homosexual does not per se render a parent unfit to have custody of his or her child.

Source: Sharon Bottoms v. Pamela Kay Bottoms, Court of Appeals Record No. 1930-93-2.

Kay Bottoms was disappointed by reversal of the decision and appealed the case to the Virginia Supreme Court. The Supreme Court sided with Kay and reversed the decision of the appellate court in 1995. Kay was awarded custody of Tyler. Sharon Bottoms, exhausted by the process to gain her son back, finally gave up.

Although the presumption favoring a parent over a non-parent is strong, it is rebutted when certain factors, such as parental unfitness, are established by clear and convincing evidence. . . . Other important considerations include the nature of the home environment and moral climate in which the child is to be raised. . . . Conduct inherent in lesbianism is punishable [under the Virginia sodomy law] as a Class 6 felony in the Commonwealth, Code 18.2–361; thus that conduct is another important consideration in determining custody. . . . The record shows a mother who, although devoted to her son, refuses to subordinate her own desires and priorities to the child's welfare. . . . Living daily under conditions stemming from active lesbianism practiced in the home may impose a burden upon a child by reason of the social condemnation attached to such an arrangement, which will inevitably afflict the child's relationships with his peers and with the community.

Source: Sharon Lynne Bottoms v. Pamela Kay Bottoms, Virginia Supreme Court, Record No. 941166.

Document 104

LESBIANAS UNIDAS (1994)

All people have multiple identities. Typically, the most common identities include racial, cultural, ethnic, and gender identities. Oftentimes identities also include employment, religious, marital identities, and more. For LGBT people, discovering that they are not part of the heterosexual norm sends them on a lifelong search for community. Unfortunately, the gay community can often be as racist and sexist as the straight community. Lesbians of color face multiple challenges in finding where they feel at home. Being women, lesbians have much in common with all women yet many women and women's organizations are decidedly antilesbian. Being a person of color should open community with other persons of color, but too often these communities are antihomosexual. And, being lesbian should open doors to the homosexual community, but, there too, is found sexists' exclusion. In response to feeling not welcomed, many lesbians of color have organized their own community and support groups. Lesbian Unidas was a Latina lesbian group active between 1984 and the mid-1990s in Los Angeles. The following is a statement from its 10th anniversary celebration.

As Latinas and as women we are hidden from history. . . . Our herstory is scattered here and there in boxes, file cabinets and garages. . . . In 1978 a group of Asian, African American, Latina and Native Americans gathered to form Lesbians of Color (LOC). It was the first time in L.A. . . . that lesbians of color organized specifically for the purpose of politically and publicly demanding recognition. . . . On another front, Gay Latinos was formed in 1981 by a small group of men who felt the need to create an organization that was culturally and politically relevant to who they were. . . . Eventually a few Latina lesbians joined the group . . . the (Lesbian Task Force) was formed to encourage more Latina participation . . . the name of the [larger] organization was changed to include the word lesbian and became Gay and Lesbian Latinos Unidos . . . [in] 1984, the name of the [lesbian] task force was changed to Lesbianas Unidas.

Lesbianas Unidas (LU) was initially formed to serve as a support group and to address the specific needs of politicized, feminist Latina lesbians (many of whom were also lesbian separatists). Our original stated purpose included not only working for the elimination of negative stereotypes but also working to address racism, classism, homophobia and sexism which was then (and which remains now) present both in society as well as our own communities. . . .

It is important to note a few of our accomplishments . . . an annual retreat since 1984, [marching] in the 25th anniversary of the Chicano Moratorium, marches with César Chavez and Jesse Jackson against the Simpson-Mazolli bill [to prevent "illegal" immigration], Dia de La Mujer [Woman's Day celebration], Primer Encuentro de Lesbianas Feministas de Latinoamerica y el Caribe [First Gathering of Feminist Lesbians from Latin America and the Caribbean] . . . support groups . . . donations of money and labor [to]: Project 10 [a high school lesbian and gay support program], a hospital in Nicaragua, a lesbian group in Mexico [working] with earthquake victims . . . LU continues to provide the space and encouragement for Latina lesbians to develop their potential as leaders and organizers. Que viva[n] lesbianas Caribenas, que viva[n] lesbianas Chicanas, Que viva[n] lesbianas Latinas [long live Caribbean lesbians, long live Chicana lesbians, long live Latina lesbians].

Source: Lesbianas Unidas 10th Anniversary Program, 1994.

Document 105

"COCKTAIL" HELPS MANAGE HIV INFECTION TRANSFORMING AIDS INTO A CHRONIC DISEASE INSTEAD OF A DEATH SENTENCE (1995)

In the early 1980, becoming infected with HIV was a death sentence. Typical incubation period was three years, and most people had no natural immunity. Death was virtually guaranteed. AZT was the first antiviral medication that could kill the virus, but it had terrible side effects and was not completely successful when used by itself. After much more research, medical scientist found a combination of AZT (Retrovir, the first drug licensed to treat Aids) and 3TC, both made by Glaxo-Wellcome, along with Norvir, one of a new class of drugs, protease inhibitors proved to be very effective at keeping the virus level so low as to be "undetectable" with far fewer side effects. By 1996, studies proved the effectiveness of this approach. The cocktail was heralded by scientists as a "new chapter" in the AIDS pandemic.

1995

- On November 20, **FDA granted accelerated approval for Epivir (lamivudine, 3TC) for use in combination with Retrovir (zidovudine, AZT)** in treating AIDS and HIV infection.

- On December 6, **FDA approved Invirase (saquinavir) the first protease inhibitor**, for use in combination with other nucleoside analogue medications. This application received approval only 97 days after FDA received the application for marketing.

1996

- On March 1, **FDA granted full approval for Norvir (ritonavir)** for use alone or in combination with nucleoside analogue medications in people with advanced HIV disease. Norvir also received accelerated approval for less advanced HIV disease.

- On March 13, **FDA granted accelerated approval for Crixivan (indinavir)** for use alone or in combination with nucleoside analogue medications in people with HIV or AIDS. FDA approved the drug in just 42 days after receiving its application for marketing.

. . . .

It would be another almost 20 years before it was shown in clinical studies that taking certain HIV medications on a daily basis could prevent infection. This is known as pre-exposure prophylaxis (or PrEP). Similarly, if someone was exposed to the virus, taking HIV medication immediately after exposure (known as PEP: post-exposure prophylaxis) for a few days, infection could be thwarted. Insurance companies and many city and state health agencies became active in promoting PrEP/PEP and absorbing the costs since it was far more cost-effective to prevent infection from HIV than treating patients with HIV.

Source: "HIV/AIDS Historical Timeline 1995–1999." U.S. Food & Drug Administration. https://www.fda.gov/forpatients/illness/hivaids/history/ucm151079.htm

Document 106
THE LESBIAN AVENGERS (1995)

In 1992, six New York women founded the Lesbian Avengers. Similar to ACT UP and, later Queer Nation, the Lesbian Avengers was an activist group whose goal was to use dramatic nonviolent actions to bring attention to lesbian and gay issues. Many lesbians were tired of the continual work on AIDS and abortion—important issues but not typically of direct impact for lesbians. They wanted to bring attention to their specific issues and the misogyny found in the LGBT community.

At the time the New York public schools were reviewing a change in curriculum to include greater diversity. The "Children of the Rainbow" curriculum (better known as the "Rainbow Curriculum") received praise for including gay and lesbian concerns, but conservatives attempted to block its adoption. The Lesbian Avengers conducted an action to support the Rainbow Curriculum. The group met at Queens School District 24 where conservatives held power and paraded through the neighborhood with an all-lesbian band. They stopped at a local elementary school and handed out lavender balloons speaking with children and parents to "Ask about Lesbian Lives." Some wore T-shirts with the words "I was a lesbian child" printed on them.

Lesbian Avengers members created actions that had strong visual presence coordinated with local media. They also eschewed permits. They didn't believe they needed to "ask" for permission to express themselves. Also, they were pragmatic that if they asked for permits, they could be denied. Lesbian Avengers used fire-eating demonstrations at many events—so much so that fire-eating became somewhat its symbol. The organization established the Dyke March in coordination with the many gay pride parades around the country.

Maxine Wolfe, one of the original participants of the Avengers, was interviewed about the founding of the organization:

We decided that we would give out club cards at Gay Pride, which was coming up in June. We each chipped in thirty-three dollars to pay for the making of eight thousand club cards. Sarah [Schulman] and someone else wrote the original text of the club card, which said something like "Lesbians, dykes, gay women: Cold-blooded liars like George Bush in the White House—what did they ever do for us? Religion. The State. Who cares. We want revenge and we want it now. What have you got to lose?" And then we put down the phone number of the telephone in the upstairs part of my house and set up a tape machine. When you called the number, the tape said "You have reached the Lesbian Avengers. We're planning our first action for the first day of school in September against the community school boards that have refused to accept the Rainbow curriculum. If you want to be part of the planning, come to our first meeting." . . . We gave the cards out only to lesbians who were not in the March. We did not want women who were already committed to nine thousand other groups. We wanted to reach women who were new. Seventy lesbians showed up. . . .

We decided that the only way to do anything about this was to do something that nobody else would do. The women who came to the first meeting were all willing to do this. They were risk-takers. They had called a number they knew nothing about that they got from a card handed to them by someone they did not know. They knew that they were coming to a meeting about doing something on the first day of school about the Rainbow curriculum. Then word-of-mouth kicked in, and every week new women would show up. And what were their biggest issues? Their biggest issues were, "Aren't we using children, who are going to school on the first day, when it's already so chaotic and so upsetting to them already, and isn't this going to be terrible for kids?" And I said, "As someone who has two kids, this is what's going to happen. The first day of school is going to be great. The first day of school, these kids are going to get balloons and marching bands. They're going to think, 'Wow! This is fantastic!' And then the second day of school we're not going to be there and they're going to think, 'Oh my God. This is so boring. I can't believe it.'" . . .

The other issue was that we had come up with this idea to make balloons that said "Ask about lesbian lives." People were really upset about that—these new women who would come in later weeks to the planning meeting. And we would have to go through the same argument again and again. They said "How can you give those balloons to children? That's really manipulating them." And I would then say, "What if the balloons said 'Save the Whales'?" The trademark of what the Avengers wanted to do was to be in a place and confront the issue that is the "no-no." Gay people connected to kids. That's where everyone falls apart—especially in Queens suburbs. . . . So we actually marched around the school and the kids were coming in for the first day of school and we handed out balloons and we had a marching band and sang songs like "We Are Family." . . .

That became our trademark—to do cutting edge stuff—out in places where people don't want us to be out. . . .

Source: Interview with Maxine Wolfe by Laraine Sommella. "This Is about People Dying: The Tactics of Early ACT UP and Lesbian Avengers in New York City." *Queers in Space: Communities, Public Spaces, Sites of Resistance.* Edited by Gordon Brent Ingram, Anne-Marie Bouthillette, and Yolanda Retter. Seattle: Bay Press, 1997, 407–437. Used by permission of Maxine Wolfe.

Document 107

DISCRIMINATION BY PRIVATE ORGANIZATIONS: *HURLEY V. IRISH-AMERICAN GAY, LESBIAN, AND BISEXUAL GROUP OF BOSTON* (1995)

A gay marching contingent applied to participate in the Boston St. Patrick's Day Parade and wanted to carry a banner indicating gay pride. The organizers refused the application and barred the group from the event because of its intent to express a message in the parade contrary to that of the parade organizers. The gay contingent sued. The U.S. Supreme Court upheld the First Amendment right of the organizers to exclude gays from their event, not because they were gay but because they intended to promote a political belief contrary to the beliefs of the private organizers of the event. The Court said that parades are a "form of expression" and private sponsors cannot be forced to include groups that "impart a message the organizers do not wish to convey."

HURLEY et al. v. IRISH AMERICAN GAY, LESBIAN AND BISEXUAL GROUP OF BOSTON et al.
CERTIORARI TO THE SUPREME JUDICIAL COURT OF MASSACHUSETTS

Petitioner South Boston Allied War Veterans Council, an unincorporated association of individuals elected from various veteran groups, was authorized by the city of Boston to organize and conduct the St. Patrick's Day Evacuation Day Parade. The Council refused a place in the 1993 event to respondent GLIB, an organization formed for the purpose of marching in the parade in order to express its members' pride in their Irish heritage as openly gay, lesbian, and bisexual individuals, to show that there are such individuals in the community, and to support the like men and women who sought to march in the New York St. Patrick's Day parade. GLIB and some of its members filed this suit in state court, alleging that the denial of their application to march violated, *inter alia*, a state law prohibiting discrimination on account of sexual orientation in places of public accommodation. In finding such a violation and ordering the Council to include GLIB in the parade, the trial court, among other things, concluded that the parade had no common theme other than the involvement of the partici-pants, and that, given the Council's lack of selectivity in choosing parade partici-pants and its failure to circumscribe the marchers' messages, the parade lacked any expressive purpose, such that GLIB's inclusion therein would not violate the Council's First Amendment rights. The Supreme Judicial Court of Massachusetts affirmed.

Held: The state courts' application of the Massachusetts public accommodations law to require private citizens who organize a parade to include among the march-ers a group imparting a message that the organizers do not wish to convey violates the First Amendment. Pp. 8–24.

(a-d). . . .

(e). . . . Since every participating parade unit affects the message conveyed by the private organizers, the state courts' peculiar application of the Massachusetts law essentially forced the Council to alter the parade's expressive content and thereby violated the fundamental First Amendment rule that a speaker has the autonomy to choose the content of his own message and, conversely, to decide what not to say. . . .

418 Mass. 238, 636 N.E. 2d 1293, reversed and remanded.

Souter, J., delivered the opinion for a unanimous Court.

Source: No. 94–749. Argued April 25, 1995–Decided June 19, 1995.

Document 108

COMMUNICATIONS DECENCY ACT (1996)

The U.S. Congress attempted, for the first time, to regulate pornographic material on the Internet by passing the Communications Decency Act of 1996 (CDA). The act was added to the Telecommunications Act of 1996 under Title V. It attempted to regulate both indecency (when children had access) and obscenity in cyberspace. Section 230 of the act provided protection to Internet Service Providers (ISP) to not consider them as publishers of third-party material.

The Internet became fully commercialized in the 1990s. With this expansion of access came a flood of pornography. Some people believe pornography is harmful for children and want to limit the access to pornography on the Internet. TV and radio broadcasting were already regulated by the Federal Communications Commission (FCC). "Offensive speech" and other "adult" activities were restricted to certain hours when children were less likely to view. The Internet was completely unregulated and worldwide making it impossible to impose FCC-like rules apply. In response to parental concerns, politicians crafted the CDA to restrict access to pornography on the Internet. It made it a crime to make available or send to a person under age 18 any "comment, request, suggestion, proposal, image, or other communication that, in context, depicts or describes, in terms patently offensive as measured by contemporary community standards, sexual or excretory activities or organs." Also, it criminalized the transmission of materials that were "obscene or indecent" to underage minors.

The act was immediately challenged by the American Civil Liberties Union (ACLU) and others. They argued many points: (1) speech already protected under the First Amendment (like books) would now become illegal because of the availability online, (2) the law would have a "chilling" effect on medical information, (3) the term patently offensive (which was used for the first time in a U.S. law) was not defined, (4) it would infringe upon the free speech rights of adults, and (5) it denied the rights of parents to decide what material is available to their children, and other concerns. A panel of federal judges blocked implementation of the CDA in 1996. Months later a U.S. federal court in New York struck down similar portions of the CDA. On June 26, 1997, the U.S. Supreme Court upheld the lower court rulings stating the indecency provisions were unconstitutional and an abridgement of the First Amendment right to free speech (Reno v. American Civil Liberties Union).

Congress amended the CDA to remove the indecency provisions to overcome the previous problems, but this, too, did not pass Supreme Court oversight (Reno v. ACLU II, 2003). A third attempt to overcome the obscenity provisions was summarily rejected by a federal court in New York in 2005 (Nitke v. Gonzales, 2006).

47 USC § 223—OBSCENE OR HARASSING TELEPHONE CALLS IN THE DISTRICT OF COLUMBIA OR IN INTERSTATE OR FOREIGN COMMUNICATIONS
(a) Prohibited acts generally
   Whoever—

(1) in interstate or foreign communications—

    (A) by means of a telecommunications device knowingly—

        (i) makes, creates, or solicits, and

        (ii) initiates the transmission of, any comment, request, suggestion, proposal, image, or other communication which is obscene or child pornography, with intent to abuse, threaten, or harass another person;

    (B) by means of a telecommunications device knowingly—

        (i) makes, creates, or solicits, and

        (ii) initiates the transmission of, any comment, request, suggestion, proposal, image, or other communication which is obscene or child pornography, knowing that the recipient of the communication is under 18 years of age, regardless of whether the maker of such communication placed the call or initiated the communication;

    (C) makes a telephone call or utilizes a telecommunications device, whether or not conversation or communication ensues, without disclosing his identity and with intent to abuse, threaten, or harass any specific person;

    (D) makes or causes the telephone of another repeatedly or continuously to ring, with intent to harass any person at the called number; or

    (E) makes repeated telephone calls or repeatedly initiates communication with a telecommunications device, during which conversation or communication ensues, solely to harass any specific person; or

(2) knowingly permits any telecommunications facility under his control to be used for any activity prohibited by paragraph (1) with the intent that it be used for such activity, shall be fined under title 18 or imprisoned not more than two years, or both.

(b) Prohibited acts for commercial purposes; defense to prosecution

. . . .

(c) Sending or displaying offensive material to persons under 18
Whoever—

. . . .

(d) Violations of law required; commercial entities, nonprofit libraries, or institutions of higher education

. . . .

Source: 47. U.S.C. § 223.

Document 109

BRANDON TEENA MURDER TRIAL (1996)

People who cross-dress have always run the risk of being found out and ostracized or worst. Brandon Teena was a young man who was murdered for crossing the gender lines.

Teena Brandon was born in 1972 as a female. Family members described Teena as a tomboy. By adolescent, Teena began identifying as a male and chose to cross-dress and pass as a male. He dated girls from his high school. In 1992, he underwent psychiatric evaluation whereupon it was concluded that Teena suffered from severe "sexual identity crisis." Teena revealed in to his mother that he had been sexually raped by a male relative when he was a small child.

Teena moved from Lincoln, Nebraska, to a nearby small town of Falls City in 1993. There he lived full time as a male using the name Brandon Teena. He easily passed as a man and soon befriended ex-convicts John Lotter and Marvin Nissen. Brandon also dated one of the local girls, 19-year-old Lana Tisdel. Brandon was arrested for passing bad checks. The police noticed that his driver's license indicated that Brandon was a female and conducted a physical inspection to verify the information. The police released the arrest information to the local newspaper including that he was legally a female. Tisdel posted his bail and that is when Brandon told her that he was transgendered hoping for a sex-change operation in the future.

Lotter and Nissen read the story in the paper and confronted Brandon at a Christmas Eve party after he was released from jail. They forcibly stripped Brandon to confirm that he was female. They then forced him into a car, drove to a meatpacking plant, and assaulted and raped Brandon to show their disgust and exert dominance. Brandon went to the police to report the rape and seek protection. He also went to the emergency medical room to be tested for rape (unfortunately the rape kit was later lost). Three days later the police questioned Lotter and Nissen but let them go for lack of evidence.

A few days later, on New Year Eve, Nissen and Lotter searched for Brandon and broke into the home of Lisa Lamberthouse—a woman friend of Brandon and where Brandon had been living. There they found Brandon, Lisa, and another male friend (Phillip DeVinde). Nissen and Lotter shot and killed all three adults in front of Lambert's toddler. Because Brandon was twitching after being shot, Lotter grabbed a knife and stabbed him to make sure he was dead. Nissen and Lotter were soon apprehended and charged with murder. Both men are serving life in prison for the murders and may be executed once all the appeals are extinguished.

The murder was made into a documentary film The Brandon Teena Story *and the Academy Award–winning 1999 film* Boys Don't Cry. *The following documents are comments from Davina Anne Grabriel from FTM International.*

The Brandon Teena murder shocked us all, even though it should have come as no real surprise to any of us. I think back on it today, and even now it fills me with rage. . . . [It] is a good example of just what is wrong with the world we live in. Brandon Teena was someone who was trying to live his own life in the only way he knew how. He made a lot of mistakes, but none of them deserved a death sentence. . . .

Richardson County sheriff Charles B. Laux . . . stat[ed] of Brandon that "you can call it 'it' as far as I'm concerned. . . ." Local authorities have denied that their outing of Brandon in any way contributed to his killers' motives, and have declined to classify it as a hate crime. However, Lotter's sister has confirmed that both Lotter and Nissen were enraged after learning that Brandon was anatomically female, but had been living as a man and was even dating a local woman. . . .

When one is willing to kill a "friend" who violates the gender binary system, it makes one realize how strong it is. Leslie Feinberg [stated] . . . "It's fair to ask if Brandon Teena would still be alive today if authorities and the local newspaper had not forcibly outed him after he had successfully passed as a male. . . ." Riki Anne Wilchins of Transexual Menace says, "He died for the right to be a man—to be Brandon Teena."

Source: Davina Anne Gabriel. "Brandon Teena Murderer Sentenced." 1996. Internet Web site (http:// songweaver.com/gender/teena-sentencing.html) posted on February 21. See also http:// www.ftm-intl.org/Hist/Bran/

Document 110

PROTECTION FROM DISCRIMINATION FOR LGBT CITIZENS: *ROMER V. EVANS*—OVERTURNING COLORADO "AMENDMENT 2" (1996)

This landmark case for gay rights marked the first decisive legal victory at the Supreme Court level following the disappointment of the 1986 Hardwick decision. In Romer, the Supreme Court held that lesbians and gay men could not be excluded from the scope of state legal protections or prohibited from using the political process to obtain antidiscrimination protections.

ROY ROMER, GOVERNOR OF COLORADO, ET AL. PETITIONERS v. RICHARD G. EVANS ET AL.
CERTIORARI TO THE SUPREME COURT
OF COLORADO No. 94–1039
Argued October 10, 1995
Decided May 20, 1996

After various Colorado municipalities passed ordinances banning discrimination based on sexual orientation in housing, employment, education, public accommodations, health and welfare services, and other transactions and activities, Colorado voters adopted by statewide referendum "Amendment 2" to the State Constitution, which precludes all legislative, executive, or judicial action at any level of state or local government designed to protect the status of persons based on their "homosexual, lesbian or bisexual orientation, conduct, practices or relationships." Respondents, who include aggrieved homosexuals and municipalities, commenced this litigation in state court against petitioner state parties to declare Amendment 2 invalid and enjoin its enforcement. The trial court's grant of a preliminary injunction was sustained by the Colorado Supreme Court, which held that Amendment 2 was subject to strict scrutiny under the Equal Protection Clause of the Fourteenth Amendment because it infringed the fundamental right of gays and lesbians to participate in the political process. On remand, the trial court found that the Amendment failed to satisfy strict scrutiny. It enjoined Amendment 2's enforcement, and the State Supreme Court affirmed. *Held:* Amendment 2 violates the Equal Protection Clause. Pp. 4–14.

Source: 517 U.S. 620 (1996).

Document 111

HARASSMENT OF GAY STUDENTS: *NABOZNY V. PODLESNY* (1996)

Jamie Nabozny experienced terrible abuse from other students while attending an Ashland, Wisconsin, high school. He was wrestled to the classroom floor while his teacher was out of the room, and then two boys pretended to rape him while 20 other students watched and laughed. He was also urinated on in a bathroom and kicked so badly that he required surgery to stop the internal bleeding. His parents complained, but a school official told them that he "had to expect that kind of stuff" because he was a homosexual. Jamie eventually moved to Minneapolis, where he graduated with an equivalency degree, but he sued the Ashland School District in 1995. Initially, the case was dismissed, but the Seventh U.S. Circuit Court of Appeals could not find any rational reason for permitting one student to assault another based on the victim's sexual orientation and thus allowed the suit to continue. A jury found that school officials violated Jamie's rights under the Fourteenth Amendment's equal protection clause, and the district was forced to pay $962,000 in damages.

Nabozny v. Podlesny
U.S. Court of Appeals, Seventh Circuit
ESCHBACH, Circuit Judge.
July 31, 1996

Jamie Nabozny was a student in the Ashland Public School District (hereinafter "the District") in Ashland, Wisconsin throughout his middle school and high school years. During that time, Nabozny was continually harassed and physically abused by fellow students because he is homosexual. Both in middle school and high school Nabozny reported the harassment to school administrators. Nabozny asked the school officials to protect him and to punish his assailants. Despite the fact that the school administrators had a policy of investigating and punishing student-on-student battery and sexual harassment, they allegedly turned a deaf ear to Nabozny's requests. Indeed, there is evidence to suggest that some of the administrators themselves mocked Nabozny's predicament. Nabozny eventually filed suit against several school officials and the District pursuant to 42 U.S.C. Section 1983 alleging, among other things, that the defendants: 1) violated his Fourteenth Amendment right to equal protection by discriminating against him based on his gender; 2) violated his Fourteenth Amendment right to equal protection by discriminating against him based on his sexual orientation; 3) violated his Fourteenth

Amendment right to due process by exacerbating the risk that he would be harmed by fellow students; and, 4) violated his Fourteenth Amendment right to due process by encouraging an environment in which he would be harmed.

[The court report details over many pages the years of abuse Nabonzy experienced at all level of schooling.]

Conclusion

We conclude that, based on the record as a whole, a reasonable fact-finder could find that the District and defendants Podlesny, Davis, and Blauert violated Nabozny's Fourteenth Amendment right to equal protection by discriminating against him based on his gender or sexual orientation. Further, the law establishing the defendants' liability was sufficiently clear to inform the defendants at the time that their conduct was unconstitutional. Nabozny's equal protection claims against the District, Podlesny, Davis, and Blauert are reinstated in toto. . . .

[Comments: Of course, Bowers will soon be eclipsed in the area of equal protection by the Supreme Court's holding in Romer v. Evans, *517 U.S. 620 (1996).* Romer, *which was decided following the oral argument in this case, struck down on equal protection grounds a Colorado constitutional amendment that discriminated against homosexuals. Although* Romer *bolsters our analysis in this case to some extent, we do not rely on it. To do so would be especially inappropriate in the context of rejecting the defendants' qualified immunity argument.]*

Source: 92 F.3d 446.

Document 112
DEFENSE OF MARRIAGE ACT (DOMA) (1996)

Same-sex marriage did not become an issue for the United States until a suit filed by three couples in Hawaii challenged the status quo in 1990. Hawaii is the most ethnically and racially diverse state in the Union and its constitution contains a strong equal protection clause. The couples claimed the state constitution did not directly prohibit same-sex marriage but rather custom had restricted marriage to opposite-sex couples. The case, Baehr v. Lewin *(later renamed* Baehr v. Miike*), was initially dismissed by the first court. They appealed to the Supreme Court of Hawaii. The court sided with the plaintiffs concluding restrictions on same-sex marriages constituted discrimination based on sex and, thereby, violated the state's equal protection clause. Instead of immediately ordering same-sex marriage, it remanded the case back to the trial court to see if the state could demonstrate denying same-sex couples from marrying met a "compelling state interest." If the state failed to convince the court, then same-sex marriages would be allowed.*

The prospects of Hawaii granting same-sex couples the right to marry sent shock waves through American politics. Conservatives and the Religious Right quickly joined forces and crafted legislation at the federal level to stop same-sex marriages. Georgia representative Bob Barr (Republican) proposed legislation that would allow states to: (1) prohibit same-sex marriages, (2) refuse to recognize same-sex marriages performed elsewhere, and (3) disenfranchise same-sex marriages from any state or federal benefits (like filing joint income taxes, or survivor benefits from Social Security). Barr stated in the Congress—"The bill amends the U.S. Code to make explicit what has been understood under federal law for over 200 years; that a marriage is the legal union of a man and a woman as husband and wife, and a spouse is a husband or wife of the opposite sex." The bill was known as the Defense of Marriage Act (DOMA). The bill was fast-tracked and approved with a veto-proof margin in 1996. President Clinton reluctantly signed the bill for political expediency. He did not hold the traditional bill signing ceremony nor allow photographs to be taken. Soon after federal DOMA was passed, many states passed their own version of DOMA. Eventually 29 states would pass amendments to their state constitutions prohibiting same-sex marriage and an additional four states would pass a simpler DOMA statute.

Many legal analysts predicted that DOMA would not hold up in court once challenged. The federal government had never crafted legislation concerning the creation of marriage until the advent of DOMA. Before then, marriage was a state function and the federal government accepted marriages performed in any state and granted more than 1,138 additional rights and protections to those who were legally married that were not available to the unmarried. DOMA seemed to be in conflict with the Fourth, Fifth, Tenth, and Fourteenth Amendments to the U.S. Constitution. Over the next decade, numerous challenges were filed against both the federal and state DOMA.

Finally, a simple and clear case was mounted in New York against federal DOMA. Edith "Edie" Windsor and Thea Spyer were residents of New York and married in Toronto, Ontario, where same-sex marriages are legal. The women had lived together for 40 years and built up significant financial assets. Spyer died in 2009. Windsor was required to pay $363,053 in federal estate taxes on the inheritance from her wife's portion of the estate. If they had been opposite-sex couples and married, there would have been no inheritance tax. Windsor sued and the U.S. Supreme Court took the case (United States v. Windsor). The Court ruled that Section 3 of DOMA, which specified that the term spouse applied only to opposite-sex couples, denied due process for same-sex couples. As such, DOMA was determined to be unconstitutional. Since then, many federal courts have struck down various state DOMA and constitutional amendments on similar grounds.

The following are two documents on this topic. The first is a speech Congressman Henry Waxman gave before the House of Representatives in 1996. He saw DOMA as a political move to create a wedge issue for Republicans and was unnecessary. The second speech was made by Senator Jesse Helms to the Senate in 1996. He considered DOMA necessary to save the traditional institution of marriage from the homosexual agenda.

Speech by Congressman Henry Waxman to House of Representatives in 1996

The proponents of H.R. 3396 would have us believe that this legislation is necessary to save the institution of marriage. The real purpose of H.R. 3396 is to create a wedge issue for Republicans in the upcoming elections. In a shameless attempt to divide the American public, the Republican party is espousing official bigotry. It is promoting discrimination against individuals who seek the same responsibilities and opportunities other Americans seek when they form a lifelong union with someone they love. It is scapegoating a segment of our society to fan the flames of intolerance and prejudice. And it is doing this to try to improve its standings in the polls.

Discrimination against people who are gay and committed to one another does nothing to defend marriage or to strengthen family values. It does, however, continue to deny them legal rights that married couples simply take for granted—inclusion in a spouse's health insurance plan, pension and tax benefits, the ability to participate in medical decisions, and the right to visit a dying spouse in the hospital. . . .

Source: Congressman Henry Waxman (D–California), speech before the House of Representative in Committee of the Whole House, July 17, 1996. *Congressional Record*, E1299. http:// www.house.gov/waxman/issues/issues_gay_rights.htm

Senator Jesse Helms Speech to the Senate in 1996

"God created Adam and Eve—not Adam and Steve. . . ." Homosexual and lesbian leaders . . . are demanding that homosexuality be considered as just another lifestyle—these are the people who seek to force their agenda upon the vast majority of Americans who reject the homosexual lifestyle. Indeed, Mr. President, the pending bill—the Defense of Marriage Act—will safeguard the sacred institutions of marriage and the family from those who seek to destroy them and who are willing to tear apart America's moral fabric in the process.

Isn't it disheartening, Mr. President, that Congress must clarify the traditional definition of marriage? But inch by inch, little by little, the homosexual lobby has chipped away at the moral stamina of some of America's courts and some legislators, in order to create the shaky ground that exists today that prompts this legislation. . . . Homosexuals and lesbians boast that they are close to realizing their goal—legitimizing their behavior.

Mr. President, Bill Bennett has championed the cause of preserving America's culture; he contends that we are already reaping the consequences of the devaluation of marriage. And he warns that "it is exceedingly imprudent to conduct a radical, untested, and inherently flawed social experiment on an institution that is the keystone and the arch of civilization."

Bill Bennett is everlastingly right, and I believe the American people in the majority understand that the Defense of Marriage Act is vitally important. It will establish a simple, clear federal definition of marriage as the legal union of one man and one woman, and it will exempt sovereign states from being compelled by a half-baked interpretation of the U.S. Constitution to recognize same-sex marriages wrongfully legalized in another state. . . .

Mr. President, at the heart of this debate is the moral and spiritual survival of this nation. . . . We will decide whither goeth America. It is solely up to us.

Source: Senator Jesse Helms (R–NC), speech in the Senate, July 11, 1996, *Congressional Record*, pp. S10067–S10068.

Document 113
GALLUCCIO-HOLDEN ADOPTION LAWSUIT (1997)

Adoption by homosexuals has always been a challenge in the United States. Adoption agencies give preference to heterosexual couples who are married. Unmarried couples have always had a harder time to adopt. Because many states do not allow same-sex marriages, it has been much more difficult for unmarried same-sex couples to adopt children, even in cases where the child is the biological child of one of the couple. The second partner of an unmarried same-sex couple is usually denied the right for a second-parent adoption.

Michael Galluccio and Jon Holden attempted to adopt a sickly three-month-old boy in 1997. The boy's liver was enlarged, his lungs filled with fluid, and assumed to be infected with HIV because his mother was dying from AIDS. The boy was not named. The men took him in as a foster child and named him Adam. They nursed him back to health and were relieved to learn he was not infected with HIV.

The mother died and the men decided to formally adopt Adam. Although New Jersey did not have an issue with the men being gay, they were prohibited by law from granting an adoption to them as a couple since no unmarried couple (whether same or opposite sex) were allowed to adopt jointly. It would have been possible for one of the men to first adopt Adam and then the second man go through the exact same process. The double process would have taken twice as long, cost twice as much, and give the second man only stepparent status. The ACLU became involved and filed suit against New Jersey in 1997. Judge Sybil R. Moses decided in favor of the men and awarded joint adoption, saying that it was in the best interest of Adam to have two legal fathers. Initially the decision was limited to this one case, but a few months later Judge Moses expanded her ruling allowing joint adoptions of unmarried couples in New Jersey.

Most states now allow same-sex couples, whether married or not, to jointly adopt children. The ACLU has been instrumental in convincing judges and legislatures to review and update their adoption programs to allow homosexuals to adopt. The following is the introduction to the original ACLU lawsuit.

. . . .

4) Under DYFS's regulation a qualified married couple can jointly adopt a child, but a qualified unmarried couple like Plaintiffs HOLDEN and GALLUCCIO must go through a cumbersome and costly two-step process: first, one member of the couple must petition for adoption with the consent of the State, and then the other parent must file a petition for a "second parent adoption" with the courts. This regulation is

not authorized by New Jersey's adoption statute, but instead conflicts with the statute because it does not serve the best interests of children. It is therefore ultra vires
and invalid.

5) In addition, by allowing a qualified married couple to jointly adopt, requiring a
qualified unmarried couple to adopt through a cumbersome and costly two-step
process, the DYFS regulation creates a classification that treats unmarried couples
differently from married couples. Because there is no rational basis for this differential treatment, the DYFS regulation violates the Equal Protection guarantees of the
United States and New Jersey Constitutions. Plaintiffs HOLDEN, GALLUCCIO and
LAMBDA FAMILIES therefore file this class action for injunctive relief and ask this
Court to declare the DYFS regulation invalid and enjoin its enforcement.

Source: Available online at the Galluccio Family homepage, http://bunny.arvixe
.com/~gallucci/lawsuit.html

Document 114

GAY AND LESBIAN ALLIANCE AGAINST
DEFAMATION (1997)

*Media has great power to influence a culture and society. The choices of images, words,
and stories help mold public opinion. For example, at one time our media referred to
homosexuals as "deviants," "sexual predators," and more. Those terms only reinforced
negative stereotypes and perpetrated false information. Before the 1970s, the few movies
that contained homosexual characters always presented them as depressed, sad, pathetic
people who were either murdered or committed suicide. There were no happy successful gay people presented in the media at that time. Gay activism exploded in the 1970s
and with it challenges to the status quo. The Gay Activists Alliance (GAA) in New York
was the first to take on antigay stereotypes perpetrated by the media in 1973. From that
organization grew many other groups that, to this day, monitor the media for antigay
portrayals. Peter Nardi, sociology professor at Pitzer College, was president of the Los
Angeles chapter of the Gay and Lesbian Alliance Against Defamation and writes about
this decades-long effort to overcome antigay stereotyping in the media.*

Attitudes are shaped by the media, and if the media persist in presenting images
favorable to the status quo, then is it any wonder that a variety of groups with least
access to the control of the media and least visibility in the media should be activists
and advocates of reform? . . . Individuals can have a big effect on the media through
letters and calls, [but] it often helps to have the clout and legitimacy of larger organizations and media. Several strategies that have been very successful in combating
homophobia and heterosexism include the development of media watchdog organizations and the creation of media by and for lesbian and gay people.

In 1973 the Gay Activists Alliance (GAA) in New York was one of the first organizations to take on the media when it confronted executives at ABCTV about
unfavorable treatment of homosexuality. A group of GAA members later split to

form the National Gay Task Force (NGTF), which then formed a Gay Media Task Force (GMTF) in Los Angeles, under the direction of Newt Deiter. The Association of Gay and Lesbian Artists (AGLA) also started in the early 1980s as a support group of gay media people to lobby the industry, consult on projects, and present awards for positive depictions of gays and lesbians.

Although GMTF and AGLA no longer exist, their efforts led to the formation of the Gay and Lesbian Alliance Against Defamation (GLAAD), begun in New York in 1985, then in 1988 in Los Angeles. Today GLAAD is the largest and most influential national organization, with chapters around the country devoted to monitoring the media's portrayals of gays and lesbians, responding with organized letter-writing actions and protest marches, and consulting with [media] executives and creative staff.

In addition to organizations structured to resist and change stereotypical images, another form of response has been the creation of lesbian and gay media. From cable TV public access shows to computer E-mail, the Internet, newspapers, and slick magazines, gays have developed an impressive communications network.

With the beginning of the modern homophile movement in the early 1950s in Los Angeles, *ONE* became the first widely circulated homosexual magazine . . . [which] helped create an incipient sense of community. The tradition carries on with . . . many [national and] local lesbian and gay newspapers.

With the growing power of openly gay and lesbian filmmakers, television and newspaper reporters, and writers, a most effective form of resistance to the hegemonic force of the dominant media is occurring, namely to speak for oneself. However, there is no lesbian or gay equivalent to the Christian cable networks or the numerous syndicated conservative religious radio and television shows that mobilize thousands of followers to write or call politicians instantly. For gays and lesbians, access remains limited, especially in the powerful electronic national media.

Source: Peter Nardi. "Changing Gay and Lesbian Images in the Media." *Overcoming Heterosexism and Homophobia: Strategies That Work.* Edited by James T. Sears and Walter L. Williams. New York: Columbia University Press, 1997, 430, 440–441. Reprinted with permission of the publisher.

Document 115

TRANSSEXUAL NAME CHANGE: *IN RE MCINTYRE* (1996)

Until recently, only transsexuals who completed or nearly completed changing over, including surgery, could have their names changed. With the case of Robert Henry McIntyre, the Pennsylvania Supreme Court granted permission to Robert to change his name to Katherine Marie McIntyre even though he had not begun surgical reassignment. The court followed the reasoning in Commonwealth v. Goodman *and* In re Grimes *that the main purpose of name change statutes is to prohibit fraud by those attempting to avoid financial obligations. Furthermore, in* In re Eck *the court determined that it is not a matter of governmental concern when someone wants to change a traditionally female or traditionally male name. Thus, in* In re McIntyre *the court found no public interest in denying McIntyre's request for a name change and determined that his transgender status had no bearing on the matter.*

IN RE: Robert Henry McINTYRE. Appeal of Robert Henry McINTYRE.
OPINION
—July 21, 1998

Appellant, a fifty-three year old male, is a pre-operative transsexual who is undergoing hormonal therapy and psychotherapy in anticipation of sex-reassignment surgery. He has been struggling with personal gender identity issues since the age of ten. Appellant is the father of two adult sons and has been divorced since 1983.

In 1991, Appellant began dressing as a woman and held himself out to the community as a woman in all respects with the exception of his employment as a maintenance worker for the Harrisburg Parking Authority. He is generally known as Katherine Marie McIntyre, the name under which he leases his apartment, maintains various bank accounts and credit cards and is enrolled in membership in local organizations.

On August 25, 1995, Appellant filed a petition to change name from Robert Henry McIntyre to Katherine Marie McIntyre pursuant to 54 Pa.C.S. §§ 701–705.

. . . . We must keep in mind, however, that the primary purpose of the Judicial Change of Name Statute, other than with regard to minor children, is to prohibit fraud by those attempting to avoid financial obligations. Commonwealth v. Goodman, 544 Pa. 339, 676 A.2d 234 (1996); see also In re: Grimes, 530 Pa. 388, 609 A.2d 158 (1992) (necessity for judicial involvement in name change petition centers on governmental concerns that individuals not alter their identity to avoid financial obligations).

. . . .

Here, it was undisputed that Appellant was judgment free and was not seeking a name change to avoid any financial obligations or commit fraud. The fact that he is a transsexual seeking a feminine name should not affect the disposition of his request.

. . . .

Likewise, we find that there is no public interest being protected by the denial of Appellant's name change petition. The details surrounding Appellant's quest for sex-reassignment surgery are not a matter of governmental concern. As the name change statute and the procedures thereunder indicate a liberal policy regarding change of name requests, In re: Grimes, 530 Pa. 388, 609 A.2d 158 (1992), we see no reason to impose restrictions which the legislature has not.

Accordingly, because Appellant has satisfied the statutory requirements, the trial court abused its discretion in denying his name change petition. The Order is reversed and the petition is granted.

Source: Supreme Court of Pennsylvania, *IN RE: Robert Henry McIntyre,* July 21, 1998.

Document 116

AIDS AND THE AMERICANS WITH DISABILITIES ACT: *BRAGDON V. ABBOT* (1998)

Sidney Abbot went to the dental office of Randon Bragdon for an examination. She revealed that she was HIV-positive on the patient registration form. Dr. Bragdon performed a routine examination, determined that she had a cavity, and told her that he would not fill the tooth in his office because of his HIV policy. Rather, filling the tooth should be done in a hospital setting and at her expense. She declined his conditions and filed a complaint under Americans with Disabilities Act (ADA) and the Maine Human Rights Act (MHRA).

Both lower courts determined that Abbot's asymptomatic HIV was a physical impairment and that she was disabled as a matter of law under the ADA. The U.S. Supreme Court used the case-by-case method of analysis—first used in Ennis v. National Ass'n of Business and Education Radio, Inc. *in 1995 where the Court decided that the plain language of ADA required each case to be analyzed by itself.*

The Court decided that HIV infection is an "impairment from the moment of infection" (Bragdon v. Abbot, 2203–04). Second, the Court agreed that HIV infection "substantially limits . . . [a] major life activit[y]" [42 U.S.C. § 12102(2) (1997)]. The Court noted that this position was further supported by the Equal Employment Opportunity Commission (EEOC) regulation for Title 1, which states that a physical or mental impairment is "[a]ny physiological disorder, or condition, . . . affecting any one or more of [a number of listed body systems]" [29 C.F.R. §1630.2 (h)(1) (1997)]. The Court upheld Abbot's claim of discrimination under ADA.

The Bragdon *decision is exemplary for finding asymptomatic HIV a disability under ADA. However, the Court failed to explicitly state that HIV infection is a disability per se. Although a few lower courts have accepted the argument that HIV infection is a disability per se* (Hoepfl v. Barlow), *only the future will reveal if the U.S. Supreme Court agrees.*

No. 97–156
RANDON BRAGDON, PETITIONER v. SIDNEYABBOTT
ET AL . ON WRIT OF CERTIORARI TO THE UNITED STATES COURT
OF APPEALS FOR THE FIRST CIRCUIT
[June 25, 1998]

Respondent is infected with the human immunodeficiency virus (HIV), but had not manifested its most serious symptoms when the incidents in question occurred. At that time, she went to petitioner's office for a dental examination and disclosed her HIV infection. Petitioner discovered a cavity and informed respondent of his policy against filling cavities of HIV-infected patients in his office. He offered to perform the work at a hospital at no extra charge, though respondent would have to pay for use of the hospital's facilities. She declined and filed suit under, inter alia, the Americans with Disabilities Act of 1990 (ADA), which prohibits discrimination against any individual "on the basis of disability in the . . . enjoyment of the . . . services . . . of any place of public accommodation by any person who . . . operates [such] a place," 42 U.S.C. 12182(a), but qualifies the prohibition by providing: "Nothing [herein] shall require an entity to permit an individual to participate in or benefit from the . . . accommodations of such entity where such individual poses a direct threat to the health or safety of others," 12182(b)(3). The District Court granted respondent summary judgment. The First Circuit affirmed, agreeing with the lower court that respondent's HIV was a disability under the ADA even though her infection had not yet progressed to the symptomatic stage, and that treating her in petitioner's office would not have posed a direct threat to the health and safety of others. In making the latter ruling, the court relied on the 1993 Dentistry Guidelines of the Centers for Disease Control and Prevention (CDC) and on the 1991 American Dental Association Policy on HIV.

Held: 1. Even though respondent's HIV infection had not progressed to the so-called symptomatic phase, it was a "disability" under 12102(2)(A), that is, "a physical . . . impairment that substantially limits one or more of [an individual's] major life activities." Pp. 3–21.

Source: 524 U.S. 624 (1998).

Document 117

SAME-SEX MARRIAGE EQUALITY: *BAKER V. VERMONT* (1999)

The Baker *case is a true milestone for the lesbian and gay rights movement. For the first time, a state was ordered by its highest court to provide same-sex couples with all the rights and duties of heterosexual marriage. Moreover, this judicial remedy was based on the court's reading of equality provisions in that state's constitution. The solution fashioned in this instance by Vermont's legislature in response to the court's decision is creative and flexible, pointing the way to future efforts to equalize the status of same-sex couples without raising people's fears about the future of heterosexual marriage.*

Stan BAKER, et al. v.
STATE of Vermont, et al.
170 Vt. 194, 744 A.2d 864, 81 A.L.R.5th 627
No. 98–032.
Dec. 20, 1999

Same-sex couples brought action against State, city, and town, seeking declaratory judgment that refusal to issue them marriage licenses violated marriage statutes and State Constitution. The Chittenden Superior Court, Linda Levitt, J., dismissed complaint. Couples appealed. The Supreme Court, Amestoy, C.J., held that exclusion of same-sex couples from benefits and protections incident to marriage under state law violated common benefits clause of State Constitution.

Reversed.

Dooley, J., concurred and filed opinion.

Johnson, J., concurred in part and dissented in part and filed opinion.

III. Conclusion

While many have noted the symbolic or spiritual significance of the marital relation, it is plaintiffs' claim to the secular benefits and protections of a singularly human relationship that, in our view, characterizes this case. The State's interest in extending official recognition and legal protection to the professed commitment of two individuals to a lasting relationship of mutual affection is predicated on the belief that legal support of a couple's commitment provides stability for the individuals, their family, and the broader community. Although plaintiffs' interest in seeking state recognition and protection of their mutual commitment may—in view of divorce statistics—represent "the triumph of hope over experience," (FN16) the essential aspect of their claim is simply and fundamentally for inclusion in the family of State-sanctioned human relations.

The past provides many instances where the law refused to see a human being when it should have. See, e.g., Dred Scott, 60 U.S. at 407(concluding that African slaves and their descendants had "no rights which the white man was bound to respect"). The future may provide instances where the law will be asked to see a human when it should not. See, e.g., G. Smith, Judicial Decision making in the Age of Biotechnology, 13 Notre Dame J. Ethics & Pub. Policy 93, 114 (1999) (noting concerns that genetically engineering humans may threaten very nature of human individuality and identity). The challenge for future generations will be to define what is most essentially human. The extension of the Common Benefits Clause to acknowledge plaintiffs as Vermonters who seek nothing more, nor less, than legal protection and security for their avowed commitment to an intimate and lasting human relationship is simply, when all is said and done, a recognition of our common humanity.

The judgment of the superior court upholding the constitutionality of the Vermont marriage statutes under Chapter I, Article 7 of the Vermont Constitution is reversed. The effect of the Court's decision is suspended, and jurisdiction is retained in this Court, to permit the Legislature to consider and enact legislation consistent with the constitutional mandate described herein.

Source: 744 A.2d 864 (Vt. 1999).

Document 118
OVERTURNING STATE SODOMY LAWS (1999)

Gay activist filed lawsuits that finally broke through the stigma of being homosexual. Many states modernized and eliminated their sodomy laws. Then the U.S. Supreme Court in Bowers v. Hardwick *(1986) slammed the door shut to overturning sodomy throughout the country. The Court upheld Georgia's right to enforce its sodomy laws against homosexuals. Gay activists coordinated with the American Civil Liberties Union and Lambda Legal Defense to attack the remaining sodomy laws state by state. This became a time-consuming and expensive process but yielded significant results by the end of the twentieth century. By the new millennium, only 13 states still had sodomy laws on their books, and they were rarely enforced. However, their existence made life difficult for LGBT people residing in those states. Because sodomy laws classified homosexuals as criminal, they were barred from adopting children, from many occupations (e.g., teaching and counseling), and the like. Sodomy was effectively overruled in 2003 when the U.S. Supreme Court declared homosexual antisodomy laws to be discriminatory and unconstitutional* (Lawrence v. Texas, 2003).

Legal challenges to state sodomy laws met with astonishing success in 1999. The tone was set before the year began, in November 1998, when the Georgia Supreme Court ruled that Georgia's sodomy statute violates the right to privacy under that state's constitution. This case was a sweet victory after repeated unsuccessful attempts to bring down the Georgia law, which became the "crown jewel" of sodomy laws after the U.S. Supreme Court's infamous 1986 decision in *Bowers v. Hardwick* upholding the statute.

The [ACLU] Lesbian and Gay Rights Project rang in the new year with a January 1999 consent decree invalidating two Maryland statutes which created felonies for anybody engaging in anal sex and for gays and lesbians engaging in oral sex. . . . After the Baltimore County Circuit Court ruled in favor of the ACLU challenge . . . Maryland agreed to enter into a global consent decree eliminating both laws.

The action continued in February 1999, when a trial judge issued a promising decision rejecting a motion by Puerto Rico's Department of Justice to dismiss an ACLU challenge to Puerto Rico's sodomy statute. That same month, a Louisiana appellate court reversed a man's conviction for engaging in sodomy with a woman, holding that Louisiana's sodomy statute violated the state constitution's right to privacy. Two Louisiana trial courts quickly followed suit, striking down the statute in a civil challenge brought on behalf of lesbians and gay men. . . . And in April 1999, the conservative Arkansas Supreme Court rejected state efforts to dismiss a challenge to Arkansas' sodomy statute filed by Lambda [Legal Defense]. . . .

Why the sudden surge forward? There are probably several explanations. First, we have spent the 1990s building a solid foundation for sodomy challenges with hard-won decisions striking down sodomy statutes in Kentucky (1993), Tennessee (1996), and Montana (1997). We may be starting to reap the benefits of this growing body of case law in our favor. Second, some of the recently successful sodomy challenges (Georgia, Louisiana) have been brought on behalf of heterosexuals who have become entangled in sodomy statutes. Courts in conservative states may find it easier to strike down sodomy statutes in cases that don't raise the gay rights flag. And finally, the success of our sodomy challenges may be improving as a result of increasing social acceptance of gay men and lesbians. Indeed, even the decisions striking down sodomy statutes in cases involving heterosexuals may evidence this, since those courts have made no efforts to distinguish between gay and straight people but instead have assumed that the same constitutional protections apply to all. Whatever the explanation, it's safe to say we're on a roll.

Source: "A Banner Year for Attacking Sodomy Statutes." *Lesbian & Gay Rights, AIDS/ HIV, 2000: An ACLU Report.* New York: American Civil Liberties Union, 2000, 22–23. Used by permission of the American Civil Liberties Union.

Document 119

STUDENT RIGHTS TO FORM GAY CLUBS: *EAST HIGH GAY/STRAIGHT ALLIANCE V. BOARD OF EDUCATION* (1999)

In 1995, a group of lesbian and gay students at East High in Salt Lake City, Utah, submitted an application to form a gay-straight alliance on campus. The school denied the application. The students sued, citing the Equal Access Act. This act requires federally funded public schools that provide access to noncurricular clubs to extend the opportunity to all clubs without discrimination. In April 1996, the board terminated 46 school clubs not directly linked to the curriculum in an effort to block the alliance from meeting on school property. The clubs that were terminated included Students against Drunk Driving and the Young Republicans. Many in the community blamed the gay students and "gay agenda" for the cancellation of the extracurricular activities. The lesbian and gay students still met, but off campus.

However, when they learned that at least one noncurricular club was allowed to meet on school property in the 1997–1998 school year, they sued again. Federal district court judge Bruce S. Jenkins ruled that the school district had violated the federal Equal Access Act and the students' First Amendment rights ("Gay/Straight Alliance's Lawsuit to Proceed against Salt Lake School Board" 1999).

A few months later, a federal judge dismissed the student lawsuit against the Salt Lake City School Board because school officials produced definitive policy guarantees that allowed the right to express pro-gay opinions. However, the lesbian and gay students still wanted to meet on campus. Thus, they reorganized their original club to link directly with the curriculum. In February 2000, the students petitioned the school to form the People Respecting Important Social Movements (PRISM) academic club. The goal of the club was to discuss history through gay and lesbian issues and expand and enhance the study and understanding of American history and government. The school denied the application. The students sued. U.S. judge Tena Campbell granted PRISM a preliminary injunction because school officials had violated their own policy and the Constitution.

East High Gay/Straight Alliance v. Board of Education COMPLAINT
Civil No: 2:98CV001193
Judge Bruce Jenkins

. . . .

First Claim for Relief

Right to Equal Access

(Violation of Equal Access Act, 20 U.S.C. §§ 4071 et seq., Violation of Civil Rights Act of 1871, 42 U.S.C. §§ 1983 and 1988, and Declaratory Relief pursuant to 28 U.S.C. §§ 2201–02)

4. The Equal Access Act further provides, at 20 U.S.C. § 4071(a), that: It shall be unlawful for any public secondary school which receives Federal financial assistance and which has a limited open forum to deny equal access or a fair opportunity to, or discriminate against, any students who wish to conduct a meeting within that limited open forum on the basis of the religious, political, philosophical, or other content of the speech at such meetings.

5. Defendants have allowed two sets of noncurriculum related student groups to meet during noninstructional time on the premises of public secondary schools in the District: (1) those actually noncurriculum related student groups that Defendants call curriculum related by placement on Defendants' lists of "approved" clubs, and (2) those noncurriculum related student groups that Defendants permit to meet based on Defendants' approval of the content of those groups' speech, even though Defendants have not classified those clubs as "approved" or curriculum related.

6. Through their conduct, Defendants have created and are maintaining a limited open forum, within the meaning of the federal Equal Access Act, at the public secondary schools within the District, including East High School, Highland High School, and West High School.

7. Defendants have violated and are continuing to violate the federal Equal Access Act by providing an opportunity for one or more noncurriculum related student groups to meet during noninstructional time on the premises of public secondary schools in the District that receive federal financial assistance, while denying equal access to and discriminating against students, including the Plaintiffs, who wish to conduct meetings on the same terms as those student groups Defendants allow to meet, and basing such denial of equal access on the religious, political, philosophical, or other content of the speech at such meetings. Defendants also have violated the federal Equal Access Act by sponsoring the meetings of those noncurriculum related student groups that Defendants have placed on their "approved" lists.

Second Claim for Relief

Freedoms of Expression and Association and Rights to Due Process and Equal Protection (Violation of the First and Fourteenth Amendments to the United States Constitution, Violation of Civil Rights Act of 1871, 42 U.S.C. §§ 1983 and 1988, and Declaratory Relief pursuant to 28 U.S.C. §§ 2201–02)
. . . . Defendants are a government body and government officials and are therefore subject to the Fourteenth Amendment to the United States Constitution, as well as to the First Amendment to the United States Constitution by virtue of the Fourteenth Amendment to the United States Constitution. . . . Under the Fourteenth Amendment to the United States Constitution, Defendants may not deny due process of law or equal protection of the laws to students enrolled at public secondary schools within the District, including the Plaintiffs.

44. Pursuant to 42 U.S.C. § 1988, the Plaintiffs are entitled to an award against Defendants of the Plaintiffs' reasonable attorneys' fees incurred in connection with this action.

Source: 81 F. Supp.2d 1166, 1197 (D. Utah 1999).

Document 120

HUMAN RIGHTS CAMPAIGN STATEMENT ON WHY REPARATIVE THERAPY AND EX-GAY MINISTRIES FAIL

The Human Rights Campaign (HRC) is one of the largest and most powerful lesbian and gay civil rights organizations in the United States. Here, from 1999, are its comments on reparative therapy.

Why Reparative Therapy and Ex-Gay Ministries Fail

By Kim I. Mills, Education Director, HRC, 1999.

The purveyors of "reparative therapy" are well outside mainstream research and thinking in the psychotherapeutic world. They rail constantly that their work is being subverted by the professional associations, which they claim were hijacked in the 1970s by activist gay members into removing homosexuality from the official lists of mental disorders.

We question how it could be that the American Psychiatric and American Psychological Associations—the pre-eminent professional associations in their fields—could have been held captive by these so-called gay activists for more than 20 years. Surely if there were clinical evidence that homosexuality *per se* were a mental illness, this information could not have been suppressed by so many bright minds for so long. In addition, the "reparative therapists" protest loudly and often that homosexuality was removed from the *Diagnostic and Statistical Manual* without empirical research. We submit that it was placed in the *DSM* originally without such evidence.

It is our studied belief that the purveyors of "reparative therapy" refuse to confront the underlying reasons for the apparent unhappiness of many of the gay people who seek their help. They presume that all gay people are mentally unwell, ignoring the hundreds of thousands of happy, well-adjusted, successful lesbians and gay men across this nation.

As for ex-gay ministries, our research found that many of them dangle impossible promises before troubled people in order to lure them into their programs. The clearest evidence that these programs are not effective are the "ex-ex gay" testimonials of people who once participated in them—and the fact that so many of the most prominent ex-gay leaders returned to their former gay lives, only to be replaced by people who were never gay themselves and therefore cannot create new public relations disasters. Like the so-called reparative therapists, these ministries play to guilt and unhappiness that have their roots in something other than people's intrinsic sexual natures.

Source: Used by permission of Human Rights Campaign.

Document 121

DIVERSITY TRAINING: *ALTMAN V. MINNESOTA DEPARTMENT OF CORRECTIONS* (1999)

Often, employees are required to attend diversity training courses. In Minnesota, three prison employees protested having to attend workplace training on sexual orientation. They believed that the mandatory program was "state-sponsored propaganda" promoting homosexuality. The three men said that homosexuality went against their religious beliefs and that same-sex intimacy was sinful. The men took their Bibles to the training program and read silently during class. They were not confronted about reading the Bible during the workshop. Afterward, the employees received written reprimands for violating prison policies prohibiting improper conduct and prejudicial behavior. Supervisors further charged that the protest was an attempt to impede efforts to prevent sexual orientation harassment. The men sued. In August 1999, U.S. district judge Ann D. Montgomery of Minnesota ordered the state to withdraw the disciplinary notices. Judge Montgomery decided that the employees' First Amendment right to free expression of religion and the Minnesota Constitution's freedom of conscience clause had been violated by the prison's actions.

Thomas ALTMAN; Kristen Larson; Kenneth Yackly, Plaintiffs-Appellants/
Cross Appellees, v. MINNESOTA DEPARTMENT OF CORRECTIONS,
et al., Defendants-Appellees/Cross Appellants.
No. 00–1168, 00–1489.
—May 29, 2001

. . . .

Background i

In mid-1997, MCFS's training director persuaded Warden Connie Roehrich to include in the next regular one-day training session a program dealing with issues of gays and lesbians in the workplace. When the agenda for the training session was published to MCFS staff, Altman sent Roehrich an e-mail objecting to the mandatory nature of this program and protesting that it would "raise deviant sexual behavior for staff to a level of acceptance and respectability." Faced with this protest, and rumors that other staff members objected to this part of the mandatory training session, Roehrich issued a memorandum to all staff explaining that the gays-and-lesbians-in-the-workplace program was part of "the facility's strong commitment to create a work environment where people are treated respectfully, regardless of their individual differences." The training is not "designed to tell you what your personal attitudes or beliefs should be," the memorandum continued, but all employees must attend.

Prior to the training session, Appellants reviewed the training materials for the gays-and-lesbians-in-the-workplace program and concluded the training would be, in the words of their complaint, "state-sponsored indoctrination designed to sanction, condone, promote, and otherwise approve behavior and a style of life [Appellants] believe to be immoral, sinful, perverse, and contrary to the teachings of the Bible."

Immediately prior to the session, Appellants met and decided to read their Bibles during this program as a silent protest and as support because of the discomforting subject matter. During the program, Appellants read their Bibles, copied scripture, and participated to a limited extent. They did not disrupt the trainers' presentation. Numerous supervisors attended the program; none complained about Appellants' behavior or told them to stop reading their Bibles.

After the program, two of the trainers reported Appellants' behavior, and the Following an internal MCFS Affirmative Action Officer filed a complaint. The reprimands were based on Appellants' conduct during this discipline. The reprimands made Appellants ineligible for portion of the training session. The summary judgment record includes deposition promotion for two years. testimony by numerous witnesses that, to their knowledge, prison officials have never disciplined other employees who were inattentive during training sessions, for example, by sleeping or reading magazines.

Free Speech, Equal Protection, and Title Vii Claims ii

. . . Appellants argued that reading their Bibles during the training program was nonverbal conduct that qualifies as speech for First Amendment purposes, an issue defendants do not contest for summary judgment purposes. . . . Defendants argued that Appellants were reprimanded for insubordination—refusing to be trained— not for their nonverbal speech.

Free Exercise of Religion/Freedom of Conscience Claims iii

Appellants claim that reprimanding them for reading their Bibles during the training program violated their First and Fourteenth Amendment rights to freely exercise their religion. . . . Appellants alleged in their complaint that they opposed the training program as "little more than state-sponsored propaganda promoting the acceptance of homosexuality," behavior they "sincerely believe is immoral and sinful." Accepting that these are faith-based beliefs, we note that Warden Roehrich's memorandum assured all employees that their employer was not telling anyone what to believe. Thus, the only burden placed on Appellants was a requirement they attend a seventy-five-minute training program at which they were exposed to widely-accepted views that they oppose on faith-based principles. This is not, in our view, a substantial burden on their free exercise of religion.

. . . . Therefore, we should grant the MCFS's cross-appeal on the free exercise claim and reverse the district court's judgment. I further agree that we should reverse the district court judgment on the free speech, Title VII, and equal protection claims. While the majority would remand all three claims for a trial, I would remand only the Title VII and equal protection claims, granting judgment to the plaintiffs on their free speech claim as a matter of law.

LOKEN, Circuit Judge.

Source: United States Court of Appeals, Eighth Circuit, No. 00–1168, 00–1489. May 29, 2001.

Further Reading

Bransford, Stephen. 1994. *Gay Politics vs. Colorado and America: The Inside Story of Amendment 2.* Cascade, CO: Sardis Press.

Gross, Larry. 1993. *Contested Closets: The Politics and Ethics of Outing.* Minneapolis: University of Minnesota Press.

Herman, Didi. 1997. *The Antigay Agenda: Orthodox Vision and the Christian Right.* Chicago, IL: University of Chicago Press.

Ingram, Gordon Brent, Anne-Marie Bouthillette, and Yolanda Retter (eds.) *Queers in Space: Communities, Public Spaces, Sites of Resistance.* Seattle, WA: Bay Press.

Lesbian & Gay Rights, AIDS/HIV, 2000: An ACLU Report. New York: American Civil Liberties Union, 2000.

Sear, James T. and Walter L. Williams. 1997. *Overcoming Heterosexism and Homophobia: Strategies That Work.* New York: Columbia University Press.

Signorile, Michaelangelo. 1993. *Queer In America.* New York: Random House.

Stewart, Chuck. 1999. *Sexually Stigmatized Communities—Reducing Heterosexism and Homophobia: An Awareness Training Manual.* Newbury Park, CA: SAGE Publishing.

Chapter 10

2000s

Same-sex antisodomy laws were finally ruled unconstitutional by the U.S. Supreme Court—overturning centuries of persecution against homosexual sexual behaviors. This was a very important milestone since the existence of such laws caste homosexuals automatically as criminal and not deserving of equal rights and protections. Their existence allowed some cities and states, for example, to deny homosexuals from adopting children, provided the rationale to deny homosexuals from obtaining certain licenses (school teaching credential, nursing, psychologist, etc.), and more. At the same time, the battle over same-sex marriage heated up in the 2000s with many courts ruling against legislative bands and antigay constitutional amendments claiming they violated equal protection afforded all citizens. A few states approved same-sex marriage setting up a federal showdown over marriage equality.

As conservative leaders were losing the marriage battle, they shifted some of their efforts to demonizing transgender people. Transgender issues began to gain greater media attention. Inadvertently, this attention helped educate the public, and most importantly the courts, about the differences between sex, gender, sex roles, gender roles, and more, that academics in gender studies had explored for decades concerning identity politics.

The escalating hate from conservatives and the Religious Right was met with even greater activism from the gay community. The tragic and shocking death of Matthew Shepard in 1998 led to the passage of a federal hate crime bill by the late 2000s. The more antigay forces tried to stop the swell of equal rights for LGBT people, the more they lost ground.

Document 122

THE WESTBORO BAPTIST CHURCH AND ITS MESSAGE OF HATE

The Westboro Baptist Church, located in Topeka, Kansas, a small church unaffiliated with any Baptist group, has drawn condemnation for its messages of hatred for LGBT people, for Jews, and for anyone who disagrees with it. Famous for picketing at military funerals and for tying the deaths of men and women in the armed service to God's punishment to the United States for allowing gay rights, they have been sued, picketed themselves, and banned from entering several countries. The church's members are all from the Phelps family, whose father, Fred Phelps, was their pastor. Phelps died on March 19, 2014. The following statements are taken from its Web site.

Meaning of "God Hates Fags," from the Westboro Baptist Church

"GOD HATES FAGS"—though elliptical—is a profound theological statement, which the world needs to hear more than it needs oxygen, water and bread. The three words, fully expounded, show:

1. the absolute sovereignty of "**GOD**" in all matters whatsoever (e.g., Jeremiah 32:17, Isaiah 45:7, Amos 3:6, Proverbs 16:4, Matthew 19:26, Romans 9:11–24, Romans 11:33–36, etc.),

2. the doctrine of reprobation or God's "**HATE**" involving eternal retribution or the everlasting punishment of most of mankind in Hell forever (e.g., Leviticus 20:13,23, Psalm 5:5, Psalm 11:5, Malachi 1:1–3, Romans 9:11–13, Matthew 7:13,23, John 12:39–40, 1 Peter 2:8, Jude 4, Revelation 13:8, 20:15, 21:27, etc.), and

3. the certainty that all impenitent sodomites (under the elegant metaphor of "**FAGS**" as the contraction of faggots, fueling the fires of God's wrath) will inevitably go to Hell (e.g., Romans 1:18–32, 1 Corinthians 6:9–11, 1 Timothy 1:8–11, Jude 7, etc.).

The only lawful sexual connection is the marriage bed. All other sex activity is whoremongery and adultery, which will damn the soul forever in Hell. Heb. 13:4. Decadent, depraved, degenerate and debauched America, having bought the lie that It's OK to be gay, has thereby changed the truth of God into a lie, and now worships and serves the creature more than the Creator, who is blessed forever. Amen! Rom. 1:25. But the Word of God abides. Better to be a eunuch if the will of God be so, and make sure of Heaven. Mat. 19:12. Better to be blind or lame, than to be cast into Hell, into the fire that never shall be quenched. Mk. 9:43–48. Abstain, you fools.

Source: Westboro Baptist Church Web site. www.godhatesfags.com.

Document 123

STUDENT GROUP RIGHTS TO UNIVERSITY FUNDING: *BOARD OF REGENTS OF THE UNIVERSITY OF WISCONSIN SYSTEM V. SOUTHWORTH* (2000)

Some students with antigay religious convictions have sued their universities to stop fund-ing LGBT groups. They claimed their money was being used to fund organizations of which they morally disapproved, and this violated their First Amendment right to free speech and association. In a unanimous decision in 2000 by the U.S. Supreme Court, the Court upheld university-funding systems that use student fees for all student groups. Because students contribute to a neutral fund that supports all viewpoints rather than a particular ideology, the Court ruled that the university did not compel any speech or violate the First Amendment.

BOARD OF REGENTS OF THE UNIVERSITY OF WISCONSIN SYSTEM *v.*
SOUTHWORTH ET AL.
CERTIORARI TO THE UNITED STATES COURT OF APPEALS FOR THE
SEVENTH CIRCUIT

No. 98–1189. Argued November 9, 1999–Decided March 22, 2000

Petitioner, Board of Regents of the University of Wisconsin System (herein-after University), requires students at the University's Madison campus to pay a segregated activity fee. The fee supports various campus services and extracurric-ular student activities. In the University's view, such fees enhance students' edu-cational experience by promoting extracurricular activities, stimulating advocacy and debate on diverse points of view, enabling participation in campus adminis-trative activity, and providing opportunities to develop social skills, all consistent with the University's broad educational mission. Registered student organizations (RSO's) engaging in a number of diverse expressive activities are eligible to receive a portion of the fees, which are administered by the student government subject to the University's approval. The parties have stipulated that the process for review-ing and approving RSO applications for funding is administered in a viewpoint-neutral fashion. RSO's may also obtain funding through a student referendum. Respondents, present and former Madison campus students, filed suit against the University, alleging, *inter alia,* that the fee violates their First Amendment rights, and that the University must grant them the choice not to fund RSO's that engage in political and ideological expression offensive to their personal beliefs.

Held:

1. The First Amendment permits a public university to charge its students an activ-ity fee used to fund a program to facilitate extracurricular student speech, provided that the program is viewpoint neutral. The University exacts the fee at issue for the sole purpose of facilitating the free and open exchange of ideas by, and among, its students. Objecting students, however, may insist upon certain safeguards with respect to the expressive activities they are required to support. . . .

Source: Board of Regents of Univ. of Wis. System v. Southworth (98–1189) 529 U.S. 217 (2000) 151 F.3d 717, reversed and remanded.

Document 124

GAY RIGHTS TO BELONG TO A GROUP: *BOY SCOUTS OF AMERICA V. DALE* (2000)

The Boy Scouts has come under a number of legal challenges in the past 20 years. Courts often ruled against the Scouts for removing openly gay troop leaders only to see these decisions overruled by higher courts. Finally, the crucial issue of whether the Boy Scouts could discriminate against homosexual members and leaders was reviewed in 2000 by the U.S. Supreme Court in Boy Scouts of America v. Dale. *(See* Boy Scouts of America v. Dale *[2000], next.)*

The lawsuit was brought by James Dale who had been involved with the Boy Scouts for 12 years. He obtained the rank of Eagle Scout, was elected to the Order of the Arrow, and became assistant troop leader in 1990 at age 20. He never made his homosexuality known to the Scouts, nor did he mention or discuss the topic of homosexuality. That same year, he was interviewed in a college newspaper and was identified as the co-president of a lesbian and gay student group at Rutgers University. The paper ran a photo of him marching in the local gay pride parade. When the Scouts Monmouth Council in New Jersey discovered this fact, they expelled him from the organization. The Scouts told Dale that it "does not admit avowed homosexuals to membership in the organization" (Asseo 2000). Dale was not expelled for inappropriate conduct "on" or "off duty," but rather for simply being identified as a homosexual.

Dale sued the Monmouth Council and the national organization in 1992. He contended that their actions violated New Jersey's antidiscrimination law. The state court threw the case out stating that the Boy Scouts was not a public accommodation and therefore was not bound by state antidiscrimination laws. The case was appealed, and the New Jersey Supreme Court ruled in Dale's favor (1999) (as Dale v. Boy Scouts of America). The court rejected the Scouts' position that allowing homosexuals to participate would violate the Scouts Oath's to remain "morally straight" and "clean." The court decided the Boy Scouts was a public accommodation and was subject to state regulation.

This issue polarized America. Together, 71 organizations filed briefs in this case. Every major civil rights organization including the NAACP and the American Bar association joined with states, cities, deans of divinity schools, youth organizations, mental health and social services organizations, and rabbinical institutions. The Religious Right, including Orthodox Jewish groups, supported the Boy Scouts.

There are two basic arguments to this issue.

For the Boy Scouts: The Boy Scouts have a First Amendment right to determine and promote the moral goals of a private organization. This includes the right to choose leaders who reflect the organization's goals. A few court cases back this position. For example, in Hurley v. Irish-American Gay, Lesbian and Bisexual Group of Boston, the Court upheld the First Amendment right of the organizers of the Boston St. Patrick's Day Parade to exclude gays from their event. The gay marching contingent was not barred from participating because of its gay identity, but rather because it intended to express a message in the parade contrary to that of the parade organizers.

For James Dale: Because of the size and institutional nature of the Boy Scouts, it is a public organization subject to state laws. As such, if state laws prohibit discrimination based upon sexual orientation, then the Boy Scouts should not be allowed to prohibit lesbian or gay members or leaders. This position is supported by three recent cases all dealing with all-male organizations. In Roberts v. United States Jaycees, the Supreme Court allowed the state of Minnesota to require that females be accepted as members into the once, all-male, Jaycees. In general, the courts found the clubs existed for commercial purposes and that the exclusion of women was not part of their self-described mission.

The Boy Scouts asserted that by donning the Scout uniform, James Dale would celebrate his identity as an openly gay scout leader precisely as did the gay Irish marchers who attempted to conscript the Boston St. Patrick's Day Parade for their own purpose. However, Dale argued that "learning that someone is gay tells you nothing about his or her political party, religious beliefs, lifestyle, or moral code." Thus, his exclusion from the Boy Scouts is the same discrimination based on status that the court rejected in the all-male club cases.

The balance between First Amendment rights to free speech and association and government regulation of discrimination is distinguished between identity-based and speech-based discrimination. The Boy Scouts is free to express its point of view in pamphlets, speeches, and other ways. However, it has chosen not to do so. Heterosexual troop leaders and entire troops have publicly stated that discrimination against homosexuals is wrong and that homosexuality is moral; yet the Boy Scouts has not acted against them. Only those who are openly gay have been expelled. This is conduct discrimination that the courts have held to be unconstitutional for private nonsecular organizations that are deemed public accommodations.

Note: In 2013, the Boy Scouts of America voted to allow gay boys to join the Boy Scouts, but continued to disallow gay men as leaders.

The following is an excerpt from the unanimous ruling of the New Jersey Supreme Court concurring opinion of Justice C. J. Poritz and Justice J. Handler:

Justice C. J. Poritz, writing for a unanimous Court.

The issue in this appeal is whether New Jersey's Law Against Discrimination (LAD) prohibits Boy Scouts of America (BSA) from expelling a member solely because he is an avowed homosexual. . . .

James Dale became a member of BSA in 1978 at the age of eight. He remained a youth member of BSA until his eighteenth birthday in 1988. Dale was an exemplary scout. During his long membership, he earned many badges and honors, including the award of an Eagle Scout Badge, an honor achieved by only the top three percent of all scouts. On March 21, 1989 . . . BSA accepted and approved his application for the position of Assistant Scoutmaster of Troop 73, where he served for approximately sixteen months.

In July 1990 . . . Dale's photo appeared in the *Star-Ledger* [local newspaper] with a caption identifying him as co-president of the Rutgers University Lesbian/Gay Alliance. Later that month, Dale received a letter from BSA Monmouth Council Executive James W. Kay, revoking Dale's BSA membership [and indicating] that the standards for leadership established by the BSA specifically forbade membership to homosexuals. . . . In July 1992, Dale filed suit against BSA. . . .

We find that . . . Dale's expulsion constituted discrimination based solely on his status as an openly gay man. The United States Supreme Court has not hesitated to uphold the enforcement of a state's antidiscrimination statute against an expressive association claim based on assumptions in respect of status that are not a part of the group members' shared expressive purpose. . . .

When contrasted with its all-inclusive policy, Boy Scouts' litigation stance on homosexuality appears antithetical to the organization's goals and philosophy. The exclusion of members solely on the basis of their sexual orientation is inconsistent with Boy Scouts' commitment to a diverse and representative membership. More-over, this exclusionary practice contradicts Boy Scouts' overarching objective to reach all eligible youth. We are satisfied that Boy Scouts' expulsion of Dale is based on little more than prejudice and not on a unified Boy Scout position; in other words, Dale's expulsion is not justified by the need to preserve the organization's expressive rights.

The invocation of stereotypes to justify discrimination is all too familiar. Indeed, the story of discrimination is the story of stereotypes that limit the potential of men, women, and children who belong to excluded groups. By way of example, we observe that certain claimed propensities of character were once invoked to advocate the subjugation of women. . . . The human price of this bigotry has been enormous. At a most fundamental level, adherence to the principle of equality demands that our legal system protect the victims of invidious discrimination. New Jersey has long been a leader in this effort. . . . Thus, even if Dale's membership works some slight infringement on Boy Scouts' members right of expressive association, we find that the infringement is justified because it serves New Jersey's compelling interest in eliminating discrimination based on sexual orientation. . . .

Justice J. Handler, concurring opinion.

Dale's statement of his [gay] identity does not express a view about homosexuality . . . any more than a Scout admitting he is Catholic amounts to a teaching that Catholicism is the only proper religion. As the Court recognizes, Dale has never used his leadership position or membership to promote homosexuality, or any message inconsistent with Boy Scouts' policies. . . . Dale appears to have heeded and lived by Boy Scouts' dictate that individual conscience should guide a Scout's moral decision making.

. . . One particular stereotype that we renounce today is that homosexuals are inherently immoral. That myth is repudiated by decades of social science data. . . . [Stereotypes] reveal nothing about that individual's moral character, or any other aspect of his or her personality. . . . Plaintiff's exemplary journey through the BSA ranks is testament enough that these stereotypical notions about homosexuals must be rejected. . . .

Another particularly pernicious stereotype about homosexuals is implicit in Boy Scouts' arguments: the sinister and unspoken fear that gay scout leaders will somehow cause physical or emotional injury to scouts. The myth that a homosexual male is more likely than a heterosexual male to molest children has been demolished. . . . [Research studies show] that the adult heterosexual male constitutes a greater sexual risk to underage children than does the adult homosexual male. . . . In light of this evidence, the belief that a gay scoutmaster poses a risk to young boys because of his sexual orientation is patently false, and . . . must be rejected as an unfounded stereotype. . . .

Sources: James Dale v. Boy Scouts of America 160 N.J. 562 (Decided August 4, 1999) and reversed by the U.S. Supreme Court in *Boy Scouts of America et al. v. Dale*, 530 U.S. 640 (2000); Asseo, Laurie. 2000, January 15. "Gays, Free Speech Mark Boy Scout's Case." The Associate Press in *Amarillo Globe-News.*

Document 125

TRANSGENDER RIGHTS AND THE ACLU (2000)

Transgendered and transsexual people often face overt hostile discrimination particularly if they were first known as one gender and then they begin cross-dressing as the other gender. Discrimination against transgender can result in loss of job, housing, child custody, marriage, and other benefits. The American Civil Liberties Union became actively involved in representing transgendered people in the 1990s and devoted significant resources to the effort. The following is the 2000 annual report of the ACLU Lesbian and Gay Rights Project explaining the need for legal support for transgendered:

Transgender issues are important to our work on two levels: both as part of the larger struggle for civil liberties, and as an element of the struggle for lesbian, gay and bisexual civil rights. The ACLU's mission is to preserve individual civil liberties. That includes protecting our rights to make choices about our bodies and about how we define ourselves, without interference or discrimination on account of those choices. Fighting prejudice against transgendered individuals fits closely within that commitment.

But transgender issues also challenge one of society's most closely held (though fluid) notions: what it is to be male, and what it is to be female. The hate and disgust that transgendered people can provoke is a fear of people who do not fit stereotypes of appropriate sex roles. And that is the same fear that often fuels discrimination against lesbian and gay people. The butch woman and the effeminate man do not conform; they stir fears that our ideas of what a woman or a man is "supposed" to be may not be fixed and reliable. And indeed, they are not. Making society comfortable with that idea is at the heart of all our work in the LGBT community.

Source: "Why Do We Work on Transgender Issues?" *Lesbian & Gay Rights, AIDS/ HIV, 2000: An ACLU Report.* New York: American Civil Liberties Union, 2000, 23. Used by permission of the American Civil Liberties Union.

Document 126

TRANSSEXUAL RIGHTS: SCHWENK V. HARTFORD (2000)

Douglas Schwenk, a self-identified preoperative transsexual who went by the name Crystal and dressed as a woman, received repeated unwanted sexual overtures from prison guard Robert Mitchell. Mitchell attempted to rape Crystal anally in her prison cell. She filed a federal lawsuit claiming violation of her civil rights under the Eighth Amendment (cruel and unusual punishment) and the Gender-Motivated Violence Act (GMVA). Judge Stephen Reinhardt of the Ninth Circuit Court of Appeals concluded that Schwenk was protected under the Eighth Amendment since precedent had been set in prior transsexual prisoner cases (Farmer v. Brennan, 1996). *He rejected Mitchell's argument that*

GMVA did not apply to the case because it was part of the Violence against Women Act (VAWA) and Schwenk was a man. Reinhardt noted that members of Congress made opinions that supported the terms of GMVA to protect all residents of the United States from gender-motivated violence. Reinhardt found that the Supreme Court had, in fact, collapsed the concept of sex and gender into one broad category—gender identity.

SCHWENK v. HARTFORD
Douglas W. SCHWENK, Plaintiff-Appellee, v. James HARTFORD; Steve Sinclair; Robert Mitchell, Defendants-Appellants.
No. 97–35870.
Argued and Submitted March 11, 1999—February 29, 2000

Robert Mitchell, a Washington state prison guard, appeals the district court's denial of his motion for summary judgment in a case in which a male-to-female transsexual prisoner, Douglas ("Crystal") Schwenk, sought damages as a result of Mitchell's alleged attempt to rape her. Following the alleged assault, Schwenk sued various prison officials including Mitchell both under Section 1983, for a violation of her Eighth Amendment rights, and under the Gender Motivated Violence Act (GMVA). Mitchell's summary judgment motion was based on qualified immunity.

With respect to Schwenk's Section 1983 claim, Mitchell argues that he is entitled to qualified immunity because the allegations amount only to sexual harassment and not to the sort of sexual attack proscribed by the Eighth Amendment. With respect to Schwenk's GMVA claim, Mitchell asserts that he is entitled to qualified immunity because the constitutionality of the Act was not clearly established and its applicability under the circumstances of this particular assault was far from clear. For the reasons set forth below, we hold that the district court properly denied Mitchell's motion on the Section 1983 claim, but erred with respect to the GMVA.

 . . . . Mitchell raises three points regarding the first ground. First, Mitchell asserts that the acts of which he was accused do not satisfy the statutory definition of a crime of violence. Second, he asserts that Schwenk is male and that the GMVA does not protect men who are raped or sexually assaulted by other men. Third, Mitchell argues that in general, transsexuals are not covered by the act. In particular, Mitchell argues that Schwenk's allegations do not constitute a claim that the attack was based on gender, as required by the statute, but rather on transsexuality. Therefore, Mitchell claims, the requisite gender motivation and animus are absent. . . . The district court rejected all of Mitchell's contentions, and this interlocutory appeal followed.

Conclusion

In conclusion, the facts and allegations in the record clearly make out a claim for relief under both Section 1983 and the GMVA. Mitchell is not entitled to qualified immunity from Schwenk's claim under Section 1983 for violation of her

Eighth Amendment rights. It was well established prior to the attack that Mitch-ell's alleged conduct constituted a violation of the Eighth Amendment, and no reasonable prison official could have believed otherwise. Although the GMVA does cover Mitchell's alleged conduct, the law regarding the scope and applicability of that statute was not clearly established at the time of the assault on Schwenk, at least with respect to questions of gender motivation and animus. Accordingly, we reverse the district court's denial of qualified immunity to Mitchell with respect to the GMVA claim.

The decision of the district court is therefore AFFIRMED in part and REVERSED in part.

Source: Schwenk v. Hartford, 204 F.3d 1187 (9th Cir. 2000).

Document 127
ANTIGAY HATE CRIMES IN HIGH SCHOOLS (2000)

It is estimated that children hear 25 antigay remarks each day in public schools. These include word such as faggot, dyke, *or the slang expression* That's so gay. *And when slurs are made in front of teachers, many times teachers make no effort to stop the attacks.*

Too often, what begins as antigay remarks escalates into physical and sexual harass-ment of lesbian and gay students. Until the landmark case Nabozny v. Podlesny, *1996, it was not clear the responsibilities schools had in preventing such harassment.*

In the mid-1990s, Jamie Nabozny attended a public high school in Ashland, Wis-consin. While there, he experienced terrible physical and verbal abuse from other stu-dents. In one instance, while his teacher was out of the classroom, two boys attacked and wrestled Jamie to the floor where they mock-raped him in front of 20 other students who laughed at his screams. In another time, he was cornered in the bathroom, uri-nated upon, and kicked so badly that he was hospitalized and given surgery to stop the internal bleeding. Both Jamie and his parents complained to the school but was told by the school official that he "had to expect that kind of stuff" because he was known to be homosexual. For his safety, the family moved to Minneapolis and Jamie graduated with an equivalency degree. In 1995, Jamie sued the Ashland School District and the case was dismissed. Until then, no court had ever held schools responsible for student upon student violence when motivated by gay hate. Jamie appealed to the Seventh U.S. Circuit Court of Appeals who agreed the case had merit and permitted the suit to continue. Ultimately, a jury found the school officials were negligent in protecting Jamie and violated Jamie's rights under the Fourteenth Amendment's equal protection clause. The district was forced to pay almost $1 million in damages to Jamie. This case opened a floodgate of lawsuits and, perhaps more importantly, the threat of lawsuits from gay students who experienced sexual harassment in schools.

A second case, Aurelia Davis v. Monroe County Board of Education, *1999, further clarified that school districts may be liable if school employees are deliberately indifferent to complaints of peer-to-peer sexual harassment. In this case, Davis was a girl who was continually harassed by boys, the harassment taking the form of sexual comments and gestures. School employees ignored her complaints. She sued and won.*

The Office of Civil Rights for the U.S. Department of Education in March 1997 released new guidelines for educators on Title IX. This is the federal statute that bars sex discrimination in public schools that receive federal funding. These guidelines make clear that one form of antigay harassment in schools—namely harassment that creates a sexually hostile environment—is illegal under Title IX. The following is an article by Jennifer Middleton and Matt Coles published in the ACLU 2000 annual report addressing the issue of hate crimes and school responsibility.

We heard a lot in the press this year about hate crimes. The brutal murder of Matthew Shepard was the most notorious anti-gay crime, but there were many others. Billy Joe Gaither was tortured and burned in his small rural hometown in Alabama for being gay. Gary Matson and Winfield Scott were killed in their bed in Happy Valley, California because they were gay. And these are only the crimes that were widely reported: unknown numbers more have been assaulted, beaten, left to die in anti-gay attacks around the nation.

Many politicians and members of the lesbian and gay community responded by calling for new laws which would impose tougher sentences for crimes motivated by hate, so-called "hate crime" laws.

Hate crime laws are not a bad idea. Their critics to the contrary, being beaten in a random attack and being beaten because you are black or Asian or Jewish or gay is not the same thing to the victim. Victims of hate crimes are more depressed, lose more of their sense of safety, and have a harder time adjusting back to a normal life.

Perhaps more important, one of the major reasons why we have hate crimes is the widespread belief that society does not value some lives much, if at all. Perpetrators often think that the society in which they live really does not think there is much wrong with assaulting minorities, including gay people. A hate crime law is one way to begin reversing that perception. . . .

But if hate crimes laws are a decent start on dealing with the problem of hate violence, they are no more than a start. The message that society does not value the lives of lesbians and gay men much will not get undone until society says in a meaningful way that discrimination based on sexual orientation is wrong, and that lesbians, gay men, bisexuals and transgendered people are entitled to the same basic respect every citizen gets. We need comprehensive anti-discrimination laws. . . .

There may be no more important place to begin getting that message of respect out than in our schools. . . . One of the purposes of school is to teach society's values. Simply leaving respect for gay people out of the curriculum would send the wrong message in itself. But in all too many schools, the problem is not just omission: schools are not a safe place for lesbian, gay, bisexual and transgendered students.

A study of Massachusetts high school students just published in the journal *Pediatrics* reported that more than 25% of gay teens had recently missed school because of fear for their safety. When compared to heterosexual students, they are four times as likely to be threatened with a weapon at school, four times as likely to be assaulted to the point that medical attention is needed. And school authorities themselves are part of the problem: another study showed that 53% of high school students report hearing homophobic slurs such as "faggot" from their teachers.

If schools are the most important place to teach values based on equality and respect for all, most schools, at least until very recently, want nothing so much as to avoid dealing with the problems of lesbian and gay students entirely. The avoidance option is disappearing. Several high profile [legal] cases have ruled that schools have a responsibility to make their environments safe for all students, gay and straight alike. If they do not, the administrators may be liable for damages. The Supreme Court ruled this past year that schools can be liable if they let sexual harassment flourish unnoticed, even when the harassment comes from other students.

School-by-school litigation is not the answer. It takes far too long, and it is much too expensive. But a few cases can make school districts realize that failure to do something about abuse of lesbians, gay men, bisexuals and transgendered students can lead to protracted litigation with expensive outcomes. The next step is to help them take action. At the start of the school year in 1999, the [ACLU Lesbian and Gay Rights] Project and GLSEN (the Gay, Lesbian, Straight Education Network) published a piece collecting the most often asked questions about school non-discrimination and harassment policies, and providing clear answers. Together we mailed it to every school district in America. . . .

The process of getting America's schools to teach respect will not be finished overnight. But it's worth being persistent, because in the long run, it is likely to be the most effective answer to hate.

Source: Jennifer Middleton and Matt Coles. "Is High School the Answer to Hate Crimes?" *Lesbian & Gay Rights, AIDS/HIV, 2000: An ACLU Report.* New York: American Civil Liberties Union, 2000, 18–19. Used by permission of the American Civil Liberties Union.

Document 128

MILLENNIUM MARCH ON WASHINGTON (2000)

Several hundreds of thousands of people attended the April 30, 2000, "March for Equality." This was the fourth such event where gays and lesbians marched on Washington in the name of gay and lesbian rights. The name change reflected the newer goals of the gay rights movement to demand absolute and total equality. C-SPAN television channel broadcast the speeches to a national audience. Lorri L. Jean, executive director of the Los Angeles Gay and Lesbian Center and later director of the National Gay and Lesbian Task Force, gave a speech that clearly stated the "gay agenda"—"to be treated fairly and equally in all aspects of our society; to have the same rights and responsibilities as every other American." In many ways, this event shows the progress gay rights have made. In just two generations, gays have gone from being immediately classified as "criminal" and being arrested because of sodomy laws to publicly demanding full and equal rights.

Today we have heard from some of the most venerable pioneers in our movement, and some of the most vivacious young people. Some say that these youth are our future. I say that they are our here and now, and together, we must work to create a future that is worthy of all of us.

That's why we're here today—we're fighting for our future. And that's important. It's good to stand up for what is right. And sometimes we even have fun doing it. But I am *not* having fun today. I am not having fun because I'm mad. I marched here for our rights in 1979; I had just come out and I was afraid. I marched again in 1987, without fear and full of pride. I marched again in 1993, filled with excitement about the promise of a new President. But now it's the year 2000, and I'm not afraid and I'm not excited.

I'm tired. I'm tired of marching. And I'm MAD! I'm mad because we should not have to be here.

We have seen the dawning of a new millennium and in a country that is supposed to be the freest on earth, we are still having to march. We are still having to fight for the most basic freedoms that every single one of our straight brothers and sisters take for granted. That's wrong, and I'm mad as hell about it!

I am mad that we live in a society where it is still permissible to discriminate against millions of people simply because of our sexual orientation. In some states, it is legal to take away our homes. In others, it is legal to break up our families and take away our children. In 39 states, it is still legal to fire us from our jobs for no reason other than who we love. And still, in the final years of the Clinton Administration, we have no federal laws to guarantee these most basic of protections. ALL OF THESE THINGS ARE WRONG.

All we want is the freedom to love. The freedom to love whomever we choose, without fear, without bigotry, without discrimination. That's it. LOVE. Why is there such a big fuss about love?

If you ask Pat Robertson or Jesse Helms, they don't talk about love. Their hearts are so full of hatred that they're *afraid* of love. Instead, they say we have "a gay agenda." Well, let's admit it. We DO have a gay agenda, and it's the very one upon which this nation was founded: liberty, equality. That's all. We simply want to be treated fairly and equally in all aspects of our society; to have the same rights and responsibilities as every other American.

But not everyone believes in freedom and fairness and equality. That's why we HAVE to march. In fact, some have the gall to look us right in the eyes and say that they *believe* that we should be second class citizens, without equal rights, like the right to marry. And these aren't just our enemies, sometimes these are politicians who claim to be our friends.

Well, to these enemies and so-called friends, I say this: there is no such thing as *partial* freedom or virtual equality. If we are not entirely free, then we are not really free at all. If we do not have the *same* rights, we do not have equal rights. And we're not going to go away until we do. We are not going away, not now, not *ever*.

So, as we enter the new millennium, it is time for a new vision, a new message. A message that is worthy of those who started this battle decades ago, and of the youngest among us who have picked up their torch.

From this point forward, let us adopt a policy of ZERO TOLERANCE. Zero tolerance of discrimination, zero tolerance of bigotry and ignorance, zero tolerance for elected officials who refuse to support our full and complete participation in this society—especially those politicians who take our money! It is *not* OK to tell us that, on one hand, we are welcome to join "the big tent," but on the other hand, we don't deserve the same rights as our tent mates. I say it again, if we are not *completely* free, then we are not really free at all.

This is the agenda that our movement leadership should be promoting, boldly and without compromise. We must stop settling for crumbs. We must stop being apologists for allies who refuse to promote our FULL equality. We must never, *never* be willing to compromise our own freedom, or give others permission to do so. Because if WE fail to stand firm for true justice, others will think they don't have to either. If we won't stand up for total justice for ourselves, how can we expect anyone else to do so?

Some might say that it's not the right time to demand full equality. I say that if we had listened to those who said that it wasn't the right time, or that it couldn't be done, we'd never be where we are today. Freedom can *never* come too soon. It *can* be done! It *must* be done! It *will* be done! This is not a radical message, it is the only acceptable message. We must never lose sight of the fact that what we want and what we demand and what we deserve and what we WILL have is full equality—full equality and nothing less.

Let this be our rallying cry for the new millennium—full equality and nothing less. This is our *birth right*. We are *entitled* to it. And ours is a noble cause because we are engaged in a fight for the very promise of America. Let us not forget that this is a patriotic battle of the highest order, a battle to secure the principle that forms the bedrock of our society, and upon which our nation was founded: life, liberty and the pursuit of happiness.

We must follow the vision of Dr. Martin Luther King, Jr. when he said: "No! No! We are not satisfied until justice rolls down like water and righteousness like a mighty stream."

FULL EQUALITY & NOTHING LESS!

Let this message ring through the land to friend and foe alike. We deserve to participate in the promise of America, and we will not be denied. Whether it takes 20 years or 200 years, we will never give up. And rest assured, we WILL win, because right is on *our* side. History will judge harshly those foes who opposed our freedom, just as it will those friends who lacked the courage and the character to do what is right.

So, when you return home to towns and cities all over this nation, do not forget our message for the new millennium: ZERO TOLERANCE!

FULL EQUALITY, NOTHING LESS!

We demand it, we deserve it and we WILL have it!

Source: Remarks of Lorri L. Jean, Millennium March on Washington. Used by permission of Lorri L. Jean.

Document 129

DR. ROBERT SPITZER CLAIMS SEXUAL ORIENTATION CAN BE CHANGED. TWELVE YEARS LATER HE RESCINDS HIS RESEARCH AND ISSUES A FORMAL PUBLIC APOLOGY (2003)

In 2003, Dr. Robert Spitzer published an academic article in the prestigious Archives in Sexual Behavior *that claimed, "highly motivated" homosexuals could change their sexual orientation. This was significant because Dr. Spitzer was a highly regarded expert and considered "unbiased" since he was part of the effort in 1973 to have the American Psychological Association declassify homosexuality as a mental disorder. Immediately the Religious Right held up his work as proof that homosexuals could change if they really wanted to. However, therapists heard more and more horror stories about sexual orientation change efforts (SOCE) therapy from their clients. For example, a friend of John Evans (one of the founders of Love in Action) committed suicide due to his inability to change. Evans stated in a 1993 interview with* The Wall Street Journal *that SOCE destroyed people lives and proponents were living in a fantasy world. Every major psychology organization came out against SOCE claiming that it not only didn't work but that it also caused emotional harm in those attempting to change.*

Abstract: Position statements of the major mental health organizations in the United States state that there is no scientific evidence that a homosexual sexual orientation can be changed by psychotherapy, often referred to as "reparative therapy." This study tested the hypothesis that some individuals whose sexual orientation is predominantly homosexual can, with some form of reparative therapy, become predominantly heterosexual. . . . The majority of participants gave reports of change from a predominantly or exclusively homosexual orientation before therapy to a predominantly or exclusively heterosexual orientation in the past year. Reports of complete change were uncommon. Female participants reported significantly more change than did male participants. Either some gay men and lesbians, following reparative therapy, actually change their predominantly homosexual orientation to a predominantly heterosexual orientation or some gay men and women construct elaborate self-deceptive narratives (or even lie) in which they claim to have changed their sexual orientation, or both. For many reasons, it is concluded that the participants' self-reports were, by-and-large, credible and that few elaborated self-deceptive narratives or lied. Thus, there is evidence that change in sexual orientation following some form of reparative therapy does occur in some gay men and lesbians.

Source: R. L. Spitzer. *Archives of Sexual Behavior* 32 (2003): 403. doi:10.1023/A:10 25647527010. https://link.springer.com/article/10.1023%2FA%3A1025647527010

Between 2012 and 2013, the SOCE industry collapsed. Alan Chambers, president of Exodus International, told the Gay Christian Network in 2012 that all efforts to change sexual orientation were failures and potentially harmful. Exodus International publicly apologized for all the harm they caused and disbanded. Similarly, Dr. Spitzer published a letter in Archives of Sexual Behavior *in 2012 apologizing to the gay community. He acknowledged that his 2003 research was flawed, that sexual orientation cannot be changed, and SOCE harm clients.*

LETTER TO THE EDITOR
  Spitzer Reassesses His 2003 Study of Reparative Therapy of Homosexuality
  Robert L. Spitzer
  Several months ago, I told the *Editor of Archives of Behavior* that, because of my revised view of my study of reparative therapy changing sexual orientation (Spitzer, 2003a), I was considering writing something that would acknowledge that I now judged the major critiques of the study as largely correct. After discussing my revised view of the study with Gabriel Arana, a reporter for *The American Prospect*, and with Malcolm Ritter, an Associated Press science writer, I decided that I had to make public my current thinking about the study. Here it is.

Basic Research Question

From the beginning, it was: Can some version of reparative therapy enable individuals to change their sexual orientation from homosexual to heterosexual? Realizing that the study design made it impossible to answer this question, I suggested that the study could be viewed as answering the question: How do individuals undergoing reparative therapy describe changes in sexual orientation? A not very interesting question.
  The Fatal Flaw in the Study: There Was No Way to Judge the Credibility of Subject Reports of Change in Sexual Orientation
  I offered several (unconvincing) reasons why it was reasonable to assume that the participants' reports of change were credible and not self-deception or outright lying. But the simple fact is that there was no way to determine if the participants' accounts of change were valid.
  I believe I owe the gay community an apology for my study making unproven claims of the efficacy of reparative therapy. I also apologize to any gay person who wasted time and energy undergoing some form of reparative therapy because they

believed that I had proven that reparative therapy works with some "highly motivated" individuals.

Source: R. Spitzer. "Spitzer Reassesses His 2003 Study of Reparative Therapy
of Homosexuality." *Archives of Sexual Behavior*—Letter to the Editor, May 24, 2012.
doi: 10.1023/A:1025647527010. http://www.spolekmedikuceskych.cz/dokumenty/
Spitzr_apology.pdf

Document 130

THE SUPREME COURT RULES THAT ANTISODOMY LAWS ARE UNCONSTITUTIONAL: *LAWRENCE V. TEXAS*, 539 U.S. 558 (2003)

*On March 26, 2003, the U.S. Supreme Court heard arguments in the case of John Ged-
des Lawrence and Tyron Garner, Petitioners versus the state of Texas, on appeal from
a decision made by the U.S. Court of Appeals for the Fourteenth District of Texas. The
case involved an arrest by officers of the Harris County (Houston) police department of
two men engaged in sex in the home of one of the men. The question at hand was whether
the Fourteenth Amendment of the U.S. Constitution provided same-sex couples with
the same guarantee of privacy as it did for opposite-sex couples. In the case, the Court
was also asked to overrule its previous, precedent-setting case of Bowers v. Hardwick
(478 U.S. 186, 1986). The Court agreed with the plaintiffs in their decision and, at the
same time, rejected its earlier ruling in Bowers v. Hardwick. Writing for the majority, Justice Kennedy began his decision by noting that "liberty protects the person from
unwarranted government intrusions into a dwelling or other private places."*

LAWRENCE ET AL. v. TEXAS
CERTIORARI TO THE COURT OF APPEALS OF TEXAS, FOURTEENTH
DISTRICT
No. 02–102. Argued March 26, 2003–Decided June 26, 2003
Responding to a reported weapons disturbance in a private residence, Houston
police entered petitioner Lawrence's apartment and saw him and another adult man,
petitioner Garner, engaging in a private, consensual sexual act. Petitioners were
arrested and convicted of deviate sexual intercourse in violation of a Texas statute
forbidding two persons of the same sex to engage in certain intimate sexual conduct. In affirming, the State Court of Appeals held, *inter alia,* that the statute was not
unconstitutional under the Due Process Clause of the Fourteenth Amendment. The
court considered *Bowers* v. *Hardwick*, 478 U.S. 186, controlling on that point.
Held: The Texas statute making it a crime for two persons of the same sex
to engage in certain intimate sexual conduct violates the Due Process Clause.
pp. 564–579.

   (a) Resolution of this case depends on whether petitioners were free as adults to engage
   in private conduct in the exercise of their liberty under the Due Process Clause. . . .

The liberty protected by the Constitution allows homosexual persons the right to choose to enter upon relationships in the confines of their homes and their own private lives and still retain their dignity as free persons. Pp. 564–567.

(b) Having misapprehended the liberty claim presented to it, the *Bowers* Court stated that proscriptions against sodomy have ancient roots. 478 U.S., at 192. It should be noted, however, that there is no longstanding history in this country of laws directed at homosexual conduct as a distinct matter. Early American sodomy laws were not directed at homosexuals as such but instead sought to prohibit nonprocreative sexual activity more generally, whether between men and women or men and men. . . . American laws targeting same-sex couples did not develop until the last third of the 20th century. . . .

(c) *Bowers'* deficiencies became even more apparent in the years following its announcement. . . . In the United States, criticism of *Bowers* has been substantial and continuing, disapproving of its reasoning in all respects, not just as to its historical assumptions. . . .

(d) *Bowers'* rationale does not withstand careful analysis. . . .

Source: Lawrence v. Texas, 539 U.S. 558 (2003).

Document 131
UNITING AMERICAN FAMILIES ACT (2007)

Under U.S. immigration law, a man or woman may sponsor his or her wife or husband from a country other than the United States to live and work permanently in this country. Same-sex spouses do not have the same privilege. Even couples who have been legally married in the United States or some other country are not eligible to take advantage of the privileges offered by immigration law to heterosexual couples. In 2007, Senator Patrick Leahy (D-VT) sponsored legislation to revise immigration law so that it would apply to same-sex couples as well as to opposite-sex couples. The extract of Leahy's bill next shows how changes in definition and terminology in the original immigration laws would accomplish this objective.

Section 2 of the bill provides the fundamental changes required to make the necessary adjustments in existing immigration law.

SEC. 2. DEFINITIONS OF PERMANENT PARTNER AND PERMANENT PARTNERSHIP.
Section 101(a) (8 U.S.C. 1101(a)) is amended—

(1) in paragraph (15)(K)(ii), by inserting "or permanent partnership" after "marriage"; and

(2) by adding at the end the following:

"(52) The term 'permanent partner' means an individual 18 years of age or older who—

"(A) is in a committed, intimate relationship with another individual 18 years of age or older in which both individuals intend a lifelong commitment;

"(B) is financially interdependent with that other individual;

"(C) is not married to, or in a permanent partnership with, any individual other than that other individual;

"(D) is unable to contract with that other individual a marriage cognizable under this Act; and

"(E) is not a first, second, or third degree blood relation of that other individual.

"(53) The term 'permanent partnership' means the relationship that exists between 2 permanent partners."

SEC. 3. WORLDWIDE LEVEL OF IMMIGRATION.
Section 201(b)(2)(A)(i) (8 U.S.C. 1151(b)(2)(A)(i)) is amended—

1. by "spouse" each place it appears and inserting "spouse or permanent partner";

2. by striking "spouses" and inserting "spouse, permanent partner,";

3. by inserting "(or, in the case of a permanent partnership, whose permanent partnership was not terminated)" after "was not legally separated from the citizen"; and

4. by striking "remarries." and inserting "remarries or enters a permanent partnership with another person."

SEC. 4. NUMERICAL LIMITATIONS ON INDIVIDUAL FOREIGN STATES.

1. PER COUNTRY LEVELS.—Section 202(a)(4) (8 U.S.C. 1152(a)(4)) is amended—

   1. in the paragraph heading, by inserting ", PERMANENT PARTNERS," after "SPOUSES";

   2. in the heading of subparagraph (A), by inserting ", PERMANENT PARTNERS," after "SPOUSES"; and

   3. in the heading of subparagraph (C), by striking "AND DAUGHTERS" inserting "WITHOUT PERMANENT PARTNERS AND UNMARRIED DAUGHTERS WITHOUT PERMANENT PARTNERS."

2. RULES FOR CHARGEABILITY.—Section 202(b)(2) (8 U.S.C. 1152(b)(2)) is amended—

   1. by striking "his spouse" and inserting "his or her spouse or permanent partner";

   2. by striking "such spouse" each place it appears and inserting "such spouse or permanent partner"; and

   3. by inserting "or permanent partners" after "husband and wife."

[Following sections make changes in the allocation of immigrant visas, procedures for granting immigrant status, admission of immigrants for emergency purposes, inadmissible aliens, conditional permanent resident status, and related issues.]

Source: 110th Congress, 1st Session. S. 1328. (Washington, DC: Government Printing Office, May 8, 2007.)

Document 132

MATTHEW SHEPARD ACT (2007)

A number of federal laws currently protect a person from attacks based on race, color, religion, or national origin (so-called hate crimes), when that person is engaged in a federally protected activity. Those laws date to 1969 (encoded as 18 U.S.C. § 245(b)(2)) and have been amended and updated a number of times. Gender, gender orientation, and gender identity (as well as disability) are not currently included in federal hate crime legislation. For a number of years, efforts have been made to amend federal hate crimes laws to include these categories. In 2007, Representative Barney Frank (D-MA) introduced H.R. 1592, summarized here. The act was officially entitled the Local Law Enforcement Hate Crimes Prevention Act of 2007 and was popularly known as the Matthew Shepard Act, in honor of the Wyoming student murdered in 1998 because of his sexual orientation. That act passed the House of Representatives and the Senate as an amendment to the 2008 Department of Defense authorization bill. President Obama signed the bill into law on October 28, 2009, thereby extending federal hate crime law to include crimes motivated by the victim's perceived or actual sexual orientation, gender, gender identity, or disability. Section 6 of the bill, reprinted next, contains new provisions for those who are to be covered by this bill and by existing federal legislation on hate crimes.

110th CONGRESS
  1st Session
  H. R. 1592 AN ACT
  To provide Federal assistance to States, local jurisdictions, and Indian tribes to prosecute hate crimes, and for other purposes.
  Be it enacted by the Senate and House of Representatives of the United States of America in Congress assembled,
  SEC. 1. SHORT TITLE.
  This Act may be cited as the 'Local Law Enforcement Hate Crimes Prevention Act of 2007.'
  [Section 2 defines terms used in the bill.]
  [Section 3 is the core of the bill, outlining the types of support that the bill provides for various governmental agencies in the campaign against hate crimes.]
  [Section 4 describes the nature of grants to be awarded for the purposes of achieving the goals of this bill along with the mechanisms for awarding those grants.]
  [Section 5 authorizes funds for carrying out provisions of this bill.]
  SEC. 6. PROHIBITION OF CERTAIN HATE CRIME ACTS.
  (a) In General—Chapter 13 of title 18, United States Code, is amended by adding at the end the following:
  Sec. 249. Hate crime acts
  (a) In General—

  (1) OFFENSES INVOLVING ACTUAL OR PERCEIVED RACE, COLOR, RELIGION, OR NATIONAL ORIGIN—Whoever, whether or not acting under color of law,

willfully causes bodily injury to any person or, through the use of fire, a firearm, or an explosive or incendiary device, attempts to cause bodily injury to any person, because of the actual or perceived race, color, religion, or national origin of any person—

(A) shall be imprisoned not more than 10 years, fined in accordance with this title, or both; and

(B) shall be imprisoned for any term of years or for life, fined in accordance with this title, or both, if—

   (i) death results from the offense; or

   (ii) the offense includes kidnaping or an attempt to kidnap, aggravated sexual abuse or an attempt to commit aggravated sexual abuse, or an attempt to kill.

(2) OFFENSES INVOLVING ACTUAL OR PERCEIVED RELIGION, NATIONAL ORIGIN, GENDER, SEXUAL ORIENTATION, GENDER IDENTITY, OR DISABILITY—

(A) IN GENERAL—Whoever, whether or not acting under color of law, in any circumstance described in subparagraph (B), willfully causes bodily injury to any person or, through the use of fire, a firearm, or an explosive or incendiary device, attempts to cause bodily injury to any person, because of the actual or perceived religion, national origin, gender, sexual orientation, gender identity or disability of any person—

   (i) shall be imprisoned not more than 10 years, fined in accordance with

   (ii) this title, or both; and

   (iii) shall be imprisoned for any term of years or for life, fined in accordance

   (iv) with this title, or both, if—

      (I) death results from the offense; or

      (II) the offense includes kidnaping or an attempt to kidnap, aggravated sexual abuse or an attempt to commit aggravated sexual abuse, or an attempt to kill.

(B) CIRCUMSTANCES DESCRIBED—For purposes of subparagraph (A), the circumstances described in this subparagraph are that—

   (i) the conduct described in subparagraph (A) occurs during the course of, or as the result of, the travel of the defendant or the victim—

      (I) across a State line or national border; or

      (II) using a channel, facility, or instrumentality of interstate or foreign commerce;

   (ii) the defendant uses a channel, facility, or instrumentality of interstate or foreign commerce in connection with the conduct described in subparagraph (A);

   (iii) in connection with the conduct described in subparagraph (A), the defendant employs a firearm, explosive or incendiary device, or other weapon that has traveled in interstate or foreign commerce; or

(iv) the conduct described in subparagraph (A)—

   (I) interferes with commercial or other economic activity in which the victim is engaged at the time of the conduct; or

   (II) otherwise affects interstate or foreign commerce.

[The remainder of this section deals with additional definitions and provisions for enforcing this section of the act.]

[Section 7 is a standard part of many bills, indicating that, should any one section be found to be unconstitutional, that decision does not affect the remaining portions of the act.]

[Section 8 notes that no provision of this act is to infringe on a person's right of free speech.]

Source: 110th Congress, 1st Session, H.R. 1592.

Document 133

IN RE MARRIAGE CASES: OPINION (2008) CALIFORNIA'S BAN ON SAME-SEX MARRIAGES IS UNCONSTITUTIONAL

One of the most important legal breakthroughs in the matter of same-sex marriages was the decision by the California Supreme Court in May 2008 that state bans on such marriages are unconstitutional. In a 121-page, 4–3 decision, Chief Justice Ronald M. George laid out the majority's reasoning for this opinion. All citations in the following extract are omitted.

In *Lockyer v. City and County of San Francisco* . . ., this court concluded that public officials of the City and County of San Francisco acted unlawfully by issuing marriage licenses to same-sex couples in the absence of a judicial determination that the California statutes limiting marriage to a union between a man and a woman are unconstitutional. Our decision in *Lockyer* emphasized, however, that the substantive question of the constitutional validity of the California marriage statutes was not before this court in that proceeding, and that our decision was not intended to reflect any view on that issue. . . . The present proceeding, involving the consolidated appeal of six cases that were litigated in the superior court and the Court of Appeal in the wake of this court's decision in *Lockyer*, squarely presents the substantive constitutional question that was not addressed in *Lockyer*.

In considering this question, we note at the outset that the constitutional issue before us differs in a significant respect from the constitutional issue that has been addressed by a number of other state supreme courts and intermediate appellate courts that recently have had occasion, in interpreting the applicable provisions of their respective state constitutions, to determine the validity of statutory provisions or common law rules limiting marriage to a union of a man and a woman. . . . These courts, often by a one-vote margin . . ., have ruled upon the validity of statutory schemes that contrast with that of California, which in recent years has enacted comprehensive domestic partnership legislation under which a same-sex couple may enter into a legal relationship that affords the couple virtually all of the same substantive legal benefits and privileges, and imposes upon the couple virtually all of the same legal obligations and duties, that California law affords to and imposes upon a married couple. Past California cases explain that the constitutional validity of a challenged statute or statutes must be evaluated by taking into consideration all of the relevant statutory provisions that bear upon how the state treats the affected persons with regard to the subject at issue. . . . Accordingly, the legal issue we must resolve is not whether it would be constitutionally permissible under the California Constitution for the state to limit marriage only to opposite-sex couples while denying same-sex couples any opportunity to enter into an official relationship with all or virtually all of the same substantive attributes, but rather whether our state Constitution prohibits the state from establishing a statutory scheme in which both opposite-sex and same-sex couples are granted the right to enter into an officially recognized family relationship that affords all of the significant legal rights and obligations traditionally associated under state law with the institution of marriage, but under which the union of an opposite-sex couple is officially designated a "marriage" whereas the union of a same-sex couple is officially designated a "domestic partnership." The question we must address is whether, under these circumstances, the failure to designate the official relationship of same-sex couples as marriage violates the California Constitution. . . .

First, we must determine the nature and scope of the "right to marry"—a right that past cases establish as one of the fundamental constitutional rights embodied in the California Constitution. Although, as an historical matter, civil marriage and the rights associated with it traditionally have been afforded only to opposite-sex couples, this court's landmark decision 60 years ago in *Perez v. Sharp* (1948) 32 Cal.2d 7114—which found that California's statutory provisions prohibiting interracial marriages were inconsistent with the fundamental constitutional right to marry, notwithstanding the circumstance that statutory prohibitions on interracial marriage had existed since the founding of the state—makes clear that history alone is not invariably an appropriate guide for determining the meaning and scope of this fundamental constitutional guarantee. The decision in *Perez*, although rendered by a deeply divided court, is a judicial opinion whose legitimacy and constitutional soundness are by now universally recognized.

Furthermore, in contrast to earlier times, our state now recognizes that an individual's capacity to establish a loving and long-term committed relationship with another person and responsibly to care for and raise children does not depend upon the individual's sexual orientation, and, more generally, that an individual's sexual orientation—like a person's race or gender—does not constitute a legitimate basis upon which to deny or withhold legal rights. We therefore conclude that in view of the substance and significance of the fundamental constitutional right to form a family relationship, the California Constitution properly must be interpreted to guarantee this basic civil right to all Californians, whether gay or heterosexual, and to same-sex couples as well as to opposite-sex couples.

. . . . We therefore conclude that although the provisions of the current domestic partnership legislation afford same-sex couples most of the substantive elements embodied in the constitutional right to marry, the current California statutes nonetheless must be viewed as potentially impinging upon a same-sex couple's constitutional right to marry under the California Constitution . . . we conclude that strict scrutiny nonetheless is applicable here because (1) the statutes in question properly must be understood as classifying or discriminating on the basis of sexual orientation, a characteristic that we conclude represents—like gender, race, and religion—a constitutionally suspect basis upon which to impose differential treatment, and (2) the differential treatment at issue impinges upon a same-sex couple's fundamental interest in having their family relationship accorded the same respect and dignity enjoyed by an opposite-sex couple.

Accordingly, we conclude that to the extent the current California statutory provisions limit marriage to opposite-sex couples, these statutes are unconstitutional.

Source: In re Marriage Cases (2008). 43 Cal.4th 757 [76 Cal.Rptr.3d 683, 183 P.3d 384]. Available online at: http://www.courtinfo.ca.gov/opinions/documents/ S147999.PDF.

Document 134
IN RE MARRIAGE CASES: DISSENT (2008)

In the previous case, In re Marriages, *a dissenting opinion was offered by Associate Justice Marvin R. Baxter. His fundamental position is outlined in the following extract from his dissent.*

The majority opinion reflects considerable research, thought, and effort on a significant and sensitive case, and I actually agree with several of the majority's conclusions. However, I cannot join the majority's holding that the California Constitution gives same-sex couples a right to marry. In reaching this decision, I believe, the majority violates the separation of powers, and thereby commits profound error.

Only one other American state recognizes the right the majority announces today. So far, Congress, and virtually every court to consider the issue, has rejected it. Nothing in our Constitution, express or implicit, compels the majority's startling conclusion that the age-old understanding of marriage—an understanding recently confirmed by an initiative law—is no longer valid. California statutes already recognize same-sex unions and grant them all the substantive legal rights this state can bestow. If there is to be a further sea change in the social and legal understanding of marriage itself, that evolution should occur by similar democratic means. The majority forecloses this ordinary democratic process, and, in doing so, oversteps its authority.

The majority's mode of analysis is particularly troubling. The majority relies heavily on the Legislature's adoption of progressive civil rights protections for gays and lesbians to find a constitutional right to same-sex marriage. In effect, the majority gives the Legislature indirectly power that body does not directly possess to amend the Constitution and repeal an initiative statute. I cannot subscribe to the majority's reasoning, or to its result.

[At this point, Baxter acknowledges the points on which he agrees with the majority opinion. He then goes on to say, however, that:]

However, I respectfully disagree with the remainder of the conclusions reached by the majority.

The question presented by this case is simple and stark. It comes down to this: Even though California's progressive laws, recently adopted through the democratic process, have pioneered the rights of same-sex partners to enter legal unions with all the substantive benefits of opposite-sex legal unions, do those laws nonetheless violate the California Constitution because at present, in deference to long and universal tradition, by a convincing popular vote, and in accord with express national policy . . ., they reserve the label "marriage" for opposite-sex legal unions? I must conclude that the answer is no. The People, directly or through their elected representatives, have every right to adopt laws abrogating the historic understanding that civil marriage is between a man and a woman. The rapid growth in California of statutory protections for the rights of gays and lesbians, as individuals, as parents, and as committed partners, suggests a quickening evolution of community attitudes on these issues. . . .

But a bare majority of this court, not satisfied with the pace of democratic change, now abruptly forestalls that process and substitutes, by judicial fiat, its own social policy views for those expressed by the People themselves. Undeterred by the strong weight of state and federal law and authority, the majority invents a new constitutional right, immune from the ordinary process of legislative consideration. The majority finds that our Constitution suddenly demands no less than a permanent redefinition of marriage, regardless of the popular will.

Source: In re Marriage Cases (2008). 43 Cal.4th 757 [76 Cal.Rptr.3d 683, 183 P.3d 384]. Available online at: http://www.courtinfo.ca.gov/opinions/documents/ S147999.PDF.

Further Reading

Asseo, Laurie. 2000, January 15. "Gays, Free Speech Mark Boy Scout's Case." The Associate Press, *Amarillo Globe-News.*

Hoad, Neville. 2007. *African Intimacies: Race, Homosexuality, and Globalization.* Minneapolis: University of Minnesota Press.

Piontek, Thomas. 2006. *Queering Gay and Lesbian Studies.* Urbana: University of Illinois Press.

Ridinger, Robert B. (ed.). 2004. *Speaking for Our Lives: Historic Speeches and Rhetoric for Gay and Lesbian Rights (1892–2000).* New York: Harrington Park.

Schwarz, A. B. Christa. 2003. *Gay Voices of the Harlem Renaissance.* Bloomington: Indiana University Press.

Somerville, Siobhan B. 2000. *Queering the Color Line: Race and the Invention of Homosexuality in American Culture.* Durham, NC: Duke University Press.

Stewart, Chuck. 2001. *Homosexuality and the Law.* Boulder, CO: ABC-CLIO Publishers.

Stewart, Chuck. 2003. *Gay and lesbian Issues: A Contemporary Resource.* Boulder, CO: ABC-CLIO Publishers.

Stewart, Chuck. 2009. *The Greenwood Encyclopedia of LGBT Issues Worldwide.* Boulder, CO: Greenwood Publishing Group.

Chapter 11

2010s

Many long-time LGBT issues came to a head in the 2010s. After decades of controversy and ruining the lives of hundreds of thousands of LGBT military personnel, President Obama repealed "Don't Ask, Don't Tell" policy in 2010. Now openly LGBT people could serve in the military without fear of dishonorable discharge or brutal discrimination. Same-sex marriage also worked its way to the U.S. Supreme Court, and a majority of the judges ruled that disallowing same-sex couples the right to marry was a violation of the equal protection clause and therefore unconstitutional. LGBT people could now marry the person of their choice in all states. Of course, there was much brouhaha from conservatives and the Religious Right over same-sex marriage, and some clerks got their 15 minutes of fame for refusing to issue marriage licenses to same-sex couples. In each case, federal courts upheld the Supreme Court decision and enforced marriage equality.

There is a long history of attempts to change sexual orientation and make gay people "straight" (never the reverse). International organizations teamed up with religious conservatives and created "conversion" or "reparative" (to "repair" the spiritual damaged that causes someone to be homosexual) therapies. Many religious parents forced their children to attend conversion camps. All professional medical and psychological associations clearly state that the attempts to change sexual orientation are never successful and only lead to psychic trauma. Alan Chambers, the president of Exodus International, publicly apologized for the harm his organization caused in trying to change sexual orientation and further stated that it was never successful. Building on this momentum, California passed legislation forbidding licensed therapists from attempting to change the sexual orientation of minors. Similar legislation was passed in a number of other states and has been upheld in all courts.

With all these wins for equal rights, conservatives changed their focus away from same-sex marriage and the military to influencing state legislatures to pass versions of Religious Freedom Restoration Act (RAFA). Under the guise of supporting religious freedoms, RAFA allows businesses and government employees to discriminate against classes of people. The discussion invariably involves allowing discrimination against LGBT people. As of 2017, more than 100 antigay bills were pending in local and state legislatures. Tied to this backlash were attempts to prevent transgender people from using the bathroom that best suits their gender expression. "Bathroom" bills showed up in North Carolina, Texas, and other states.

In June 2016, a lone gunman entered the Pulse gay nightclub located in Orlando, Florida, and killed 49 people and wounded another 53. This was the worst mass murder in U.S. history and the worst hate crime committed against the

LGBT community. The motivation of the gunman was never discovered, and he was not identified as a terrorist, but his goal was to kill people within a gay bar. Although great strides have been made toward equal rights for all, conservative backlash and outright violence poses a constant threat.

Document 135

THE REPEAL OF "DON'T ASK, DON'T TELL" (2010)

"Don't Ask, Don't Tell" (DADT) was a policy signed into law in October 1993 by President Bill Clinton. He had promised during his presidential campaign to eliminate the barriers for homosexual men and women to serve in the military and to end the punishment of courts-martial for any service member found guilty of homosexual actions. The idea was a compromise by which the armed services would not seek to determine if a service member was homosexual.

In 2010, with the repeal of DADT, all servicemen and woman are free to serve in the military openly, regardless of their sexual orientation. On December 22, 2010, President Barack Obama signed the bill into law, though it was not officially enacted until September 20, 2011. The repeal of DADT has farther-reaching effects beyond those for active-duty homosexual service members. A result of this repeal is that servicemen and women who were discharged previously can re-enlist into the military if they so choose. Veterans who were separated from the military with a "less than honorable" or "dishonorable" discharge because of DADT as well as the pre–DADT era can have their discharge upgraded to "honorable" status, their records amended, and receive VA benefits.

Don't Ask, Don't Tell Repeal Act of 2010
An Act

To amend the Small Business Act with respect to the Small Business Innovation Research Program and the Small Business Technology Transfer Program, and for other purposes. <<NOTE: Dec. 22, 2010—[H.R. 2965]>>

Be it enacted by the Senate and House of Representatives of the United States of America in Congress assembled, <<NOTE: Don't Ask, Don't Tell Repeal Act of 2010. 10 USC 654 note.>>

SECTION 1. SHORT TITLE.

This Act may be cited as the "Don't Ask, Don't Tell Repeal Act of 2010."

SEC. 2. DEPARTMENT OF DEFENSE POLICY CONCERNING HOMOSEXUALITY IN THE ARMED FORCES.

(a) Comprehensive Review on the Implementation of a Repeal of 10 U.S.C. 654.—

(1) In general.—On March 2, 2010, the Secretary of Defense issued a memorandum directing the Comprehensive Review on the Implementation of a Repeal of 10 U.S.C. 654 (section 654 of title 10, United States Code).

(2) Objectives and scope of review.—The Terms of Reference accompanying the Secretary's memorandum established the following objectives and scope of the ordered review:

(A) Determine any impacts to military readiness, military effectiveness and unit cohesion, recruiting/ retention, and family readiness that may result from repeal of the law and recommend any actions that should be taken in light of such impacts.

(B) Determine leadership, guidance, and training on standards of conduct and new policies.

(C) Determine appropriate changes to existing policies and regulations, including but not limited to issues regarding personnel management, leadership and training, facilities, investigations, and benefits.

(D) Recommend appropriate changes (if any) to the Uniform Code of Military Justice.

(E) Monitor and evaluate existing legislative proposals to repeal 10 U.S.C. 654 and proposals that may be introduced in the Congress during the period of the review.

(F) Assure appropriate ways to monitor the workforce climate and military effectiveness that support successful follow-through on implementation.

(G) Evaluate the issues raised in ongoing litigation involving 10 U.S.C. 654. [[Page 124 STAT. 3516]]

Source: 111th Congress, Public Law 111–321.

Document 136

LAWSUIT BY *SEXUAL MINORITIES UGANDA V. SCOTT LIVELY* FOR PUSHING HIS ANTIGAY HATE IN A FOREIGN COUNTRY (2012)

Scott Lively, founder and president of Abiding Truth Ministries, traveled to Uganda in early 2000s to spread his gospel of hatred for gays. By 2009, the Ugandan legislator David Bahati sponsored the "Anti-Homosexuality Bill" that would have imposed the death sentence for anyone convicted of being a homosexual or supporting human rights for homosexuals. World leaders spoke out against the law, and it was shelved for a while.

In 2012, the Sexual Minorities Uganda (SMUG) filed suit in the United States against Lively stating that he conspired with Ugandan political and religious leaders to incite violence against LGBT people by whipping up antigay hysteria. Uganda experienced an increase in violence (including murder) against LGBT people because of Lively's activism. Inciting violence and persecution of lesbians and gay men is a violation of international law. The Alien Tort Statute (ATS) in the United States allows foreigners to sue in American court when international law is violated.

In late 2013, the Ugandan legislature passed a modified bill that eliminated the death provision but still imposed life imprisonment. As expected, violence against lesbians and gays increased significantly in Uganda.

UNITED STATES DISTRICT COURT
DISTRICT OF MASSACHUSETTS
SPRINGFIELD DIVISION
SEXUAL MINORITIES UGANDA
Plaintiff,
v.
SCOTT LIVELY, individually and as President of Abiding Truth Ministries
Defendant.

Introduction

1. This case is brought by SEXUAL MINORITIES UGANDA, an umbrella organization located in Kampala, Uganda, which represents the interests of its constituent member organizations in advocating for the rights of lesbian, gay, bisexual, transgender and intersex people ("LGBTI") in Uganda. It is brought against defendant Scott LIVELY, a U.S.-based attorney, author, evangelical minister and self-described world-leading expert on the "gay movement," for the decade-long campaign he has waged, in agreement and coordination with his Ugandan counterparts, to persecute persons on the basis of their gender and/or sexual orientation and gender identity.

2. The case is brought under the Alien Tort Statute ("ATS"), 28 U.S.C. §1350, which provides federal jurisdiction for "any civil action by an alien, for a tort only, committed in violation of the law of nations or a treaty of the United States." United States Supreme Court has affirmed the use of the ATS as a remedy for serious violations of international law norms that are widely accepted and clearly defined. *Sosa v. Alvarez-Machain,* 542 U.S. 692 (2004).

3. Persecution, as a crime against humanity that is universally proscribed and clearly defined in international law, is such a violation. Persecution is defined in international law as the "intentional and severe deprivation of fundamental rights contrary to international law by reason of the identity of the group or collectivity." *Rome Statute of the International Criminal Court,* Art. 7(2)(G). The prohibition on persecution protects individuals on the basis of their identity and punishes those who act in concert to deprive the rights of others on the basis of that identity.1 Persecution, by definition, is a group crime; it cannot be committed by one person acting alone.

4. Plaintiff also asserts tort claims which are cognizable under Massachusetts state law.

5. In very large part due to defendant LIVELY's contributions to the conspiracy to persecute LGBTI persons in Uganda, plaintiff SEXUAL MINORITIES UGANDA, as an entity, as well as its individual staff-members and member organizations, have suffered severe deprivations of fundamental rights. Their very existence has been criminalized and their physical safety threatened through a coordinated campaign, which LIVELY has largely initiated, instigated and directed, to strip way basic fundamental rights from people on the basis of their sexual orientation and gender identity and those who advocate on their behalf. To aid in doing so, LIVELY frequently attributes to the "genocidal" "gay movement" an irrepressible predilection to commit rape and child sexual abuse.

6. As set out in more detail below, SEXUAL MINORITIES UGANDA and the community they represent have endured severe discrimination in virtually every meaningful aspect of their civil and political lives; their association has been criminalized; their advocacy on issues central to their health and political participation has been suppressed and punished; and they have been subjected to cruel, inhuman and degrading treatment. Plaintiff's meetings and trainings have been raided and disbanded and its staff members have been arrested, subjected to humiliating and degrading treatment. Sexual Minorities Uganda has had to devote substantial resources and time in dealing with precarious and emergent situations in response to crises of individual LGBTI persons in the community who have been threatened, assaulted, harassed, falsely arrested and/or made homeless because of their real or perceived status as lesbian, gay, bisexual, transgender or intersex. Many individual members of SMUG and its constituent organizations live in persistent fear of harassment, arbitrary arrest and physical harm, even death.

7. According to LIVELY'S own admissions, his influence and work in Uganda date back at least a decade when he visited Uganda twice in 2002 to coordinate with his Ugandan counterparts, Stephen LANGA, a prominent and extremist anti-gay community leader and pastor, and Martin SSEMPA, also an anti-gay extremist activist and minister, to implement his strategies to dehumanize, demonize, silence, and further criminalize the LGBTI community. While their efforts were largely effective between 2002 and 2009, LIVELY's work took on a whole new level of urgency after a December 2008 court victory for LGBTI advocates which affirmed that they are entitled to the basic protections of law.

8. Spurred to action to counter the prospect of basic legal protections for LGBTI individuals, LIVELY and his co-conspirators, LANGA, SSEMPA, Minister of Ethics and Integrity James BUTURO and Member of Parliament David BAHATI, coordinated a dramatic, far-reaching response, which LIVELY and LANGA would later boast had the "effect of a nuclear bomb." LIVELY'S 2009 work in Uganda and his call to arms to fight against an "evil" and "genocidal," "pedophilic" "gay movement," which he likened to the Nazis and Rwandan murderers, ignited a cultural panic and atmosphere of terror that radically intensified the climate of hatred in which LIVELY's goals of persecution could advance. Shortly after LIVELY'S pivotal 2009 work in Uganda, one Member of Parliament expressed, "We must exterminate homosexuals before they exterminate society."

9. Among the shocking, repressive measures undertaken after 2009, is the introduction of the Anti-Homosexuality Bill (also referred to as the "Kill the Gays Bill"), which proposed the *death penalty* for a second conviction of consensual sex between adults of the same gender, and imprisonment for failure to report on others suspected of being "homosexual," and for advocacy in any way on issues related to homosexuality. While LIVELY has half-heartedly tried to distance himself from the death penalty provision of the bill, he still considers it the "lesser of two evils" as compared to recognizing the humanity of LGBTI individuals or permitting their speech or advocacy.

10. In 2010, a tabloid newspaper—parroting characterizations of gays and lesbians repeatedly made to Ugandan officials by LIVELY—published an article "outing" SEXUAL MINORITIES UGANDA Advocacy Officer David Kato (and others), under the headline, "HANG THEM." Some of the advocates featured in that article received

heightened death threats, and one of them, Mr. Kato, is now dead. In February and June of 2012, trainings on human rights for LGBTI organizations were raided by Ugandan government officials who declared the gatherings "illegal." In February 2012, the Minister of Ethics and Integrity called those gathered there "terrorists." One of the organizers had to flee in order to avoid arrest and detention.

11. This case seeks to challenge LIVELY'S conduct through his involvement in a conspiracy to severely deprive people of their fundamental rights on the basis of their identity. It is not, therefore, premised on his anti-gay speech or writings. LIVELY'S prolific, willfully misinformed and inflammatory rhetoric about the "evil" gay movement with his frequent depictions of gay people as "genocidal," "psychopathic," "exceptionally brutal and savage" and as child predators in Uganda and elsewhere, are relevant pieces of evidence insofar as they demonstrate his overall discriminatory purpose and the shared intent of the conspiracy to persecute in which he is intimately involved. They do not form an independent basis for a cause of action.

12. The context of LIVELY's actions is important. His insidious rhetoric and attempts at overt discrimination against, and ultimately eradication of, a minority community might not take hold in many places not also struggling in the way Uganda has been in the battle against the spread of HIV/AIDS, poverty and armed conflict. Yet, it is specifically because he knew Uganda presented fertile ground and—through his willing accomplices with access to political power—a realistic opportunity to meaningfully provoke and bring about the persecution of the LGBTI community, that he focused much of his decade-long efforts there.

13. SEXUAL MINORITIES UGANDA seeks a judgment declaring that LIVELY's actions are illegal, in violation of international law and Plaintiff's fundamental human rights. SEXUAL MINORITIES UGANDA also seeks compensatory and punitive damages for violations of their fundamental rights, and injunctive relief enjoining the Defendant from undertaking further actions to strip away and/or deprive Plaintiff and LGBTI community in Uganda of their fundamental rights, including their rights to freedom of expression, association and assembly, to be free from torture and other cruel, inhuman and degrading treatment, and arbitrary arrest and detention, as part of his effort to enshrine and legalize discrimination on the basis of sexual orientation and gender identity.

14. By seeking to enjoin, punish, and deter LIVELY's actions, SEXUAL MINORITIES UGANDA acts now to prevent the further escalation of persecution in Uganda before it reaches an even more lethal stage.

Source: Sexual Minorities Uganda v. Scott Lively, individually and as President of Abiding Truth Ministries, U.S. District Court Massachusetts, 3;12-CV-30051, July 13, 2012. https://ccrjustice.org/sites/default/files/assets/files/SMUG-Amended-Complaint.pdf

The suit was dismissed in June 2017 by U.S. District Court judge Michael Ponsor on a technical issue. In 2013, the U.S. Supreme Court limited the extraterritorial reach of the Alien Tort Statute (ATS). As such, the suit did not provide sufficient evidence that the actions taken by Lively were taken on American soil. Judge Ponsor issued a scathing ruling affirming SMUG's charges against Lively of "bigotry' and that Lively "aided and abetted a vicious and frightening campaign of repression against LGBTI persons in Uganda."

Anyone reading this memorandum should make no mistake. The question before the court is not whether Defendant's actions in aiding and abetting efforts to demonize, intimidate, and injure LGBTI people in Uganda constitute violations of international law. They do. The much narrower and more technical question posed by Defendant's motion is whether the limited actions taken by Defendant on American soil in pursuit of his odious campaign are sufficient to give this court jurisdiction over Plaintiff's claims. Since they are not sufficient, summary judgment is appropriate for this, and only this, reason.

Source: Sexual Minorities Uganda v. Scott Lively, U.S. District Court Massachusetts, 12-cv-30051-MAP, June 5, 2017. https://ccrjustice.org/sites/default/files/attach/2017/06/350_2017-06-05_ORDER%20granting%20Def%27s%20MSJ_2.pdf

Document 137

CALIFORNIA'S LAW BANS SEXUAL ORIENTATION CHANGE EFFORTS (SOCE): SENATE BILL NO. 1172 (2012)

A major recent achievement in gay civil rights in California was the approval of SB 1172 in 2012. It prohibited mental health providers from using "conversion" therapy on persons under the age of 18 (also known as sexual orientation change effort—SOCE). Conversion (also known as "reparative") therapy claims to help LGBT people become heterosexual. Every reputable medical and psychology professional organization agrees that it is not possible to change a person's sexual orientation or gender identity and such treatments increase feelings of worthlessness that may proceed to suicide. The legality of the bill was upheld by the Ninth Circuit court, and the U.S. Supreme Court affirmed in 2014. A number of other states have implemented similar legislation that has been upheld in state courts. The National Center for Lesbian Rights is the organization providing leadership in assisting states to adopt similar bills to stop SOCE.

An act to add Article 15 (commencing with Section 865) to Chapter 1 of Division 2 of the Business and Professions Code, relating to healing arts.

[Approved by Governor September 30, 2012. Filed with Secretary of State September 30, 2012.]

Legislative Counsel's Digest

SB 1172, Lieu. Sexual orientation change efforts.

Existing law provides for licensing and regulation of various professions in the healing arts, including physicians and surgeons, psychologists, marriage and family therapists, educational psychologists, clinical social workers, and licensed professional clinical counselors.

This bill would prohibit a mental health provider, as defined, from engaging in sexual orientation change efforts, as defined, with a patient under 18 years of age. The bill would provide that any sexual orientation change efforts attempted on a patient under 18 years of age by a mental health provider shall be considered unprofessional conduct and shall subject the provider to discipline by the provider's licensing entity.

The bill would also declare the intent of the Legislature in this regard.

Source: California Senate Bill No. 1172 (2012).

Document 138

PRESIDENT OF EXODUS INTERNATIONAL APOLOGIES FOR THE HURT, PAIN, AND FAILURE CAUSED BY THEIR DECADES-LONG EFFORT TO CHANGE SEXUAL ORIENTATION (2013)

"Love in Action" was an "ex-gay" ministry founded in 1973 San Francisco that provided spiritual counseling for gay men wishing to reduce their homosexual feelings and become heterosexual. Often referred to as "reparative" therapy (i.e., to "repair" their "broken" sexual orientation), an international organization formed to help coordinate worldwide change efforts. Exodus International would grow to include over 270 ministries. Various psychological techniques were used to attempt to change a person's sexual orientation including shock therapy, talk therapy, behavioral modification, aversion therapy, and prayer (often humorously referred to as "pray away the gay").

In June 2013, Exodus International announced that they were shutting down their original operation and restarting a separate ministry for a new generation. In the announcement, Alan Chambers, then president of Exodus, issued a letter in which he apologized for decades of suffering inflicted onto LGBT people in trying to change their sexual orientation.

To Members of the LGBTQ Community:

In 1993 I caused a four-car pileup. In a hurry to get to a friend's house, I was driving when a bee started buzzing around the inside of my windshield. I hit the bee and it fell on the dashboard. A minute later it started buzzing again with a fury. Trying to swat it again I completely missed the fact that a city bus had stopped three cars in front of me. I also missed that those three cars were stopping, as well. Going 40 miles an hour I slammed into the car in front of me causing a chain reaction. I was injured and so were several others. I never intended for the accident to happen. I would never have knowingly hurt anyone. But I did. And it was my fault. In my rush to get to my destination, fear of being stung by a silly bee, and selfish distraction, I injured others.

I have no idea if any of the people injured in that accident have suffered long term effects. While I did not mean to hurt them, I did. The fact that my heart wasn't malicious did not lessen their pain or their suffering. I am very sorry that I chose to be distracted that fall afternoon, and that I caused so much damage to people and property. If I could take it all back I absolutely would. But I cannot. I pray that everyone involved in the crash has been restored to health.

Recently, I have begun thinking again about how to apologize to the people that have been hurt by Exodus International through an experience or by a message. I have heard many firsthand stories from people called ex-gay survivors. Stories of people who went to Exodus affiliated ministries or ministers for help only to experience more trauma. I have heard stories of shame, sexual misconduct, and false hope. In every case that has been brought to my attention, there has been swift action resulting in the removal of these leaders and/or their organizations. But rarely was there an apology or a public acknowledgement by me.

And then there is the trauma that I have caused. There were several years that I conveniently omitted my ongoing same-sex attractions. I was afraid to share them as readily and easily as I do today. They brought me tremendous shame and I hid them in the hopes they would go away. Looking back, it seems so odd that I thought I could do something to make them stop. Today, however, I accept these feelings as parts of my life that will likely always be there. The days of feeling shame over being human in that way are long over, and I feel free simply accepting myself as my wife and family does. As my friends do. As God does.

Never in a million years would I intentionally hurt another person. Yet, here I sit having hurt so many by failing to acknowledge the pain some affiliated with Exodus International caused, and by failing to share the whole truth about my own story. My good intentions matter very little and fail to diminish the pain and hurt others have experienced on my watch. The good that we have done at Exodus is overshadowed by all of this.

Friends and critics alike have said it's not enough to simply change our message or website. I agree. I cannot simply move on and pretend that I have always been the friend that I long to be today. I understand why I am distrusted and why Exodus is hated.

Please know that I am deeply sorry. I am sorry for the pain and hurt many of you have experienced. I am sorry that some of you spent years working through the shame and guilt you felt when your attractions didn't change. I am sorry we promoted sexual orientation change efforts and reparative theories about sexual orientation that stigmatized parents. I am sorry that there were times I didn't stand up to people publicly "on my side" who called you names like sodomite— or worse. I am sorry that I, knowing some of you so well, failed to share publicly that the gay and lesbian people I know were every bit as capable of being amazing parents as the straight people that I know. I am sorry that when I celebrated a person coming to Christ and surrendering their sexuality to Him that I callously celebrated the end of relationships that broke your heart. I am sorry that I have communicated that you and your families are less than me and mine.

More than anything, I am sorry that so many have interpreted this religious rejection by Christians as God's rejection. I am profoundly sorry that many have walked away from their faith and that some have chosen to end their lives. For the rest of my life I will proclaim nothing but the whole truth of the Gospel, one of grace, mercy and open invitation to all to enter into an inseverable relationship with almighty God.

I cannot apologize for my deeply held biblical beliefs about the boundaries I see in scripture surrounding sex, but I will exercise my beliefs with great care and respect for those who do not share them. I cannot apologize for my beliefs about marriage. But I do not have any desire to fight you on your beliefs or the rights that you seek. My beliefs about these things will never again interfere with God's command to love my neighbor as I love myself.

You have never been my enemy. I am very sorry that I have been yours. I hope the changes in my own life, as well as the ones we announce tonight regarding Exodus International, will bring resolution, and show that I am serious in both my regret and my offer of friendship. I pledge that future endeavors will be focused on peace and common good.

Moving forward, we will serve in our pluralistic culture by hosting thoughtful and safe conversations about gender and sexuality, while partnering with others to reduce fear, inspire hope, and cultivate human flourishing.

Source: Melissa Steffan. "Alan Chambers Apologizes to Gay Community, Exodus International to Shut Down." *Christianity Today*, June 21, 2013. http://www.chris tianitytoday.com/news/2013/june/alan-chambers-apologizes-to-gay-community-exodus.html

Document 139

U.S. SUPREME COURT LETS BAN AGAINST PROPOSITION 8 STAND, ALLOWING SAME-SEX MARRIAGE IN CALIFORNIA: *HOLLINGSWORTH ET AL. V. PERRY ET AL.* (2013)

In 2008, the California Supreme Court held that limiting marriage to opposite-sex couples violated the California Constitution, but soon after that state voters passed Proposition 8, a ballot initiative that amended the state constitution to define marriage as a union between a man and a woman. In the six months between the ban being lifted, and Proposition 8 again banning same-sex marriage, some 18,000 marriage licenses were issued. However, in 2010, Judge Vaughn R. Walker ruled that the ban against same-sex marriage was unconstitutional since it violated both the due process and equal protection clauses of the U.S. Constitution; however, he stayed his decision to allow supporters of Proposition 8 to prepare an appeal.

Governor Arnold Schwarzenegger and Attorney General Jerry Brown of California refused to officially appeal on behalf of the ban, and so representatives of the proponents for Proposition 8 appealed to the Supreme Court. On June 26, 2013, the Court refused the appeal based on their decision that the petitioners did not have standing to official appeal the ban. As such, same-sex marriages resumed.

SUPREME COURT OF THE UNITED STATES
  Syllabus
  HOLLINGSWORTH et al. v. PERRY et al. certiorari to the united states court of appeals for the ninth circuit No. 12–144. Argued March 26, 2013–Decided June 26, 2013
  After the California Supreme Court held that limiting marriage to opposite-sex couples violated the California Constitution, state voters passed a ballot initiative known as Proposition 8, amending the State Constitution to define marriage as a union between a man and a woman. Respondents, same-sex couples who wish to marry, filed suit in federal court, challenging Proposition 8 under the Due Process and Equal Protection Clauses of the Fourteenth Amendment, and naming as defendants California's Governor and other state and local officials responsible for enforcing California's marriage laws. The officials refused to defend the law, so the District Court allowed petitioners—the initiative's official proponents—to intervene to defend it. After a bench trial, the court declared Proposition 8 unconstitutional and enjoined the public officials named as defendants from enforcing the law. Those officials elected not to appeal, but petitioners did. The Ninth Circuit certified a question to the California Supreme Court: whether official proponents of a ballot initiative have authority to assert the State's interest in defending the constitutionality of the initiative when public officials refuse to do so. After the California Supreme Court answered in the affirmative, the Ninth Circuit concluded that petitioners had standing under federal law to defend Proposition 8's constitutionality.

Source: Perry v. Brown, 671 F.3d 1052 (9th Cir. 2012) renamed Hollingsworth v. Perry (formerly Perry v. Brown and Perry v. Schwarzenegger), 570 U.S._____ (2013) (Docket No. 12–144).

Document 140

SUPREME COURT RULES THAT DOMA IS UNCONSTITUTIONAL: *UNITED STATES V. WINDSOR, EXECUTOR OF THE ESTATE OF SPYER, ET AL.* (2013)

Edith Windsor had been married in Toronto, Canada, to Thea Spyer. When Spyer died in 2009, Windsor could not claim the federal estate tax exemption for surviving spouses, because of the federal Defense of Marriage Act (DOMA), which excludes same-sex *partners. Instead, she had to pay $363,053 in estate taxes. On June 26, 2013, the U.S. Supreme Court ruled that the DOMA, which President Bill Clinton had signed into law in 1996, is unconstitutional. The Court found the act to be in violation of the due process clause of the Fifth Amendment. The ruling, a landmark, paves the way for further legislation on behalf of same-sex marriage.*

UNITED STATES v. WINDSOR, Executor of the ESTATE OF SPYER, et al. (2013)

SUPREME COURT OF THE UNITED STATES
Syllabus
UNITED STATES v. WINDSOR, executor of the ESTATE OF SPYER, et al.
certiorari to the United States court of appeals for the second circuit
No. 12–307. Argued March 27, 2013–Decided June 26, 2013

The State of New York recognizes the marriage of New York residents Edith Windsor and Thea Spyer, who wed in Ontario, Canada, in 2007. When Spyer died in 2009, she left her entire estate to Windsor. Windsor sought to claim the federal estate tax exemption for surviving spouses, but was barred from doing so by §3 of the federal Defense of Marriage Act (DOMA), which amended the Dictionary Act—a law providing rules of construction for over 1,000 federal laws and the whole realm of federal regulations—to define "marriage" and "spouse" as excluding same-sex partners. Windsor paid $363,053 in estate taxes and sought a refund, which the Internal Revenue Service denied. Windsor brought this refund suit, contending that DOMA violates the principles of equal protection incorporated in the Fifth Amendment. While the suit was pending, the Attorney General notified the Speaker of the House of Representatives that the Department of Justice would no longer defend §3's constitutionality. In response, the Bipartisan Legal Advisory Group (BLAG) of the House of Representatives voted to intervene in the litigation to defend §3's constitutionality. The District Court permitted the intervention. On the merits, the court ruled against the United States, finding §3 unconstitutional and ordering the Treasury to refund Windsor's tax with interest.

The Second Circuit affirmed. The United States has not complied with the judgment.

Held:

. . . .

2. DOMA is unconstitutional as a deprivation of the equal liberty of persons that is protected by the Fifth Amendment. Pp. 13–26.

   (a) By history and tradition the definition and regulation of marriage has been treated as being within the authority and realm of the separate States. . . . DOMA rejects this long-established precept. . . .

   (b) By seeking to injure the very class New York seeks to protect, DOMA violates basic due process and equal protection principles applicable to the Federal Government. . . .

Opinion

Justice Kennedy delivered the opinion of the Court.

I. . . . Section 3 is at issue here. It amends the Dictionary Act in Title 1, §7, of the United States Code to provide a federal definition of "marriage" and "spouse." Section 3 of DOMA provides as follows:

"In determining the meaning of any Act of Congress, or of any ruling, regulation, or interpretation of the various administrative bureaus and agencies of the United States, the word 'marriage' means only a legal union between one man and one woman as husband and wife, and the word 'spouse' refers only to a person of the opposite sex who is a husband or a wife." 1 U.S.C. §7.

It held that §3 of DOMA is unconstitutional and ordered the Treasury to refund the tax with interest. . . .

The class to which DOMA directs its restrictions and restraints are those persons who are joined in same-sex marriages made lawful by the State. DOMA singles out a class of persons deemed by a State entitled to recognition and protection to enhance their own liberty. It imposes a disability on the class by refusing to acknowledge a status the State finds to be dignified and proper. DOMA instructs all federal officials, and indeed all persons with whom same-sex couples interact, including their own children, that their marriage is less worthy than the marriages of others. The federal statute is invalid, for no legitimate purpose overcomes the purpose and effect to disparage and to injure those whom the State, by its marriage laws, sought to protect in personhood and dignity. By seeking to displace this protection and treating those persons as living in marriages less respected than others, the federal statute is in violation of the Fifth Amendment. This opinion and its holding are confined to those lawful marriages.

The judgment of the Court of Appeals for the Second Circuit is affirmed.

It is so ordered.

Source: United States v. Windsor, 570 U.S. ___ (2013).

Document 141

ARIZONA'S ATTEMPTED LEGISLATION TO ALLOW DISCRIMINATION BASED ON RELIGIOUS FREEDOM: SB1062 (2014)

On February 20, 2014, the Arizona state legislature approved SB1062, a bill described by its proponents as preserving religious freedom. Opponents to the bill described it as promoting discrimination against LGBT people, as it would allow business owners legally to refuse service to anyone based on the business owners' religious beliefs. There was a large and concerted protest against the bill, supported by LGBT people, some members of clergy, other concerned citizens, and probably most tellingly, by Arizona business organizations, including the Phoenix Chamber of Commerce, who did not want to see conventions and tourists boycott the state. The NFL and Super Bowl organizers also threatened to pull out of the 2015 Super Bowl game to be played in Glendale, a suburb of Phoenix, if the bill had been signed into law. The bill was sent to the Republican governor, Jan Brewer, for her signature on February 24, but, on February 26, she vetoed it. Many other states, however, are planning such legislation, and on April 3, 2014, Mississippi passed a similar law, called the Mississippi Freedom Act, signed by the governor.

An Act

amending sections 41–1493 and 41–1493.01, Arizona Revised Statutes; relating to the free exercise of religion.

Be it enacted by the Legislature of the State of Arizona:

Section 1. Section 41–1493, Arizona Revised Statutes, is amended to read:

41–1493. Definitions

In this article, unless the context otherwise requires:

1. "Demonstrates" means meets the burdens of going forward with the evidence and of persuasion.

2. "Exercise of religion" means the practice or observance of religion, including the ability to act or refusal to act in a manner substantially motivated by a religious belief, whether or not the exercise is compulsory or central to a larger system of religious belief.

3. "Government" includes this state and any agency or political subdivision of this state.

4. "Nonreligious assembly or institution" includes all membership organizations, theaters, cultural centers, dance halls, fraternal orders, amphitheaters and places of public assembly regardless of size that a government or political subdivision allows to meet in a zoning district by code or ordinance or by practice.

5. "Person" includes any individual, association, partnership, corporation, church, religious assembly or institution, estate, trust, foundation or other legal entity.

6. "Political subdivision" includes any county, city, including a charter city, town, school district, municipal corporation or special district, any board, commission or agency of a county, city, including a charter city, town, school district, municipal corporation or special district or any other local public agency.

7. "Religion-neutral zoning standards":

   (a) Means numerically definable standards such as maximum occupancy codes, height restrictions, setbacks, fire codes, parking space requirements, sewer capacity limitations and traffic congestion limitations.

   (b) Does not include:

      (i) Synergy with uses that a government holds as more desirable.

      (ii) The ability to raise tax revenues.

8. "Suitable alternate property" means a financially feasible property considering the person's revenue sources and other financial obligations with respect to the person's

exercise of religion and with relation to spending that is in the same zoning district or in a contiguous area that the person finds acceptable for conducting the person's religious mission and that is large enough to fully accommodate the current and projected seating capacity requirements of the person in a manner that the person deems suitable for the person's religious mission.

9. "Unreasonable burden" means that a person is prevented from using the person's property in a manner that the person finds satisfactory to fulfill the person's religious mission.

Sec. 2. Section 41–1493.01, Arizona Revised Statutes, is amended to read: 41–1493.01. Free exercise of religion protected; definition

1. Free exercise of religion is a fundamental right that applies in this state even if laws, rules or other government actions are facially neutral.

2. Except as provided in subsection C of this section, state action shall not substantially burden a person's exercise of religion even if the burden results from a rule of general applicability.

3. State action may substantially burden a person's exercise of religion only if the opposing party demonstrates that application of the burden to the person's exercise of religion in this particular instance is both:

(a) In furtherance of a compelling governmental interest.

(b) The least restrictive means of furthering that compelling governmental interest.

4. A person whose religious exercise is burdened in violation of this section may assert that violation as a claim or defense in a judicial proceeding, regardless of whether the government is a party to the proceeding. The person asserting such a claim or defense may obtain appropriate relief. A party who prevails in any action to enforce this article against a government shall recover attorney fees and costs.

5. For the purposes of this section, the term substantially burden is intended solely to ensure that this article is not triggered by trivial, technical or de minimis infractions.

6. For the purposes of this section, "state action" means any action by the government or the implementation or application of any law, including state and local laws, ordinances, rules, regulations and policies, whether statutory or otherwise, and whether the implementation or application is made or attempted to be made by the government or nongovernmental persons.

Source: Arizona SB1062 (2014).

Document 142

THE NATIONAL ASSOCIATION FOR RESEARCH AND THERAPY OF HOMOSEXUALITY (NARTH) AND ITS PURPOSE (2014)

The National Association for Research and Therapy of Homosexuality states that it promotes psychological understanding of the cause, treatment, and behavior patterns associated with homosexuality and its cure. It has long sought to show that "homosexuals" can be cured and homosexuality is not an identity and orientation that people are born with.

NARTH's Purpose

During the last 25 years, powerful political pressures have done much to erode scientific study of homosexuality. As a result, there is now great misunderstanding surrounding this issue. Because of the angry tenor of the debate, many researchers have been intimidated, we believe, into trading the truth for silence.

As clinicians, we have witnessed the intense suffering caused by homosexuality, which many of our members see as a "failure to function according to design." Homosexuality distorts the natural bond of friendship that would naturally unite persons of the same sex. It threatens the continuity of traditional male-female marriage—a bond which is naturally anchored by the complementarily of the sexes, and long been considered essential for the protection of children.

In males, homosexuality is associated with poor relationship with father; difficulty individuating from mother; a sense of masculine deficit; and a persistent belief of having been different from, and misunderstood by, same-sex childhood peers. In adulthood we also see a persistent pattern of maladaptive behaviors and a documented higher level of psychiatric complaints.

Professionals who belong to NARTH comprise a wide variety of men and women who *defend the right to pursue change of sexual orientation.* Most NARTH members consider homosexuality to be developmental in origin. Others simply defend the right to psychological care regardless of the genesis of homosexuality. They have joined NARTH because they know the client's right to choose his own direction of treatment must be protected.

It is NARTH's aim to provide a different perspective. Particularly, we want to clarify that homosexuality is not "inborn," and that gays are not "a people," in the same sense that an ethnic group is "a people"—but instead, they are (like all of us) simply individuals who exhibit particular patterns of feelings and behavior.

Source: National Association for Research & Therapy of Homosexuality, http:// narth.com/ menus/statement.html. Used by permission of NARTH.

Document 143
SAME-SEX MARRIAGE LEGALIZED (2015)

After years of struggle and the slow acceptance by many states to license and recognize same-sex marriage, a split existed between the circuit courts about the legality of same-sex marriage and the requirement to recognize such marriages from other states. By early 2015, 36 states and the District of Columbia and Guam issued marriage licenses to

same-sex couples. However, the Sixth Circuit ruled that the ban against same-sex mar-
riage enforced by Minnesota and litigated in Baker v. Nelson was constitutional.

In a 5–4 decision, the U.S. Supreme Court ruled that marriage is a fundamental right
that could not be denied to same-sex couples. The Obergefell v. Hodges decision over-
turned Baker v. Nelson. The equal protection clause, due process clause, and Fourteenth
Amendment to the U.S. Constitution were interpreted to allow marriage equality.

OBERGEFELL ET AL. v. HODGES, DIRECTOR, OHIO DEPARTMENT OF HEALTH, ET AL.

CERTIORARI TO THE UNITED STATES COURT OF APPEALS FOR THE SIXTH CIRCUIT

No. 14–556. Argued April 28, 2015–Decided June 26, 2015*

Held: The Fourteenth Amendment requires a State to license a marriage between two people of the same sex and to recognize a marriage between two people of the same sex when their marriage was lawfully licensed and performed out-of-State. Pp. 3–28.

(a) Before turning to the governing principles and precedents, it is appropriate to note the history of the subject now before the Court. Pp. 3–10.

(1) The history of marriage as a union between two persons of the opposite sex marks the beginning of these cases. To the respondents, it would demean a timeless institution if marriage were extended to same-sex couples. But the petitioners, far from seeking to devalue marriage, seek it for themselves because of their respect—and need—for its privileges and responsibilities, as illustrated by the petitioners' own experiences. Pp. 3–6.

(2) The history of marriage is one of both continuity and change.

Changes, such as the decline of arranged marriages and the abandonment of the law of coverture, have worked deep transformations in the structure of marriage, affecting aspects of marriage once viewed as essential. These new insights have strengthened, not weakened, the institution. Changed understandings of marriage are characteristic of a Nation where new dimensions of freedom become apparent to new generations.

This dynamic can be seen in the Nation's experience with gay and lesbian rights. Well into the 20th century, many States condemned same-sex intimacy as immoral, and homosexuality was treated as an illness. Later in the century, cultural and political developments allowed same-sex couples to lead more open and public lives. Extensive public and private dialogue followed, along with shifts in public attitudes. Questions about the legal treatment of gays and lesbians soon reached the courts, where they could be discussed in the formal discourse of the law. In 2003, this Court overruled its 1986 decision in Bowers v. Hardwick, 478 U.S. 186, which upheld a Georgia law that criminalized certain homosexual acts, concluding laws making same-sex intimacy a crime "demea[n] the lives of homosexual persons." Lawrence v. Texas, 539 U.S. 558, 575. In 2012, the federal Defense of Marriage Act was also struck down. United States v. Windsor, 570 U.S. ___. Numerous same-sex marriage cases reaching the federal courts and state supreme courts have added to the dialogue. Pp. 6–10.

(b) The Fourteenth Amendment requires a State to license a marriage between two people of the same sex. Pp. 10–27.

(1) The fundamental liberties protected by the Fourteenth Amendment's Due Process Clause extend to certain personal choices central to individual dignity and autonomy, including intimate choices defining personal identity and beliefs. See, e.g., Eisenstadt v. Baird, 405 U.S. 438, 453; Griswold v. Connecticut, 381 U.S. 479, 484–486. Courts must exercise reasoned judgment in identifying interests of the person so fundamental that the State must accord them its respect. History and tradition guide and discipline the inquiry but do not set its outer boundaries. When new insight reveals dis- cord between the Constitution's central protections and a received legal stricture, a claim to liberty must be addressed.

Applying these tenets, the Court has long held the right to marry is protected by the Constitution. For example, Loving v. Virginia, 388 U.S. 1, 12, invalidated bans on interracial unions, and Turner v. Safley, 482 U.S. 78, 95, held that prisoners could not be denied the right to marry. To be sure, these cases presumed a relationship involving opposite-sex partners, as did Baker v. Nelson, 409 U.S. 810, a one-line summary decision issued in 1972, holding that the exclusion of same-sex couples from marriage did not present a substantial federal question. But other, more instructive precedents have expressed broader principles. See, e.g., Lawrence, supra, at 574. In assessing whether the force and rationale of its cases apply to same-sex couples, the Court must respect the basic reasons why the right to marry has been long protected. See, e.g., Eisenstadt, supra, at 453–454. This analysis compels the conclusion that same-sex couples may exercise the right to marry. Pp. 10–12.

(2) Four principles and traditions demonstrate that the reasons marriage is fundamental under the Constitution apply with equal force to same-sex couples. The first premise of this Court's relevant precedents is that the right to personal choice regarding marriage is inherent in the concept of individual autonomy. This abiding connection between marriage and liberty is why Loving invalidated interracial marriage bans under the Due Process Clause. See 388 U.S., at 12. Decisions about marriage are among the most intimate that an individual can make. See Lawrence, supra, at 574. This is true for all persons, whatever their sexual orientation.

A second principle in this Court's jurisprudence is that the right to marry is fundamental because it supports a two-person union unlike any other in its importance to the committed individuals. The intimate association protected by this right was central to Griswold v. Connecticut, which held the Constitution protects the right of married couples to use contraception, 381 U.S., at 485, and was acknowledged in Turner, supra, at 95. Same-sex couples have the same right as opposite-sex couples to enjoy intimate association, a right extending beyond mere freedom from laws making same-sex intimacy a criminal offense. See Lawrence, supra, at 567.

A third basis for protecting the right to marry is that it safeguards children and families and thus draws meaning from related rights of childrearing, procreation, and education. See, e.g., Pierce v. Society of Sisters, 268 U.S. 510. Without the recognition, stability, and predictability marriage offers, children suffer the stigma of knowing their families are somehow lesser. They also suffer the significant material costs of being raised by unmarried parents, relegated to a more difficult and uncertain family life. The marriage laws at issue thus harm and humiliate the children of same-sex couples. See Windsor, supra, at ___. This does not mean that the right to marry is less meaningful for those who do not or cannot have children. Precedent protects the right of a married couple not to procreate, so the right to marry cannot be conditioned on the capacity or commitment to procreate.

Finally, this Court's cases and the Nation's traditions make clear that marriage is a keystone of the Nation's social order. See Maynard v. Hill, 125 U.S. 190, 211. States have contributed to the fundamental character of marriage by placing it at the center of many facets of the legal and social order. There is no difference between same- and opposite-sex couples with respect to this principle, yet same-sex couples are denied the constellation of benefits that the States have linked to marriage and are consigned to an instability many opposite-sex couples would find intolerable. It is demeaning to lock same-sex couples out of a central institution of the Nation's society, for they too may aspire to the transcendent purposes of marriage.

The limitation of marriage to opposite-sex couples may long have seemed natural and just, but its inconsistency with the central meaning of the fundamental right to marry is now manifest. Pp. 12–18.

(3) The right of same-sex couples to marry is also derived from the Fourteenth Amendment's guarantee of equal protection. The Due Process Clause and the Equal Protection Clause are connected in a profound way. Rights implicit in liberty and rights secured by equal protection may rest on different precepts and are not always co- extensive, yet each may be instructive as to the meaning and reach of the other. This dynamic is reflected in Loving, where the Court invoked both the Equal Protection Clause and the Due Process Clause; and in Zablocki v. Redhail, 434 U.S. 374, where the Court invalidated a law barring fathers delinquent on child-support payments from marrying. Indeed, recognizing that new insights and societal understandings can reveal unjustified inequality within fundamental institutions that once passed unnoticed and unchallenged, this Court has invoked equal protection principles to invalidate laws imposing sex-based inequality on marriage, see, e.g., Kirchberg v. Feenstra, 450 U.S. 455, 460–461, and confirmed the relation between liberty and equality, see, e.g., M. L. B. v. S. L. J., 519 U.S. 102, 120–121.

The Court has acknowledged the interlocking nature of these constitutional safeguards in the context of the legal treatment of gays and lesbians. See Lawrence, 539 U.S., at 575. This dynamic also applies to same-sex marriage. The challenged laws burden the liberty of same-sex couples, and they abridge central precepts of equality. The marriage laws at issue are in essence unequal: Same-sex couples are denied benefits afforded opposite-sex couples and are barred from exercising a fundamental right. Especially against a long history of disapproval of their relationships, this denial works a grave and continuing harm, serving to disrespect and subordinate gays and lesbians. Pp. 18–22.

(4) The right to marry is a fundamental right inherent in the liberty of the person, and under the Due Process and Equal Protection Clauses of the Fourteenth Amendment couples of the same-sex may not be deprived of that right and that liberty. Same-sex couples may exercise the fundamental right to marry. Baker v. Nelson is overruled. The State laws challenged by the petitioners in these cases are held invalid to the extent they exclude same-sex couples from civil marriage on the same terms and conditions as opposite-sex couples. Pp. 22–23.

(5) There may be an initial inclination to await further legislation, litigation, and debate, but referenda, legislative debates, and grassroots campaigns; studies and other writings; and extensive litigation in state and federal courts have led to an enhanced understanding of the issue. While the Constitution contemplates that democracy is the appropriate process for change, individuals who are harmed need not await legislative action before asserting a fundamental right. Bowers, in effect, upheld state action that denied gays and lesbians a fundamental right. Though it was eventually repudiated, men and women suffered pain and humiliation in the interim, and the effects of these injuries no doubt lingered long after Bowers was overruled. A ruling against same-sex couples would have the same effect and would be unjustified under the Fourteenth Amendment. The petitioners' stories show the urgency of the issue they present to the Court, which has a duty to address these claims and answer these questions. Respondents' argument that allowing same-sex couples to wed will harm marriage as an institution rests on a counterintuitive view of opposite-sex couples' decisions about marriage and parenthood. Finally, the First Amendment ensures that religions, those who adhere to religious doctrines, and others have protection as they seek to teach the principles that are so fulfilling and so central to their lives and faiths. Pp. 23–27.

(c) The Fourteenth Amendment requires States to recognize same-sex marriages validly performed out of State. Since same-sex couples may now exercise the fundamental right to marry in all States, there is no lawful basis for a State to refuse to recognize a lawful same-sex marriage performed in another State on the ground of its same-sex character. Pp. 27–28.

772 F. 3d 388, reversed.

Source: Obergefell v. Hodges, 576 U.S. ___ (2015). https://www.supremecourt.gov/opinions/14pdf/14-556_3204.pdf

Document 144

COUNTY CLERK KIM DAVIS RELEASED FROM JAIL FOR DEFYING COURT ORDER TO ISSUE MARRIAGE LICENSES TO SAME-SEX COUPLES (2015)

County Clerk Kim Davis of Rowan County, Kentucky, made international news when she denied marriage licenses to same-sex couples following the U.S. Supreme Court ruling in favor of same-sex marriage in Obergefell v. Hodges (2015). Davis cited God and her *faith when defending her decision, refusing to sign any marriage licenses or supply any marriage certificates.*

In response, the ACLU and four couples whom Davis denied filed a lawsuit against the County Clerk (Miller v. Davis). However, while the plaintiffs won the case, Davis refused to follow court orders and issue marriage licenses. She was held in contempt and sent to jail for five days, then released after vowing not to interfere with her fellow clerks as they issued marriage licenses to same-sex couples. The couples won and the court ordered Davis to comply with the decision and issue marriage licenses. She refused, was held in contempt of court, and placed in jail. The other clerks in the office took over her duties and issued marriage certificates to both same- and opposite-sex couples. Her actions came to world attention, and conservatives, religious leaders, and Republican politicians rushed to Kentucky to hold press conferences in her support. After five days, she was released once she promised not to interfere with the other deputy clerks performing their lawful duties in issuing marriage licenses.

In May 2017, a Cincinnati federal appeals court granted the right for the plaintiffs to sue Davis for damages. The case is still pending. The following is an excerpt from the original court case that, eventually, landed Davis in jail.

Source: Alan Blinder and Richard Perez-Pena. "Kentucky Clerk Denies Same-Sex Marriage Licenses, Defying Court." *The New York Times*, September 1, 2015. Retrieved September 1, 2015. https://www.nytimes.com/2015/09/02/us/same-sex-marriage-kentucky-kim-davis.html?_r=0

UNITED STATES DISTRICT COURT EASTERN DISTRICT OF KENTUCKY NORTHERN DIVISION AT ASHLAND

APRIL MILLER et al. ALL OTHERS SIMILARLY SITUATED, Plaintiffs,

v.

KIM DAVIS, both individually and in her official capacity as Rowan County Clerk, and ROWAN COUNTY, KENTUCKY,

PROPOSED CLASS ACTION

COMPLAINT Preliminary Statement

1. In this 42 U.S.C. § 1983 class action suit, Plaintiffs assert claims on their own behalves as well as on behalf of the putative class for the constitutional violations resulting from the Rowan County Clerk's policy of refusing to issue marriage licenses to applicants who are otherwise legally permitted to marry. Specifically, because Rowan County Clerk Kim Davis objects on religious grounds to the Supreme Court's decision recognizing that states cannot deny the privileges of marriage to same-sex couples, Defendant Davis has adopted a policy and/or practice of refusing to issue marry licenses to any couple, same-sex or different-sex, even though they are otherwise legally entitled to marry.

Plaintiffs are two same-sex couples and two different-sex couples who are in committed relationships. They assert individual and official capacity as-applied claims against Defendant Davis. They seek compensatory and punitive damages for Defendant Davis' refusal to issue them marriage licenses in violation of their rights under the Fourteenth Amendment's Due Process Clause, and they request preliminary and permanent injunctive relief compelling Defendant Davis to receive and process their applications and issue them marriage licenses. Plaintiffs also assert a claim pursuant to Monell v. Dept. of Social Services, 436 U.S. 658 (1978), against Defendant Rowan County, Kentucky for damages due the uncon-stitutional policy or practice adopted by Defendant Davis, a county official with final policymaking authority. . . .

Factual Allegations

. . . .

16. On Monday, June 29, 2015, Defendant Davis adopted an official policy of refusing to issue any marriage licenses. [Plaintiffs' Exhibit 1: J. CHEVES, *Several Kentucky county clerks defy same-sex marriage ruling, refuse to issue marriage licenses* ("Pl. Exh. 1"), at 2.] Defendant Davis declared that the policy was adopted because of "deep religious convictions" which would not "allow" her to issue same-sex marriage licenses. [Plaintiffs' Exhibit 2: ANDREW WOLFSON, *Gay marriage ruling defied by some Ky clerks* ("Pl. Exh. 2"), at 2.]

Source: Miller et al. v. Kim Davis, US District Court Eastern District of Kentucky, 2015. https://www.aclu-ky.org/sites/default/files/wp-content/uploads/2015/07/Rowan-complaint.pdf

Document 145

BAPTIST PASTOR CALLS ON GOD TO KILL MORE GAYS AFTER THE PULSE GAY NIGHTCLUB MASSACRE IN ORLANDO, FLORIDA (2016)

In the early morning of June 12, 2016, Omar Mateen, a U.S. born citizen, used a semi-automatic rifle and pistol to kill 49 and wound another 53 people at the Orlando, Florida, gay nightclub—Pulse. At the time, it was the deadliest mass shooting by a single shooter in U.S. history. Immediately the media claimed this was a terrorist attack and "straight washed" the event failing to mention that it was a gay nightclub.

Why did Omar Mateen attack the people at Pulse? It will most likely remain a mys-tery. The FBI interviewed over 500 people and concluded that he was born in the United States to immigrant parents, pledged allegiance to Hezbollah, ISIS, and Al-Qaeda (three organizations that are at war with each other indicating how ignorant he was of Middle East politics), was not radicalized through directed effort, was not religious, admired authority (including NYPD) and obsessed with guns and violence, was racist, a school bully who was expelled often for violence, beat his two wives and was seeing another woman who was not his current wife, expressed antigay sentiments although witnesses claimed to have seen him at the gay nightclub many times before the shooting, did not have an account with any of the gay dating or hookup sites, and, perhaps, struggled with his own same-sex attraction.

But does it matter? This was an attack on gay people in a gay establishment with a high-power weapon by someone who purposefully wanted them dead. It really doesn't

matter if the gunman was Muslim, or it was an act of "terror," or the results of gay self-loathing. They were gay people (and some friends and parents) enjoying each other's company in a safe place; and they were killed for being at the gay club. This was an antigay hate crime.

Yet, within the first 24 hours of the massacre, right-wing talking heads, church leaders, puffed up conservative TV and radio pundits, and political opportunists tried to blame Muslims for the deaths. The comments from some religious leaders were shocking. Just days after the shooting, Pastor Roger Jimenez of Verity Baptist Church in Sacramento released a YouTube video of a speech he made claiming Christians shouldn't mourn the "death of 50 sodomites. . . . The tragedy is that more of them didn't die . . . I think that's great" (Bever 2016). The same day, preacher Steven Anderson in Tempe, Arizona, celebrated the mass murders by posting his own YouTube video (Parkman 2016), saying that "there are 50 less pedophiles in this world," and later added, "There's no tragedy. I wish the government would round them [gays] all up, put them up against a wall, put a firing squad in front of them and blow their brains out" (Tribune Media Wire 2016; Joe.My.God 2016). In Fort Worth, Pastor Donnie Romero of the Stedfast Baptist Church prayed that god would finish off the shooting victims in intensive care (Foster 2016).

Christian Pastor Calls Orlando Massacre "Good News"

Claiming "homosexuals are a bunch of disgusting perverts," Pastor Steven Anderson celebrates the Orlando nightclub shooting.

In a twisted video recently uploaded to YouTube, Pastor Steven Anderson of Faithful Word Baptist Church argues that the mass shooting that left at least 50 dead and scores more wounded at a gay nightclub in Florida is "good news" because "homosexuals are a bunch of disgusting perverts."

In his hateful rant Pastor Anderson says he is "not sad," and says he is "not gonna cry" about the horrific massacre, because the victims were just "disgusting homosexuals at a gay bar."

The following is an excerpt from his hateful rant:

> The good news is that there's 50 less pedophiles in this world, because, you know, these homosexuals are a bunch of disgusting perverts and pedophiles. That's who was a victim here, are a bunch of, just, disgusting homosexuals at a gay bar, okay?
>
> But the bad news is that this is now gonna be used, I'm sure, to push for gun control, where, you know, law-abiding normal Americans are not gonna be allowed to have guns for self-defense. And then I'm sure it's also gonna be used to push an agenda against so-called "hate speech." So Bible-believing Christian preachers who preach what the Bible actually says about homosexuality—that it's vile, that it's disgusting, that they're reprobates—you know, we're gonna be blamed. Like, "It's all extremism! It's not just the Muslims, it's the Christians!" I'm sure that that's coming. I'm sure that people are gonna start attacking, you know, Bible-believing Christians now, because of what this guy did.

Now let me just be real clear: I've never advocated for violence. I don't believe in, you know, taking the law into our own hands. I would never go in and shoot up a gay bar—so-called. I don't believe it's right for us to just be a vigilante. . . . But I will say this: The Bible says that homosexuals should be put to death, in Leviticus 20:13. Obviously, it's not right for somebody to just, you know, shoot up the place, because that's not going through the proper channels. But these people all should have been killed, anyway, but they should have been killed through the proper channels, as in they should have been executed by a righteous government that would have tried them, convicted them, and saw them executed. Because, in Leviticus 20:13, God's perfect law, he put the death penalty on murder, and he also put the death penalty on homosexuality. That's what the Bible says, plain and simple.

So, you know, the good news is that at least 50 of these pedophiles are not gonna be harming children anymore. The bad news is that a lot of the homos in the bar are still alive, so they're gonna continue to molest children and recruit people into their filthy homosexual lifestyle.

. . .

I'm not sad about it, I'm not gonna cry about it. Because these . . . 50 people in a gay bar that got shot up, they were gonna die of AIDS, and syphilis, and whatever else. They were all gonna die early, anyway, because homosexuals have a 20-year shorter life-span than normal people, anyway . . .

For those unfamiliar with Pastor Anderson, he is an obnoxious Christian extremist with a history of preaching a hateful and extreme Christian fundamentalism. Previously the Arizona pastor has called for the public execution of gays and lesbians, and more recently prayed for the death of Caitlyn Jenner.

In addition, the controversial pastor has used the Bible to explain why women should not have the right to vote, the right to work outside the home, or the right to seek a divorce.

Bottom line: Pastor Anderson is a dangerous Christian extremist who takes the Bible literally, even when doing so leads to morally reprehensible positions, such as defending slavery, or defending the death penalty for gays.

Source: Michael Stone. "Christian Pastor Calls Orlando Massacre 'Good News.'" *Patheos,* June 12, 2016. http://www.patheos.com/blogs/progressivesecularhuman ist/2016/06/christian-pastor-calls-orlando-massacre-good-news/. The original video by Steven Anderson may be viewed at: https://www.youtube.com/watch?v=w83k IAfuKoE

Document 146

BILLS TO RESTRICT TRANSGENDER PEOPLE FROM USING PUBLIC BATHROOMS PASSED IN NORTH CAROLINA (2016)

As the LGBT rights movement makes strides toward equality, there are often back-lashes from conservatives and the Religious Right in the form of passing local and state

ordinances against LGBT people or behavior. In the mid-2010s, a rash of "bathroom bills" were considered and passed by some states that targeted transgender people. North Carolina passed "An Act to Provide for Single-Sex Multiple Occupancy Bathroom and Changing Facilities in Schools and Public Agencies and to Create Statewide Consistency in Regulation of Employment and Public Accommodations" (commonly referred to as "House Bill 2" or HB2) in March 2016. The bill legislated that individuals may only use bathrooms and changing facilities that match the sex on their birth certificates. Obviously, such laws impact transgender people since their gender presentation is different from the sex recorded on their birth certificates. Proponents of such laws view them as "common sense" to provide safety in bathrooms from sexual predators whereas LGBT people see them as discriminatory. The "safety" claim is a smokescreen. There has never been a recorded case of a transgender person accosting someone in a bathroom, whereas, in contrast, many Republican politicians have been arrested and convicted of solicitation in public bathrooms. People already use bathrooms that accommodate all genders (like the portable bathrooms found at outdoor sporting or musical events, or bathrooms located in small businesses or bathrooms at home) without incident. Likewise, how does one administer such a law? Is there to be a monitor at all bathrooms to check birth certificates? And does this monitor require you to disrobe to check genitalia? The law provided no funding or guidance about how it was to be enforced. Police departments in Asheville, Greensboro, Raleigh, and Wilmington expressed discontent over the vagueness of the law. The law is unenforceable and reveals its true political goal—to legalize discrimination against transgender people.

After the passage of HB2, there was a great outcry of complaints against North Carolina legislature and governor. The U.S. Department of Justice sued Governor Pat McCrory, claiming the law violated Title VII of the Civil Rights Act, Title IX of the Education Amendments of 1972, and the Violence Against Women Act. Because of the law, many states issued travel bans for government employees to not visit North Carolina. Many private businesses (film, sports, musical events) pulled out of the state, and many announced their intention to not conduct business in the state. The ACLU, Lambda Legal, and Equality North Carolina filed suit against the bill. Besides the lawsuits, economic threats, and great pressure applied by the National Collegiate Athletic Association (NCAA), the governor and legislature issued a partial repeal of HB2 in March 30, 2017. The partial repeal did not satisfy either conservative or equal-rights groups.

Similar bills are working their way through many state legislatures.

GENERAL ASSEMBLY OF NORTH CAROLINA
SECOND EXTRA SESSION 2016
SESSION LAW 2016–3
HOUSE BILL 2

AN ACT TO PROVIDE FOR SINGLE-SEX MULTIPLE OCCUPANCY BATHROOM AND CHANGING FACILITIES IN SCHOOLS AND PUBLIC AGENCIES AND TO CREATE STATEWIDE CONSISTENCY IN REGULATION OF EMPLOYMENT AND PUBLIC ACCOMMODATIONS.

. . . .

The General Assembly of North Carolina enacts:

PART I. SINGLE-SEX MULTIPLE OCCUPANCY BATHROOM AND CHANGING FACILITIES

SECTION 1.1. G.S. 115C-47 is amended by adding a new subdivision to read: "(63) To Establish Single-Sex Multiple Occupancy Bathroom and Changing Facilities.—Local boards of education shall establish single-sex multiple occupancy bathroom and changing facilities as provided in G.S. 115C-521.2."

SECTION 1.2. Article 37 of Chapter 115C of the General Statutes is amended by adding a new section to read:

"§ 115C-521.2. Single-sex multiple occupancy bathroom and changing facilities.

(a) Definitions.—The following definitions apply in this section:

(1) Biological sex.—The physical condition of being male or female, which is stated on a person's birth certificate.

(2) Multiple occupancy bathroom or changing facility.—A facility designed or designated to be used by more than one person at a time where students may be in various states of undress in the presence of other persons. A multiple occupancy bathroom or changing facility may include, but is not limited to, a school restroom, locker room, changing room, or shower room.

(3) Single occupancy bathroom or changing facility.—A facility designed or designated to be used by only one person at a time where students may be in various states of undress. A single occupancy bathroom or changing facility may include, but is not limited to, a single stall restroom designated as unisex or for use based on biological sex.

(b) Single-Sex Multiple Occupancy Bathroom and Changing Facilities.—Local boards of education shall require every multiple occupancy bathroom or changing facility that designated for student use to be designated for and used only by students based on their biological sex.

(c) Accommodations Permitted.—Nothing in this section shall prohibit local boards of education from providing accommodations such as single occupancy bathroom or changing facilities or controlled use of faculty facilities upon a request due to special circumstances, but in no event shall that accommodation result in the local boards of education allowing a student to use a multiple occupancy bathroom or changing facility designated under subsection (b) of this section for a sex other than the student's biological sex.

(d) Exceptions.—This section does not apply to persons entering a multiple occupancy bathroom or changing facility designated for use by the opposite sex:

(1) For custodial purposes.

(2) For maintenance or inspection purposes.

(3) To render medical assistance.

(4) To accompany a student needing assistance when the assisting individual is an employee or authorized volunteer of the local board of education or the student's parent or authorized caregiver.

(5) To receive assistance in using the facility.

(6) To accompany a person other than a student needing assistance.

(7) That has been temporarily designated for use by that person's biological sex."

. . . .

Approved 9:57 p.m. this 23rd day of March, 2016

Source: General Assembly of North Carolina, Second Extra Session, 2016, House Bill 2. http://www.ncleg.net/Sessions/2015E2/Bills/House/PDF/H2v4.pdf

Document 147

NATIONAL CENTER FOR LESBIAN RIGHTS SUES UTAH OVER "NO-PROMO HOMO" LAW (2016)

Public school curricula have always been a battleground between opposing forces of what should and should not be taught using taxpayer money. One contentious area has been instruction on human sexuality and, in particular, anything that does not conform to heterosexist norms about marriage and sexuality. Many states have written specific guidelines in their statewide curricula restricting information about homosexuality. These "no promo homo laws" not only prevent any positive discussion about homosexuality, but they, instead, also present homosexuality as diseased, deviant, and a mental illness, and promote heterosexuality and marriage between one man and one woman as the desirable way to live. States such as Alabama, Arizona, Louisiana, Mississippi, Oklahoma, South Carolina, and Texas have specific guidelines that are anti-LGBT.

For example, Utah Education Code required materials adopted by local school boards to "comply with state law and state board rules emphasizing abstinence before marriage and fidelity after marriage, and prohibiting instruction in the advocacy of homosexuality" Utah Code § 53A-13-101. Equality Utah filed a lawsuit against the Utah State Board of Education in October 21, 2016, to strike the offending language. After much pressure and national media, the state legislature passed SB196 to remove the phrase "the advocacy of homosexuality" from the law.

EQUALITY UTAH et al v. UTAH STATE BOARD OF EDUCATION

Complaint for Declaratory and Injunctive Relief

Introduction

1. This action seeks to enjoin enforcement of Utah laws that infringe upon the constitutional rights of students and teachers by facially targeting lesbian, gay, and bisexual persons for disparate treatment, by prohibiting positive student and teacher speech about "homosexuality," while permitting positive speech about

the sexual orientation of heterosexual persons, and by prohibiting the equal treatment of student clubs that are supportive of students who are lesbian, gay, bisexual, or transgender ("LGBT"). The state laws and regulations challenged in this action—hereinafter the "Anti-Gay School Laws"—expressly prohibit speech that "advocat[es] homosexuality" in public school classrooms and student clubs. Moreover, some local school officials have applied the Anti-Gay School Laws to speech about transgender persons as well and, in at least one instance, have refused to protect a gender non-conforming student from bullying and harassment. Facially and as applied, the Anti-Gay School Laws violate Title IX of the Education Amendments of 1972, 20 U.S.C. §§ 1681–1688 ("Title IX"), the Equal Access Act, 20 U.S.C. §§ 4071–4074 ("EAA"), and the Equal Protection Clause of the Fourteenth Amendment to the United States Constitution.

2. The Anti-Gay School Laws violate the Equal Protection Clause of the Fourteenth Amendment by expressly singling out a class of persons—those who are "homosexual"—for negative treatment by prohibiting classroom instruction and extracurricular activities that "advoca[te] . . . homosexuality" without imposing any comparable restriction on speech about heterosexuality. This discriminates against students and teachers on the basis of sexual orientation and sex in violation of the Equal Protection Clause of the Fourteenth Amendment.

3. In addition, the Anti-Gay School Laws violate the Free Speech Clause of the First Amendment by prohibiting student and teacher speech that expresses a positive view about "homosexuality." In practice, these laws are used by some school officials to silence virtually any reference even to the existence of LGBT persons, while imposing no such restrictions on speech about heterosexuality or heterosexual persons or on speech that expresses negative views about "homosexuality" or LGBT persons. These restrictions constitute impermissible content and viewpoint discrimination and also impose an overbroad and impermissibly vague restriction on protected speech, all in violation of the Free Speech Clause of the First Amendment.

4. The Anti-Gay School Laws also violate Title IX by creating a hostile environment for LGBT students and by discouraging and, in some cases, preventing teachers and other school officials from appropriately supporting LGBT students or protecting them against bullying and harassment.

5. The Anti-Gay School Laws also violate the EAA by prohibiting the equal treatment of, and imposing impermissible restrictions upon the speech of, student clubs that address the topic of "homosexuality," while imposing no such restrictions on student clubs addressing heterosexuality or heterosexual persons.

6. Research has found that laws that prohibit the expression of positive views about "homosexuality" in public schools, like the Anti-Gay School Laws here, "can have a significant negative effect on the actions of teachers and other school staff toward LGBT students.". . . Such laws foster school climates that stigmatize and isolate LGBT youth, putting them at heightened risk of bullying and discouraging and preventing them from participating openly and equally in school activities.

7. The Anti-Gay School Laws were enacted in order to express moral disapproval of "homosexuality" and of LGBT persons and to discriminate against them. They do not serve any legitimate state interest.

8. In sum, the Anti-Gay School Laws single out "homosexuality" and LGBT persons for negative treatment, improperly restrict student and teacher speech about

"homosexuality" and LGBT persons, and create a culture of silence and non-acceptance for LGBT students and teachers, all of which puts LGBT students at heightened risk of isolation, harassment, and long-term negative impacts on their health and well-being while serving no legitimate state interest. Plaintiffs have sustained severe and irreparable harm due to the Anti-Gay School Laws. Accordingly, the Court should declare the Anti-Gay School Laws unconstitutional and in violation of federal education law, and enjoin their enforcement.

. . . .

Source: Equality Utah v. Utah State Board of Education. US District Court of Utah, Central Division, October 2016. http://www.nclrights.org/wp-content/uploads/2016/10/Equality-Utah-v.-Utah-State-Board-of-Education-Complaint.pdf

Document 148

APOLOGY FOR PAST ANTIGAY DISCRIMINATION MADE BY STATE DEPARTMENT REMOVED FROM WEB SITE WHEN DONALD TRUMP ASSUMES THE U.S. PRESIDENCY (2017)

For decades, open lesbians and gay men were prevented from working at the U.S. Department of State. If employees were discovered to be LGBT, their employment would be terminated and future benefits withheld. Only in the past decade has the restriction on LGBT employees been relaxed through presidential executive orders.

John Kerry was appointed as secretary of state by President Obama. In 2015, Kerry created a Special Envoy for the Human Rights of LGBTI Persons—the first time such a specific task group was created in the State Department. It is from that task force that specific recommendations were put into action to protect the rights of LGBT employees in the State Department. John Kerry issued a formal apology for past discriminations in January 2017 that was posted to the State Department's Web site. Within just a few weeks and the after the inauguration of President Trump, the apology was removed from the State Department's Web site with no explanation. Many other Web pages disappeared from government Web sites after Trump took charge including any dealing with LGBT issues, civil rights, climate change, as well as pages in other languages such as Spanish.

Apology for Past Discrimination toward Employees and Applicants Based on Sexual Orientation

Press Statement
John Kerry
Secretary of State
Washington, DC
January 9, 2017

Throughout my career, including as Secretary of State, I have stood strongly in support of the LGBTI community, recognizing that respect for human rights must include respect for all individuals. LGBTI employees serve as proud members of the State Department and valued colleagues dedicated to the service of our country. For the past several years, the Department has pressed for the families of LGBTI officers to have the same protections overseas as families of other officers. In 2015, to further promote LGBTI rights throughout the world, I appointed the first ever Special Envoy for the Human Rights of LGBTI Persons.

In the past—as far back as the 1940s, but continuing for decades—the Department of State was among many public and private employers that discriminated against employees and job applicants on the basis of perceived sexual orientation, forcing some employees to resign or refusing to hire certain applicants in the first place. These actions were wrong then, just as they would be wrong today.

On behalf of the Department, I apologize to those who were impacted by the practices of the past and reaffirm the Department's steadfast commitment to diversity and inclusion for all our employees, including members of the LGBTI community.

Source: John Kerry. Apology for Past Discrimination toward Employees and Applicants Based on Sexual Orientation. U.S. Department of State, January 9, 2017. Available at: https://www.state.gov/secretary/remarks/2017/01/266711.htm

Document 149

FEDERAL APPEALS COURT RULES THE 1964 CIVIL RIGHTS ACT PROTECTS LGBT EMPLOYEES FROM WORKPLACE DISCRIMINATION (2017)

Title VII of the 1964 Civil Rights Act included "sex" as a protected class from discrimination in the workplace. Unfortunately, the term sex was not defined. Courts relied upon common understanding when cases claiming sex discrimination reached their dockets. The academic understanding of "sex" has expanded and deepened considerably in the past 50 years. Sex may encompass sexual orientation, gender, gender presentation, sex roles, primary and secondary sexual characteristics, transgender and intersex people, and other intersectionalities and descriptions. Slowly, courts gained a greater understanding of these refinements and applied Title VII to an ever-greater number of classes of Americans.

A truly pivotal court case was decided by the Seventh District Court of Appeals. Here, Kimberly Hively sued Ivy Tech Community College over being fired for being a lesbian. Hively was an instructor at Ivy Tech and was seen kissing her then-girlfriend in the parking lot of the school. Her first suit was dismissed by the court when it claimed Title VII did not protect employees from antigay discrimination. Lambda Legal helped with her appeal to the Seventh Circuit Court in April 2015. The three-judge panel ruled against Hively, and she requested a rehearing by the full panel. The panel reached an 8–3 ruling in favor of Hively in April 2017. Chief Judge Diane Wood wrote:

". . . Hively represents the ultimate case of failure to conform to the female stereotype (at least as understood in a place such as modern America, which views heterosexuality as the norm and other forms of sexuality as exceptional): she is not heterosexual. Our panel described the line between a gender nonconformity claim and one based on sexual orientation as gossamer-thin; we conclude that it does not exist at all. Hively's claim is no different from the claims brought by women who were rejected for jobs in traditionally male workplaces, such as fire departments, construction, and policing. The employers in those cases were policing the boundaries of what jobs or behaviors they found acceptable for a woman (or in some cases, for a man)."

At this time, less than half the states have antidiscrimination laws. This ruling would effectively extend workplace protection for LGBT employees from antigay discrimination in all states. It is anticipated that this ruling will be challenged in other federal courts and eventually the U.S. Supreme Court.

United States Court of Appeals For the Seventh Circuit
No. 15–1720 KIMBERLY HIVELY,
Plaintiff-Appellant,
v.
IVY TECH COMMUNITY COLLEGE OF INDIANA, *Defendant-Appellee.*
Appeal from the United States District Court for the Northern District of Indiana, South Bend Division. No. 3:14-cv-1791—**Rudy Lozano**, *Judge.*
ARGUED NOVEMBER 30, 2016–DECIDED APRIL 4, 2017
Title VII of the Civil Rights Act of 1964 makes it unlawful for employers subject to the Act to discriminate on the basis of a person's "race, color, religion, sex, or national origin. . . ." 42 U.S.C. § 2000e-2(a). For many years, the courts of appeals of this country understood the prohibition against sex discrimination to exclude discrimination on the basis of a person's sexual orientation. The Supreme Court, however, has never spoken to that question. In this case, we have been asked to take a fresh look at our position in light of developments at the Supreme Court extending over two decades. We have done so, and we conclude today that discrimination on the basis of sexual orientation is a form of sex discrimination. We therefore reverse the district court's judgment dismissing Kimberly Hively's suit against Ivy Tech Community College and remand for further proceedings.

I

Hively is openly lesbian. She began teaching as a part-time, adjunct professor at Ivy Tech Community College's South Bend campus in 2000. Hoping to improve her lot, she applied for at least six full-time positions between 2009 and 2014. These efforts were unsuccessful; worse yet, in July 2014 her part-time contract was not renewed. Believing that Ivy Tech was spurning her because of her sexual orientation, she filed a pro se charge with the Equal Employment Opportunity Commission on December 13, 2013. It was short and to the point:

> I have applied for several positions at IVY TECH, fulltime, in the last 5 years. I believe I am being blocked from fulltime employment without just cause. I believe I am being discriminated against based on my sexual orientation. I believe I have been discriminated against and that my rights under Title VII of the Civil Rights Act of 1964 were violated.

. . . .

That is not because the Supreme Court has left this subject entirely to the side. To the contrary, as the panel recognized, over the years the Court has issued several opinions that are relevant to the issue before us. Key among those decisions are *Price Waterhouse v. Hopkins*, 490 U.S. 228 (1989), and *Oncale v. Sundowner Offshore Servs., Inc.*, 523 U.S. 75 (1998). *Price Water-house* held that the practice of gender stereotyping falls within Title VII's prohibition against sex discrimination, and *Oncale* clarified that it makes no difference if the sex of the harasser is (or is not) the same as the sex of the victim. Our panel frankly acknowledged how difficult it is "to extricate the gender nonconformity claims from the sexual orientation claims." 830 F.3d at 709. That effort, it commented, has led to a "confused hodge-podge of cases." *Id.* at 711. It also noted that "all gay, lesbian and bisexual persons fail to comply with the sine qua non of gender stereotypes—that all men should form intimate relationships only with women, and all women should form intimate relationships only with men." *Id.* Especially since the Supreme Court's recognition that the Due Process and Equal Protection Clauses of the Constitution protect the right of same-sex couples to marry, *Obergefell v. Hodges*, 135 S.Ct. 2584 (2015), bizarre results ensue from the current regime. As the panel noted, it creates "a paradoxical legal landscape in which a person can be married on Saturday and then fired on Monday for just that act." 830 F.3d at 714. . . .

II

A

. . . . We must decide instead what it means to discriminate on the basis of sex, and in particular, whether actions taken on the basis of sexual interpretation thus well within the judiciary's competence. . . . Many courts, including the Supreme Court, appear to have used "sex" and "gender" synonymously. . . . Moreover, the agency most closely associated with this law, the Equal Employment Opportunity Commission, in 2015 announced that it now takes the position that Title VII's prohibition against sex discrimination encompasses discrimination on the basis of sexual orientation. . . .

Hively alleges that if she had been a man married to a woman (or living with a woman, or dating a woman) and everything else had stayed the same, Ivy Tech would not have refused to promote her and would not have fired her. . . . This describes paradigmatic sex discrimination. To use the phrase from *Ulane*, Ivy Tech is disadvantaging her *because she is a woman*. . . .

Viewed through the lens of the gender non-conformity line of cases, Hively represents the ultimate case of failure to conform to the female stereotype (at least as understood in a place such as modern America, which views heterosexuality as the norm and other forms of sexuality as exceptional): she is not heterosexual. Our panel described the line between a gender nonconformity claim and one based on sexual orientation as gossamer-thin; we conclude that it does not exist at all. Hively's claim is no different from the claims brought by women who were rejected for jobs in traditionally male workplaces, such as fire departments, construction, and policing. The employers in those cases were policing the boundaries of what jobs or behaviors they found acceptable for a woman (or in some cases, for a man). . . .

Source: Kimbery Hively v. Ivy Tech Community College of Indiana, US Court of Appeals 7th Circuit, No. 15–1720 April 4, 2017.

Further Reading

Bever, Lindsey. 2016, June 15. "Pastor Refuses to Mourn Orlando Victims: 'The Tragedy Is That More of Them Didn't Die.'" *Washington Post.* Retrieved September 1, 2016, from https://www.washingtonpost.com/news/acts-of-faith/wp/2016/06/14/pastor-refuses-to-mourn-orlando-victims-the-tragedy-is-that-more-of-them-didnt-die

Dickel, Simon. 2012. *Black/Gay: The Harlem Renaissance, the Protest Era, and Constructions of Black Gay Identity in the 1980s and 90s.* East Lansing: Michigan State University Press.

Foster, Stephen. 2016, June 20. "Texas Pastor Cheers Orlando Mass Shooting, Prays God Will Finish Off Those in ICU." *Addicting Information.* Retrieved June 20, 2016, from http://www.addictinginfo.org/2016/06/20/watch-texas-pastor-cheers-orlando-mass-shooting-prays-god-will-finish-off-those-in-icu

Frank, Nathaniel. 2017. *Awakening: How Gays and Lesbians Brought Marriage Equality to America.* Cambridge, MA: The Belknap Press of Harvard University Press.

Joe My God. 2016, June 14. "Christian Pastor Celebrates Orlando Massacre: Round Up All the Gays and Blow Their Brains Out." Retrieved October 1, 2016, from http://www.joemygod.com/2016/06/14/christian-pastor-celebrates-orlando-massacre-round-up-all-the-gays-and-blow-their-brains-out-video

Kaplan, Roberts and Lisa Dickey. 2015. *Then Comes Marriage.* New York: WW. Norton Company.

Parkman, David. 2014, December 4. "Baptist Pastor in Arizona Calls for the Death of All Gays." *David Parkman Show.* Retrieved June 14, 2016, from https://www.youtube.com/watch?v=w83kIAfuKoE

Pearl, Monica B. 2013. *AIDS Literature and Gay Identity: The Literature of Loss.* New York: Routledge.

Rifkin, Mark. 2012. *The Erotics of Sovereignty: Queer Native Writing in the Era of Self-Determination.* Minneapolis: University of Minnesota Press.

Stewart, Chuck. 2014. *Proud Heritage.* Santa Barbara, CA: ABC-CLIO.

Tribune Media Wire. 2016, June 15. "Sacramento Pastor Defends Hate-Filled Sermon on Orlando Shootings." *KTLA5 News.* Retrieved September 1, 2016, from http://ktla.com/2016/06/15/pastor-defends-hate-filled-sermon-on-orlando-shootings

Index

About the Author

Chuck Stewart, PhD, is an independent researcher and writer on LGBT topics. His published works include ABC-CLIO's: *Proud Heritage: People, Issues, and Documents of the LGBT Experience*; *The Greenwood Encyclopedia of LGBT Issues Worldwide*; *Issues in Focus—Understanding Controversy and Society* (online database); *Gay and Lesbian Issues: A Reference Handbook*; and *Homosexuality and the Law: A Dictionary*. He also wrote *Sexually Stigmatized Communities—Reducing Heterosexism and Homophobia: An Awareness Training Manual* that was used to create training programs used by the Los Angeles Police Academy. Stewart also published the legal self-help book—*Bankrupt Your Student Loans and Other Discharge Strategies*—besides books and training manuals on environmental issues in residential real estate. Stewart holds a doctorate in education with a certificate in women's studies from the University of Southern California. His first degrees were in physics and math, and he worked for many years in aerospace. He has taught at all levels of education and currently teaches math and statistic courses for National University. Surprisingly, he was a classical ballet dancer for 25 years and for the past 20 years has taught ballroom and Western dancing to the gay and lesbian community. He founded and guided Out Dancing Ballroom from 2000 to 2006, a Los Angeles dance troupe dedicated to same-sex couple ballroom dancing.